CONSCIENCE
AND
CAPTIVITY

JANICE BROUN, an Oxford University graduate living in Scotland, is a free-lance journalist specializing in religion in Communist countries. She has written more than two hundred articles for many journals, including *Religion in Communist Lands, America*, the *Journal of Church and State, Commonweal,* and *Freedom at Issue,* and has contributed chapters to several books.

GRAŻYNA SIKORSKA was born in Poland and received an M.Sc. from the University of Katowice. In 1979 she joined the staff of Keston College, near London, where she does research on religion in her native land. Her book about Father Jerzy Popiełuszko, *A Martyr for the Truth,* appeared in 1985 and has been translated into five languages.

THE COVER: The Western monk Benedict and the Eastern monks Cyril and Methodius were proclaimed co-patron saints of Europe by Pope John Paul II. Czechoslovak Catholics have portrayed this message of spiritual unity on a card, circulated underground, that shows the three saints standing on a map of Europe.

CONSCIENCE
AND
CAPTIVITY
Religion in Eastern Europe

Janice Broun
Grażyna Sikorska

ETHICS AND PUBLIC POLICY CENTER

Library of Congress Cataloging in Publication Data
Broun, Janice
Conscience and captivity.

  Bibliography: p.
  Includes index.
  1. Europe, Eastern—Religion 2. Religion and state—
Europe, Eastern. I. Sikorska, Grazyna. II. Title.
BL980.E852B76   1988   209'.47   88-30942
ISBN 0-89633-129-6 (alk. paper)
ISBN 0-89633-130-X (pbk. : alk. paper)

Distributed by arrangement with:
University Press of America, Inc.
4720 Boston Way
Lanham, MD 20706

3 Henrietta Street
London WC2E 8LU England

Ethics and Public Policy Center
1030 Fifteenth Street N.W.
Washington, D.C. 20005
(202) 682-1200

*This book is dedicated to
those who bear the mark of the Cross
on their foreheads*

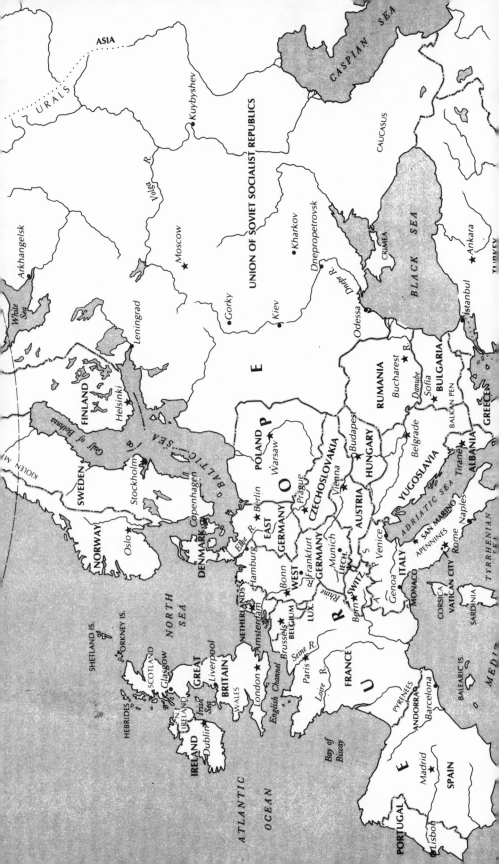

Contents

Appendixes

MAP SOURCES ◆ Europe (p. vi) and seven country maps (pp. 44, 66, 102, 126, 162, 198, and 244), from *The New Columbia Encyclopedia,* by permission of Columbia University Press (© 1975, Columbia University Press). ◆ Europe before and after World War II (pp. 7, 10), from *The Twentieth Century*, History of Mankind, vol. 6, by Caroline Ware, K. M. Panikkar, and J. M. Romein (© 1960, UNESCO). ◆ Albania (p. 22), from *Area Handbook for Albania,* Eugene K. Keefe et al. (1971, U.S. Government Printing Office). ◆ Yugoslavia, ethnic distribution (p. 251), from *Yugoslavia: A Multinational State*, by Jack C. Fisher (© 1966, Chandler Publishing Co.; by permission of Harper & Row). ◆ Yugoslavia, religious distribution (p. 258), from *Church and State in Yugoslavia*, by Stella Alexander (© 1979, Cambridge University Press).

Preface

I BECAME deeply interested in life under Communism many years ago at the Free Europe Society at Oxford, where I met many refugees from Eastern Europe and many former Communists. There I also met my husband, now a canon in the Scottish Episcopal Church, who has shared my interest. Later, during the 1960s, my concern for the plight of Christians under persecution, particularly in the Soviet Union under Khrushchev, was deepened by my meeting Metropolitan Anthony of Sourozh and the Reverend Michael Bordeaux, and by a gift subscription to *Religion in Communist Dominated Areas* from an American priest, the late John Foster Savidge, who had heard my husband preach in Edinburgh Cathedral.

From modest beginnings my work expanded, and many of my articles were published in the United States. I am very grateful to Robert Royal and the Ethics and Public Policy Center for commissioning, and thus making available to the general public as well as to academics, this wide and detailed coverage of an area that is too little known. I am also grateful to my two dedicated editors, Carol Griffith and Patricia Bozell, who have cooperated enthusiastically.

This book would have been impossible without the information Keston College provides through its publication *Religion in Communist Lands*, the Keston News Service, and its archives, as well as much help and advice I have received from Keston researchers over the years. I would particularly like to thank Michael Bordeaux for encouragement and inspiration, and Grażyna Sikorska, an experienced Keston researcher and author, for writing the chapter on Poland. Others at Keston or associated with Keston whom I must thank for their help with particular chapters are: Alexander Tomsky and Morven MacLeod (Czechoslovakia), Arvan Gordon (GDR), Bob Hoare (Bulgaria), Paul Booth (Romania), John Eibner (Hungary), and Muriel Heppel and Stella Alexander (Yugoslavia); also Malcolm Walker for help in the library and archives, and Philip Walters for general oversight. I must stress that although Keston researchers are in full agreement with the general lines of my arguments, the views I express and any errors I make are entirely my own and are not the responsibility of anyone at Keston.

I am grateful, too, to many other people: for Yugoslavia, Ljubo Sirc, Stevan Pavlovic, and the trainee monk in Belgrade who unwittingly taught me some of the problems of the Serbian Orthodox Church; for Romania, Paddy Georgescu and the late Horia Georgescu, Adriana and Fr. Gheorghe Calciu-Dumitressa, Ion Ratiu, Mgr. Traian Crisan; for Bulgaria, Spas Raikin; for Albania, over many years, Gjon Sinishta. I would also particularly like to thank Sergiu Grossu and his Paris newspaper *Catacombes*; Fr. Pierre Delooz and Pro Mundi Vita, Belgium; Bob Lockwood of *Our Sunday Visitor*, Illinois; also the staffs of the Hungarian Institute for Sociology, Vienna, of La Chiesa Del Silenzio, Pesaro, Italy, and of *L'Altra Europa*, Bergamo, Italy, which of all the European journals I am familiar with now has the best coverage of religion in Eastern Europe.

Special mention must also be made of Pedro Ramet of Washington University, Seattle, who has thoughtfully provided extra documentation throughout; also of my Lithuanian émigré friends Mgr. Vincas Mincevicius in Rome and Ginte Damusis and Fr. Casimir Pugevicius in Brooklyn, who by their indefatigable labors in providing the world with information on the Lithuanian Catholic Church have made me long familiar with problems faced by a church struggling to continue under Communism and foreign domination.

I owe much to the support and encouragement of various personal friends and the prayer group in our last parish for what has been a long and largely lone task; to my sister-in-law Helena, the best and most intelligent typist an untidy author could want; to my daughter Katherine and son Alasdair for their criticism; and of course to my long-suffering husband Claud, without whose hours of preliminary typing and continual criticism of style and spelling this book would not have been possible.

Finally I must not forget certain people who have helped more than I can express but whose names, sadly, I am unable to reveal, since they or their relatives must continue to live on the other side. It is to their courage and Christian love that I dedicate this book. After all these years I am privileged to be able to make a small return for all the inspiration they have provided for me and, I hope, for all who read this book. It is my earnest hope that what follows in these pages will do something toward enabling us in the West to be more sensitive to, and even to share in, the problems of those who live behind the Iron Curtain.

JANICE BROUN

Greyfriars Rectory
Kirkcudbright, Galloway, Scotland

Introduction

E IGHT VERY DIFFERENT countries—Albania, Bulgaria, Czechoslovakia, the German Democratic Republic (GDR), Hungary, Poland,
Romania, and Yugoslavia—lie between the "Iron Curtain" and the Soviet
Union. The West tends to lump them together as Eastern Europe. Although
this label is disputed by the Hungarians, Poles, Czechoslovaks, and
Slovenes, who consider themselves Central Europeans, and by the East
Germans, who might be classed as Western Europeans, it is nonetheless
useful. The eight countries have in common the fact that in recent decades
they have been under the influence, if not the control, of the Soviet Union,
and that they are ruled by parties claiming to apply Marxism-Leninism. An
inevitable consequence is that, despite professions of complete separation of
church and state, the state interferes in church life in a generally hostile and
limiting manner.

There are two common misconceptions, however. One, fostered by certain Western evangelical groups, is that all East European followers of religion are persecuted; the other, propagated by official church delegations and
the Christian Peace Conference, is that the state interferes not at all.

Both views are erroneous. Believers under Communism certainly do not
enjoy full religious liberty. Yet, except in Albania, churches, mosques, and
synagogues do exist, and some religious bodies and practices are officially
recognized. Widespread discrimination against the religious faithful persists,
but open persecution has leveled off.

A third misconception is to consider the situation the same in the
Soviet Union and throughout Eastern Europe. There is considerable varia-
tion among the East European countries. Six of the eight are Soviet satel-
lites; they are members of the Warsaw Pact (the Soviet-bloc military al-
liance) and COMECON (Council for Mutual Economic Assistance—the
Soviet-bloc trade alliance). Two, Yugoslavia and Albania, have left the
Soviet bloc to pursue vastly different courses. Yugoslavia, exposed to the
West, is generally more tolerant; Albania, successively in thrall to
Stalinism and Maoism, is the world's first self-proclaimed atheistic state.

Among the six Soviet satellites, there is a common negative attitude
toward religion—and a shared stock of methods to minimize it—but con-

siderable diversity in the intensity of anti-religious activity. The pressure on believers has varied according to a plethora of circumstances, internal and external. During some periods—notably the five years preceding Stalin's death in 1953—religion has suffered repression severe enough to warrant the term "persecution." Except in Albania, these periods tend to be followed by times of relative relaxation. Relaxation may in turn give way to repression, such as that which followed the Hungarian revolt in 1956, the Prague Spring of 1968, and the Polish bids for freedom in 1956, 1970, and during the Solidarity years. What the state gives with one hand it may take away with the other. The result is a deep sense of insecurity among believers.

There is perhaps a fourth misconception: that Communist governments provide reliable statistics. Many statistics will be quoted in this book; they have been checked as far as possible, but they contain irreconcilable figures and should be approached with care. Communist governments are very reluctant to release figures on matters they find embarrassing or unpalatable, and religious practice and church membership are high on that list. Membership figures tend to be on the low side. Often the most basic statistics are either not available or totally outdated. In the German Democratic Republic, the most efficient of the lot, the latest official publication of church statistics is from 1964.

In general, statistics on smaller churches, particularly Protestant ones, are the most reliable, those for the Orthodox churches the least. The Orthodox are vague on such matters, and, in Eastern Europe, their membership is usually inextricably tied to nationalism. In Yugoslavia, for example, most Serbs (who make up somewhat more than a third of the population), apart from Communist party members, claim to be Orthodox, but only a small proportion attend church regularly. In regard to statistics or any other information from the Communist world, it takes years of experience, a large amount of common sense, and the ability to read between the lines to arrive anywhere near the elusive truth.

There are no doubt factual and interpretative errors of other kinds also in the chapters that follow. The scope of the book is large, its subject complex. During 1987–88, some of the countries have been taking their first tentative steps toward change, though Westerners should not be misled: in religion, almost nothing has changed. In a part of the world where there is still no press freedom, and where information does not flow freely, facts are often difficult to verify, cases difficult to follow up. The book should be taken as a kind of mosaic of religion in Eastern Europe, presenting a valid overall picture even though some pieces may be out of place, wrongly colored, or missing.

The fallibility of human nature has given religion a negative as well as a positive side. The negative aspects will be emphasized in the brief historical survey in chapter one, to show how religion appeared to new rulers of territories that are now a part of Eastern Europe. The positive side, including the remarkable contribution to society that many believers are making today, despite all odds, will become evident later, in the country-by-country surveys.

1

Eastern Europe to 1975

TO UNDERSTAND the wide diversity of peoples, languages, cultural heritages, and religious affiliations that make up Eastern Europe, some knowledge of the past is needed. Elements in this complex history have been crucial to the survival of religion under the various Communist governments.

In the early years of Christendom, Greek and Roman colonists founded churches in various places in Europe, but they were scattered and of little importance. As the Roman Empire disintegrated, successive waves of invading tribes from the east swept around the Carpathian Mountains across the great north European plain or up the Danube valley. The most widely dispersed of these invading tribes, the Slavs, began to arrive in the area we now call Eastern Europe in the seventh century. Much of the region remained pagan until the end of the first millennium, and parts of it for another two or three hundred years. (Pockets of Albanians, Bulgarians, and Vlachs with pagan practices persisted until the beginning of this century.)

In 395 the Roman Empire was divided into the Eastern Roman or Byzantine Empire, with Constantinople as its capital, and the Western Roman Empire, with Rome as its capital. The subsequent division—beginning in the ninth century and culminating in the fifteenth—of the Christian Church into Orthodox, linked with Constantinople, and Catholic, linked with Rome, had far-reaching consequences. Each of the two had its distinctive ethos and worship and used a liturgical language alien to most East European converts. Until the twelfth or thirteenth century, many local rulers, whose conversions were initially superficial, fluctuated in their allegiance, confused by the conflicting claims of the Orthodox and the Catholic missionaries.

Saints Cyril and Methodius

Had the Western church's rulers possessed greater vision at one crucial moment in history, schism might have been averted. In 863, Rastislav,

1

ruler of Moravia (now part of Czechoslovakia), asked the Byzantine emperor to send missionaries to instruct his people in Slavonic, their own tongue, for German missionaries using Latin had made little headway. The emperor chose two Greek brothers, born in Thessalonika, who were familiar with Slavonic. Methodius, a monk, and Constantine, a teacher and philologist of genius, had already worked among heathen Asiatic tribes using the native languages. Constantine rapidly produced a Slavic alphabet, known as Glagolitic, and translated basic biblical readings into Slavonic.

After three years of success in Moravia, the brothers went to Rome and submitted the new Slavonic translations of both Byzantine and Roman liturgies for the approval of Pope Hadrian II. Constantine, who took monastic vows under the name Cyril, died in Rome in 869. Methodius returned to Central Europe as archbishop of Pannonia, entrusted with building up the church under papal jurisdiction in what is now Czechoslovakia and Hungary, using his Slavonic liturgy. Unfortunately, narrow-minded German clergy opposed him relentlessly until his death in 885.

Shortly thereafter, the disciples of Methodius were arrested and forced to leave the area. Some went to Croatia (in what is now Yugoslavia), where the Slavonic Roman rite was widely used. Others were welcomed by the rulers of Bulgaria, whose empire at that time extended farther north and west than today. These rulers adopted the Slavonic version of the Byzantine liturgy. There, in 893, the Glagolitic alphabet was officially replaced by one closer to Greek, misleadingly called the Cyrillic alphabet.

The work of the brothers Cyril and Methodius and of their disciples reached far and wide. Their literary and liturgical legacy spread across the Balkans to Serbs, Romanians, and eventually Russians, whose literary, cultural, and religious foundations were laid in the course of the Orthodox missionary work. Had the vernacular literature and teaching not ultimately been replaced by Latin, European history might have been very different.

By the late Middle Ages, the various national groups, with the exception of the Turks, were approximately as they stood at the outbreak of World War II. Slavs were predominant, with *Poles*, *Czechs*, and *Slovaks* making up the northern Slavs, and *Slovenes*, *Serbs*, and *Croats* the southern. To the northwest were the *Germans*—Teutonic in origin—and to the south the *Bulgarians*, who, though of Turkish-Mongol origin, adopted Slavonic, intermarried, and considered themselves Slavs. Among the Slavs were three other main groups: (1) the *Albanians* along the Adriatic coast north of Greece, probably former Illyrians; (2) the *Romanians*, who occupied the lower Danube area and whose language was Latin in origin; and (3) the *Hungarians*, a self-contained Finno-Ugrian people who settled in the Danube plains and set up a powerful kingdom that divided the northern from the southern Slavs. Although the Hungarians and the Albanians spoke languages with little affinity to that of their Slav neighbors, they and the Romanians intermarried to some extent with the Slavs.

The Coming of the Turks

Starting with the fourteenth century, Christendom was threatened, where not swamped, by the Ottoman Turks' militant form of Islam. Greece, Bulgaria, Albania, and much of what is now Yugoslavia succumbed after often heroic resistance. The Romanians, as vassals of the Turks, retained some self-rule, and Romanian Christianity was not threatened by Islam.

Farther north, Poland and Lithuania, a united Catholic kingdom, were free of the main Turkish threat, though they were troubled sporadically by the Tatars (Muslims) in the east and by the Teutonic Knights, a German military-religious order. Hungary became the key battleground for the struggle between the Turks and the rising Austro-Hungarian Empire. The struggle continued into the late seventeenth century, when the Turkish tide was finally rolled back.

Turkish rule over the Balkans (today Albania, Bulgaria, Greece, Romania, and Yugoslavia) and their Orthodox churches had significant long-term effects. At its height, the Ottoman Empire was relatively tolerant, inducing conversions to Islam through social status and exemption from taxes. Generally the conversions were only skin-deep, and religious commitment remains rather tepid among the Muslims of Eastern Europe, except for the Turks who stayed in Bulgaria after its independence. Today there are only about eight million Muslims in all of Eastern Europe.

The long-term effect of Turkish rule was to reduce the Balkans to a backwater. Slipping into decline, the Ottoman Empire by the nineteenth century was notorious for its maladministration, poverty, and brutality. A deep cultural as well as economic gap had opened between the Central European Catholic world, including Croatia, and the East European Orthodox world, including the Serbs—a grave problem in the making for the future Yugoslavia.

Effects of Turkish Rule on Orthodoxy

Under Turkish rule the Orthodox churches were isolated from the repercussions of the Reformation and Counter-Reformation. They remained severely traditionalist. Unless they traveled west, they were deprived of access to scholarship, and the great written treasury of the early Church Fathers, the Philokalia, was not to be rediscovered until the end of the eighteenth century. Most Orthodox knew little of the Bible, except what was recited during the liturgy and what they could learn from the carefully arranged paintings on their church walls, from festivals, and from family rites. Priests lacked the systematic training Catholic priests and Protestant pastors came to have. There was an almost instinctive interaction of ecclesiastical and domestic ritual, for Orthodoxy is a way of life as well as a religion, with an ethos all its own.

Another legacy of the Turks helped to mute the Orthodox response to Communism. Orthodoxy regards the state not as a rival institution but as a means ordained by God to maintain law and order. Within the Ottoman Empire the church was made responsible for collecting taxes and for local administration. So bishops became accustomed to working within a state with an alien ideology, as they have had to do under Communism. During the latter years of the empire, when the churches became the guardians of the national heritage, the clergy, especially the monks, promoted the cause of independence and nationhood. When the Balkan nations achieved independence, bishops tended to work closely with the governments—they were employed as much by the state as by the church—and were thus vulnerable to Communist rule. They were moreover traditionally grateful to Russia, with which they shared a common religion and which, of all the big powers operating in the Balkans, seemed to offer the most help against the crumbling Ottoman Empire. Thus there wasn't the head-on collision between church and state that occurred in Catholic countries such as Poland and, to some extent, Hungary.

The Orthodox bishops seem to some observers to be too compromising. This is to misunderstand the nature of Orthodox resistance, which is to preserve the church and the faith, even at the cost of humiliation and disdain. Nevertheless, it is significant that there has not been a rebellion against Communism in any of the Orthodox countries.

One other important factor in the development of East European religion: Orthodoxy tends to regard all matters *sub specie aeternitatis.* Empires rise, empires fall, but the church, unchanged and unchanging, preserves the Christian faith forever. What then are a few decades of persecution or enforced collaboration?

The Reformation and Counter-Reformation

The Catholic Church, dominant in those parts of Eastern Europe untouched by the Ottoman Empire or won back, was in dire need of reform. When reform came, it divided Christians between Protestants (Reformation) and Catholics (Counter-Reformation).

The Reformation began not in Germany but in Bohemia and Moravia in the early fifteenth century. Inspired by the Bohemian Jan Hus, it was espoused, despite persecution and his martyrdom in 1415, by virtually all his countrymen. The protest was aimed at social and religious corruption and urged a vernacular liturgy, communion under both species (i.e., bread and wine), and popularization of the Bible.

Martin Luther's sixteenth-century Reformation found ready soil in Central Europe among Germans, Hungarians, Czechs, Slovaks, and even Poles, for the large united Catholic kingdom of Poland and Lithuania was a model of tolerance. Reformation teaching spread far but had no appeal whatsoever to the Orthodox.

The Counter-Reformation rejuvenated the Catholic Church. The outburst of spiritual fervor was partially turned toward the reconversion of Protestants, sometimes forcibly. Where the church was backed by civil power—as in the Habsburg Austro-Hungarian Empire—some far-reaching consequences ensued. Protestantism almost disappeared, and Catholics suffered—like the Orthodox—from being tied to the state.

As a result, only East Germany (the GDR) has a Protestant majority. Czechoslovakia, western and central Yugoslavia, Hungary, and Transylvania (then part of Hungary but incorporated into Romania—to whose nationality the majority of Transylvanians belong—in 1918) bear the imprint of Habsburg rule, where the Catholic hierarchy became part of a conservative, feudal establishment. Catholic intolerance tended in the long run to discredit the religion. By the end of the nineteenth century, the Czech part of Czechoslovakia (i.e., Bohemia and Moravia) was as secularized as any other place in Europe. Later, Czech and Hungarian Catholicism, having shallower roots, lost ground more quickly to Communism than did Polish Catholicism.

Tolerance in Poland withered under external threats to national liberty. With Poland partitioned among Austria, Prussia, and Russia in the eighteenth century, Catholicism and nationalism became intertwined.

Eastern Rite Catholic Churches

Historically, the Catholic Church has tried to take advantage of Orthodox when they have become vulnerable, so the Orthodox as well as the Protestants were pressured by the Habsburg Empire to convert to Catholicism. Various agreements, in which the Orthodox had little choice, were reached, the most important being the Union of Brest in 1596, involving Poles and Ukrainians, and that of Alba Iulia in 1698, involving Transylvanian Romanians. The results were new "hybrid" churches, often referred to as Uniate, though they prefer the name Eastern Rite or Greek Catholic. In these churches, Orthodox forms of worship in their customary language were retained along with a married priesthood, but Rome's jurisdiction was acknowledged.

Though many members returned to Orthodoxy when they could, the new churches developed their own ethos and devotion to Rome. Orthodox in rite but Catholic in loyalty, they became the special target of Communist attack. In Romania and Czechoslovakia, they were "voluntarily" absorbed into the Orthodox Church; in Poland and Hungary, they survive uneasily within the Catholic Church. The Slovak church, however, was rehabilitated after the Prague Spring of 1968. A small Eastern Rite church in Bulgaria has kept its separate identity.

The Protestant Churches

The traditional Protestant churches—with their majority in what is now the GDR and their substantial minorities in Hungary, Czechoslovakia, and the Transylvanian region of Romania—though at first radical, in their turn became predominantly conservative, part of the establishment. The Erastian Lutheran churches, named after the Swiss theologian Thomas Erastus, believed in the dominance of the state over the church; like the Orthodox, they were especially prepared to accommodate to Communist rule.

Some Protestant churches, however, have tried to maintain their distance from the government. The provincial Protestant churches of the GDR have attempted to dissociate themselves from the pro-Nazi movement, giving much weight to the witness of the heroic minority "Confessing Church," which opposed Nazism. Some members of the Evangelical Czech Brethren Church have tried to carry on the ideals of Jan Hus.

The other Protestant churches—such as Baptist and Pentecostal—are relative newcomers. Almost all owe their origins to Western missions during the late nineteenth and early twentieth centuries. Regarded as foreign imports, they are numerically small, are apolitical, and have not had a great impact. The only country where they have grown substantially is Romania, where their tradition of sturdy independence and antipathy to state control has brought them under fire from the authorities. Romanian Baptists particularly, through their defiance of the state and their fearless evangelization, have become the largest of their denomination in all Europe.

The Link Between Nationalism and Religion

As we have noted, in several countries nationalism and religion are closely linked. In Poland this strengthens the church *vis-à-vis* the government, whereas in Romania and Bulgaria the state has complete control over Orthodox churches, which are tacitly still recognized as the national churches.

The church-nationalism link presents the most problems in Yugoslavia, an artificially created country containing three major religious

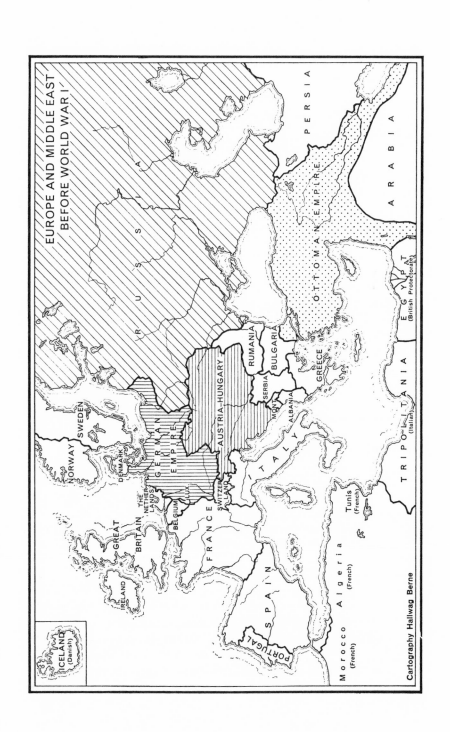

EUROPE AND MIDDLE EAST
BEFORE WORLD WAR I

RUSSIA

NORWAY

SWEDEN

DENMARK

GREAT
BRITAIN

IRELAND

ICELAND
(Danish)

THE
NETHER-
LANDS

BELGIUM

LUX.

GERMAN
EMPIRE

SWITZER-
LAND

FRANCE

SPAIN

PORTUGAL

Morocco
(French)

Algeria
(French)

Tunis
(French)

ITALY

TRIPOLITANIA
(Italian)

AUSTRIA-HUNGARY

RUMANIA

SERBIA

MONT.

ALBANIA

BULGARIA

GREECE

OTTOMAN EMPIRE

PERSIA

ARABIA

EGYPT
(British Protectorate)

Cartography Hallwag Berne

groupings and several nationalities that often are mutually antagonistic, as are the Orthodox Serbs and Catholic Croats as a result of appalling atrocities committed by Croats against Serbs in World War II. The Yugoslav government fears the potential divisive force of nationalism and is suspicious of religious activity because of its close ties to nationalist movements. At present the Muslim Albanian minority causes the greatest concern.

The Czechoslovak government fears Slovak nationalism, which, like the Hungarian and Croatian, was exploited by the Nazis during the war. In addition, Slovakia has a solid Catholic majority that has developed close links with Polish Catholics. Only Hungary and the GDR have no internal nationality problems. In some cases the state by its chauvinistic behavior creates greater problems. In Bulgaria the government has turned savagely on its Turkish Muslim minority. In Romania Hungarians are currently under great pressure.

National feeling is often a cause of friction among East European countries. There is little love lost among the leaders. The Soviet Union attempts to keep national rivalry among Warsaw Pact allies within manageable bounds.

Communism—Return to Authoritarianism

Eastern Europe has had little experience of democratic government, largely because it has lacked the stable conditions conducive to democracy. Except for Germany, which evolved from a union of several small states autocratically governed, East European history has been riddled with despotic foreign rulers—Germans, Austrians, Russians, Turks. Some countries achieved independence in the late nineteenth century; most waited until after World War I, but their glimpse of freedom was overshadowed by the threat of Nazi Germany.

Until 1939, most of these countries were ruled by autocratic governments; in some, full religious toleration (particularly toward the evangelical Protestant churches) was not granted. Although many Romanians and Serbs had democratic ideals and some experience of parliamentary government, only one country, Czechoslovakia, achieved true democracy and complete religious freedom for any length of time. This of course makes the Czechoslovak people's fate today all the more difficult to bear.

The Communists came to power in countries where the tradition of coexistence between church and state was deeply rooted and the experience of democracy and toleration was limited. Communist rule was therefore a reversion to type—even to the widespread subordination of church to state.

Among the traumatic effects of World War II on Eastern Europe were the deaths caused by the fighting, the famine, and the forces of occupation (one-fifth of Poland's population perished); the millions of refugees and displaced persons; the wholesale destruction of property. The substantial Jewish presence was all but wiped out; those who survived were allowed to emigrate to Israel. People had little time to recover—physically, mentally, or spiritually—before the Communists, backed by the Soviet occupational forces, swept away any attempts at democratic government.

By the end of 1948, the Communists controlled Eastern Europe and faced the gigantic task of rebuilding. They made considerable improvements in the poorer sections of society, and until the mid-sixties, life expectancy rose and infant mortality fell. Nonetheless, the standard of living in most countries—notably Czechoslovakia and Romania—is now probably much lower than it would have been without Communism. The churches' devastated property was left untouched in the rebuilding.

Post-War Persecution

Following the Communist takeovers, the churches came under direct attack. The Catholic Church, with its property, influence, and Western control and orientation, received the brunt of the hostility, which Rome initially returned. Communism and Catholicism were viewed as absolutely irreconcilable.

On July 13, 1949, Pope Pius XII issued "Acta Apostolicae Sedis"—a threat to excommunicate Catholics who belonged to or supported a Communist party, or propagated Communist ideas. The order was unenforceable, however, and caused Catholics great difficulty. For their part, Communist governments pressured the local churches to sever their ties with Rome and form national Catholic churches. But despite ruthless programs of arrests, confiscations, closures—particularly of schools and religious houses—and, of course, intimidation, the repression failed, except in Albania, where the government resorted to deception. The attitude of the Polish church can be summed up in Cardinal Wyszyński's dictum: "I learned to say no to Communism, lock, stock, and barrel."

Tolerable personal relations between the new state leaders and the churches existed to some extent in the GDR; institutional links and a delicate diplomacy with the West German churches helped protect the East German churches from attack and individuals from persecution, though not from discrimination.

The Protestant churches, a vulnerable minority in most countries outside the GDR, were cowed into docility by their witness of the merciless treatment of the Catholics. As for the Orthodox, after the war the newly established Moscow patriarchate proved itself an obedient arm of the Kremlin in its strenuous efforts to dominate Eastern Europe. With the Russian

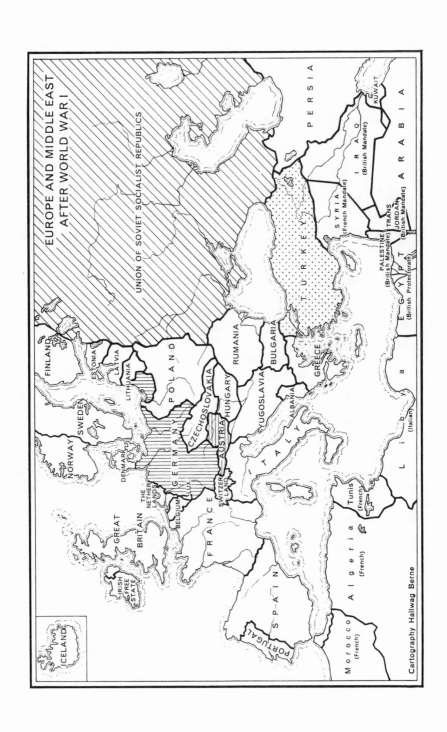

EUROPE AND MIDDLE EAST
AFTER WORLD WAR I

UNION OF SOVIET SOCIALIST REPUBLICS

PERSIA

KUWAIT

I R A Q
(British Mandate)

A R A B I A

SYRIA
(French Mandate)

JORDAN
(British Mandate)

TRANS

PALESTINE
(British Mandate)

E G Y P T
(British Protectorate)

FINLAND

ESTONIA

LATVIA

LITHUANIA

P O L A N D

CZECHOSLOVAKIA

RUMANIA

HUNGARY

BULGARIA

YUGOSLAVIA

ALBANIA

GREECE

T U R K E Y

SWEDEN

NORWAY

DENMARK

G E R M A N

AUSTRIA

SWITZER
LAND

THE
NETHER-
LANDS

BELGIUM

LUX.

F R A N C E

I T A L Y

L i b y a
(Italian)

GREAT
BRITAIN

IRISH
FREE
STATE

ICELAND

S P A I N

PORTUGAL

Morocco
(French)

A l g e r i a
(French)

Tunis
(French)

Cartography Hallwag Berne

church parading its ability to coexist, the Orthodox hierarchies succumbed to Communist control more easily than the Catholics.

The initial persecutions died down after Stalin's death, as the various governments recognized the need to gain the support of the people. Religion was too ingrained in the people to be suppressed by force. Besides, an open persecution created martyrs and stiffened resistance. Other methods had to be discovered.

The Period of Détente

As East-West relations began to improve, Paul VI, who became pope in 1963, in conjunction with his secretary of state, Agostino Casaroli, initiated the Vatican *"Ostpolitik"* to open communications with Catholic churches isolated from Rome since 1948. Casaroli concentrated on three objectives: the appointment of bishops in vacant dioceses; the survival of seminaries to fill out the thinned ranks of the clergy; and the religious instruction of children. The policy accepted a reality: the churches would not be restored to full freedom. The failure of the 1956 Hungarian revolt (and the failure of the West to support it) persuaded a disillusioned Eastern Europe that Communism was there to stay.

The governments tried to undermine the church by, among other measures, sponsoring the Peace Priests movement, from whose ranks emerged bishops and religious leaders willing to compromise with the regime to preserve a modicum of church life. From the Communist viewpoint, the effort succeeded in Hungary and Czechoslovakia but failed in Poland. Yugoslavia and Albania went their own very different ways, with Albania "abolishing" religion in 1967.

In Czechoslovakia, "socialism with a human face" seemed to offer some hope for a genuine Christian-Marxist dialogue, until the crushing of the Prague Spring in 1968 wiped out hopes for reconciliation. Christian-Marxist dialogue today is meaningless to most East Europeans; it is found officially only in Yugoslavia and Hungary and among a few intellectual dissidents in Poland and Czechoslovakia.

The churches drew some benefit during the period of détente between East and West, largely through those leaders who stood up to state pressure. By 1970 the churches in the GDR, Poland, and Yugoslavia had gained some real autonomy. In Poland, the indomitable Cardinal Wyszyński brought the church relatively unscathed through struggles with the state. There, after 1973, to the resentment of the local church, Vatican *Ostpolitik* had the government conferring with the Vatican over the heads of the local hierarchy.

The Vatican's new policy was most successful in Yugoslavia. In return for Vatican recognition of Tito, Yugoslavia recognized the Holy See's jurisdiction in 1966, and the Yugoslav bishops were allowed unimpeded communication with Rome. To cement the agreement, the Vatican endorsed the ban on clergy involvement in politics and promised to cooperate with the government should violence occur.

Stirrings Within the Churches

Meanwhile, a new generation, untouched by the traumas of the 1940s and 1950s, was growing up in Eastern Europe. These young people were less cowed than their parents and ready to question the church-state status quo, among other aspects of life. Within the churches, too, with the emergence of a new generation, discontent surged—most often where a docile hierarchy had driven a wedge of distrust between church leaders and the laity.

The dissatisfaction was particularly visible where Paul VI's *Ostpolitik* had failed, as when the Vatican accepted government nominees to fill vacant sees, something it had previously resisted. In 1970, Czech dissident Ivan Medek wrote to the Vatican complaining that the new policy was creating a spiritual crisis in which believers felt deprived of leadership.

In 1975, the Helsinki Accords were signed by the USSR, Bulgaria, Czechoslovakia, the GDR, Hungary, Poland, Romania, and Yugoslavia. Though systematically broken by the Communists, the accords gave East Europeans a way of measuring their actual against their supposed freedom and furthered the impetus to dissent, and the monitoring groups provided a platform, however shaky, for protest.

The election in 1978 of Polish Cardinal Wojtyła as pope came as the optimism of détente waned. Wojtyła gave new heart to all the people of Eastern Europe; even the Orthodox welcomed the election of a man who had experienced from the inside the problems the churches faced. Developments since the Helsinki Accords and the election of Pope John Paul II will be the main focus of succeeding chapters.

2

Eastern Europe Today

T HE CHURCHES of Eastern Europe have suffered losses not only from persecution and propaganda but also from the same secularization that has swept the West. Secularization has been most pervasive in the more sophisticated areas—the German Democratic Republic, Hungary, Slovenia in Yugoslavia, and the Czech part of Czechoslovakia. It has even made inroads into Poland, regarded by many as the most deeply Catholic of nations.

Religious attachment has remained stronger in the traditionally peasant societies—such as Catholic Slovakia and Orthodox Romania—but it is being eroded there too as people are uprooted and forced to work in factories and live in dreary housing blocks where new churches are banned.

Some of the governments have noted that in the West, as prosperity increased, religion withered. Sensing a replay of the Western experience, they are willing to become more tolerant of religion, if not of religious education. Whereas in the West religious education has largely gone by default, in the Communist bloc it has been suppressed or hedged by difficulties. Whether by neglect or by suppression, the result is the same: an anti-religious view of life has corrupted the behavior of the young.

The ideological attitude of the Communist parties is the same in Eastern Europe as in the Soviet Union. This "scientific" attitude regards religion as a distorted reflection of reality that prevents the human race from seeking its true salvation in materialism and the humanistic society. Religion is merely a temporary historical phenomenon, and will wither away, but nevertheless it must be removed from any field that might affect society, such as politics or education. Moreover, the churches, often virtually the only non-state organizations permitted, provide a focus for potential dissent. Therefore the governments have set up special bodies whose purpose is to keep religion under control.

The two Eastern countries outside the Soviet bloc, Yugoslavia and Albania, have different policies. Yugoslavia generally avoids interfering in

13

strictly ecclesiastical matters, while Albania bans religion altogether. The rest follow the Soviet pattern of having a department of religious affairs, or its equivalent, to control religious life. (In Bulgaria, religion is supervised by a department in the foreign office, but it amounts to the same thing.) These departments provide the official link between religious bodies and the government. Except in Poland, their official status is rather low. They are headed, as in the USSR, by people hostile to religion who work closely with the ministry of the interior and the security services.

The departments are rarely referred to in official publications, their regulations are published only in part, and their activities are usually given little publicity. The reasons are obvious: to give as little coverage as possible to religious survival, and to avert criticism of the departments' questionable activities. The departments control all the actions of religious groups—channel funds, administer ecclesiastical legislation, coordinate the many organs of state that have legal powers in religious matters, and give legal opinions wherever necessary. They evaluate religious data, which are published only if it suits the state. There is evidence that they may also infiltrate certain religious establishments—clergy and theological colleges, for instance.

The differences among these bodies are not so much in the way they work as in their degree of involvement in religious affairs. This involvement will be examined in more detail in succeeding chapters. First a few general observations.

Until 1987 the most oppressive policy was pursued by the Soviet Union, followed by Czechoslovakia, Romania, and Bulgaria. In Czechoslovakia, for example, the State Office of Church Affairs often makes decisions on strictly religious questions for reasons of political expediency. Since these decisions are nowhere fixed by statute, the lawless treatment of religion hides behind a patently thin veil of dubious legality.

At the other end of the scale, the Secretariat of State for Church Affairs in the GDR acts as a link between the government and the churches rather than as an organ of state interference. In between come the Hungarian and Polish religious-affairs departments, which have limited legal powers. In Poland, the powers of the state with respect to the Catholic Church have never been properly clarified. Such legal powers as the department claims exist to a large extent on paper only, since the church succeeds in disregarding regulations.

Whether East European policy toward the churches is directed and coordinated by Moscow is a moot question. Some experts who maintain that it is point to the joint meetings held two or three times a year by the Eastern-bloc religious-affairs departments. At these meetings, it is claimed, countries that have made concessions to the churches are criticized unless they can show that the moves were tactical and temporary. Others, however, believe that because conditions vary from one country to another, the meetings serve mainly for the exchange of information.

If the departments do not operate entirely negatively—the official contacts they maintain do in some cases serve the interests of the church concerned—the suppression nevertheless continues. In practice if not in theory, there is no separation of church and state, no neutrality by the state toward religion. On the contrary, except in the GDR, the state seeks to exert as full control as possible.

Aspects of Church Life

In contrast, however, with the situation in the USSR (though there may be some loosening there through Gorbachev's reform program), the East European churches in general have legal status and can own property and carry on activities beyond worship. Most permit religious instruction for minors. Let us look at some aspects of church life and how they are handled in the Eastern bloc.

1. *Official Status.* East European governments are less strict than the USSR in registering congregations, although new congregations or denominations are discouraged to various degrees. As in the Soviet Union, however, entire churches have been banned. The most important—certain Eastern Rite Catholic churches—were forced into the Orthodox Church by Moscow; but, except in Romania and, in very individual circumstances, in Poland, they have now been reinstated. Some small churches have also been banned, including Jehovah's Witnesses, except in Poland and Yugoslavia; and Romania has banned a more sizable group, the Lord's Army.

2. *Church Property.* Although East European governments allow the churches to own buildings, they control the construction of new churches and the repairs of existing ones. Where churches have been closed, as in Romania and Bulgaria, it is often on the pretext that they hinder urban development. Nevertheless, in contrast with the Soviet Union, East Europeans are generally adequately supplied with churches.

3. *Religious Instruction.* In the Soviet Union, the formal religious instruction of minors is banned and is a punishable offense. In Eastern Europe—except for Bulgaria—instruction is permitted, sometimes only on church premises, sometime also in schools after hours. But owing to strict regulations and warnings to parents that their children's future may be jeopardized, the proportion of children receiving official religious instruction is very low, except in Poland and Yugoslavia. Hungary permits a handful of denominational schools, and Poland a few educational institutions. All this,

of course, in no way compensates for the loss of church schools nationalized by the Communists.

Generally, adult religious instruction is not allowed. Theological education of laity is permitted, however, in Poland, the GDR, and Yugoslavia, which have university theological faculties. Lately, Hungary has allowed part-time courses.

4. *Seminaries*. Most churches are allowed to have seminaries to train their future clergy, though in Bulgaria only the Orthodox Church is allowed a seminary. But where the state subsidizes the seminaries—Hungary, Czechoslovakia, Bulgaria, and Romania—it assumes the right to decide who may attend. The government's aim is clear: to produce second-rate clergy who can be manipulated. Mediocre candidates are preferred over persons of higher quality or of uncompromising nature. In certain seminaries, students are subjected to blackmail and intimidation.

The state's arm reaches further—it often imposes restrictions on the number of seminarians, no matter how many the applicants or how drastic the need for them. Theological training goes on relatively unimpeded only in the GDR, Poland, and Yugoslavia. Poland alone has a surplus of clergy.

5. *Control of the Clergy*. Except in the GDR, Poland, and Yugoslavia, the state not only selects and trains the future clergy but also controls the appointment and dismissal of the existing clergy. (Though technically this is true in Poland, the government has never been able to apply it.) State pressures may be exercised to demoralize the clergy. Stipends are paid by the state and are low—half the national average in Czechoslovakia. The governments undermine solidarity among the clergy by inducing them to join state-sponsored organizations, such as the Peace Priests, which bring benefits in pay, promotion, and travel.

6. *Finances*. Financial independence is closely tied to institutional freedom. Many churches, badly hit by war, persecution, and secularization, are strapped for money, which leaves them vulnerable to state control through subsidies. Only Yugoslav and Polish churches and non-Orthodox churches in Bulgaria receive no state assistance. In several countries, the churches have been rendered dependent on state subsidies for their survival and must submit their financial accounts for state approval.

7. *Political Activity*. Although church participation in politics is generally not permitted, the GDR and Poland allow a Christian political party in parliament with a designated number of seats; members have even voted against government policies. In Romania and Hungary, religious leaders in favor with the regime may be rewarded with seats in the parliament. But since power rests with the party and not with the parliament, these appointments carry little force.

8. *Congregational Activities.* In the Soviet Union, religious bodies are officially restricted to worship, a practice followed in Romania and Bulgaria; for all practical purposes, the Catholic Church in Czechoslovakia is limited in the same manner. Elsewhere some normal congregational activities are allowed, though they vary from place to place, as do the penalties for illegal meetings. In the GDR and Poland, the scope of church activities exceeds what might be expected in a Communist country.

Charitable activities, forbidden to Soviet churches, are permitted in Poland, in Yugoslavia, to a small extent in Hungary, and, again to an unprecedented extent, in the GDR, where the churches make a remarkable contribution to the nation's welfare. Generally, however, states that permit works of charity see that the benefits are channeled to those members of society whom they consider superfluous, such as the handicapped and the elderly.

9. *Religious Orders.* Much of the charitable work is done by members of religious orders, which in Poland, Yugoslavia, and the GDR—the only countries with no restrictions on religious vocations—form a valuable pool of cheap labor.

In Hungary and Romania, the state imposes rigid numerical restrictions; in Romania, where all religious houses are under strict government scrutiny, only the Orthodox (not Catholics) are allowed to become monks and nuns. In Czechoslovakia, religious orders have not been able to accept novices since 1971. Resentment against the restrictions is high, for monasticism is a traditional and vital element in church life, and religious (i.e., members of religious orders) have provided outstanding Christian witness in labor camps. As for the religious, only a few survivors of the Communist takeover are still active in church life, but many others ostensibly in the secular world exercise their vocation in private, sometimes in secret.

10. *Religious Literature.* Control of religious writing is vital to Communist policy. Most religious bodies in Eastern Europe are allowed their own press, but they must submit to some degree of censorship and to a limited circulation. In Poland, Yugoslavia, and the GDR, the church press is relatively free, but even there "offensive" material can be cut back at the will of the state. Elsewhere the situation is much worse. An authentic Catholic press is all but non-existent in Czechoslovakia, non-existent in Bulgaria and Romania.

Believers throughout Eastern Europe are deliberately kept short of basic literature—Bibles, hymnbooks, and catechisms. The worst shortages exist in Czechoslovakia, Romania, and Bulgaria, where people can be imprisoned for importing or producing "unofficial" literature, such as Bibles. And in Albania, of course, religious literature of all kinds is officially non-existent.

11. *Persecution and Imprisonment.* Religious persecution, fairly continuous in the Soviet Union since the 1917 Revolution, peaked in the 1930s, and visible religious life all but vanished. But during World War II Stalin was forced to come to terms with the religious remnants. As a result, Christian and Muslim bodies, after a reign of terror tactics and intense atheistic indoctrination, have compliant leaders. Those who seek greater religious freedom are dealt with severely by the state, which exercises strict control over all religious matters.

In Eastern Europe, once the first phase of frontal attack and terror was over, the Communist governments (with the exception later of Albania) adopted less drastic measures. They chose a pragmatic policy so as not to alienate those of their subjects who were deeply religious, and did not usually imprison people for strictly religious offenses, as did the USSR. For this reason, the number of people in prisons, labor camps, and psychiatric hospitals for religious offenses was lower in most of Eastern Europe than in the USSR, though sometimes still high in relation to their much smaller populations.

In 1986, before Gorbachev's relaxation and subsequent releases, there were about four hundred *known* religious prisoners in the USSR (Natan Sharansky estimates between five and six thousand). By December 1987 there were, according to Keston College, approximately 240. In the GDR, Hungary, Poland, and Yugoslavia, there are barely any. In Albania, the number could run to the thousands, although recent estimates have reduced it to hundreds. In Romania and Czechoslovakia, the increased religious activity in the mid-1970s resulted in the jailing of several dozen people. Thanks to protests from the West, most have been released. Reports in the mideighties, however, however, speak of up to four hundred Romanians being "treated" in psychiatric hospitals, and there, occasionally people simply disappear and are never heard from again.

Only a few Christians have been imprisoned in Bulgaria since the late 1960s. Islam has become the chief target—first the Bulgarian Muslims, more recently their Turkish brethren. At least five hundred prisoners from the Bulgarian Muslim communities were reported in the 1970s; and with the campaign begun in 1984 to force Turks to change their names to Bulgarian ones, the number may be even higher in the 1980s.

Some believers have been imprisoned for political offenses, such as the many Polish Catholics involved in the Solidarity movement that struck out for political and social reform. While Yugoslavia tends to impose short sentences for religious offenses, conscientious objectors and those who are charged with political infractions receive harsher treatment. In Hungary, Poland, and the GDR, the number of religious prisoners is low and consists in the main of conscientious objectors who refuse to do national service.

12. *Discrimination.* While active persecution now affects only a small proportion of believers, discrimination continues to be a grim reality throughout Eastern Europe. The effects are all the more insidious in that much of it is neither official nor automatic. Those higher up the social or professional scale—teachers in particular—are more liable to suffer, but Christians at any level may forfeit promotions, social benefits, educational advancement, housing, or pensions. The arbitrary punishments range from lower wages for churchgoers in Hungary to degrading jobs for activist Christian intellectuals in Czechoslovakia. Believers have no legal redress against discrimination since it is applied illegally in the first place.

The evangelicals—Baptists, Pentecostals, and other conservative Protestant groups—often take the lead in professing their faith openly. Some believers, however, wait until retirement to attend church, or attend furtively and baptize their children in secret. Churchgoers in small communities, lacking the anonymity of urban areas, are particularly vulnerable. The courage of those people who openly confess their faith—such as the teenagers in the GDR who refused to swear allegiance to the state in the "Youth Dedication" ceremony—is something the West can only admire from a distance.

The greatest pain to parents is caused by the discrimination leveled against their children, who can be excluded from higher education or suffer intolerable pressures at school if they receive formal religious education. Therefore from an early age children are trained to conceal their beliefs. A German girl, asked by a visitor if she was a Christian, said, "Yes, after two o'clock" (i.e., outside school). Nearly all children are thus initiated early into the pernicious system of "double-think." Aware of the strains, some clergy—even Catholic priests—advise parents to educate their children in religion at home, which is difficult given the lack of basic religious literature.

Infringements of human rights are common, but their nature and manner of application are such that open protests are rarely made. Church authorities are usually powerless or unwilling to help, except in Poland, Yugoslavia, and the GDR. Arrests and house searches are commonly reported.

13. *Sources of Information.* Everywhere official church sources of news are censored. Reports discrediting the authorities or airing the views of dissidents rarely appear except in Poland, the GDR, and Yugoslavia, where the church press offers some diversity of opinion. In Poland and Yugoslavia, it is now possible to discuss some controversial and religious matters in the media. Elsewhere, believers send information to the West through reliable personal channels. Poles, Hungarians, and Yugoslavs have the best access to

the West, but fear of reprisals sometimes inhibits the transmission of "hot" news.

In most countries, the people who are allowed to meet foreign visitors or whose views are reported in the official church press are generally state-approved representatives. In some cases, they are the only ones permitted to speak for the churches. One of the most insidious outcomes of Communist rule has been the wedge driven between the leadership and the ordinary church members. Few leaders are not compromised to some extent, and fewer dare to speak out when they should. Leaders willing to criticize government policies are found only in Poland, Yugoslavia, and the GDR—the three countries where the state does not control church appointments—and, recently, with a transformed Cardinal Tomášek, in Czechoslovakia.

Reports by officially sponsored Western visitors and delegations—who are shown the more positive side of church life—must therefore be treated with caution, especially as there are, of course, church leaders known to be government stooges and polite as well as credulous visitors, particularly among the Western intelligentsia. But even these very restricted visits can foster a measure of contact with the outside world and may be of help to the churches.

In Albania, gathering news of the churches through personal contact has been impossible. The few Albanians who are allowed to visit abroad or who escape are terrified to talk for fear of repercussions back home. Since East Germans (church personnel seem to have some priority), Poles, Hungarians, and Yugoslavs have some freedom to travel, and Westerners can also visit those countries fairly easily, a valuable network of contacts has been built. Yugoslavs are somewhat inhibited, for their secret police sometimes arrest citizens for making statements abroad.

In some countries, Romania and Bulgaria in particular, most people are too afraid to speak freely to visitors. In Romania, for example, the people are forbidden to provide personal hospitality to foreign visitors, and since 1986 everyone has had to report any foreign contact to the police. Information from these more closed countries is therefore less complete. If there is little news of arrests, harassments, and violations of human rights, it does not mean that such things are not taking place. What reaches the West is often only the tip of the iceberg.

14. *The Role of Samizdat.* The mushrooming of religious *samizdat* (material reproduced and circulated clandestinely) since the early 1970s has proved vital to the religious ferment and has happened everywhere. Even in Poland, because the religious press practices self-censorship, a lot of the best writing circulates in *samizdat*, though more openly than in Czechoslovakia. The news, opinions, sermons, letters, and protests detailing

violations of rights are sometimes privately circulated, sometimes deliberately aimed at the West. The latter reach various reliable contact points, of which the best known in the English-speaking world is Keston College in Kent, England, where trained experts translate and assess material before releasing it. Its reliability can be attested by the risks entailed—house searches, possible arrest—in getting it out of the country.

Samizdat is a means of breaking the state monopoly of news. It generally expresses the views of ordinary believers, though it may be written by experienced writers. In Czechoslovakia, the intelligentsia is so sickened by official writing, and church people are so frustrated by the bias of the church press, that almost everything worth reading is written for *samizdat*. The quality of *samizdat* writing on religious issues is exceptional there, as it is in Poland. Bulgaria produces virtually no *samizdat*; almost all reports are oral. Information there is harder to come by than anywhere else, except Albania.

In such an atmosphere, rumor flourishes; research centers like Keston must sometimes withhold news because it cannot be substantiated. We can give only a partial picture because so much material has disappeared irretrievably. In Poland, many popular ideas have recently been revised since the publication of an authoritative biography of Cardinal Wyszyński, which he himself checked before his death. Our knowledge of the situation in less open countries is likely to be even more inaccurate. For this and other reasons—including the inaccessibility of original documents—it is almost impossible to write a scholarly book on Eastern Europe.

Communism thrives on falsifications of history. Not only have many primary documents disappeared or been ruthlessly destroyed, but standard textbooks have been rewritten and distorted beyond a semblance of reality, so that even nationals cannot discover the truth. With the press censored and governments turning out disinformation, people behind the Iron Curtain are often unaware of events in their own country. They rely on Western sources like Radio Free Europe and Vatican Radio to get some idea of the truth.

Despite the many burdens, church life in Eastern Europe goes on, at times flickering, but at other times glowing with the true fervor of faith. The following chapters will survey this life country by country. In the appendixes, Czechoslovak, Hungarian, Polish, and Romanian believers speak for themselves.

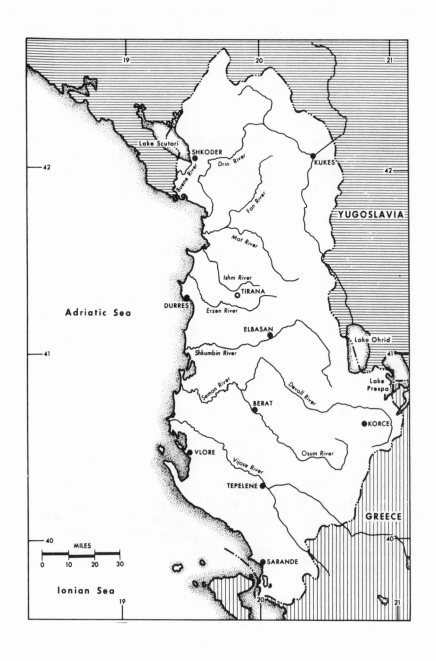

19 20 21

Lake Scutari

SHKODER

Drin River

KUKES

Buena River

42 42

Fan River

YUGOSLAVIA

Mat River

Ishm River

TIRANA

Adriatic Sea

DURRES

Erzen River

ELBASAN

Lake Ohrid

Shkumbin River

41 41

Lake
Prespa

Seman River

Devoll River

BERAT

KORCE

VLORE

Osum River

Vijose River

TEPELENE

GREECE

40 40

MILES

0   10   20   30

SARANDE

Ionian Sea

19 20 21

3

Albania

NO COUNTRY in Europe today is more impenetrable in its self-imposed isolation, or more paranoid in its attitude toward the outside world, than Albania during and since the four-decade rule of Enver Hoxha. The country, very mountainous and only 13,000 miles square, is forgotten and neglected. Although it lies between Yugoslavia and Greece (and is only fifty miles across the Adriatic from Italy), no railway linked it to the outside world until 1986. As a rule, journalists and Americans cannot enter; tours are few and stringently regulated. The Albanian language is so difficult that few foreigners learn it. The only sources of information about the country are the official press and broadcasts plus observant tourists and the handful of Albanians who have managed to leave. For these reasons it is almost impossible to assess how religion has fared since 1967, when Hoxha proudly proclaimed Albania the world's first atheistic state and banned all religious practice.

Albanians are largely descendants of the Illyrians, who occupied most of the Balkans before the Slavs. In the time of Rome, Illyricum was possibly better governed, more prosperous, and more integrated into European culture than the area has been at any time since. Missionary visits from St. Paul and St. Andrew have been claimed as part of the religious heritage. In A.D. 66, the bishopric of Durrachium (Durres)—consisting of seventy Christian families—was established; its bishop, Astio, was one of the earliest Christian martyrs. St. Jerome was also Albanian. Notable religious figures in this century who were of Albanian origin are the late ecumenical patriarch of Constantinople, Athenagoras, who reopened Orthodox discussions with Pope Paul VI in 1967, and Mother Teresa of Calcutta, born of Albanian parents in Skopje, Macedonia, a province of Yugoslavia.

The Slav invasions (A.D. 600 to 800) destroyed much of Roman civilization, but Christianity survived. By the eleventh century, however, the church had split—southern Albania came under the sway of the Orthodox patriarch of Constantinople while the north stood with Rome, though few Albanians were aware of the doctrinal differences.

23

Partial Conversion to Islam

In 1385 the Turks invaded. Despite fierce resistance under a leader known as Skanderberg (1405-68), Albania was engulfed by the Islamic Ottoman Empire. Skanderberg, a former hostage and commander in the Turkish army, reverted to Christianity and helped save Western Europe from the Turkish onslaught. Many Albanians fled; others were selected to serve as janissaries (members of an elite guard of Turkish troops)—Albanians are born fighters—where a disproportionate number became the high officials called grand viziers, a testimony to their ability.

Today about as many Albanians live outside as inside the country—three million outside, an estimated three million inside (as of 1986). The largest outside group, now approaching three million, lives in Yugoslavia, in the Kossovo and Macedonia regions, as a result of a partition in 1913.

Conversion to Islam was slow and at first involved only feudal landowners eager to retain their property and status. In the fifteenth century, the Catholic Church in particular was still active and well organized, and in 1616 the bishop of Bar was able to report that only 10 per cent of Albanians had converted to Islam. By the end of the seventeenth century, however, with a decline in pastoral standards, higher taxes on Christians, and increased coercion, there were more conversions.

Under such conditions, it was hardly surprising that among Albanians, who are not naturally a religious people, Islam rarely went very deep. Some of the Christians who conformed outwardly to Islam continued to use their Christian prayers secretly. These Laramani, as they were called, were unable to integrate fully with either the Christian or the Muslim community. Others joined the Bektashis (more popularly known as the Dervishes), a pantheistic, charismatic, tolerant, and heretical Muslim sect. Since Bektashis mix pagan, Christian, and Muslim elements, Albanians found them congenial. The Albanian version is a compound of popular mysticism and Masonic-style secret signs.

Even into this century, many Albanians, especially in remote mountain valleys in the north, clung tenaciously to their pagan beliefs, and both Islam and Christianity were only a veneer. Many villages had neither mosque nor church, neither hodja (Muslim cross between a priest and a local judge) nor priest. There the ancient Law of Lek had a far greater hold than any religion and stood in the way of the people's understanding religious concepts such as the soul and sin. Honor, loyalty, and vengeance were the most important values. Blood feuds lasted for generations. Many pagan customs and superstitions persist to this day, as even government sources admit. Over in Kossovo (Yugoslavia), where resident Albanians are not pressured to conform to Communism, children are still on occasion victims of blood feuds.

The religious background of Albania is thus quite complex. A religious census taken in 1945 shows that of the 1.1 million population, 73 per cent was Muslim, 17 per cent, mainly in the south near the Greek border, Orthodox Christian, and 10 per cent, mainly in the more backward north, Roman Catholic. But each of these categories could cover a wide spectrum of belief and superstition.

Deterioration Sets In

As the Ottoman Empire declined, corruption grew and overall conditions deteriorated; Albania was left backward and neglected. During the nineteenth century the various religious groups, which have very cordial relations with one another, cooperated in the struggle for independence. At the same time Albania became more open to foreign influences, and, with the influx of Jesuits and Franciscans (many of them descendants of Albanian refugees known as Arberesh, long settled in Italy), the Catholic Church was institutionally reestablished.

Albania gained independence in 1912, but with the proviso that it remain under the supervision of the Great Powers. In 1913 nearly half of the lands where Albanians were settled were allotted by the London Conference to the Montenegrins and Serbs to the north, and so became part of Yugoslavia. Albania was never free from the threat of further partition, a factor that helps explain the almost paranoiac suspicion of foreigners under the Hoxha regime. It also continued to suffer from misrule. During the reign of King Zog, a clan chief who seized power in 1924, it became a puppet of Mussolini's Italy, which was allowed to exploit it as a colony. When Italy invaded in 1939, over 80 per cent of the population was illiterate and the country had no university. Health problems abounded; half the babies born died in their early months of life. Government corruption was notorious. Even by Balkan standards Albania was primitive.

The Churches During Independence (1912-39)

When it became independent, Albania was the only predominantly Muslim country in Europe. The churches were neither privileged nor wealthy. The Orthodox Church had about 220,000 members in 200 parishes, with 29 monasteries. It was trying to shake off identification with Greeks and to introduce services in Albanian. Although it declared itself autonomous in 1922, it was not recognized as such by Constantinople till 1937. The Albanian Orthodox Church had a few articulate, cultured leaders. Bishop Fan Noli, for instance (later, as an émigré, to head the Albanian Orthodox Church in the United States), was the Liberal prime minister before

Zog took over. But there was a considerable gap between them and the poorly educated parish priests.

The Catholic clergy were better trained and equipped to lead any resistance against the Communist onslaught against religion. In 1939 the church had 124,000 members in 123 parishes, served by 152 priests, 32 lay monks, and 135 nuns. It operated a seminary, 15 schools, 134 orphanages, and a lively press. Franciscans and Jesuits made heroic attempts to reconcile and pacify warring clans in the mountains. Living in remote villages, they acted as judges and as doctors, trudging from deathbed to deathbed during epidemics, and were greatly beloved. Nuns helped pioneer the education of girls and staff the few hospitals.

Foreign Relations Under Communist Rule

The Albanian Communists emerged victorious from the upheaval of World War II—the chaos of invasion and civil war. Their victory was due in part to the support they got both from their big neighbor Yugoslavia's Communist Party and from the Allies, but also to their own discipline and military effectiveness under a brilliant, ruthless commander, Mehmet Shehu, later to become prime minister. Albania had the distinction of being the only East European country where the Red Army played no part in "liberation." But after the war its new rulers were only too aware of Albania's vulnerability, owing to its relatively small size, its poverty, and its strategic position.

Enver Hoxha had become the first secretary of the Communist Party, and thus Communist party chief, in 1941, three years before the Communists took over the the country. In 1948, the West attempted to destroy Hoxha's fledgling regime by sending in agents to stir up guerrilla warfare—a scheme revealed to the USSR by Kim Philby, the British intelligence agent who was a Soviet spy. In the same year, Tito (who had become the head of Yugoslavia in 1945) was expelled from the Cominform—the organization of Communist parties—for challenging Soviet supremacy. The first of these developments caused Hoxha's anti-Western attitude to harden, and the second increased his justifiable fear of being taken over by Yugoslavia. As a result, Albania became a Soviet satellite.

Hoxha revered Stalin, whose shrewdness and ruthlessness matched his own, but when Khrushchev succeeded Stalin, Hoxha despised him as a revisionist. He removed Albania from the Soviet camp and allied it with China. China was looking for suitable allies to provide a window on Europe and was willing to provide some technical aid, and the huge distance between Albania and China allowed Hoxha to retain full control. Hoxha was a great admirer of Mao Tse-tung's ideology and his brain-washing techniques. When he closed all places of worship in 1967, he was to some extent inspired by China's 1966 "Cultural Revolution." Meanwhile, Albania withdrew from the Warsaw Pact as a protest against the invasion of Czechoslovakia in 1968. In July 1975, Albania refused to participate in the Helsinki Conference, which produced the Helsinki Accords on human rights.

Hoxha became deeply disturbed by the rapprochement between China and the United States in 1972 and the ensuing subtle diplomacy of Prime Minister Zhou Enlai. For its part, the Chinese government decided that Albania was politically expendable. Relations deteriorated. In 1978, after Mao's death and with the emergence of Deng Xiaoping's less doctrinaire rule, Albania broke off relations with China, for it too had betrayed true Marxism-Leninism. Ideologically isolated from the whole Communist world, Hoxha was forced to rely on such "hostile" neighbors as Greece and Italy for trade.

Since the 1960s, Albania's relations with Yugoslavia have improved, thanks to their common fear of Soviet hegemonism and their mutual economic needs. But relations cooled in the spring of 1981 after Yugoslav police brutally subdued rioting Albanian students in Kossovo, causing a number of deaths and many arrests.

Living Conditions Today

Hoxha, highly intellectual (and thus unique among post-war Communist leaders) and French-educated, maintained until his death in 1985 a totalitarian regime unparalleled in any other Communist state. The longest surviving original Communist leader in Eastern Europe, he was able to keep Albania on a constant course—ideologically independent, based on a Stalinist model, equipped to defend itself against enemies. Although the country is still backward in the eyes of the West (for instance, only two thousand favored party members have the use of cars), a remarkable social uniformity has been achieved along with a rise in living standards. Food supplies seem adequate, better than Romania's in 1987. All children, boys and girls together, go to school. Considerable strides have been made in education and culture.

Most diseases have been tackled, with some success. A common language was introduced in 1971 to help bridge the language gap and the animosity between the northern Gheg and southern Tosk tribes. The government has taken steps to emancipate women from their deplorable status and to foster their self-esteem. Traditionally under the Law of Lek they were treated as chattels and regarded as unintelligent beings, who had to obey males, even small boys. They did almost all the manual work but were not allowed to eat with men. However, sexual equality proves elusive. Most of the laborers seen working in the fields are women, who are rarely seen taking part in public social life. Life is very puritanical. Official sources claim that there is no alcoholism, drug addiction, sexual abuse, pornography, or terrorism. Homosexuality is punished by a five-year sentence.

Political Conditions Today

In 1987, out of 1.8 million votes there was only one dissent. The party "protects" its people from "contamination" from the outside world by printing its own censored versions of such foreign books as are permitted. From an early age, Albanians are trained to hate foreigners and to use guns—traditionally, the Albanian's "best friend." In no other Communist country are soldiers and pill-boxes so much in evidence. Albanians are on a permanent military footing.

The whole country is riddled with secret police and is full of distrust and suspicion. Children are encouraged to denounce parents who follow forbidden practices, such as worshipping privately in their homes. Failure to denounce religious practices is punishable by a sentence in the labor camps, where there are reportedly 12,000 prisoners.

In its 1984 report on Albania, Amnesty International pointed out that brutality, torture, and beatings to extort confessions are common and that security agents deliberately trap people into criticizing the regime. Anyone caught trying to leave the country can be sentenced to death, a punishment much used by the Hoxha regime. The relatives of those who try to flee can be interned. Internees are crowded into unheated concrete barracks with straw mattresses for beds. Work hours are from 4:30 A.M. to 10:00 P.M., and the food is sparse and poor.

Purge follows purge. Anyone who "represents a danger to the social system," Amnesty reports, can be banished or sentenced to forced labor. No indication is given of the criteria used, and indeed the victims may have committed no offense whatsoever. The report points out that penal legislation is explicitly ideological and is officially characterized as a "weapon" in the class struggle. There is no ministry of justice; there are no defense lawyers.

Apart from the party elite, some academic and cultural groups, a few students, truck drivers, and relatives of Albanians living in Kossovo (Yugoslavia), no one is allowed to travel outside the country. Those who do are terrified of giving information that might endanger their families. Albanians are denied all opportunities to compare their situation with that of others. Even watching television programs from Yugoslavia, Greece, or Italy is a punishable offense; one person was imprisoned for watching a football game televised from Yugoslavia.

THE SUPPRESSION OF RELIGION

Why is Albania the one East European country where Communist policy has been taken to what some regard as its logical conclusion, that is, the banning of all religion?

The answer lies in Enver Hoxha—a doctrinaire Marxist from a Muslim background who saw religion as a negative force in his country's history, the chief source of reaction and division. In his view, Albanians were at heart atheists, and all religions were guilty of opening Albania to the influence of foreign exploiters. The Muslims had strong links with Turkey and the Muslim world; the Orthodox, ruled by Constantinople, were under Greek sway, even if unwillingly; the Catholics were under papal jurisdiction, a third of their clergy were Italian, and most Albanian priests completed their education in Italy. For centuries Albanians had had to worship in Arabic, Greek, and Latin.

Hoxha's assessment of the general effect of religion was not completely fair. He branded all Catholics as Fascists, though only a minority collaborated with Mussolini. Catholics and Bektashi, in particular, had provided much of the leadership in the independence movement. The first books in Albanian had been printed and the first Albanian schools opened by the Catholic Church. Hoxha made great use of a statement by a leading nineteenth-century Catholic intellectual, Vaso Pashko: "The religion of Albanians is Albanianism."

Hoxha also regarded religion as responsible for the pronounced backwardness of Albanian society, particularly its fatalism and its gross inequality between men and women, which were due largely to the Law of Lek and to Islam.

The First Stage, 1944–51

Hoxha's campaign against religion was conducted in three clear stages. In the first stage, the government, as in most other Communist states, attempted to "nationalize" the churches. In 1945, land reform nationalized most church property. Believers who actively opposed state policies were treated harshly. Fake trials, torture, and open murder were among the tactics used.

The Muslims. Islam never presented Hoxha with a serious obstacle. He split the Muslims by officially recognizing the Bektashis as separate, executed any leaders who opposed him, and flaunted those who accepted his changes to show the Muslim world that Communists and Muslims could coexist. The Ded, spiritual head of the world's seven million Bektashis, who had his seat in Albania's capital, Tirana, was exploited in this way. The

Bektashis' 260 monasteries, with 65 superiors and 468 monks, were closed, and in 1949 their schools were shut down.

The Orthodox Church. A number of the Orthodox lower clergy had actively supported the Communist partisans during World War II, hoping thereby to be allowed to continue their religious activity unobstructed. In 1945, they joined the Union of Orthodox Priests, an organization used as a ploy by the state to divide the lower clergy from the bishops. Hoxha also tried to exploit the traditional patriotism of the Orthodox by infiltrating their churches and monasteries with Communist agents and sympathizers. As a result, one of their two seminaries was closed, their schools were nationalized (1949), and the church was brought to its knees, though not without a struggle.

Those who opposed the changes were quickly dealt with. Archbishop Kristofor Kissi was deposed in April 1949 and tortured to death. The other archbishop, three bishops, and a number of priests who opposed the Communists were arrested and disappeared in the labor camps. As a final insult, a pro-Communist militant, Pais Vodica, was appointed to replace Kissi, although he was married and therefore canonically ineligible to be a bishop. When Albania came under Soviet domination in 1948, Hoxha was pressured to subordinate the Orthodox Church to the Moscow Patriarchate. The autonomy the church had fought so long and so hard to achieve was surrendered in 1950, and for over a decade its representatives were forced to attend peace conferences promoted by Moscow.

The Catholic Church. The brunt of the early persecution, however, fell on the Catholic Church. As Hoxha had foreseen, the Catholic Church put up a far stronger fight owing to its superior organization and its fierce loyalty to Rome. Guerrilla resistance lasted longest in the more Catholic northern regions.

Hoxha responded by launching a propaganda campaign to discredit the church—arresting or eliminating its leaders and branding them as "a fifth column of Italian Fascists," or as Vatican or American spies. Leading Jesuits and Franciscans—key figures in the church and national culture—were executed. In 1945, in a slight shift of tactics, he tried to persuade the two archbishops, Gaspar Thaci and Vincent Prendushi, to separate from Rome by promising them material help to form a "national" church. They refused. Thaci was murdered in 1946, and Prendushi, sentenced to twenty years' hard labor, died in prison, possibly in 1949, certainly after torture. Bishop Fran Gjini, who made a particularly courageous stand, and two other bishops were executed. By 1950, Bernardin Shllaku, a septuagenarian, was the sole surviving Catholic bishop in Albania.

Nuns were publicly humiliated—many forced to walk naked through the streets—and forty-three were sent to labor camps. All schools, orphanages, and charitable institutions were confiscated. An infuriated government watched as a large crowd of grateful Albanians, including many Muslims, turned out to say goodbye to the 120 Italian clergy who were expelled in 1946. That same year, some leading priests and laity who had printed and distributed leaflets calling for a democratic union to oppose the Communists in the coming elections were executed.

An estimated thirty Franciscans, thirteen Jesuits, sixty parish priests, ten seminarians, and eight nuns either were executed or died in the appalling conditions in the labor camps, whose inmates were mainly employed in draining malarial swamps in the coastal plains. An outstanding young Muslim lawyer, Mustafer Pipa, who undertook the defense of the Franciscans knowing that he thereby signed his own death warrant, was martyred. In addition, many Catholic intellectuals were shot, while other lay people, including young women, perished in the course of guerrilla resistance or in the camps. Many died martyrs' deaths, praying for their enemies and for their beloved country.

The loss of so many leaders was a blow to the small Catholic Church. Even so, it took two and a half years of lengthy negotiations between the government and the surviving clergy, about thirty in number, before the church on July 30, 1951—under intimidation and long after the other religious bodies—finally accepted a statute legalizing its position. Eventually, the clergy had to accept nationalization, but only after insisting that their church was founded by Jesus Christ, and that, tied to Rome or not, they would never renounce the spiritual authority of the pope. When the clergy discovered that the government had acted in bad faith—falsifying the published text and refusing to reopen the seminary or allow children to receive religious instruction—they courageously denounced the betrayal.

The Second Stage: 1951–67

With the state in complete control of the churches, active persecution slackened, although between 1959 and 1965 more than a dozen Catholic priests, religious, and laymen were executed and a dozen others were sent to labor camps. Only the priests who signed the statute were allowed to function.

In line with Soviet legislation, religious activity after 1948 was restricted strictly to services conducted in places of worship, which allowed believers a minimal security. With the advent of the 1960s, however, antireligious propaganda intensified. Many mosques and most madrasahs (Muslim seminaries) were closed. All the clergy were pressured to become vehicles of Communist indoctrination.

Catholic priests were united in resisting the new offensive, and the Catholic Church was taking steps to ensure its survival. In or after 1951, Shllaku, the one remaining bishop, consecrated four new bishops to fill the four vacant sees, an act not strictly canonical but recognized because of the catacomb circumstances. More than a dozen ex-seminarians were secretly trained and ordained to the priesthood.

As the years went by, churchgoers were increasingly subjected to harassment, mockery, and crude, humiliating anti-religious propaganda. Church councils were dissolved, choirs disbanded. In response, many Christian congregations had people—including many teachers and students—flocking to their services in larger numbers than ever. But the repression took its toll. Harry Hamm, a German newsman visiting Albania in 1961, reported on the decay of the churches and mosques. The faces of the surviving clergy, he said, were "full of despair and resignation." But especially in the Catholic areas, he added, Albanians remained defiantly attached to religion and continued to attend church.

As Mao did in China, Hoxha concentrated on the coming generation with an intense atheistic indoctrination in the schools. By all reports it was an uphill task. According to Albanian sources, many students, while trotting out standard atheistic replies at school, observed religious rites at home and attended church regularly.

Between 1965 and 1967, in conjunction with the Cultural Revolution and the completion of the collectivization of agriculture, Hoxha set in motion a carefully engineered campaign led by those students who had been "liberated" from "reactionary" beliefs. Religion, they claimed, was outdated, a routine performance of superstitious rites that obstructed the development of a modern and genuinely socialist Albania. Redundant places of worship should be closed and, where possible, converted to more useful purposes. Parasitic clergy should be put to work in a productive capacity.

A campaign unparalleled in post-war Eastern Europe saw numerous mass meetings at which representatives of all sections of society publicly renounced all belief in God and the saints, reviled the clergy as parasites, exploiters, and frauds, and pledged never again to engage in worship or to observe religious festivals. In certain cases children even denounced their clergymen fathers. "Thunder sheets" appeared in the streets attacking parents who had named their children after saints, as was customary among Christians.

It was all very similar to what was going on in the Chinese Cultural Revolution at the same time—people tried to outdo one another in the vehemence of their denunciations, in dread of being singled out and punished. The Albanian Communist Party even published volumes of denunciations.

The Third Stage: 1967 to the Present

The anti-religious campaign culminated in 1967—Hoxha's target had been achieved. All existing decrees on religion had been repealed, and religious observance from then on was regarded as illegal. All 2,169 mosques and churches (about 600 of them Orthodox and 327 Catholic) had been closed, often with considerable violence by hot-headed students. The students were rebuked—but not punished—for their lack of respect for the elderly: their deeds included burning four elderly Franciscans to death in their church. The remaining Orthodox seminary was suppressed.

Almost overnight the face of Albania was changed. Mosques and churches became storage barns, cafes, youth centers, movie theaters, even public lavatories. In Shkodra, for example, the cathedral was converted into a sports complex, and a convent church became the headquarters of the secret police. Perhaps because of their greater historical and architectural merit, more Orthodox churches were left untouched, although some later became museums.

Under great pressure, many of the Muslim mullahs and Orthodox priests—but not one Catholic priest—renounced their "parasitic" past. Of the clergy from all three groups who resisted, 217 were sent to prison or labor camps for "reeducation," many for the second time. At least one, Father Zef Bici, was accused of sabotage and shot. A few managed to go into hiding. Many, especially the well educated, were given unpleasant manual jobs. Ernesto Coba, for instance—one of the four bishops consecrated by Shllaku—much beloved for his ministry to the poor, the sick, and the orphaned, was beaten unconscious when he refused to deny his faith and was later seen wheeling a dustcart. Two old priests, deprived of their ration cards, starved to death.

Anti-Religious Legislation

Although all existing decrees that allowed the religious communities minimal existence were repealed in November 1967, it took years for the legal situation to clarify. In 1976, a new constitution formally forbade any activity of a religious nature and proclaimed that the Albanian state does not recognize any religion whatsoever. The new penal code of 1977 imposed sentences of three to ten years for "religious propaganda" and the "storage, production, or distribution of religious literature."

An extraordinary decree in 1975 announced that all people with names that "do not conform to the political, ideological, or moral standards of the state are to change them." This was directed against Christian names, regarded by the regime as alien. Muslim names, apparently, are acceptable, possibly in deference to Hoxha's background—*hoxha* is the Muslim word for clergyman. Parents were forbidden to give their children Christian names, a stricture many disobeyed. The press was soon complaining that children from religious families used a secular name at school but reverted to their saint's name at home.

The Continuing Persecution

This anti-religious legislation represented the most radical social policy ever carried out under Communism in Eastern Europe. But if Hoxha thought his herculean efforts could immediately eradicate religion, he was mistaken. More than a decade later, the persecution of believers continues. Details are scarce, and the reports that reach the West are often months or even years late.

Little is known about the fate of the Orthodox, the youngest and institutionally weakest of the churches. The only sure information is discouraging: the primate elected in 1966, Damien Kononessi, was imprisoned in 1967 and died in 1973 at the age of eighty; by 1975 the entire hierarchy and most of the clergy were in prison. The Albanian Orthodox are probably the most neglected Christian group in Eastern Europe. Influential church and rightist circles in Greece have expressed concern over their fate since 1981, but émigré Albanians suspect chauvinism in this because of the former territorial claims of Greece to parts of Albania and also because of the insistence of some Greeks that members of the Orthodox Church are Greek nationals.

There are indeed 35,000 Greeks in Albania, some of whom are certainly devout Christians, though the figure could be nowhere near the 400,000 the Greek bishops claim. Subject to large-scale resettlement away from the border area and even to forced marriages with former Muslims, they are even worse off than Albanians. According to a book written by the metropolitan of Konitsa in northern Greece, there are no priests functioning. A few courageous women, young as well as old, still light candles outside former churches when all is dark, but most Greeks are so terrified that when pensioners visit relatives in Greece they don't dare even make the sign of the cross, convinced that the Albanian secret police can still track them down. In most families, religious instruction has lapsed; yet, according to young refugees, the majority are Christian at heart.

Most of the information about the suffering Catholic Church comes from the few who have gotten out, specifically two Catholics who escaped, one in 1972 and the other in 1979. These sources report that the three surviving Catholic bishops were sentenced to labor camps for conducting services in private. Antonin Fishta died around 1973. Ernesto Coba, who was rearrested in 1974, celebrated a secret Easter Mass in 1979 at the request of fellow prisoners, who prepared the simple furnishings and vestments. They were caught and beaten up. Frail and nearly blind, the old bishop died the next day. The only bishop presumed still alive is Nikoll Troshani, who is in his seventies.

Perhaps another thirty priests and religious are alive, twelve of whom have been identified. Because of their advanced age, most may not live out their sentences, though by now some should have been released. In 1972, 74-year-old Father Stefen Kurti, well known for his opposition to government policy, was executed for secretly baptizing a fellow prisoner's baby at the mother's request. This case, unlike the others, received wide Western publicity. This evoked a torrent of invective from the Albanian government against the Vatican, for which Father Kurti was said to be working as "a subversive agent." In 1980, Father Ndjoc Luli, S.J., while working as a laborer on a collective farm, was sentenced to "life until death" for a similar offense: baptizing his twin nephews at the insistence of his sister-in-law, who received eight years. According to reports from refugees, Father Luli was executed.

In 1977, Father Fran Mark Gjoni was sentenced to twelve years in a labor camp when some Bibles and other religious literature were discovered in his attic. Under torture he admitted that he had found them in parks and on the seashore and was storing them in anticipation of the day when religion would once again be legal. Although not reported by the press, his trial aroused much interest among Albanians, many of whom are aware that certain Christian groups of the West "float" literature in plastic bags that wash up on the Albanian coast.

Father Filip Mazrreku, a Franciscan, died in 1985 in Ballsh Camp, the special camp for elderly prisoners where Bishop Troshani is held. Father Mazrreku, a highly regarded teacher of music, was arrested in the early 1950s. During his thirty-five-year imprisonment, his fellow prisoners loved him for his cheerful tenderness.

No one knows how many of the laity are in prison for religious offenses. It is reliably reported, however, that a large number of "political" prisoners—perhaps several thousand—are in fact believers.

THE SURVIVAL OF RELIGION

Even the party media admit that certain deeply held religious practices still survive. Although officially there are no Muslims, many Albanians fast during Ramadan, do not eat pork, and submit male babies to the Muslim circumcision. And though officially there are no Christians, some Albanians fast during Lent, six weeks during which former Orthodox areas show a sharp drop in the consumption of meat and milk products. Many more people refuse to work on the major feast days, especially Easter.

The authorities play down these lingering practices as superstition. There is certainly some truth in that, given the background of centuries of Albanian pagan customs, which, in all societies under Communism, have remained the most persistent rites of passage. These customs, for example, might account for the particular tenacity of burial practices. The towns are full of notices openly inviting people to funeral services conducted in homes, with prayers led by the laity. Muslims are buried apart, facing Mecca; the Orthodox say prayers on the ninth and fortieth days after death; and many Christians light candles for the departed souls. These all suggest the old Albanian belief that unpropitiated souls can harm the living, and they are akin to the primitive practices intended to ward off illnesses or drive away evil spirits—practices that also continue to this day.

Within the tiny Jewish community—about 2,000 to 2,500—eating traditional sweets in memory of the dead is the only surviving communal religious practice.

At traditional markets and fairs, people gather to celebrate saints' days and Muslim feasts. In place of icons, now unavailable, people buy postcards that show some of the more famous icons in the guise of national relics. Tourists have seen men and women, whether from superstition or genuine devotion, using Muslim prayer mats and beads, and others crossing themselves and reciting the rosary. The rosary, in fact, is almost certainly the most widespread religious practice for Catholics.

Disguised pilgrimages to the former popular shrines have alarmed the authorities, especially when miraculous healings are reported, as was the case with two Catholic shrines, since obliterated. One of the reported miracles involved the healing of the incurably ill son of a prominent member (now deceased) of the Politburo. The government understands that even among seemingly committed party members, atheism may well be only skin-deep.

A pragmatic atheism is particularly likely among Muslims. Islam is more flexible than Christianity and has certainly not been so severely repressed. The principle of *taqiya* permits Muslims under persecution to conceal or even to deny their faith; thus a Muslim can work publicly as an official of the Party while in secret carrying out the five basic rules of Islam. The maneuver has been successful in the USSR for years. It is nevertheless strange that, with few exceptions, Muslim communities abroad whose governments trade with Albania seldom voice any objection to Albania's war on religion.

The Resistance

It is all but impossible to determine to what extent deep religious convictions survive today in Albania. The continuing harsh sentences for recalcitrant believers—along with articles in the press against religion, the Pope, and Orthodox patriarchs—suggest that religion is still strong enough to disquiet the government. Official pronouncements in the media acknowledge that the process of "liberating the people's consciousness from unfounded religious faiths" is incomplete.

Resistance is not restricted to the ignorant and elderly, who, party propagandists admit, could hardly be expected to know any better or to change their ways. It appears that some supposedly "emancipated" young people have become infected with religious beliefs, apparently transmitted by some of the older generation and former priests. Obviously, conditions vary tremendously from place to place. On the one hand, there is evidence that priests, some of them well-educated laymen who have been secretly ordained, continue to say Mass and administer the sacraments secretly. Lay people too are known to take the Reserved Sacrament (a portion of the consecrated bread and wine) to others at great risk. On the other hand, the young in some former Catholic families do not even know what a priest is.

Some people cling to their prayer books, crucifixes, or icons, even while knowing that the mere possession of these objects could land them in a labor camp. One of the few sources of information, Mark Ndocaj, a former seminarian who escaped in 1979, stresses the vital role of the family—traditionally strong and independent in Albania—in preserving the faith. In the absence of priests, parents or older relatives baptize babies, bless the bride and groom, and recite funeral prayers. Many believers manufacture religious objects, even commercially—in 1973 a former hodja opened a shop selling medallions—and some recite the office at home. Resourceful believers one way or another will find a place to worship—in a garden or a forest, in a cave in the mountains, even in abandoned mosques and churches.

Religious Influences From Outside

Albanians can sometimes listen to religious radio broadcasts—at the risk of a three-year sentence—that afford a lifeline to a sane outer world and occasionally make converts. These include broadcasts from Vatican Radio, Radio Florina in Greece, and evangelical Protestant stations like Radio Monte Carlo. Vatican Radio is said to have improved considerably since John Paul II became pope—previously, much of its material was criticized as "irrelevant" to the listeners' lives—but it still broadcasts Masses in Latin. Currently the messages sent to the station expressing thanks for its encouragement and information reveal a thirst for doctrine and pastoral teaching. Radio Florina's services are in Greek and therefore of limited value. Radio Monte Carlo includes attractive gospel music, evangelistic and teaching programs, and Bible readings at dictation speed.

The government continually conducts searches for religious literature that ingenious Western Christians somehow manage to smuggle in. Between 1979 and 1982, 30,000 gospels entered the country, and Western Christians have received a number of messages of thanks. "The Church of Jesus Christ is alive and growing in Albania," one letter said. "Please send us more literature." Another: "We pray not only for ourselves but for all who are suffering anywhere; what we have suffered has purified our faith." These are the most encouraging messages yet received by the few Western Christians who have been deeply concerned about religion in Albania.

Since the mid-seventies Albania has received more publicity in the Western religious press. The book *Tomorrow You Die*, by Reona Peterson, awakened widespread interest among Protestants. Peterson, a nurse from New Zealand who visited Albania in 1973, was arrested for handing a Bible to a cleaning woman in her hotel and was expelled from the country. Gjon Sinishta, a former seminarian now living in the United States, has done invaluable work with his 1976 book on the martyrdom of the Catholic Church, *The Fulfilled Promise,* and with the annual Albanian Catholic bulletin that he started in 1980. Sinishta credits the evangelical missions for consistently taking the situation in Albania more seriously than any other non-Albanian group. Pope John Paul is very concerned about Albanians, and from nearby parts of Italy across the Strait of Otranto in 1980 he asked for prayers for all persecuted believers. He has since taken every opportunity to draw attention to Albanian believers' fate. For his efforts, he has drawn continual and crudely worded attacks from the Albanian media. When Italian TV broadcasts a religious program or shows the Pope, it is jammed in Albania.

In Kossovo, Yugoslavia, in 1981, the Catholic Church produced an excellent translation of the New Testament in modern Albanian, which even some Muslims read. Many believe that the barriers into Albania will fall in the near future and that the Kossovans will be able to extend help to their long-isolated fellow Albanians.

During 1984, a Christian tourist was allowed several sessions of conversation with Albanians. The very first question asked by a man who spoke fluent English was: "Do you believe in God?" Every time the conversation strayed to other subjects, he and his wife steered it back to religion. Others said that they had Christian relatives. In response to a Christian greeting in Albanian, a woman hugged the tourist and said, "That's true."

The Failure to Eradicate Religion

By a succession of purges, Hoxha, working closely with the prime minister, Mehmet Shehu, managed to maintain his power until his death in 1985. But Shehu's mysterious death in December 1981 revealed a fundamental rift in the leadership. The official version was that Shehu committed suicide, but it now appears that Hoxha shot him. After the mandatory purge and trial, ten ministers connected with Shehu lost their jobs—some their lives as well—and several of Shehu's relatives disappeared. Hoxha claimed that Shehu had been a "supermultiple agent" for the United States, the USSR, and Yugoslavia ever since World War II. The whole episode had all the ingredients of a traditional clan feud and revealed how little some aspects of Albanian life have changed.

Traditional customs connected with religion have proved more durable than expected. In 1980, Albanian sociologists complained that 96 per cent of young Albanians were marrying persons from the same religious background, reversing a previous trend. Religious groups, the figures suggest, are deliberately insulating themselves in order to preserve their distinctive cultures from further atheistic erosion.

Hoxha was intelligent enough to realize that this indicated the failure of his policy to eradicate religion. There were, furthermore, sporadic demonstrations of believers demanding religious freedom. Religion is also continually present in Albanian literature, which cannot possibly conceal the nation's debt to religion and to heroic religious figures such as Skanderberg and the Frasheri brothers, Bektashi Muslims who fought for national independence. Even Hoxha himself, in his writings prior to his death, showed signs of nostalgia for his Muslim origins and an open admiration for Islam at its most militant—Iran's Khomeini and the Afghan guerrillas.

A Slight Opening to Outside

After suffering a stroke in 1983, Hoxha gradually disappeared from public life. Reports filtered out of increasing unrest, particularly among the younger elements. An upsurge of petty theft and begging from tourists indicated an envy of Westerners and a desire for material goods. In 1986, for example, a *London Times* reporter wrote of children in Elbasan blithely defying authority by repeatedly crossing themselves and insisting that tourists follow them to old, locked churches in return for a reward—chewing gum or a ballpoint pen. Shop windows smashed by dissatisfied customers and the growth of a Western rock cult among the young have been noted and censured by the media.

Since the early 1970s there has been considerable unrest and unease among the new intelligentsia—the first generation to be trained in modern skills and given a broad education within Albania—with regard to the state's isolationist policy. They want to participate in European culture. Hoxha, suspecting them of disloyalty, purged them in 1973.

It is apparent that Albanian society cannot be completely isolated from the outside world—Hoxha's strict puritanism is doomed. Indeed, his successor, Ramiz Alia, who took over effective control well before Hoxha's death in April 1985, was immediately aware that total insulation was no longer possible. Alia, who had been with Hoxha since the war, is a Stalinist hardliner of the same mold. The survivor of numerous purges since his return from his studies in Leningrad, he is regarded as by far the most intelligent of Hoxha's dwindling entourage. He is evidently also a realist.

Alia faces daunting problems. Since large families are both traditional and encouraged in Albania and abortion is banned, the birth rate is four times the European average. The population is expected to reach four million by A.D. 2000, and today 37 per cent of the population is under fifteen. The land and the economy are under increasing pressure, with serious food, water, and power shortages. Tourists who have managed to leave their conducted parties have noted children barefoot and in rags. There were reports in 1988 of increasing discontent with low wages, long working hours, and fairly widespread food shortages. The *London Times* correspondent commented that despite the boast of no unemployment, visible loafing and overmanning are evident everywhere. Productivity is very low, and Alia is increasingly having to modify Hoxha's policies. For instance, he is reportedly considering extending farmers' private plots.

Alia has also been forced to modify Albanian isolationism. A freight railway line linking Shkodra with Titograd in Yugoslavia opened in 1986, and Italian is once again taught in schools. People over thirty—not just fifty as in Hoxha's day—may apply for passports to visit relatives abroad. Negotiations are taking place to resume diplomatic relations with Great Britain, though not as yet with the United States or the Soviet Union.

Some tourists in 1986 described the experience of visiting Albania as like being on another planet. The atmosphere of repression created a sense of emptiness and meaninglessness. They left an Albanian gospel in their hotel room and as a result were humiliated and threatened before finally being allowed to leave the country. Tourists in 1987, however, reported a much more relaxed atmosphere, with more contact with Albanians. Also, not all parties were subjected to the usual search when entering Albania.

In foreign policy, the key problem is Kossovo. Relations with Yugoslavia over this issue are tense. The Albanian government's attitude is itself ambivalent. Historically it acquiesced in Yugoslavia's holding on to

Kossovo—it was in no position to demand its alienated territory. In theory it would like to recover the large territory, many of whose inhabitants wish to secede from Yugoslavia and rejoin Albania. But Hoxha regarded these people as potentially subversive, a corrupting element from a "rotten revisionist environment." Should Kossovo become part of Albania, its people would threaten the ideological purity of the country. Many Albanian refugees from Yugoslavia have been handed back quietly to an unpleasant fate. Alia's interests would be best served if Kossovo, at present an autonomous region in the republic of Serbia, were to be upgraded to the status of Yugoslavia's seventh republic. But if it were then to secede, Albanian Kossovans would be too undisciplined to fit comfortably into the Albania of Hoxha and Alia. Albanian Kossovans nevertheless receive increasing Albanian support.

Early in 1988 Albania was represented at the first Balkan conference, together with Yugoslavia (the host country), Romania, Bulgaria, Greece, and Turkey. This is the most significant step yet.

A Slight Softening Toward Religion?

News of religion reached the West in the spring of 1986 from an unlikely but reliable source—the Czechoslovak *samizdat* journal *Informace o Církvi*. It disclosed the most heartening news since 1967: Alia had declared that people would no longer be imprisoned or otherwise punished for praying at home. This, however, has been denied by an official, who would admit only that old people were allowed to light candles and make the sign of the cross, but not to carry out religious practices that would encourage the younger generation to participate. To mark the fortieth anniversary of the "republic," an amnesty was granted on January 11, 1986, to various categories of prisoners. Several hundred people, mostly women, who were serving terms for religious offenses were probably released. Amnesty International has concluded, however, that the amnesty applied mostly to criminal rather than to political prisoners.

The softening toward religion is very limited and the future very uncertain. As recently as December 1985, octogenarian Father Pjeter Meshkella, S.J., was arrested while celebrating Christmas Mass in a private home near Shkodra. An outspoken critic of the government's anti-religious policy, he has already served as many as thirty-four years in prison and labor camps. There are no indications that places of worship will be reopened, nor is there news of the release of any specific religious prisoners. Some Western Christians, it is true, have met Albanian Christians eager to discuss their faith, but in the main the people are still too intimidated even to accept gifts of religious literature.

There are interesting inconsistencies. The notorious Museum of Atheism in Shkodra is now closed to tourists, apparently because of the controversy that its crude exhibits aroused. In Korce and Berat, designated as Muslim cities because of their historical significance, carefully restored icons are on display. Berat's Orthodox cathedral has been beautifully restored but is open only to tourists. Meanwhile the press maintains its constant barrage of attacks against the Soviet Union, which has, in Albanian Communist eyes, betrayed the true path of Marxism-Leninism. Even in the 1960s, at a time when Christianity in the Soviet Union was under dire persecution, the press attacked "traitorous Soviet revisionists" for fostering religious revival there, and for treacherously collaborating with Washington and the Vatican. With the Soviet Union apparently entering an era of real relaxation of its religious policy, the Albanian press will have more to attack than ever.

A March 1986 article by party ideologist Hulusi Hako suggests that the basic party attitude to religion has not changed. Hako says that although the anti-religious campaign has effectively destroyed the material basis of religion, it has not yet eradicated all religious manifestations. More attention must be paid to the psychological roots of belief. At moments of difficulty or weakness, says Hako, people resort to religious practices. Many still acquiesce in the performance of funeral rites. Also, many people still give their children religious or foreign names—completely unnecessary since the 1982 Dictionary of People's Names provides 3,000 good Albanian names.

Hako acknowledges that the family has remained the stronghold of religion. Atheistic education in the schools must be militant and challenging so as to enable children to counter religious remnants in their families, he says. Young people rarely marry outside their own religious background but should be encouraged to do so. Furthermore, the small contingent of activists, including ex-clerics, who oppose the social order and are allied with the imperialists must be given harsh sentences as a deterrent.

Meanwhile, religious practices continue, particularly among Catholics. Mothers pass on the faith to their children. People use their ingenuity to find hiding places for their icons and rosaries. Laypersons can no longer expect much help from the few remaining priests, most of whom are reluctant to officiate at any clandestine religious service or even to discuss religion, for fear of being sent to labor camp. Baptisms are usually performed by the parents alone; the presence of other family members and friends might draw unwelcome attention.

The official *Zeri i Rinise* (Voice of youth) of July 29, 1987, reported that seventy youth brigades are operating throughout the country, particularly in the north, to fight "backward customs, superstitions, and recalcitrant religious practices."

Should Albania, like China, be partially opened to the West, what would emerge from this nation that has a past of religious confusion and a present in which genuine faith has undergone the purification of intense persecution? Speculation would be premature. But a nation that can produce a Mother Teresa—a living reproach to Hoxha's policy—has much to contribute to the world.

4

Bulgaria

UNTIL ITS ALLEGED involvement in the attempted assassination of Pope John Paul II, Bulgaria aroused far less interest in the West than any other Warsaw Pact country. There had been no organized movements for human rights or religious freedom to attract attention, and few Western papers maintained correspondents in the country.

As a people, Bulgarians are thorough and hard-working, if perhaps somewhat lacking in initiative and imagination. They are often disliked and distrusted by their fellow East Europeans, partly perhaps because of the close collaboration between Bulgaria and the Soviet Union.

For largely historical reasons, Bulgaria has since the end of World War II been the Soviet Union's most dependable ally in the strategically sensitive Balkans. In the nineteenth century, during Bulgaria's struggle for independence from the Turks (gained in 1878), Russia answered the call for help. The two countries had similar languages, both using the Cyrillic alphabet, and a common faith, Orthodoxy. At the end of the war, the Bulgarians welcomed the Russian troops, who helped the local revolutionists seize power. This probably saved Bulgaria from being partitioned. But the ensuing brutal regime, which liquidated so many—including the Peasant Party leaders—soon alienated the people.

Bulgarians have drawn certain material advantages from their subservience to Moscow and the stability of their leadership. Todor Zhivkov is the senior and longest reigning ruler in the Soviet bloc. Since becoming first secretary of the Party in 1954 and president in 1971, he has avoided debt, varied the economy, and provided food for the people. He is currently encouraging young blood in industry and agriculture. Having been left in an appallingly backward condition by Turkish rule, Bulgaria is now more prosperous than Poland, Romania, and the Soviet Union (though lately, as in most other East European countries, there have been signs of a deteriorating economy).

These assets are counteracted by the excessive demands their Soviet masters make on them. The resources and labor of Bulgaria's nine million

45

people are at the beck and call of the USSR, and the country, essential to Soviet strategy, is used as a pipeline for aid to Third World countries. Bulgaria is riddled with KGB high-security zones, including a camp where foreigners who are *persona non grata* in their own lands are trained in espionage. The sole legitimacy of a "security" job is a direct order from Moscow.

In 1978 Georgi Markov, a Bulgarian defector who broadcast from the BBC in London, was killed by a jab from a poisoned umbrella. During the ensuing investigation, a former senior official of the Bulgarian Intelligence Service revealed that the service was run by the KGB. Before his defection, Markov had been in close contact with Todor Zhivkov and many of his ruling elite, and his popular broadcasts gave many of their secrets away.

Markov's audience in Bulgaria was reliably estimated at five million—over half the population—confirming the belief that there is widespread hidden discontent. In 1978 a dissident group complained about violations of human rights, but such rumblings are rare. No concerted movement has opposed government policy. It is thought that the Bulgarian security forces intercepted complaints to the Belgrade and Madrid follow-up conferences on the Helsinki Accords. A letter did get through to the Vienna conference in 1987. In October 1987 an official from the U.N. Human Rights Commission visited Bulgaria and conferred with Lyubomir Popov, deputy minister of foreign affairs, and various religious leaders.

The Religious Background

Although believers have suffered the most from Bulgaria's close links with the Soviet Union, even Communists recognize that the church has played a positive and beneficial role in the nation's history.

Christianity reached the Bulgars, a Slav-speaking Turko-Mongol tribe, in the ninth century. Saints Cyril and Methodius, the originators of the mission to the Slavs and devisers of the Cyrillic alphabet, are the nation's patron saints. Of their disciples, St. Clement of Ohrid, who died in A.D. 916, laid the foundation of Bulgarian Christian culture, while Constantine (Cyril) modified the Cyrillic script at the request of Emperor Simeon. Since the nation lay within the sphere of Byzantium, Orthodoxy rather than Catholicism became its form of religion.

When in 1396 the Bulgarians became part of the Ottoman Empire, only a few were converted to Islam; the converts adopted Muslim names and were known as Pomaks. Those who remained Christian became second-class citizens. Their isolation from the rest of Europe allowed some strange practices to creep into the Orthodox Church. The church was further handicapped when, in the second half of the eighteenth century, it came to be dominated by unpopular Greeks from Constantinople. In 1878 the church unilaterally declared its independence, though this was not recognized by the Patriarch of Constantinople. The schism between the two churches was not healed until 1945, and worldwide recognition by the Orthodox of the autonomy of the Church of Bulgaria was not extended for another sixteen years.

Religion Under Communism

The church was not strong enough to provide real opposition when the Communists took over in the mid-forties. Although three-quarters of Bulgarians were proud to claim membership in the national church, it was backward and poor. It failed to give its people the moral teaching they needed; good scholarship and attention to doctrine were notably lacking. Attendance at special festivals was more popular than regular churchgoing.

About one-tenth of the population was Islamic, made up of Turks and Pomaks. There were also small communities of Catholics, Armenian Orthodox, and Protestants. Despite Bulgaria's alliance with Hitler, the Jewish community of about fifty thousand had grown during World War II, thanks to the courageous stand of King Boris and the Orthodox Church.

The new Communist government followed Soviet anti-religious policy to a considerable extent. The current Bulgarian Orthodox hierarchy appears to accept the situation, and the church offers no challenge to the state.

By 1962 the government was able to boast that the dramatic decline in religious belief in the country was unmatched in the Soviet bloc. Two million claimed to be atheist; less than a third of the population admitted to being "religious." In most places church life was stagnant and churchgoers were elderly. A 1970 survey among peasants showed that 80 per cent of those over 80, but only 15 per cent of those age 18–23, had strong religious convictions.

During the period of terror between 1948 and 1952, hundreds of believers were sent to prison and subjected to terrible treatment. After the general amnesty in 1964, most survivors were too traumatized to speak of their experiences. There had also been intense anti-religious education in schools and discrimination against professional people to dissuade them from attending church. But in the late 1960s, a village priest made the interesting comment that Communism had made little difference in people's churchgoing habits: "It's just as bad as in the old days."

Improvement in the 1970s

During the 1970s, thanks to an overall relaxation, the situation improved for all except Muslims. In 1979 the Academy of Sciences estimated that religion was holding its own—35 per cent of the population held religious beliefs, a slight gain from 1962. The state, too, was allowing the churches a more visible role by promoting the participation of their leaders in international and pan-Orthodox conferences and, more recently, bringing religious representatives together to present a united front on behalf of Soviet foreign policy, especially at the frequent peace conferences. It has spared no expense to host these conferences in Sofia.

Representatives of the Bulgarian Orthodox Church have been foremost among religious leaders propagating the Soviet line, inevitably attacking the United States and the West. They have also been active in the World Council of Churches.

The meetings do serve the purpose of reducing the isolation of religious leaders, allowing them to establish foreign friendships and even to travel abroad. But these privileges are granted only to a favored few—and can be withdrawn. It is the Ministry of Foreign Affairs that handles all church affairs through a subordinate Committee for the Affairs of the Bulgarian Orthodox Church and Religious Denominations, which monitors all contacts with the outside world. Ordinary believers still suffer from a religious seclusion more complete than that in any other East European country except Albania.

Lack of contact with the rest of the Christian world is a condition that has sapped Bulgarian religious life for centuries. The present efficient system of police surveillance and intimidation, backed by ubiquitous informers—even within congregations—has made most Christians unwilling to talk to Westerners or to accept gifts, such as religious literature or money. As recently as 1982, some Bibles donated by Western missions were turned over to the police by Christians who feared reprisals. Visitors, moreover, followed well-established tourist routes and are unable to get an overall picture of attendance at religious services.

It is all but impossible to assess the strength of religious belief and practice today, especially in the Orthodox Church. Almost no accounts of parish life are available, and such reports as do exist are often contradictory. There is virtually no religious *samizdat*. Much of the available information is about individual Protestant or Catholic churches, but together they account for only about 1 per cent of the population.

THE ORTHODOX CHURCH

The Orthodox Church failed to provide any real opposition to the Communist takeover at the end of the war. Metropolitan Stefan, exarch of the Bulgarian Church (an exarch heads an extension of a patriarchate outside its geographical limits), at first welcomed a regime that promised much-needed reforms. When he realized the full implications of the new rule and began to take countermeasures, he was forced to retire in 1948, saved by his international reputation from the fate of many Catholic and Protestant leaders. His complaints dealt with the government's encroachments on church life and the suppression of freedoms, and he suggested a national plebiscite on the matter of rights. He died in a remote village in 1957, silent to the last. (An article by Professor Spas Raikin based on hitherto unexamined material gives a far less favorable analysis of Stefan's behavior.)

In February 1948, legislation on church-state relations was introduced, predictably on Soviet models, which gave the state almost complete control over the churches. Any churchman opposing the regime could be ousted. The Orthodox Church became virtually the hostage of the government.

The church was ordered to draw up its own bylaws and submit them to the government for approval. The new exarch, Paisi, though favored by the state, fought doggedly in defense of canon laws and managed to equivocate for two years, finally resigning in exhaustion. Under pressure from the pro-government Priests' Union, the final text (approved in December 1950) included the lesser clergy and laity in its scope. This made it possible for the Communists to manipulate elections and to interfere in parish affairs.

The Church Under Kiril

Paisi's successor, Exarch Kiril, was an astute tactician and an outstanding theologian; he managed to salvage something from the wreck and ensured the survival of the church. Having at one time been a Communist, he knew how to play the Communists' own game. With state support he became the first patriarch of Bulgaria in 1953.

Originally, a significant minority had stood up to the Communists, but it was silenced by the arrest of its leaders. Out of 2,440 Orthodox priests, 316 were imprisoned in the notorious Belene Island concentration camp. Not one renounced his faith. Though some survived the torture and brainwashing, their health was often ruined.

Kiril took complete control. Promising young leaders vanished into oblivion. Kiril and many clergy nevertheless were defiant. A 1957 document referred to an upsurge of religious activity, a considerable increase in church attendance, and an effort by both clergy and laity not only to conserve but also to spread their faith.

Among the means of survival fostered by Kiril was an emphasis on preaching, a perennially weak point in Orthodox worship. Kiril himself was a great preacher and wrote a prodigious number of sermons. He provided the clergy with carefully planned sermon books, leaving them no excuse for not preaching. In the absence of church schools and religious instruction, sermons have assumed major importance and are followed intently. The standard of preaching has fallen since Kiril's death in 1971, probably owing in part to lack of guidance from Maxim, his successor.

Kiril also made sure that the church was not overlooked in national life, taking advantage of every possible opening, especially in colorful celebrations of major events in the nation's history. May 24, for example, the feast day of Saints Cyril and Methodius, continues to be observed as a major national holiday. It culminated in the 1981 celebration of the thirteenth centenary of the nation's founding, with many tributes to the saintly brothers.

Because of its "national" place in Bulgarian life—roughly 85 per cent (6.8 million) of the people are Orthodox—the Orthodox Church can function somewhat more normally than other religions, which, being of foreign origin, are suspect. It alone can train its clergy, print books, and own land. It is also subsidized by the state, which provides 13 per cent of the church's income—enough to cover the annual deficit, and to enable the state to call the tune. The Orthodox status as an almost "established" church carries its penalties—closer state control and greater pressure. The church is expected to expound the Communist viewpoint to the Bulgarian people and to act as an uncritical mouthpiece for government policy everywhere, something the Catholic and Protestant churches try valiantly to avoid.

Priests and Bibles: In Short Supply

The Orthodox clergy are trained at one seminary, which until 1987 ran five-year courses for young men and special two-year courses for older men destined to be village priests. Some students go on for further study at an academy. These two institutions are the only ones in Bulgaria providing courses in theology. Vocations are few. Students are kept under close police surveillance and are discouraged from finishing their course. Many drop out, particularly during their compulsory military service. As a result, there is an acute shortage: for 2,600 parishes and 3,720 churches, there are fewer than 1,500 priests, and the number is falling (although the figures given are notoriously unreliable; different bishops give contradictory figures).

The older generation of pre-war priests has all but died out. Under Communism many others have left the priesthood for more lucrative professions, although priests have a certain status in society, some even entering local politics. There seem to be no priests comparable to Russia's Fr. Dmitri Dudko or Romania's Fr. Gheorghe Calciu to inspire through their pastoral zeal, challenging preaching, and public attacks on state-imposed atheism. There are nevertheless some good ones whose churches are never empty. In such churches, people can be seen dropping in and out for quiet moments of reflection and meditation. But overall attendance—even with the anonymity the urban churches afford—is low. No priest wishes to be identified as a dissident. In 1986 a priest, in a unique action, phoned Radio Free Europe to complain about the (unpunished) vandalizing of his church.

The church press is allowed two regular magazines, largely of interest to the clergy. Bibles are virtually unobtainable; apart from a small issue in 1940, none were printed between 1925 and 1982. In 1980 the United Bible Societies were allowed to send in enough paper for 28,000 Bibles. The first printing was supposedly distributed to Orthodox parishes; the second batch was so badly printed as to be a waste of paper. Visitors saw no Bibles for sale. Bulgarians view the matter laconically—a propaganda exercise by the government. In like manner, the printing of a good modern (1972) Bulgarian translation of the New Testament and Psalms by Orthodox scholars and acceptable to other churches has been indefinitely postponed.

The Condition of Church Buildings

In the early years, the Communist government allowed hundreds of churches to fall into disrepair; others were deliberately destroyed. Because of the reawakened interest in national culture, however, Bulgarians began to complain of the neglect of historic church buildings. Their rulers today would not dare destroy a building as they did in 1971, when St. Spas, which had a congregation of eight hundred and was famous for its frescoes, was bulldozed to make way for a bank, despite 40,000 protestors. People lamented: "For over five hundred years we were under Turkish rule, yet they never destroyed one of our churches in Sofia. God will not be mocked!"

The advent of tourists has also played a part in persuading the state to restore various important buildings. Among them is St. John of Rila Monastery, whose restoration has, unfortunately, been mainly cosmetic. During the summer, Rila has about a thousand visitors a day. In 1977 the deputy abbot of the monastery confided to a foreign visitor: "In a socialist society where there is no religious education in school, exposure to the liturgy is exposure to the Gospel as a new fact. Many children, and some adults, too, come to be baptized, sometimes thirty or forty at a time." St. John of Rila is also a place of physical healing. In three decades, three hundred cures, validated by doctors, have taken place.

But the great days when the monasteries were the focus of the struggle for national independence have gone. The handful of monks who remain at Rila are shuffled aside to make way for noisy parties of young Bulgarian tourists who regard the monastery as a museum. There are at most two hundred Orthodox monks, some of dubious caliber, and about the same number of more devout but mostly elderly Orthodox nuns left in the country.

Some churches still noted for their excellent choral tradition—of which Bulgarians are rightly proud—are particularly well attended; their services draw tourists and persons interested in music as well as religious ones. To counter the drawing power of Orthodox worship, whatever its form, the state in the 1970s introduced substitute quasi-successful secular ceremonies—infant-naming functions and burial "services"—with a cash bonus attached.

Kiril died in 1971 and was succeeded by Maxim, a nonentity who has provided no guidance in a time of great difficulty. Whether from conviction or opportunism, the present hierarchy is subservient to the state. It follows the party line slavishly and has even attempted to neutralize opposition mounted by Bulgarian émigrés. Priests still exist, however, who deeply resent the "communization" of their church, and there are said to be underground Orthodox groups opposed to the state; but no sure information exists.

A few members are leaving the church and worshiping guardedly in house groups. As in most of the other Bulgarian churches, the majority prefer to remain docile so as to avoid harassment.

Bulgaria's Armenian community, which dates back to the seventh century, was swollen by refugees from the Turkish massacres of this century—the last large influx of 20,000 occurring in 1922. As many as 20,000 Armenians have been baptized in the ancient Armenian Orthodox Church, under an archbishop for Romania and Bulgaria whose see is in Bucharest.

THE CATHOLIC CHURCH

Bulgaria's 70,000 Catholics and 20,000 Protestants constitute a mere 1 per cent of the population, yet play a significant part in the nation's religious life. Most of the Catholics are of the Latin Rite. Although there have been Catholics in Bulgaria since the Middle Ages, the original Latin Rite church was largely the fruit of dedicated mission work in the seventeenth century among the Bogomils, a heretical Christian sect. The small but intensely patriotic church was all but wiped out by the Turks after a nationalist rising in 1688. It was revived by foreign missionaries during the last century. A small Eastern Rite Church of 10,000-15,000 dates from the 1860s, when a group of nationalist Orthodox put themselves under papal authority as a protest against chauvinist Greek domination of their church.

Because of their foreign connections, both Catholics and Protestants were automatically regarded as suspect by the Communists and persecuted with particular intensity, especially between 1948 and 1952, when their institutions were closed and their contact with the outside world cut. Such treatment was very unjust in view of their considerable contributions during the years of independence, not to mention the Catholic participation in the struggle for that independence during Turkish rule.

The Catholic Church in particular has enriched Bulgaria—its society, culture, and education—out of all proportion to its numbers. Its clergy, averaging about two hundred (including monks and some ordained lay brothers), having studied abroad, were on the whole far better educated than their Orthodox counterparts. Their high caliber and dedication stood their church in good stead under Communism. The Catholics ran two large hospitals, excellent schools, libraries, orphanages, and homes for the elderly.

More than thirty leading Catholics (clergy, laity, and nuns) received sentences during a trial in 1952, and the most energetic of the Catholic bishops, Eugene Bossilkov, was condemned to death. In an indication of the isolation of Bulgarian Christians, the Vatican did not ascertain that Bossilkov had actually been executed until 1975. Of the other two bishops in office, one was murdered, the other died in prison. The majority of priests, and some nuns, were imprisoned.

The government made one important concession. Unlike the regimes in the USSR, Romania, and Czechoslovakia, it did not force the Eastern Rite Catholic Church to merge into the Orthodox Church. Behind the leniency, the government confidently figured that the Catholic and Protestant churches would simply disappear, since their leadership had been largely liquidated, their young forbidden instruction, their seminaries closed, their literature banned, and the remnants isolated from their co-religionists. But in this they were mistaken. As an added insult, to maintain their independence, both groups rejected the offer of state subsidies. In the end, they were subjected to the same treatment as the Orthodox: police surveillance, interrogation, and intimidation.

Conditions Today

Despite confident predictions that it would die out by 1975, the Catholic Church survived. It has done so through the resourcefulness and discipline of its aging priests, not one of whom is known to have renounced his vocation, and through the deep devotion of a committed laity.

In 1970, only seventy-two priests were left. These priests were destitute and, like the nuns, had to live in makeshift accommodations—church choirs and shacks. When a West German newspaper, around 1970, printed a photograph of a bishop's episcopal palace—one small room that served as a diocesan office and chapel, with a bed and washstand behind a curtain—the authorities were furious.

Now there are only thirty-five priests, of whom seventeen are over sixty and overworked. The five seminaries remain closed, but candidates for the priesthood have been trained privately by some of the priests, and six of these have been ordained with government permission. The major problem has been teaching the young, which is a punishable offense. In 1975 Fr. Bogdan Giev was caught instructing the young and died the day after he underwent prolonged and harsh police interrogation.

Religious orders have not been disbanded, but joining is "discouraged." In 1970 police broke into the enclosed Carmelite convent in Sofia to "rescue" a novice, the daughter of a government official, who was harassed until she agreed to marry. Sixty-four Catholic nuns are left.

The laity learn their religion by closely following the excellent sermons and the new Vatican II services they hear in their churches. These services were painstakingly translated into modern Bulgarian by Bishop Kokov, one of the two bishops allowed to attend Vatican II, thanks to the wide esteem in which Pope John XXIII was held in Bulgaria. (As papal nuncio in Sofia between 1925 and 1935, with special responsibility for Eastern Rite Catholics, Angelo Roncalli, the future John XXIII, won the affection of the people.)

Restoring Contact With Rome

With the exception of the Vatican Council, between 1948 and 1975 the church had virtually no communication with Rome. Relations were resumed by chance, or providence. To prepare for the nation's thirteenth centenary celebrations in 1981, President Zhivkov had to visit the Pope in 1975 to request access to the Vatican's Bulgarian archives. Zhivkov regarded the Catholic Church in his land as so negligible that, without consulting the Ministry of Foreign Affairs, he approved the appointment of two papal nominees for the two vacant dioceses. With the gentle but uncompromising Metodi Stratiev holding on as senior bishop and exarch of the Eastern Rite Church, the Bulgarian Catholic Church was in the unusual position in Eastern Europe of having three bishops, not one of whom was a state nominee.

When the foreign minister made a follow-up visit to Pope John Paul II in 1978, the Pope emphasized the exemplary conduct of Bulgarian Catholics and gained a few concessions, such as occasional visits to Rome for a few selected Catholics, but not the unjamming of Vatican Radio. Meanwhile, Catholics had repaired their churches and other property, though the well-attended church in the Black Sea resort of Varna, closed in 1970, has not been reopened despite local petitions.

With a sympathetic Slav as pope, Bulgarian Catholics gained confidence and began to show a healthy openness toward other denominations. Most congregations are mainly old or middle-aged, female, and poor, but with a sprinkling of professional people and some intelligent young people who are drawn particularly to the Eastern Rite Church because it is closer to their traditional background.

THE PROTESTANT CHURCHES

Protestant churches appeared in Bulgaria between 1850 and 1921, founded by foreign missionaries (including Russians, who founded Baptist and Pentecostal communities). Like the Catholics, Protestants contributed much to the nation during the years of independence. With their Western orientation, the Protestant churches served as a conduit for the modern practical knowledge that was vital to Bulgaria as it strove to become a modern European nation.

There are five officially recognized Protestant churches: the *Pentecostals,* with 7,000 members, the newest and most dynamic church; the *Congregationalists,* with 5,000; *Seventh Day Adventists,* 3,000; *Methodists,* 1,300; and *Baptists,* 800. (By a sensible agreement, Congregationalists work in the south and Methodists in the north.) Some groups that the state does not recognize are: the Church of God, a 4,000-strong Pentecostal group; the Brethren, who have refused to register; and an Adventist group whose members refuse to receive medical treatment, take the military oath, or participate in social activity.

Like Catholics, Protestants were considered suspect because of their foreign connections and were greatly persecuted, especially from 1948 to 1952. In February 1949, after intensive brainwashing, all but one of the fifteen Pentecostal pastors subjected to a show trial confessed to espionage and received long sentences, drawing protests from many Western governments and the U.N. General Assembly. Details of the trial and a horrifying account of brainwashing methods can be found in *Tortured for His Faith* by Haralan Popov, who arrived in the West in 1962 with his brother, the late Ladan Popov, the one pastor who did not give way.

The Lack of Literature

Protestants suffer problems similar to those of the Catholics, but they feel the lack of Bibles more acutely. Under import laws, religious literature, classified with pornography, can be confiscated. Although many Bibles are smuggled in, the basic lack of Christian literature, particularly that dealing with modern questions, has impaired Christian life. Some Protestant women, for example, believe children are a punishment sent by God, and routinely have abortions to ease the housing problem. There has been no formal training in theology for pastors since the Communist takeover.

The official ban on instructing minors and, in many places, the unofficial ban on their attending church have been particularly disastrous for Protestants. Tourists have seen children in church in the cities, but off the beaten track congregations have been subdued by threats and often have no children at all in them. Some parents teach their children at home, but the task is made difficult by the lack of books.

Another problem is the government policy—*de facto* if not *de jure*—of reducing the Protestant presence to one interdenominational congregation per place. This makes control by the state easier and allows it to exploit differences among the various groups, thus weakening religion in general. The practice also keeps pastors and congregations in a constant state of anxiety. The Pentecostal church in Plovdiv was bulldozed in 1981, and the congregation, rather than share the Congregational church building as suggested by the authorities, squeezed into a private house until they were granted permission to build a new church. The Baptist church at Varna, demolished in 1985, is being rebuilt. There are also some flourishing congregations that the state refuses to register.

Although evangelistic activities are officially forbidden, many churches hold mission services several times a week. In 1977 a charismatic revival started spontaneously in the Pentecostal Church. Baptism in the Spirit, miraculous healings, conversions among young people—even among former party activists—have been reported. This renewal has spilled over into some other churches—even Orthodox and Catholic—and represents the most dynamic element in Bulgarian church life today; the state is helpless to control it. The Pentecostal Church is unique in having many younger clergy.

Banishment and Imprisonment

The state has special means of dealing with pastors whom it regards as too active or successful. It does not penalize them on religious grounds but instead, under various false accusations, including illegal dealings in foreign currency, banishes them to remote villages (one of the three thus punished in 1975, an outstanding pastor named Stefan Stefanov, had been instrumental in converting the daughter of a party official) or sends them to prison, as it did with five leading Pentecostals in 1979. Thanks to international publicity and protests, the Pentecostals' sentences were reduced. Under the People's Militia Law, people may be banished internally for up to three years without trial. Their freedom of movement may be restricted, and the restrictions indefinitely renewed.

Abjuring military service may also lead to imprisonment. Pentecostalist Emil Kalmakov, for example, has served four terms in prison since 1979 for refusing to bear arms. His father, Kostadin, was imprisoned for five years in 1982 for protesting the treatment of his son and of conscientious objectors generally. He had been in prison previously for refusing to work on Christmas and Easter, which he maintains should be observed as religious holidays. In 1984 at Christmas he was beaten unconscious by prison guards. The prison doctor was called but did nothing to help him. He was then thrown naked into a punishment cell for fourteen days but released after three for fear he would die of the cold.

Surprisingly few cases of imprisonment have been recorded in the past ten years, but some could have gone unreported. Certainly pressure on believers continues. Christians can be removed from their church by a change of job or have a neighbor planted to monitor their movements; informers in congregations create distrust. Some, especially pastors, have their residence permits withdrawn; the pastor of a Sofia Baptist church has to live elsewhere and travel to Sofia for services. Many devout Christians have experienced hidden suffering on account of their faith.

A particularly tense situation developed in Bulgaria's main Congregational church at Sofia, whose pastor automatically becomes chairman of the whole denomination. After Pastor Bozavaiski retired in 1984, the state named Pavel Ivanov as successor. This violates the fundamental tenet of Congregationalism—that the local congregation has authority over its own affairs. Ivanov had already effectively destroyed three churches of which he had been pastor. There were unedifying incidents within the church as Ivanov, with full government backing, attempted to assert his authority. The congregation began to dwindle. The believers' choice for pastor, Hristo Kulichev, and his brother were arrested in January 1985. They were eventually charged with "practicing a trade or profession without the requisite authorization," and, later, "misappropriation of funds." They were released, but Hristo was exiled for three years to a remote village, where he is making converts. Late in 1987 he refused to accept a conditional release from internal exile since he would have had to become an ordinary member of another church in Sofia, where he still has the support of his own congregation.

THE MUSLIM COMMUNITY

Although the government has claimed since 1956 that there are no ethnic minorities in Bulgaria, there are at least 800,000 Turks, who together with the 150,000 Pomaks (descendants of the Bulgarians who converted to Islam under Ottoman rule), the Tatars (descendants of the Mongolians who overran much of Europe and Asia under Genghis Khan), and the Gypsies make up a total of 1.2 million "Muslims." At least 60 per cent practice their religion. The estimated number of Gypsies varies from 200,000 to 460,000. Although they are classified as Muslims, apart from a few who are ardent Christians, their religious beliefs are barely perceptible.

The Muslim communities are found mostly in the northeast, where the Pomaks are concentrated, and in the southern Rhodope Mountains. They are homogeneous and geographically compact and thus are potential centers of mass resistance to Communism, although they are reportedly law-abiding people.

The Anti-Islamic Policy

As a reminder of Bulgaria's former oppressors, Muslims are looked upon with suspicion; current state policy bears the signs of pathological revenge. The situation is aggravated by their birth rate—four times higher than the (low) national average. In 1950, 250,000 Bulgarian Turks were expatriated to Turkey, but another mass exodus is unlikely since neighboring Muslim countries have their own population problems. Between 1950 and 1977, when emigration was banned, about 70,000 more emigrated.

Apart from formal top-level contact with Soviet Muslim leaders, Bulgarian Muslims have been kept isolated from the outside Muslim world. Since the early 1950s, only three have been allowed to make the pilgrimage to Mecca.

The Communists have admitted that Islam is far harder to break down than Christianity. It is a complete way of life, in which religious and secular elements cannot be separated. As a result, besides enforcing the normal limitations on religious practice, the government has singled out Muslims for extra discrimination and oppression. Fewer than 1 per cent of university graduates are Muslims; those on military service are not permitted to carry weapons; and those openly practicing their religion are liable to lose their jobs.

Whole villages have been sacked, many mosques and Korans destroyed. Schools have been closed, and starting in 1958 Turkish schools began to merge with Bulgarian schools. Since 1974 the Turkish language can no longer be taught. The once flourishing madrasah (seminary) was shut down, and the only religious publication allowed is a pocket diary.

By the early 1980s, there were only 1,300 mosques left, and the number of imams (religious leaders) had fallen from 2,715 (in 1956) to 600 (in 1981).

Since the government does not categorize prisoners as either "political" or "religious," it is impossible to ascertain how many Muslims are in prison for their faith. All sentences are for "criminal" offenses, such as currency speculation and possession of weapons. Refugees, however, report that a disproportionately large number of "politicals" in prison are Muslim, women as well as men. Some of these, including a number of imams arrested in 1977 and sent to the Belene Island camp, were imprisoned solely for maintaining their traditional beliefs and practices.

Forcing a Change of Names

The Pomaks were the first target; in the early 1970s, they were subjected to physical and psychological terror tactics to force them to adopt Slavonic names. (Their ancestors had taken Muslim names when they converted to Islam.) Many refused and were imprisoned. As of 1976, of the 1,300 prisoners on Belene Island, 500 were Pomaks. The harsh treatment stimulated a harder resistance, which in turn provoked more arrests.

The government's anti-Islamic policy gained force in 1984 when—in a ploy to give the impression of national unity for the 1985 census—it decided to Bulgarize the Turkish population by forcing them too to change their names. The reasons for this extraordinary campaign, reminiscent of Albania, seems to have been a mixture of pathological revenge on former oppressors with fear of the rising Turkish birth rate and of militant Islam. The decision to enforce name-changing was taken in secret by the party Central Committee and launched without warning. Halil Ahmedov Ibishev, a former member of the National Assembly now in the West, was told to explain that anyone who resisted would be "killed like a dog." A Yugoslav, the only foreign journalist who managed to enter the "forbidden" Muslim territory, reported on the prevailing fear and suspicion. An old man spoke of a resistance movement whose aim was to create a separate republic for Bulgarian Turks, as had happened in Cyprus. The government uncovered the plot and used it as an excuse for further vicious attacks on the Turks. The secret organization was destroyed; its leaders fled to Turkey.

The bits of information that seeped out told of troops and tanks surrounding Turkish areas without warning. Phone connections were severed. People weren't allowed to leave till the campaign was completed. Objectors were put temporarily in special camps; some were tortured. In one village, in the course of a peaceful demonstration, six people—including a two-year-old girl and her mother—were killed and forty wounded; in bitter clashes in various places, a hundred are believed to have been slain. It is impossible to verify the numbers of arrests and of casualties, though Amnesty International obtained the names of 250 arrested between December 1984 and March 1985.

Although the government has been charged with "administrative genocide," the Turkish government—the Muslims' obvious defender—has done little beyond removing the Turkish ambassador, not wishing to fall out of grace with Bulgaria and lose its main truck route to Europe.

The people have now been cowed into submission and have agreed to change their names, at least in public. There is little doubt that in private they retain their Islamic names, just as in Albania, Christian names are preserved secretly despite the official decree that Christians adopt names of Muslim origin—a strange parallel indeed.

Other Restrictions

Islamic holidays, circumcision, and other traditional ceremonies have been banned; all boys are now examined. Kalbiye Saadettinova was arrested for having two sons circumcised and was still in detention late in 1986. More mosques have been demolished; where they remain, they are open only on Fridays. Tombstones have been destroyed. Fasting during Ramadan has been condemned as a "destructive superstition that prevents people from working properly," and Muslim women must do military service along with men. Women are forbidden to wear traditional Turkish trousers. The Turkish language is banned. Most imams were cowed into submission by the threat that their mosques would be closed. At least one, Yusei Kabou, was arrested when he resisted the coversion of his mosque into a warehouse.

The state authorities reacted indignantly to accusations of persecution in the foreign media. The chairman of the Bulgarian National Assembly remarked in March 1985 that the "resumption" of Bulgarian names by citizens with "Turkish-Arabic" names had been "completed safely," and that it had taken place "speedily, spontaneously, and calmly" as a result of "historical maturity." In the Bulgarian nation "there were no parts of other people or nations." The chief mufti (judge of Muslim religious law) and leading imams, obviously under duress, followed up with an official statement in December 1985 denying any abusive treatment of Muslims. In 1987 an Islamic Conference delegation was allowed to visit Muslim areas and was reassured by the chief mufti, Miran Topchiev, that the people were free to practice their religion.

In 1986 short (six-month) training courses for imams were restarted, a reward for the loyalty of the Muslim establishment and an indication that the situation was now under control. The state has obviously decided to maintain a minimal Muslim life for cosmetic purposes.

The campaign against the Muslim minority has continued with the breaking up of some Muslim communities by compulsory resettlement and removal of protesting families under the People's Militia Law. It may be ill advised. Moscow is said to have been unhappy about it, though Soviet leaders declined a Turkish plea to intercede. Although Zhivkov is obviously confident that the police and the army can maintain control, no country can afford to have a million of its people simmering with suppressed hatred.

In contrast, the only other non-Christian group of note, the Jewish community, presents no problem at all to the government. Since 40,000 were permitted to emigrate to Israel between 1948 and 1955, only 5,500 rather elderly Jews are left, with three active synagogues and no rabbis. Only about 50 of Sofia's 3,200 Jews attend its dilapidated synagogue. Although the Jews are officially recognized as a religious body, with their own calendar and newspaper, mixed marriages are common, and assimilation and integration into the Bulgarian nation, along approved lines, is proceeding fast.

RECENT DEVELOPMENTS

Many young Bulgarians, like the young elsewhere in Eastern Europe, are becoming disenchanted with the Party and its rigid ideology. Since October 1985, the state has taken severe steps to regulate youth—including a 9:00 P.M. curfew and the use of identity cards. The young for the most part no longer turn to the USSR for inspiration but look with envy at the United States and its material goods. Some, however, as Orthodox Bishop Stefan of Velike Turnovo said back in 1970, "are searching for new answers, and they do so with great seriousness." He claimed then that "religion is finding its place again." The young whose search leads them to religion, however, must enter the churches furtively, for fear of reprisals.

At the 1982 Congress of Communist Youth, the ban on religious instruction of minors was reiterated: "education and the care of the young are the responsibility solely of the State." Significantly, the two Latin Rite Catholic bishops were selected for warning in this respect. Restrictions on Christians traveling abroad have also been renewed, though inconsistently.

The Orthodox Church

The splendor and otherworldliness of Orthodox services attract some Bulgarians; others prefer the charismatic services. Still others seek the close fellowship of unofficial prayer groups, signs of a grass-roots ecumenism unexpected in a country where relations between Christians even of the same denomination have been marred by mutual suspicion. Often these suspicions are well founded, for every congregation has informers.

Active evangelism—which proceeds despite official prohibition—is not confined to Protestants. In 1978 three Orthodox activists in Burgas were attacked in the local press for sharing their beliefs with fellow workers. One of them, Yanko Yankev, a cable-factory worker, distributed material copied from religious books, a practice considered more reprehensible than his preconversion hobby—pornographic photography.

A further ominous sign of concern by the state was the 1982 clampdown on activities that were formerly tolerated. The *bratstva* (brother-hoods), for example, have been banned. These informal parish organizations, extremely popular and active in the 1950s, shared in various church activities, such as singing in the choir, cleaning the church, studying Scripture, training lay preachers, and going on pilgrimages with the clergy to the many shrines. Now only paid employees can clean churches or sing in church choirs. (What goes on in the relatively few churches on the tourist track and what goes on in the vast majority elsewhere are entirely different matters.) In 1987, without warning, the five- and two-year courses at the seminary were replaced by a single three-year one that both older and younger men now have to follow. Some Orthodox see this as state interfer-ence to produce insufficiently prepared priests. The cut is a significant backward step at a time when the Soviet Union seems to be slightly relax-ing its religious policy.

The Catholic Church

The "Bulgarian Connection" in the attempted assassination of Pope John Paul II brought unwelcome attention to the country and has had an especially adverse effect on the Catholic Church, no matter its innocence. Individual Catholics have again suffered severe intimidation. This is particularly unfortunate, since the Vatican's relations with Bulgaria had become less strained than its relations with most other East European governments.

The principal problem—the aging of the clergy—is becoming more acute each year. The state has allowed only four younger candidates to be ordained. At present, owing to the effective state deterrents, only three can-didates are in training. Bishop Dobranov died in 1983, and despite concilia-tory moves by the Pope, for several years there were no signs of a successor. Finally in 1988, Georgi Iovchev, 38, who had been permitted to study in Rome 1980–82, became bishop of Sofia-Plovdiv. The process of beatification of Bishop Bossilkov—condemned to death in 1952—has been postponed following pressure on the Vatican from the government.

According to reports, the church is in a grave condition. One priest, for instance, who previously exercised an active ministry, has been forced to cut contacts with visitors and even with his parishioners because of death threats to his aged mother. There may be other similar cases. It seems as if the Catholic Church is being condemned to return to the ghetto existence from which it had emerged so impressively in the 1960s. In 1987 a Vatican dele-gation discussed current concerns with Lyubomir Popov, who is both deputy minister of foreign affairs and chairman of the Committee for the Affairs of the Bulgarian Orthodox Church and Religious Denominations.

The Protestant Churches

The Congregational church in Sofia continues to be run by the state-appointed Ivanov, who at first had to be escorted to the pulpit by the police.

The state has also clamped down on the Baptists. From 1984 until his death in 1987 at the age of 83, their saintly leader Ivan Angelov, who for many years was forced to live in a remote village, was the only Baptist leader in Eastern Europe not allowed to attend the European Baptist Conference. At another Sofia Baptist church, three qualified candidates were ordered out of the city, leaving the state-supported Timotei Michaelov to fill the post of pastor. When he began to preach, almost the entire congregation walked out.

The Church of God, which applies in vain for registration, continues strong, but its members have been under constant pressure and subject to physical and mental intimidation. Many have become secret believers or changed over to registered churches. In the fall of 1987, three of its leaders who had previously been sentenced, under the People's Militia Law, to three years' exile with compulsory labor were allowed to return home. Toma Spassov had served two years, Pavel Ignatov six months, and Stanislav Todorov two months. Their release seems to have been due to publicity abroad, especially in Ignatov's case. There are now indications that the authorities may be prepared to grant the Church of God official recognition under certain conditions. The influence of this church has even extended to some Orthodox priests, who now enthusiastically preach the necessity of personal conversion.

Bright Spots, But a Gloomy Prospect

There are some bright spots. Nowhere do Saints Cyril and Methodius receive such official adulation as in Bulgaria. National pride undoubtedly plays its part, as does perhaps a self-assertiveness *vis-à-vis* the Russians, whose nation and church are younger. Hence, when Patriarch Maxim observed that the Moravian mission of "the first two Slavonic teachers" had awakened Slavdom to a new life and given impetus to its progress, he added, not unexpectedly, that "it was the land of Bulgaria that saw the extraordinary spiritual advancement of the Slavs. Thus Bulgaria emerged as the cradle of Slavonic culture."

Bulgaria has continually produced some Christians of high caliber with a remarkably open approach to those from other traditions. Visitors have at times experienced a warmth and an almost tangible spiritual vitality. And the government has probably underestimated the tenacity of religious belief. Other Orthodox say, of the Bulgarians, "they *believe*," meaning that they believe even if they don't always go to church to show it. The republication, in 1986, of a 1957 document referring to the continuing vitality of the church and the shortcomings of atheistic propaganda suggests a continuing reserve of resilience and resourcefulness. Bulgarians kept the Christian faith throughout five centuries of Muslim rule, compared to which four decades of Communist rule fade into insignificance.

The state's thirteenth-centenary celebrations in 1985, although involving the Orthodox Church, were kept strictly under the aegis of the state. There were many references to the saints, even in the secular press, and a nationwide program of lectures, meetings, and cultural activities under the personal patronage of Zhivkov.

In the same year, 1985, the Bulgarian Orthodox Church hosted Emilio Castro, secretary of the World Council of Churches. Castro also met with Methodist, Congregational, Baptist, Pentecostal, and Adventist representatives—but no Catholics. Because the state wanted to give the impression that all was well with the Muslims, Castro met with the Muslims' chief mufti as well. Several topics were discussed—national and local ecumenism, religious liberty and human rights, the supply of Bibles and liturgical books, the alleged "Bulgarization" of Turkish names, and the possibility of increasing the number of Protestant students admitted to the (Orthodox) theological academy.

World attention has recently focused on the maltreatment of Bulgaria's Muslims. In 1987, when the official from the U.N. Commission on Human Rights visited Bulgaria and conferred with Lyubomir Popov, various church leaders, and the chief mufti, the Bulgarian government's defensive statements revealed its increasing sensitivity in the face of the condemnation it has received. Soviet support has been notable for its absence. The faith and culture of the second largest Muslim group in Europe is at stake, and the Soviets have generally shown restraint toward their own Muslim people. However, the Bulgarian government seems confident of its ability to control the situation.

The situation of Bulgarian Christians is unlikely to change in any major way. Bulgarians are not noted for their religious zeal, and the churches keep a low profile. In general, Christians still fear the consequences of contacts from abroad, although these could be of benefit to them; they desperately need guidance on moral problems from other Christians.

Religious activity is at a low ebb in Bulgaria, and the outlook seems gloomy. Although Bulgaria has plunged into a far-reaching program of economic and social reform, *glasnost* and *perestroika* have not reached the churches. The Orthodox Church has done its utmost to espouse the cause of Bulgarian nationalism so as to ensure its continued existence, but after forty years of Communism it has been unable to exert a dominant presence in national life. At the thirteen hundredth anniversary celebrations, Patriarch Maxim, who should have occupied a place of honor, had 114 party officials ahead of him, and Zhivkov mentioned the church only briefly and in a derogatory fashion.

Nationalism has become the dominant factor in Bulgarian life. To the foreign observer, religious survival remains an enigma.

5

Czechoslovakia

THE PRESENT PLIGHT of the Czechoslovak people is especially melancholy in light of their past. Their country was the most Westernized of the Slav nations, and they were the only people to enjoy real democracy in the years between the world wars. Talented and hard-working, they lived in a prosperous, industrialized nation.

The Communists seized power in 1948, and a harsh Stalinist period followed, with violent suppression of all opposition. Early in 1968 a liberalization movement spread through the country. The longtime Stalinist party leader was deposed and was succeeded by Alexander Dubček, a Slovak, who declared his intention to make Communism democratic. A new premier, Oldřich Černîk, and his cabinet pledged to carry out democratization and economic reforms. But in August Warsaw Pact armies invaded. Liberal leaders were ousted and press censorship was imposed. Dubček resigned in April 1969 and was succeeded by Gustav Husák. The Prague Spring was over.

Since the fall of Dubček and the imposition of a hard-line regime run by lackeys of the Soviet Union, many Czechoslovaks have spurned hard work, and the economy has stagnated. Although in standard of living they are second only to the GDR in the Eastern bloc, that standard compares unfavorably to their pre-war level. Worse still is the memory of former freedoms: a literate and lively people with a distinctive national culture has been condemned to a system that stifles individuality and creativity.

Since 1968 censorship has been total—against excellence as well as against ideological deviation. Promotion comes not from ability, intellectual or otherwise, but from political reliability; intellectuals who do not prostitute themselves may end up, as do many of the clergy, in menial jobs. The state, in complete control of the material side of life, has blackmailed people into submission. The result is a flight from social and political concerns into materialism, which has smothered the people in apathy and hopelessness.

Religion has not escaped the general demoralization. In the original heartland of the Reformation, whose people pioneered against social and religious corruption in the fifteenth century, religion is now under tight control. The nation that produced such independent thinkers as Jan Hus and whose Protestant tradition stood for freedom of conscience capitulated meekly to Communist assault.

Czechoslovakia's political and religious weakness under Soviet rule reflects its strategic vulnerability. Historically the prey of greedy neighbors—Austrians, Hungarians, Germans, and Russians—it has had only brief periods of independence since the late Middle Ages. It is also a divided nation: the population consists of about ten million Czechs, in the western and central provinces of Bohemia and Moravia, and five million Slovaks, in the eastern province of Slovakia. Although the languages are similar, the cultural gap is wide.

During the nineteenth century, Bohemia and Moravia, though under Austrian rule, underwent a great national revival and became a prosperous, literate nation. Slovakia, however, suffered by being under Hungarian rule, which was extremely chauvinistic in its attitude to non-Magyar citizens. Almost every Slovak school was closed down. Very poor and backward, Slovakia could only start to develop during the inter-war years of independence, thanks to generous help from the Czechs, including the loan of many teachers.

History helps explain the weakness of church resistance to the Communists. In the Czech lands, the Habsburg rulers of the Austro-Hungarian Empire forced the Protestant Hussites to revert to Catholicism, and Protestantism was banned between 1620 and 1781. In Slovakia, under Hungarian rule for most of its history, although repression was less severe, Protestantism could not be openly practiced. Protestants did not gain full freedom in Czechoslovakia until 1918, when the country became independent. The Catholic Church's freedom was also abridged under the Habsburgs, who turned the priesthood into a civil service and abolished the contemplative orders.

The result in the Czech area was a disillusionment with religion. In Slovakia, a predominantly peasant province, less sophisticated Catholicism remained strong. During the war Slovakia was ruled by a Nazi-backed puppet government in which Catholic priests were prominent. But in the Czech area, Catholicism had no strong roots, and Protestantism was too feeble to combat virulent secularism and left-wing thinking. In the last free elections, held in 1946, the Communists were the largest party (a situation unique in Europe), with 38 per cent of the vote. The soil was ready for the Communist takeover two years later.

Early Years Under Communism

The churches represented no obstacle to the new Communist state. Protestants, only 17 per cent of the nation, were fragmented into numerous small churches, several representing national minorities. They felt secure in the legal equality given them in 1948. The Hussite Church, the largest Protestant denomination in 1918, had declined and now came under the control of subservient clergy, led by Bishop Miroslav Novák, who actively cooperated with the government.

Some Protestant leaders, like theologian Josef L. Hromádka, a proponent of Protestant ecumenism with a sense of social commitment, were more sympathetic to the regime than Catholics. The government used these qualities to promote two "front" organizations—the Christian-Marxist Dialogue and, in particular, the Christian Peace Conference (CPC), headquartered in Prague.

A considerable number of Protestants have suffered and died in prisons, and the Evangelical Church of Czech Brethren (ECCB) in particular has a rather independent, critical element. Yet the Protestant churches as a whole, with their roughly 1.5 million members, have achieved a better *modus vivendi* under Communism than the Roman Catholic Church, with its 10 million members in a population of 15.5 million.

The state regarded the role of the Catholic Church in Czechoslovak history as reactionary and obstructive of progress. Its allegiance to Rome and, in Slovakia, some collaboration with the Nazis also made it suspect. The government determined to break up its institutional network by removing its hierarchy, drastically reducing the number of priests, and eliminating its intellectual potential by closing 11 of its 13 seminaries. In 1950, religious orders were banned; thousands of lay people, along with 3,000 of the 7,000 priests and about three-quarters of the 15,200 religious from 393 religious houses, were sent to forced labor camps. All the religious were evicted by force in the course of a single night. Eight thousand were imprisoned for an average of five years; the heads of most orders were not released until the Prague Spring of 1968. Their death rate from overwork, malnutrition, and disease was very high.

Throughout the 1960s, when the camps were being phased out, the survivors were retired or sent to designated homes or convents. Some nuns were allowed to do work that no one else would undertake, such as caring for the deformed and retarded. The church's considerable lands were confiscated, its schools closed—only a flicker remained of its institutional life. After an unsuccessful attempt was made to merge the small (320,000-strong) Eastern Rite Slovak Church with the Orthodox Church in Slovakia, the Eastern

Rite Church was completely suppressed. Church attendance fell drastically throughout the country.

During the 1968 Prague Spring under Dubček, clergy and laity resurfaced, and for a brief period anti-religious laws were relaxed and the religious orders reestablished. Some ECCB pastors, notably Jan Šimsa, spoke openly of pressures imposed on the clergy, some so extreme they led to suicide. The government-backed Catholic Peace Priests movement—an attempt to separate the Catholic Church from Rome—was dissolved.

But the spring was short-lived. In the subsequent clampdown, the Office for Religious Affairs deprived a few outspoken Protestant pastors of their parishes, though not without a struggle from the ECCB, and resurrected the Peace Priests under the name Pacem in Terris (the title of a papal encyclical), a clumsy ruse that fooled no one. In 1971, religious orders were forbidden to recruit new members. Other than the rehabilitated Eastern Rite Church, which was given legal status, all was much as before. By 1980 about a third to a half of the Catholic clergy belonged to Pacem in Terris, many because they thought it afforded extra financial security and spared them problems with state functionaries.

Absolute State Control

There is no separation of church and state in Czechoslovakia. Since 1949, the eighteen recognized churches (all, in theory, equal) have been subject to the state Office for Religious Affairs, which has a stranglehold over every aspect of church life—including finance and administration, the selection, training, and licensing of clergy, parish activities, church publications, and religious education. By 1984, the state was subsidizing the Catholic Church to the extent of $40 million annually, not counting social and health provision for the clergy.

Government restrictions are enforced less strictly against Protestants than against the Catholic Church, particularly in Slovakia. Religious practices are still an integral part of Slovak life; 70 per cent of the population believed in God as of 1970. The government began a "war of extermination" and set up an Institute of Scientific Atheism in Bratislava. A typical ploy was a crude slogan used in a Slovak high school: "There will never be prosperity until the last remaining priest is struck down by the last remaining stone from the last remaining church." The campaign initially had some success, for by 1979 only 20 per cent of Slovaks attended Mass regularly. In the country as a whole, the number attending Mass is said to have dropped from around five or six million pre-war to perhaps as low as one million in the 1970s but to have risen since then.

From the very start, state control of the church has been absolute. The state must approve entry into any of the six remaining theological colleges: two Catholic, one Orthodox (in Slovakia), and three Protestant—one (in Prague) for the Hussite churches, one (the Comenius, in Prague) for the ECCB church and all the other Protestant churches except the Lutherans, and one (in Bratislava, Slovakia) for the Lutherans. In the 1970s, the number of places was arbitrarily cut by half to 400; in 1988 the number was back up to about 700. The most able and independent-minded candidates are the least likely to be admitted. In Slovakia the number of priests dropped from 1,773 in 1979 to 1,396 in 1987. Restrictions are draconic: since 1974 no radios or foreign theological books have been allowed.

Even after ordination, there is no guarantee a priest will get his license. At any given time, 100 to 500 Catholic priests, usually the most active, are in alternative employment—often menial—because their licenses have been withheld or withdrawn. There were thought to be about 250 in 1985. From the state's viewpoint, the ideal priest does nothing apart from saying Mass. Contact between priest and parishioner is frowned upon. Since Christmas 1979, unlicensed priests have not been allowed to read the Scriptures at services or to concelebrate Mass.

Meanwhile, a predominantly elderly Catholic clergy is dying off, and the number of vacant parishes increases. The number of clergy dropped from 3,550 in 1972 to about 3,000, serving 4,336 parishes, in 1985. The number of Masses—well attended if the priest is respected—is also restricted, with the times determined by the state Office for Religious Affairs. Protestant clergy are not usually so closely watched, and they are permitted to carry out a more routine pastoral ministry. Payment of all clergy is in the hands of the state. Until fairly recently they received a mere pittance, around half the average national wage. A discretionary supplement is paid to clergy with "clean" records—i.e., those negligent in their duty. Except for a few buildings for the very small and apolitical Baptists, no new churches have been built since 1968, which leads to problems in the extensive new housing developments.

Religious Education and Literature

Religious education is permitted in schools after hours, for children from seven to about twelve years of age. Both parents must request it. Since children who study religion are reviled by fellow pupils and teachers, and may jeopardize their chance of a university education, most parents—often on advice of the clergy—do not request it. In 1976, 30 per cent of Slovak children attended religion classes, down from 70 per cent in 1968.

The persecution of children has caused deep bitterness. Children of active believers, particularly in Slovakia, often find their chosen careers barred to them. Slovak teachers are paid a bonus if they dissuade children from attending catechism classes. The victimization they suffer in school has driven at least two pre-teen children to commit suicide. In many Slovak towns, young teenagers have been forced to disclose whether they believe in God, read religious literature, or attend religion classes.

Publication of Bibles and religious literature is strictly controlled. Since the early 1970s, United Bible Societies has been allowed to send in a fairly adequate number of Bibles, but the state controls the distribution—largely through Protestant churches, to keep the Bibles away from Catholics. Each denomination is allowed to print four or five books a year, another measure that is proportionately harder on Catholics.

Each church is also allowed a magazine, but all are censored. The Catholic weekly *Katolické Noviny* is produced by Pacem in Terris and thus is largely political propaganda. Even articles by the cardinal are rejected. Despite the shortage of religious literature, stacks of *Katolické Noviny* remain at the back of the churches.

Most of the old texts have been confiscated and pulped. The texts of Vatican II are not available, and only some of its liturgical reforms have been introduced. Services are in the vernacular but are distinctly old-fashioned. Western Catholic relief organizations have been told that impoverished, isolated priests need theology more than bread. As one Christian put it, "People without books are naked, and the enemies of souls cannot be fought unarmed." Czechs, avid readers who previously had access to the whole of European literature, feel the deprivation more acutely than most other East Europeans.

Dwindling Clergy and Religious

Catholics also suffer from the forced separation of the remaining religious. The aging survivors of the years of terror were shut away in remote and forbidding convents under the control of lay government officials. Their numbers have dropped from 15,000 in 1950 to 5,000 today, and care of the sick and handicapped has fallen markedly. Although in 1977 heads of religious orders protested in writing against the threatened extinction of the religious life, pointing out its usefulness to the state, the policy has not changed. The government has deliberately avoided entering into polemics with the orders because it knows its position has no legal grounds. (An account of the plight of religious orders since 1950 is in appendix A.)

The state can prosecute anyone who works against the restraints on church life. Article 178 of the Criminal Code—"the clergy can carry out their ministry only with the prior approval of the state"—can be used against almost any activity. An unlicensed priest, for instance, can be fined or imprisoned for saying Mass privately. Article 178 applies, moreover, not only to the clergy but to "anyone engaged in pastoral activity," anyone who "obstructs" state supervision of the church. These catch-all phrases can be applied to anyone who takes part in any parish activity, no matter how normal the activity would seem elsewhere.

Discrimination in Employment

Discrimination against believers in employment is widespread, if inconsistent. Christians have virtually been driven out of the teaching profession, which is geared to propagate atheism and to pressure Christian children to deny their faith. Teachers who destroy the faith of the children or persuade them not to apply for religious instruction are given a bonus. Many Christian teachers have broken under the pressure. Job discrimination has been more effective in cutting church attendance in rural areas—though not so much in Slovakia—since anonymity is easier in the cities.

Inevitably, discrimination is reflected in rites of passage. The number of baptisms is still relatively high (46 per cent among Catholics in Moravia; 64 per cent in Slovakia). But only about 3 per cent of Catholics are married in church, for a church wedding is a barrier to professional advancement. Burial statistics are hard to get. Inside hospitals priests are prevented from visiting the sick and the dying.

Anyone suspected of circumventing restrictions on church life, or any active believer, whether clergy or lay, may be hauled in by the police for lengthy interrogations or subjected to threats, blackmail, and even violence. Some clergy are forced to become informers. Many priests joined Pacem in Terris simply to be left in peace. Once compromised, they find it almost impossible to escape the clutches of state security officials. Almost all churches and church organizations are infiltrated.

Beset on all sides, and demoralized by the growing secularism and materialism of society, religion by the mid-seventies seemed a spent force, especially in the Czech regions. Then, in 1977, world attention again focused on Czechoslovakia with the appearance of a new force.

Charter 77

The Czech tradition of independence was reasserted in 1977 when a thousand persons from all walks of life signed a charter. The document, dignified and restrained, challenged the government to abide by the agreement on human rights signed in Helsinki in 1975 and by its own laws. Charter signatories, among whom were left-wing intellectuals, eschewed all violence. Half of them were church members, including fourteen unlicensed ECCB pastors and a number of Czech Catholics. Few Slovaks signed; the charter was essentially a Czech document. Its author, Professor Jiři Hájek, summed it up: "Without freedom of belief no society can be fully human."

Many signatories lost their jobs; some were harassed, others imprisoned. Two hundred were pressed to emigrate, the rest driven to the margins of society, to work as stokers, porters, and the like. The government demanded that every organization and every citizen condemn the charter—though its text had not been printed. The official demand ran into difficulties in the churches: some church statements had to be revised several times, while ECCB leaders and Slovak Catholic bishops courageously refused to comply. ECCB leaders also refused to excommunicate the pastors who signed the charter.

The state-controlled Catholic press misrepresented the stand of the Slovak bishops, causing dismay among the faithful. The church leaders who had condemned the charter maintained that they had acted under threat by the authorities to close their churches. Cardinal František Tomášek was bitterly attacked for his compliance in a letter by a much respected theologian, Fr. Josef Zvěřina.

The Chartists set up the Committee for the Defense of the Unjustly Persecuted (VONS). The West protested in vain when its leading members were arrested, tried, and given sentences of up to five years. The Chartists, who still appoint three spokespersons each year and even now attract new members, periodically issue important documents, but in general the initiatives have been limited to a few dedicated individuals who are prepared to sacrifice everything except their integrity. "Speaking the truth out loud" is their battle cry. They say what others only dare to think. They are the conscience of the nation, but because of state restrictions the only chance most of the Czechoslovak public has of hearing about their activities is through BBC broadcasts.

Charter 77 brought to bloom a thought that had taken root among some ECCB members and Catholics—that compliance with state regulations was leading to a slow death for the churches. The situation had become so bad that nothing could be gained by silence. "Only the silence of those who were not sentenced made the terror possible," said Fr. František Lízna, who was deprived of his license, referring to the early persecution. Agonized appeals to the cardinal, to church leaders, even to the Pope, marked the beginning of *samizdat* protests that in quality, inspiration, and information are perhaps unequaled in Eastern Europe. (See appendixes A-F.)

The Chartist movement brought together for the first time people from polarized areas of society—artists, rock musicians, university professors, dissident Marxists, Catholics, Protestants. New friendships broke down barriers, particularly the traditional anti-clericalism and indifference toward religion. Owing to past persecution, the Protestant churches were still leery of the Catholic Church, but the charter united a number of Christian activists. These included leading theologians like Father Zvěřina, a Catholic, and Jakub Trojan, a Protestant (Trojan conducted the funeral of Jan Palach, the student who burnt himself to death to protest the Soviet invasion); Catholics like Father Václav Malý and philosopher Václav Benda and such Protestants as the pastors Jan Šimsa and Jan Dus.

Benda, imprisoned at the VONS trial, first formulated the theory that dissidents who sought to "live by the truth" had to create a parallel culture to foster Christian life. (His description of the plight of a dissident appears in appendix B.) Benda argued that the Chartists were handicapped by their willingness to work within the system. Some Catholics were already setting up a network of activities independent of church and state authorities alike. The election to the papacy of John Paul—who had lived in a situation like theirs—was electrifying.

THE CATHOLIC CHURCH

Before the election of John Paul II in 1978, Vatican policy on Czechoslovakia had been disastrous, focused almost entirely on matters of a regular episcopate and canonical administration. Many dioceses were vacant and administered by vicars capitular, an elective office manipulated by the government.

As a result of negotiations in 1973, five residential bishops were appointed. Two of them, Josef Vrána and Josef Feranec, were leading members of Pacem in Terris and were disdained by the faithful. Vrána severed close links with Pacem at the time of his appointment but never completely renounced allegiance to it. Vatican *Ostpolitik* then concentrated on trying to fill the other eight vacant dioceses, to emulate its success in Hungary. Most Catholics believed the policy was doomed, since the government would never accept a good, outspoken leader as bishop, and in fact no bishops were appointed between 1973 and 1987. Meanwhile, so as not to ruffle the negotiations, the Vatican did not protest the state's continuous crippling of church life, such as its refusal to allow five validly consecrated bishops to function.

Among these "ordinaries" who have not been permitted to become official bishops because they refuse to compromise is Jan Korec, regarded as a hero throughout Czechoslovakia. Korec is the unofficial spokesman for the persecuted church in Slovakia. In 1951, at the height of the Stalinist terror, he was secretly consecrated bishop at age twenty-seven. When this was discovered in 1960, he was sentenced to twelve years' imprisonment, during which he contracted tuberculosis. He was released during the Prague Spring, only to be sentenced to serve the remainder of his term in 1974. Because of his poor health and his fame abroad, his sentence was mitigated. Since then he has done manual labor in Bratislava, sweeping streets, carrying luggage, and working in factories. In 1976 the government tried to expel him, but the Vatican objected. On Vatican orders he remained in Bratislava, having refused the offer of a very remote parish.

In 1974, Cardinal Štefan Trochta, sixty-nine years old, died after a six-hour interrogation; he had refused to have priests in religious orders withdrawn from his diocese. In 1977 he was succeeded as primate by Cardinal František Tomášek, born in 1899, apostolic administrator of Prague since 1965. Tomášek had been imprisoned in 1951 but was released in 1954 since he was not regarded as dangerous. Thereafter he was confined to parish work in a remote village until 1964. He was made a cardinal *in pectore*—that is, not publicly announced—in 1976. An honest, simple man, with no College of Bishops to support him, Cardinal Tomášek mastered the art of survival without personal compromise. But in his position this was not enough. Between 1975 and 1977 alone, a hundred Catholic priests had been arrested. With ten of the thirteen dioceses administered by members of Pacem in Terris, no one in authority spoke out. Over half of the clergy were what the laity call "Pax terriers."

The Effect of John Paul II

With John Paul II, things began to change. At last East European Catholics had one of their own as leader. He was to give Vatican *Ostpolitik* an entirely new look. He put fresh heart into flagging resisters and urged believers not to be afraid to stand up for their faith. His charismatic personality inspired many, especially the young. Indeed, many Czechoslovaks have turned to Christianity since the late 1970s. Catholics who were organizing an underground church felt they had the backing of the highest authority. The events in Poland began to have an effect, particularly on the Slovaks, who feel a deeper affinity for their Polish fellow Catholics than for the Czechs.

Pope John Paul is well aware that the Communist ideology is a spent force in Czechoslovakia. But he also knows that the Communist state has the power. The church's autonomy depends on its spiritual resources. Therefore he encourages spiritual renewal and gives cautiously worded support to the growing underground church (frequently referred to as "those suffering for Christ"). The hierarchy has been quietly encouraged to resist state interference.

When John Paul condemned priests' activity in politics in general in his 1982 encyclical *Quidam Episcopi,* his proscription included Pacem in Terris. This gave some solidarity to the church and afforded Tomášek badly needed moral support.

The government counterattacked. It accused the Pope of playing a double game—forbidding "progressive" priests' associations from becoming politically involved while delving in politics himself. In 1982, in what the government saw as another "reactionary" move, the Pope appointed bishops for the émigré Czech and Slovak communities, who have frequently been attacked in the press.

In 1981, Pope John Paul's uncompromising stance broke up the drawn-out negotiations between the Vatican and the Czech government. Early in 1983, however, Karel Hruza was replaced as state secretary for religious affairs after embezzling half of the extra funds allocated to reward Pacem in Terris priests. His successor, Vladimir Janku, appears to be more honest and far more intelligent.

In 1983 the foreign minister, Bohuslav Chňoupek, made an unprecedented visit to the Vatican, and in 1984 negotiations—fruitless, as it turned out—were reopened. But there was no hope that the Vatican and the government could agree on candidates for the ten dioceses in need of regular bishops—no hope for any rapprochement—while Pacem in Terris continued. An ideologically inflexible government and a pope aware of the futility of compromise and sensitive to the feelings of Czechoslovak Catholics have little room to negotiate.

Some concessions have been made. The entry figure for the two Catholic seminaries, for example, was raised (possibly to discourage underground ordinations). There were about 520 seminary students in 1987, 75 per cent more than in 1980. The rise is partially offset by the deteriorating quality of teaching and staff, all of whom are members of Pacem in Terris, and by the high death rate among priests—fifty a year, for which the ordination of thirty new ones cannot compensate.

In an unsigned letter from Litoměřice seminary in January 1988, students alleged that members of the secret police are being trained there. They complained that many potential students are deterred by threats to themselves and their families; that during study they are subject to police interrogations and pressure to collaborate; that many teachers are not interested in their subjects but that Marxism is taught by specialists; that their course is interrupted by two years' compulsory military service; that they are completely "cut off from the life of the church," kept short of basic spiritual literature, and allowed only two spiritual directors; and that no religious festivals are observed at the seminary, whereas all Communist anniversaries are.

The Vacant Dioceses

The Czechoslovak bishops' *ad limina* visit (required of bishops every five years) to the Pope in the fall of 1987 drew attention to the abnormality of the diocesan situation. Only one bishop beside Cardinal Tomášek was able to attend; the other three were all too ill. By the end of 1987 two of the three had died: Julius Gábriš, apostolic administrator of Trnava, Slovakia, a popular man who was posthumously created an archbishop by papal decree at his well-attended funeral; and Vrána, apostolic administrator of the Moravian archdiocese of Olomouc, who was anything but popular. This left ten of the thirteen dioceses without bishops.

In an obvious emergency situation, with mounting pressure from Western Catholic bishops, from ninety-four priests in a petition, and from the church as a whole through a petition eventually signed by nearly half a million (more of this later), Janku (state secretary for religious affairs) and a delegation went to Rome in December 1987, emphasizing that prospective candidates would have to be loyal to the government. The government proposed a compromise, seeking to obtain the nomination of František Vymetal, leader of Pacem in Terris, as archbishop of Olomouc, in exchange for the nomination of two bishops acceptable to the Vatican. Vymetal is extremely unpopular with Catholics. The Vatican refused the offer. Since then, Jan Sokol, a highly respected priest nominated by the Vatican, has been confirmed by the state and consecrated as the successor to Gábriš at Trnava.

Of the thirteen dioceses (one Eastern Rite), then, only four have bishops, a situation unparalleled in any other Communist state, Albania excluded. One diocese has been vacant for forty years. Tomášek, in his late eighties, has had to run his own archdiocese of Prague and another diocese for years, almost singlehanded and usually without secretarial help. Finally, in the spring of 1988 two auxiliary bishops were appointed to help him.

By 1987 only about 10 per cent of priests—300 to 500—still belonged to Pacem in Terris, but it continues to dominate Catholic media and seminaries and to act as a mouthpiece for government policy. When some members were awarded a special "International Year of Peace" title, there was widespread consternation among Catholics. Fr. Václav Malý, although at the time sacked from his job as a stoker and thus in danger of imprisonment for being unemployed, protested, "How can they talk about peace when they have brought conflict and chaos to the church?" He was backed up by fifty-six Catholics, all of whom had suffered imprisonment or persecution by the government.

The group also sent a letter to the secretary general of the United

Nations. They said that in failing to aid persecuted Christians and priests prevented from exercising their duties, Pacem in Terris members had alienated themselves from the church and from the Czechoslovak people.

Father Malý is a 37-year-old priest, ordained in 1976, whose license was revoked after three years. He has been a spokesperson for Charter 77 and is a member of VONS. Over the last eight years he not only has spoken out fearlessly on a number of occasions, but also has been instrumental in broadcasting the outlook of Cardinal Tomášek. Imprisoned for seven months in 1979, he has been beaten up many times, has had his nose and jaw broken, has been interrogated weekly and threatened with death. In 1987 he was four times offered the chance to emigrate to the West, but he refused.

A Reinvigorated Cardinal

Nowhere is John Paul's effect on morale more clearly seen than in the behavior of the octogenarian Cardinal František Tomášek. After years of silence, when, not being given clear instructions from Paul VI, he floundered, he began to speak out, as directed, though at first his nerve sometimes failed him. He promised, for example, to offer Mass in St. Vitus Cathedral for imprisoned religious. The cathedral was packed, but he never once referred to the persecuted. The congregation was heartbroken.

But instances of courage have become more common. Following his visit to Rome in April 1980, the cardinal revealed in an interview in *Il Regno*, an Italian newspaper, that the Pope was worried about the potentially schismatic Pacem in Terris.

In April 1981 Tomášek wrote to *Katolické Noviny,* calling it the mouthpiece of Pacem in Terris. "It is quite absurd that a paper which carries the Church's *imprimatur* and calls itself Catholic should publish the views and reports of organizations forbidden by the Church," he said. The cardinal has to resort to the unofficial press to ensure that his pastoral letters get printed.

Although tending to conservatism, Cardinal Tomášek in October 1983 spoke out on behalf of two laymen who were on trial for holding charismatic gatherings in their homes. "Every committed Christian," he said, "should know that the Pentecostal movement is part and parcel of traditional devotion to the Holy Spirit." The accused men escaped with suspended sentences.

Among the state-recognized bishops, the cardinal remains a lone voice. He does have a nucleus of support in the Slovak hierarchy, several of whom refuse to compromise with the government. (In appendix C, a Catholic activist describes the situation of his church and characterizes Tomášek as "a great source of strength.")

The Eastern Rite Catholic Church

After having been forced out of existence for seventeen years, the Eastern Rite Catholic Church emerged with surprising vigor under Dubček. Despite enormous pressure, only about 10 per cent of its members had joined the small Orthodox Church. All of its three hundred priests except the thirty who became Orthodox had been imprisoned. During those seventeen years, moreover, Catholic policy prevented Eastern Rite members from receiving the sacraments in Roman Catholic churches.

After Dubček, it would have been unrealistic to attempt once again to liquidate the church. Since 1969 it has been under the good guidance of Fr. Jan Hirka, who has not been properly consecrated as bishop because he refuses to compromise with the government. Relations between Eastern Rite Catholics (mostly Ukrainians) and Roman Catholics, once very strained because of national differences, have improved greatly. This moved the state in 1974 to start a campaign to rekindle the embers of dispute, but with no success. Property disputes between Eastern Rite and Orthodox churches continue.

The Eastern Rite Church was the only one whose membership increased during the 1970s: from 315,000 in 1976 to 350,000 in 1980. After a barren period, vocations to the priesthood have surged.

PROTESTANTS, ORTHODOX, AND OTHERS

About 1.4 million Czechoslovaks belong to religious bodies other than the Catholic Church.

The *Orthodox Church,* with about 150,000 members, four dioceses, 150 parishes, and 110 priests, though predominantly Slovak and Ukrainian in membership, is proud of having existed for ten centuries as a genuinely Czechoslovak church. It resents Catholics, who forced it to become a Uniate church—i.e., one in communion with Rome—for three centuries, and it claims to represent the genuine heritage of St. Methodius. It became autocephalous in 1951 but is handicapped by its isolation, by being deprived of monks (who traditionally provide its bishops), and by its lukewarm membership. Most catechesis concentrates on adults. On the positive side, women are becoming increasingly important and may soon be allowed to become deacons.

The *Jews,* a flourishing community of about 350,000 in the 1930s, were almost wiped out by the Nazis; about 48,000 remained in 1948. Emigration to Israel, particularly after 1968—many Jews were involved in the Prague Spring—has reduced their numbers to about 5,000. They have a new young chief rabbi, Daniel Mayer, who was trained abroad. There are ten congregations in Slovakia and about twenty synagogues. The state maintains a Jewish museum and synagogues in Prague as part of the nation's heritage; they attract huge numbers of tourists.

In 1987 a group of Slovaks including Catholic Chartist Jan Carnogursky issued a statement condemning the deportation of Jews from Slovakia forty-five years ago. They expressed deep sorrow for the victims of "the greatest collective tragedy in our history," most of whom later died in Nazi camps, and regretted that in Slovakia there is not a single memorial to them. Some Slovaks collaborated with the Nazis during the war, and this is still a very sensitive topic.

Other small churches include the *Unitarian* and *Old Catholic*.

Protestant Churches

Although the Protestant churches are not so compliant as the state might wish, to prevent a united opposition the government allows them more leeway than the Catholic Church.

The *Hussite Church,* once the largest, has been sapped by liberal secularism and by its leadership's collaboration with the state. It has gone into an apparently irreversible decline.

However, the *Slovak Lutheran Church* (369,000 members) shows signs of life. Largely Hungarian in membership, it is effectively the largest Protestant church in any of the Slav nations, with about 384 places of worship and 350 ministers. The church as a whole has been revitalized by Luther Year (1984), during which it reexamined its foundations, and by evangelical clergy who are challenging its traditional formalism.

Also showing signs of life is the *Evangelical Church of the Czech Brethren* (ECCB) with 240,000 members. The ECCB was formed in 1918 by a union of Christians of the Lutheran and Reformed tradition and a few Catholics. It has a presbyterian form of government, about 521 congregations and 250 ministers; ministers and laity share responsibility at all levels. It is the main Protestant target of state oppression.

Among the smaller churches, the *Reformed Church of Slovakia*— Calvinist and Hungarian in origin—has between 130,000 and 225,000 members, more than 300 places of worship, and 150 pastors. In 1987 twenty-three pastors were ordained—the first ordination since 1976, although all were already engaged in pastoral work. Theological students have to train at the Comenius Faculty in Prague and must therefore, as Hungarians who learned Slovak, learn a third language, Czech.

The *Silesian Lutheran Church* has about 50,000 members, mostly Polish. There are two *Brethren* churches, with a total of about 16,000 members. The *Methodist Church* has 1,500 members. The state has made some concessions to the smaller, apolitical churches. The *Baptist Church,* with about 4,000 baptized members, has a vigorous youth life and is expanding far more rapidly than other Protestant churches. *Pentecostalists* have had many difficulties; some of their leaders were arrested in 1983 for "illegal activities." But in September 1984 these men were acquitted and their church was officially registered, a major breakthrough.

Repression of Protestants

The members of the ECCB—lay and clergy alike—are well trained and vigorous; they are the nucleus of the dissident Protestants. The church's leaders, though more courageous than those of the Catholic Church, were nevertheless faulted by the indefatigable ECCB pastor Miloš Rejchrt for failing to give adequate support to those who have fallen afoul of the state. Indeed, some dissident pastors lost their faith when their fellow Christians abandoned them. (The police, incidentally, went after Rejchrt by claiming he resembles a wanted rapist. This did not affect his wide unofficial ministry— he is a stoker—or his contacts with the young.) By the late 1980s, the church seemed to be taking a more cautious line. For instance, at the 1987 Synod a motion asking the state to clarify the position of church-sponsored organizations (such as youth camps) was not even discussed.

Among the ECCB pastors whose licenses were withdrawn by the government are the Brodski couple, both pastors, who have young children, and two Chartists, Tómáš Bišek and Jan Keller. After two and a half years, Bišek emigrated to Scotland so as to continue as a clergyman. Keller, who ran a youth camp, lost his license on the grounds he had promoted immorality among the young. Charged under Article 178 (anyone engaged in pastoral activity must have "the prior approval of the state") in 1983, he was brought to court in 1985 when, because of widespread protests and the unprecedented support of the ECCB Synod, the case was dropped. He still has no license. Very occasionally, a pastor is reinstated. In April 1988 Jaromír Dus was allowed to function as a pastor for the first time since his imprisonment (for encouraging people to vote according to their consciences) in the early 1970s.

Three leading Chartists, all ECCB members (and all backed by Catholics), were given up to three years in prison. Jan Šimsa was released in 1981. When Jan Litomiský was given leave after nine months' imprisonment to attend his father's funeral, he was barely recognizable. Following their release in 1984, he and sociologist Ladislav Lis became the first victims of a particularly unpleasant practice—the "preventive surveillance" law, intended for criminals. Their homes could be searched at any time, and they had to report daily to the police. The restrictions are almost impossible to keep; yet, if the person under surveillance is even a few minutes late reporting, he can be reimprisoned. Litomiský became a Chartist spokesperson for 1987.

Other hardships have been imposed. Dr. Luboš Lacho for example, a law court psychiatrist, was sentenced to sixteen months for smuggling out a letter from a prisoner condemned to death, whom he had brought to faith in God.

A most callous case involves an Adventist couple, Karel and Jindřiška Kořínek, who after their conversion were confined in a psychiatric hospital for two years (1966-68). Their four children were put in state orphanages, and in 1973 their newly born fifth child was offered for adoption. Through prolonged legal battles they managed to get back four of the children. When they attempted to reclaim the youngest child, they were diagnosed as mentally ill and allowed to stay out of a psychiatric hospital only on condition they took drugs at home. Both parents contracted Parkinson's disease, which improved dramatically when they refused further medication. After they brought suit against the authorities for depriving them of their parental rights, they were sentenced for "criminal activity" in 1985, and they went into hiding. Their friends, including the Catholic activist Augustin Navrátil, describe them as perfectly normal and reasonable people. In 1987, still in hiding, the Koříneks appealed to the Conference on Security and Cooperation in Europe to be allowed to emigrate with their whole family.

Protestants have frequently been imprisoned in cases involving religious literature. Among those arrested were members of the ECCB, the two Jan Juhaščiks senior and junior, Rudolf Sabanos, and Ladislav Rakai, who were detained near the Soviet border in 1984 when Russian Bibles were discovered in their car. They were charged with "illegal import of goods." Three were given suspended sentences when their cases finally came to trial in March 1987, but Rakai was tried in December 1985 and sentenced to thirteen months. He failed to win an appeal, and his sentence was confirmed in June 1986. Rakai suffered severe spinal injuries while in prison but lost an appeal for early release.

In another case, three Slovak Lutherans were due for trial in 1986. Two were students whose car contained a thousand Slovak children's Bibles and unofficial translations of Billy Graham's sermons. The third, Michael Hrěsko, a pastor, organized Bible-study and hymn-singing groups. They were eventually released without being brought to trial.

In July 1984 the entire editorial staff of the ECCB monthly *Český Bratr*, the best of the official church magazines, was suspended on spurious charges. Those who replaced them have managed to maintain the standards.

Peace Issues

Protestants, notably Josef L. Hromádka, played a leading part in the formation of the Christian Peace Conference (CPC) and the Christian-Marxist Dialogue, and the government gained international stature by supporting them. The events of August 1968, however, dealt both movements a crushing blow. (Hromádka died in late 1969, a disillusioned man.) Although the CPC, an international Communist front, is given a wide berth by most Czechoslovak Christians, the churches have to send observers to its meetings. Its leaders are disdained for talking "peace" while ignoring the persecution in their midst.

In 1971, ECCB pastor Miloš Rejchrt persuaded his church to withdraw from the CPC; the motion passed eighty to two, and Rejchrt's license was withdrawn by the government. During the fifth CPC meeting in 1978, attended by both Eastern and Western representatives, twenty-two ECCB members sent the conference a letter that began with a verse from Hebrews 13, "Remember them that are in bonds, as bound with them." In 1983, some prisoners in the notorious Plzeň-Bory camp, including ECCB Chartist Jan Litomiský and Fr. František Lízna, wrote to the CPC saying, "Governments that deny peace to their citizens cannot claim to be genuine in their international peace endeavors."

Open opposition to the exploitation of peace for political purposes has grown gradually. At a peace rally sponsored by the government, Cardinal Tomášek dared to speak on the nature of genuine peace. The speech was never published in the official press. The 1983 ECCB General Assembly, following the lead of the East German Protestant churches, called for multilateral disarmament and for an alternative to military service. In 1984, the Slovak bishops went one step further and refused to lay all the blame for the arms race on the United States.

By linking "peace" with individual freedom, activist church leaders have identified their churches with the Chartists. The growing number of independent "peace people" speak for the majority of the nation, especially its youth; they object to rearmament by both sides and specifically to Soviet missiles on Czechoslovak soil. In contrast, Pacem in Terris supports the Soviet missiles.

The rising tide of genuine peace efforts spells the doom of one-sided government peace initiatives. As dissident playwright Václav Havel, who wrote *Anatomy of Reticence* for the Amsterdam Peace Congress in 1985, said: "What threatens peace in Europe is not the prospect of change but the existing situation. Without free, self-respecting, and autonomous citizens, there can be no free and independent nations."

THE UNDERGROUND CHURCH

Some Czechoslovakian Christians, like their counterparts in other places and times, have decided to cope with the drastic limitations imposed by the state by going underground. The movement includes more than private worship; those involved challenge the state and its control of the church.

The underground is essentially Catholic. Protestants still distrust Catholics and are hesitant to cooperate with them; they can, moreover, fulfill most of their basic needs within existing structures. Some Protestants do, however, get involved in underground activities, where they are welcomed by Catholics who hope for far more interdenominational cooperation. The underground church in the Czech lands has at most a few thousand participants, for it requires a degree of commitment beyond that of most ordinary church members. Essentially a lay movement, it is inspired and aided by a nucleus of experienced, unlicensed priests and religious who secretly train a new generation of underground priests, monks, and nuns.

Most of the strength of the underground church lies in its loose network of strongly motivated Catholics, each with a few effective contacts. The Czechoslovak people are excellent organizers once they have overcome the prevalent apathy. In Slovakia, according to Korec (the secretly consecrated bishop persecuted by the state and not allowed to function as a bishop), the official church and the underground church are essentially one, and there are very few bad priests. Thousands of people of all ages are involved.

Hundreds of groups meet regularly in private houses under the guidance of the older generation. People, many of them young, meet to pray, meditate, study the Bible, discuss problems, and worship—sometimes in experimental ways. Informal seminars on theology and philosophy are attended by dissidents and even by sympathetic atheists. In Slovakia the groups embrace a far wider range of churchgoers than elsewhere, meeting for daily worship, communal prayer, and Bible study. Informal groups—sometimes based on the Polish "Oasis" groups, or charismatic gatherings—can mold young Catholics and Protestants into committed, grassroots ecumenists. (A fuller description, from Czechoslovakia, of the underground church appears in appendix D.)

There is little official ecumenism, and the spontaneous variety is frowned upon by the state. Brother Roger Schutz, the leader of the ecumenical Taizé community in France, was allowed to come to Prague in 1981, but he and his fellow monks had to wear ordinary clothes. Thousands turned out to meet him in both Catholic and Protestant churches. Although he was not allowed to preach, Brother Roger shook hands with them, in silence—a moving demonstration of Christian solidarity and love.

The Underground Press

The press of the underground church is a striking achievement. It provides basic religious literature of a quality unequaled in Eastern Europe. Between 1977 and 1981 alone, for instance, seven hundred titles were published. Banned writers such as Christian philosopher Václav Benda and theologian Father Zvěřina are printed as well as translations of foreign religious literature. There are also illustrated books for children and lives of the saints to inspire the young.

In addition, several magazines have appeared. The monthly *Informace o Církvi* (Church information), the largest in circulation, has made significant contributions to *samizdat* literature. It is also a major source of religious news from home and abroad. It provides a platform for independent opinion and monitors individual cases of persecution. Unfortunately, this coverage is far from comprehensive; many victims are too frightened even to report the abuses. A counterpart is published independently in Slovak.

Teologické Texty (Theological texts) is an invaluable quarterly for the clergy and educated laity. It publishes modern theological material of all kinds, as well as Protestant writings.

The circulation of the two main religious magazines is larger than that of all the secular *samizdat* put together. Hundreds of people are involved in the effort—monitoring smuggled literature, translating, typing, duplicating, and binding.

Underground Priests and Religious

The state has tried to frustrate vocations to the religious life by banning orders and limiting the numbers at seminaries. Although it claims that "religious vocation is compatible with the law as long as it is a private affair," those who secretly become priests or religious face penalties, including imprisonment, for "obstructing state supervision of the church."

Yet there is no shortage of candidates for the priesthood and the religious life. It is rumored that 200 secret priests are operating in Slovakia, many of them, because of their high caliber, seminary rejects. Many priests join orders for moral and spiritual support, since diocesan priests are isolated and at the mercy of Pacem in Terris. In 1980, the Office for Religious Affairs tried, with little success, to counter the trend by prejudicing seminarians against the orders. In 1987, under state pressure, seminarians were faced with the choice of signing a declaration that they would not join a religious order or being expelled immediately. Tomášek wrote a protest, saying that the seminary requirement "defied Vatican II."

Vocations to the religious life are also flourishing, especially among young women and in Slovakia. All secret priests and religious must, of course, live in the world and have secular employment. Thus the state's repressive policy has produced "worker priests," some in responsible professional posts, and many hundreds, perhaps thousands, of religious who can evangelize quietly at work and join in underground activities. In some places of work, nearly all the employees are religious; they do their work well and are valued employees. Some choose unofficially to serve those on the fringes of society, such as Gypsies, orphans, juvenile delinquents, and drug addicts. Their field of action is far wider than that open to most licensed clergy.

Secret nuns usually share accommodations. In most male secret religious orders, however, members know only their immediate superior and live a more isolated and dangerous life.

THE PRESENT PHASE OF REPRESSION

State reaction to the growing self-confidence and renewal among Catholics, and to the expansion of underground activities, has been all but hysterical, and largely counterproductive. In 1984 VONS, the Chartist-generated Committee for the Defense of the Unjustly Persecuted, reported 50 in-court and more than 270 out-of-court cases of persecution since 1979. Those figures would have risen considerably since then. Also, many cases are never reported because of ignorance of the existence of VONS.

The present phase of repression began September 12, 1979, when a "printing works" was discovered in the home of Jan Krumpholc near Olomouc. During the previous two years it had churned out about eight thousand copies of fifty-five *samizdat* titles, including such basic documents as the papal encyclical *Redemptor Hominis*. Eleven people were arrested, including Frs. František Lízna, Rudolf Smahel, and Josef Zvěrina. They were suddenly released four months later, probably because the state was about to reopen relations with the Vatican. But when the flow of *samizdat* continued, the case was reopened.

In September 1981, the three priests and two others were given prison sentences for "illicit trading" and "theft of socialist property." Despite attempts to keep the trial secret, a crowd of young people turned up, and Father Lízna blessed them on his way to his twenty-month sentence. This was increased by seven months when Lízna smuggled out a letter to the West, where ten thousand people signed petitions on his behalf. His inspiring letters from prison were stopped once it became apparent that he had become a national symbol. (Excerpts from several of his letters appear in appendix E.)

A lawyer said of Lízna, "It is his total insistence on his priestly vocation that seems to be at the root of the authorities' quarrel with him rather than the dissident activity of which they accuse him." In the labor camps where he had been imprisoned as a youth for tearing down a Soviet flag and later for trying to escape from Czechoslovakia, Lízna had seen priests of such caliber that he determined to become one. He later studied at a Jesuit college in England and had his chance to remain, but he chose to return to Czechoslovakia to carry on his ministry.

Article 178 also applies to people who are praying, studying the Bible, or discussing religious matters at home with three or more people present. Such meetings are a criminal offense, according to the courts, because they cannot be officially supervised. Under such an interpretation, almost any active Christian is liable to arrest; Fr. Oskar Formánek, a Jesuit, has said that Christians should accept imprisonment as a normal part of life today.

Persecution of Religious

The brunt of the persecution has fallen on the people of Slovakia and on members of religious orders. The state's treatment of religious is politically motivated, with no legal basis. To belong to an order is automatically to forfeit the basic rights of a citizen and to become subject to the threat of judicial oppression. This applies, though to a lesser extent, to the thousands of tertiaries—those who cannot take full vows but nevertheless live under a strict rule.

An example of repression for even the suspicion of belonging to a religious order is the case of Gunther Rompf, a metal worker from Bratislava, who devoted his free time to helping youth gangs who terrorized parts of the city. Rompf said his most difficult task was to eliminate the hatred of society in these young people and to develop their trust in people and institutions. Believing that only faith in God can generate faith in man, he taught them the catechism. He was arrested in 1981 and charged under Article 178 with being a member of the secret Salesians, a religious society that works with boys. When imprisoned, he refused food for twelve days, fearing he might betray his friends—anti-psychotic drugs are mixed with prisoners' food to weaken their will. Rompf was sentenced to two years, for what amounted to outstanding social work. His fortitude is typical of Czechoslovak Christians under interrogation.

A case that outraged the public occurred in the autumn of 1981, when a large number of police with dogs raided two convents of elderly nuns. The nuns were suspected of harboring an illicit press, and the police confiscated typewriters, duplicators, and every scrap of religious literature. Three of the elderly nuns died following the search. The state seems to be particularly afraid of the Franciscans, an active order that attracts more and more young people. Secret seminaries were organized by an elderly Franciscan, Fr. Jan Bárta, who previously had spent sixteen years working in a uranium mine. He died in 1982 after being rearrested.

A Change of Tactics

Today, sometimes sentences are suspended, cases are dropped, and some prisoners are released, especially when there has been widespread protest inside or outside the country. The authorities seem somewhat unsure of themselves. Arrests continue, but on a reduced scale, for the persecution of the early 1980s has backfired. On Palm Sunday 1983, for instance, the police arrested and interrogated 250 people suspected of being Franciscans. Criminal proceedings were started against twenty of them. But the outcry at home and abroad was so great that the charges were dropped. The courage, moreover, of those under interrogation and in prison attracted attention to the values for which they were prepared to suffer.

The state, of course, has not abandoned its campaign against religion. Rather, it has resorted to other methods even more oppressive than trials. People are arrested and let out on bail (as Christians they can be trusted), only to live in constant fear of a trial, or are given suspended sentences. On top of the exhausting interrogations, the methods include blackmail, slander, death threats, and even, very occasionally, internment in psychiatric hospitals and murder disguised as suicide.

Secret monks or priests are particularly vulnerable. Because they have to conceal their identities, they cannot rely on large-scale support. For example, Fr. Přemysl Coufal, a leading figure in the Slovak underground and a secret monk, was found dead in his apartment in February 1981, following threats to his life. The official ruling was suicide, which hardly explained his brutally mutilated body.

Special Measures in Slovakia

The repression is worst in Slovakia, where the religious revival is strongest. President Husák clearly feared the spread of the "Polish disease"; he said that the Catholic Church was the only opposition. People who were active in collecting signatures for an invitation to the Pope to visit in 1985 were threatened with "accidents." So too Slovakian youth, who have specially trained agents working among them to root out believers.

The press harps on the need to get rid of the patriarchal family so that "the new generation may have the opportunity to decide freely and choose a different outlook from that of its parents." Christian teachers have been fired. A major scandal erupted in 1984 when a young convert from an atheistic, Communist background, Jana Micianová, contested her dismissal. She was accused of breaking the teacher's oath when she requested religious education for her son. When she asked where this was forbidden in the oath, she was told that the prohibition was "self-evident." Micianová lost her case, but she proved another: discrimination against religion exists.

In another case, a schoolgirl who was a talented organist, Monika Kacurikova, was taken from school and interrogated for twenty-three days. During this time her parents were not once allowed to visit her. When she was released, the police spread the rumor that she had been suffering from venereal disease.

Resistance in Slovakia

Letters from young Slovak Catholics to President Husák in 1985 and 1986, though unsigned, indicate considerable boldness. They protested that soon prisons would be filled with young Christians. In a country where "parasitism" (being unemployed) is a criminal offense, active youngsters are increasingly becoming unemployed, turned away from job after job because they have no "cadre requirements." No one, however, will say what "cadre requirements" are.

Although repression is fierce in Slovakia, so too is the will to resist, as young people discover the role the church has played in shaping their national culture and history. More than ten thousand people, mostly young, have taken part in secretly organized theological courses.

Pilgrimages, a traditional feature in Slovak life, are attracting more people each year, Eastern Rite Catholics and Orthodox as well as Roman Catholics. They are also attracting varying degrees of police harassment, including the use of police dogs and helicopters. For example, in 1984, on the day of the pilgrimage to Levoča, a concert by a favorite pop singer was scheduled, and diversionary activities were arranged at schools. Meanwhile, buses and trains were canceled, oaks were felled and left lying across the road, and priests had to produce permits to hear confessions. People slept in tents and lit open fires, a convenient excuse for police to trample on pilgrims and tents alike. Yet spirits soared as thousands raised home-made crosses—a symbol of the growing defiance of Slovak Christians. There are so many of them that they know the government cannot possibly persecute them all. In 1988, more than 200,000 took part in the Levoča pilgrimage. The police did not interfere, and, unlike previous years, pilgrims were able to buy prayer books and rosaries near the shrine.

Arrests and Imprisonment

Various methods are used by the authorities to break people. Some arrested Christians are released pending trial, which often never takes place;

some are kept in prison despite their innocence; some receive extraordinarily callous treatment. Charges often bear no relation to the crime.

Petr Kozánek and his friend Zdeněk Kotrlý were sentenced to ten months' imprisonment in 1985 for attempted violation of Article 112 of the penal code, "defamation of the republic abroad." They were "conspiring" to take *samizdat* prose and poetry by Iva Kotrlá, Zdeněk's wife, out of the country for publication in England. During the trial the prosecution's chief witness described Kotrlá's works as "full of apocalyptic images construed to show the demoralization of Czech society and the transient nature of the socialist system where the only certainty is the Christian faith."

Maria Kuhilová, who had spent five months in prison in 1984, was re-arrested in 1985 and given a three-and-a-half-year sentence for "illegal trading." Interestingly enough, she was found with six thousand Russian Bibles; Czechs help Russians just as Poles help Czechs.

Most arrests are made in connection with the production of religious literature. Widespread swoops in 1985 eventually proved an embarrassment for the authorities, since thousands were involved. Some individuals are nevertheless kept in prison as an example to others.

Some leading activist priests have been defamed in bizarre ways. In 1986, two well-known Slovak priests, Frs. Anton Srholec and Stěfan Gerbóc, were tried for sexually assaulting children. Identical methods were used by the Nazis to discredit Slovak priests during the war, and the memory only exacerbates the bitterness of Slovak Catholics.

The case of Augustin Navrátil, a signal-box worker with a family of nine, brought the reputation of Czechoslovak justice to new depths. In 1977, Navrátil and Jan Pavlíček were the first Catholics to circulate a petition to church leaders suggesting how the state could improve conditions for believers. Pavlíček was sentenced without trial to eight months; Navrátil was sent to a psychiatric hospital for a few months. In 1985 Navrátil was again arrested for sending an open letter to President Husák with evidence that Father Coufal, the secret monk found dead in his apartment, had been murdered by the police. He was sentenced to indefinite confinement in a psychiatric hospital. Navrátil's final statement before entering the hospital was a challenge: "Remember that my God is also yours, and that he is not only a God of love and mercy but also a God of justice." The doctor who had "diagnosed" him died a few days later of a heart attack.

Navrátil was released in 1986. In 1987, he was brutally attacked by a gang of Gypsies who said they'd been told to get rid of him. In 1988, he was charged again after the demonstration after Mass at St. Vitus Cathedral, Prague. He was again sent to a psychiatric hospital in June but was released after two weeks.

The outspoken unlicensed ECCB pastor, Jan Dus, after sending abroad a damning analysis of church-state relations and vociferously supporting imprisoned fellow Christians, was kept in prison for over a year without trial. After protests from the West he was released in summer 1987.

Several lay Catholics were charged with producing religious literature. Their cases dragged on, and some eventually received suspended sentences. One, František Adamik, was threatened with eight years for "incitement"; after waiting two years for a trial, he was given a suspended sentence.

Maria Nechalová was the first person to be sentenced merely for *possessing* religious literature, in 1986. Maria Foltynová was charged in 1985 with trying to ruin relations between the state and foreign countries because of her alleged participation in the Czech translation of a German book on the assassination attempt on the Pope. Four months pregnant, she was sentenced to ten months in prison.

Two young Chartist activists, Petr Pospíchal and Michal Mrtvý, were victimized and imprisoned. Pospíchal, accused of "subversion of the republic," was freed largely because of Western support. Mrtvý was eventually given a three-month suspended sentence after a trial at which his pregnant wife and his supporters were brutally attacked by the police.

An 80-year old priest, Ladislav Hanuš, received a year's suspended sentence for helping out another priest by hearing confessions once a month for two years without state permission. Fr. Stefan Javorský was sentenced to eight months' imprisonment for saying Mass in a house.

In Novermber 1987, a 52-year-old Slovak Catholic technician, Ivan Polanský, was arrested after a house search; in June 1988 the father of four was sentenced to four years for "subversion." VONS described the case as "the most serious attack on independent religious and civil activity in recent years."

By 1988, only five of the 5,000 political prisoners were reported to be in prison for religious activities. One, Jiří Wolf, a Catholic convicted of sending critical literature abroad, was in the fourth year of a six-year sentence, isolated from the world, denied family visits, and the right to read newspapers or write letters.

These and other cases have brought extreme discredit to the government because of completely unrealistic charges. The fact that trials are repeatedly postponed, or held behind closed doors or in remote country towns, and that lawyers involved often express grave reservations about the charges and reliability of the witnesses produced, are signs of the hollowness of the accusations.

Western pressure helps. Chartists—of whom there are now more than 1,000—and VONS, a most reliable source, continue to do admirable work in monitoring and reporting cases to the outside world. Indeed, it is only fear of adverse publicity that prevents the government from sentencing far more religious activists. People away from Prague, at the mercy of vindictive local officials, are more vulnerable to discrimination and injustice. The fact that most believers do carry out religious activities without harassment does not always alleviate the tension and fear, for active ones know that *anyone* may be arrested. Activists like Malý and Václav Benda endure a life of constant tension, followed by the police.

VELEHRAD 1985: THE METHODIUS CELEBRATION

In July 1985, on the eleven hundredth anniversary of the death of St. Methodius, the long-suppressed feelings of Czechoslovak Christians poured out in an unprecedented fashion as between 150,000 and 250,000 Catholics assembled for a vigil and Mass at the Moravian shrine of Velehrad.

The government had tried to downplay the anniversary. The party newspaper had gone so far as to ridicule Saints Cyril and Methodius, calling them "altar boys." Despite these efforts and police violence, a petition with 20,000 signatures was issued inviting the Pope to attend the celebrations.

To ease the pressure, Cardinal Tomášek issued his own invitation, but the Vatican could not accept the government's terms for a papal visit. Otherwise, the Pope replied, he would have been delighted to accept. John Paul emphasized his Slav affinity with the Czechs and Slovaks. This provoked a counteroffensive from the government, which charged that the Pope was misusing Saints Cyril and Methodius in a new Vatican *Ostpolitik* aimed at wresting Czechoslovakia from the socialist bloc.

Tomášek wrote two strong letters to the official press and the government protesting the political misinterpretation of religious history, and asked for respect for human rights. The republic, he said, gave the impression that it was "under siege."

In an effort to distract attention from the brouhaha over the proposed visit, the state sponsored a three-day celebration by the Czechoslovak Orthodox at which the state secretary for religious affairs, Vladimir Janku, and a World Council of Churches representative were guest speakers. But to no avail. On April 10, 1985, 1,000 priests—a third of the Catholic clergy—demonstrated their solidarity with Cardinal Tomášek by attending a special ceremony at Velehrad. More than 7,000 believers, including religious, some of whom wore their habits, joined the priests to hear Tomášek read a letter from the Pope. John Paul urged the priests "in the spirit of St. Methodius to continue intrepidly on the path of evangelization and testimony, even if the present situation makes it arduous, difficult, and even bitter."

On the following day, the government launched a full-scale, nationwide attack, raiding the homes of all Catholics known to be connected with the information network.

Although the government could make it impossible for the Pope to set foot on Czechoslovak soil, it could not halt the major celebration planned for July. It took the precaution, however, of summoning a number of well-known Prague dissident Catholics for interrogation immediately before the arrival of Cardinal Casaroli, the Vatican foreign secretary, who attended as papal legate. The intention was to prevent the cardinal from meeting with anyone other than officially approved Catholics. The government also refused visas to such well-known cardinals as Basil Hume of England, Jean-Marie Lustiger of France, and Franz Koenig of Austria.

The government took steps to minimize the impact of the celebration by making use of "reliable" bishops—Vrána to head the organization, Feranec to preach a sermon on behalf of Pacem in Terris. Internal party circulars explained how the Vatican was trying to use the brothers to undermine the influence of the state. Since the Christian Peace Conference was meeting in Prague at the same time, three of its members were encouraged at attend the Czech celebration, presumably to give the impression of religious freedom. (One of them, Metropolitan Philaret of Minsk, made an excellent speech.)

Not a word about the celebration appeared in the press, and many pilgrims had to make their way on foot, since transport was deliberately curtailed. Yet on the eve of the event, thousands of young people had already congregated, summoned by clandestine leaflets. The authorities were prodigal in offering liquor, but the young people spent the night praying and singing hymns. A large contingent appeared from Slovakia, even though 100,000 Slovaks were simultaneously attending their usual pilgrimage celebration at Levoča.

An Inspiring Demonstration

The event turned out to be what the government most feared—a tremendous, inspiring demonstration of faith such as had never before been seen in the country under Communist rule. When Communist officials opened the proceedings by calling it a "peace festival," the crowd exploded, "This is a pilgrimage!" And when the minister of culture, Milan Klusák, spoke of the brothers Cyril and Methodius as cultural missionaries, omitting the title "saints," the people booed. They chanted, "We want the Pope! Faith, faith!" Klusák was finally silenced when the impatient crowd began to shout: "We want the Mass!"

One of the editors of an underground Catholic journal commented on leaving, "We have just experienced a few hours of freedom. Czech and Slovak Catholics will not forget this event for many years to come." The two groups had united in prayer, a first step in bridging the gap between them. A young pilgrim gave voice to another awesome sight at Velehrad: "For the first time I realized what it meant to see people applaud when they want to, not when they must."

Pilgrims were aware that the secret police were photographing them, but they no longer cared. The attempt to render a country totally atheistic through state oppression had boomeranged. Instead of dying, Catholicism had come alive.

Velehrad was one of the most important events in Eastern Europe, and its spirit lives on. A new Marian shrine, opened later that year at Filipov in Bohemia in a quieter celebration, was a major accomplishment for that subdued part of the country. In September of that year, 20,000 pilgrims, mostly young Slovaks and Franciscans wearing their habits, turned up at Šaštin shrine and chanted, "Christus vincit, Christus regnat, Christus imperit!" (Christ conquers, Christ reigns, Christ rules!) At the Levoča celebration in 1986, half the pilgrims were young and defiant, as they taunted the police, holding up banners with the papal emblem and the motto "Totus Tuus"— "We are totally yours." In 1987, 120,000 pilgrims, mostly young people, gathered at Velehrad to hear Cardinal Tomášek.

Cardinal Tomášek and the State

The confrontation between Cardinal Tomášek and the state has sharpened since Velehrad. The hardest exchange followed an official article that appeared in the international *World Marxist Review* attacking the church and denying that the state interferes in church affairs. In a thorny reply, Tomášek protested the charge that the church was a vehicle of Western imperialism and anti-socialist forces. "The Church here is not the center of political opposition," he wrote. "All it wishes to do is to carry on its pastoral and missionary work." The letter set off the first official public attack on the cardinal, although privately he had been referred to as "that swine."

Years earlier, the cardinal had been unhappy when his priests became involved with the Chartists, fearing that their faith might be sapped by contact with left-wing intellectuals. Now, thanks partly to long hours of discussion with Fr. Malý, who argued that Christians should defend the rights of all who are unjustly persecuted, his attitude has completely changed. He sees that it is these intellectuals who are most eagerly seeking after the faith, and he actually received a group of Chartists.

In an April 1986 letter to the Ministry of Culture, Tomášek called for a complete revision of church-state legislation—which he said was obsolete and so vaguely worded that almost any religious activity could be labeled criminal—and, for the first time, for the complete separation of church and state. Among the particular points he called for was an end to state licensing of clergy.

Tomášek also spoke out against Pacem in Terris, and he defended several persecuted Catholics. In the unofficial church press he has addressed several wider ranging issues that are of broad concern but cannot be discussed in the media, such as abortion, alcoholism, drug abuse, and environmental pollution. Tomášek publicly opposed the 1986 measure that made abortion easier to obtain. (A petition against the abortion measure gathered 15,000 signatures, despite harassment and interrogation of collectors.) He has negotiated the printing of 100,000 economy Bibles and of 10,000 breviaries, the first to appear in Czech since Vatican II.

Cardinal Tomášek is not in direct touch with the authorities. He used to meet Husák once a year for a polite minute's talk, although they lived only two hundred yards from each other. He has written letter after letter to Husák and to the Office of Church Affairs, but has never had an answer. He has never been allowed to participate in government talks with the Vatican on the appointment of new bishops. He has been deliberately snubbed on numerous occasions. The latest was in 1988, when he was not allowed to conduct two of the three ordinations in Bohemia and Moravia, despite being primate. He was superseded by the government-favored Slovak bishop Jozef Feranec, a member of Pacem in Terris. (Such actions infuriate church members.) He does, however, receive a constant stream of visitors, including foreign journalists.

Tomášek commands the almost universal support of lay Catholics, for whom he is a symbol of resistance. Pope John Paul paid him tribute a few years ago: "Every day I think of this venerable pastor who like a solid spiritual oak provides brave testimony of his fidelity to Christ, both for his flock and for the whole of the Church."

Tomášek's demands were echoed by a charter circulated by believers in Czechoslovakia that reached the West in the fall of 1987. The charter also called for: an end to state control of entrance to seminaries, and a second seminary for Moravia, at Olomouc; an end to discrimination against parents and their children for requesting religious instruction; elimination of the office of secretary of state for church affairs; restoration of religious orders; an end to state control of religious literature; free contact for Catholics with Catholics abroad; lay councils in all parishes, and lay involvement in services; church access to the media; the consecration of new bishops; the establishment of a bishops' conference; and an end to the practice of barring believers from teaching.

The December 1987 Petition

There has been considerable foreign media coverage of the issue of the empty bishoprics and of the government's treatment of its political and religious dissidents, and the government is only too aware of the bad publicity its religious policy is getting in the West. Although it is responding with violent attacks on what it calls the "secret church," accusing activists of being in the pay of "bourgeois Western centers," it is nevertheless unsure of its next move.

Key Czechoslovak Christians have decided to take advantage of the situation by pushing demands for basic reforms to produce a tolerable church life. In December 1987 a thirty-one-point petition emerged from Moravia, probably with Navrátil as the principal instigator. (See appendix F.) The response was unprecedented in the history of Czechoslovakia under Communism. By May 1988 it had been signed by more than half a million people, mainly Catholics, but Protestants, Jews, and agnostics as well. It was endorsed by Cardinal Tomášek, who in an open letter to the faithful told them it was their duty to sign the document—"cowardice and fear are not becoming to a true Christian." Many priests read the petition from the pulpit, and it was displayed at church exits.

In addition to demands made in the previous petition, this petition demanded the following: the appointment of new bishops should be an internal matter for the church and without state interference. Religious instruction of children should be allowed on church premises rather than in school. The copying and dissemination of religious texts should not be considered an illicit business activity or a legally punishable act. Priests and people should be allowed to proclaim Christian ideas in public. The construction of new churches should be allowed where necessary. All unlawfully sentenced priests and laypeople should be speedily and consistently rehabilitated. All legal regulations that make a considerable part of the activity of priests and laypeople illegal should be rescinded. A mixed body consisting of representatives of the state and the church, including laymen chosen by Tomášek, should discuss and resolve outstanding problems. (Interestingly, neither this document nor the previous one referred to Pacem in Terris.)

On March 6, 1988, a special Mass and national pilgrimage was held in St. Vitus Cathedral, Prague, in connection with the forthcoming beatification of Blessed Agnes of Bohemia and a ten-year program of spiritual renewal. It was attended by 8,000 people, hundreds of whom afterwards demonstrated beneath the cardinal's residence, shouting, "We want bishops!" and "Bring us the Pope!" After the demonstration, Navrátil was charged with "slandering the state and public authorities" and could therefore be sentenced to a year in prison.

Two days earlier, several Catholic activists had been among thirteen Chartists invited to dinner with a leading British Foreign Office official. The thirteen had been detained by the police and held without charge under the forty-eight-hour detention law, used for the first time since 1985. The intention, apparently, was to prevent them from attending the Mass. The British government issued a strongly worded protest.

On March 25 police brutally broke up a peaceful candlelit rally in which several thousand Catholics in Bratislava were calling on the authorities to allow greater civil freedom. The attack, using dogs, water cannon, and tear gas, was unprovoked and unexpectedly vicious. Some BBC and Australian TV crew members were beaten. Several governments protested the incident, as did some forty Hungarian intellectuals, including clergy. Benda cited it as proof that the government had no intention of introducing *glasnost* reforms. "Not even the most narrow-minded of policemen could have thought that girls with rosaries and candles in their hands posed a threat to Bratislava or Central Europe," commented Jan Korec, the best known and loved of the unrecognized bishops. Negotiations with the Vatican, not surprisingly, were making little progress. Cardinal Tomášek, in a letter to Prime Minister Štrougal, said, "We demand a change in the state's attitude toward the church. We want dialogue, not confrontation."

THE OUTLOOK

Evaluating the overall effect of persecution on the churches is difficult. Attendance at church is declining in certain Protestant churches and in the Czech provinces, where many Christians are disheartened and cowed. Rapprochement between the state and the Vatican is not likely, particularly since most lay Catholics want no more compromise with the government, and the Pope respects their stance.

The priesthood as a whole is not capable of providing the leadership and vision the laity needs. As Father Srholec said, "The state license is a sword of Damocles hanging over the head of every priest." Most priests, he said, in their attempts not to ruffle the state so they can continue their pastoral work, live in such a "schizophrenic state of tension" that their entire ministry suffers. Consequently the church now "is sustained by the laity," he said. Many clergy are still too afraid to get involved with the underground, even to read its press.

There are grounds for hope. There is immense solidarity among Chartists, who refuse to be intimidated. The years of suffering in the camps have borne fruit that no one can destroy. And there are limits to the lengths the state can go to enforce its anti-religious policies. A few people—the Kořineks, Micianová, and an assortment of priests—have had the courage to challenge the legality of certain state actions, sometimes successfully. These challenges have given moral encouragement to others.

Slovakia, particularly, shows increasing renewal, self-confidence, courage, and solidarity. In many churches, there is standing-room-only for Mass on weekdays. The Czechs, however, though less ebullient, may have deeper reserves of faith.

Other encouraging signs include the inspiring example set by many Christians under suffering and imprisonment; the thriving underground church; the meeting together in small groups of some Catholics and Protestants and the ecumenical rapprochement of Catholics and ECCB members in Bratislava; the vision inspired by the Pope through a rejuvenated Tomášek; the ample supply of candidates for the priesthood and the religious life; and the witness of ordinary Christians in everyday life. Wherever there are jobs that are badly paid but of great value to society, out of the limelight, there believers can be found.

In an interview with Western journalists in 1981, Karel Hruza, then state secretary for religious affairs, admitted, "In the past you saw only grandmothers in the churches, but at present there are young people there too." Government statistics for 1984 show that 36 per cent of the population over fifteen claim to be believers—30 per cent in Czech areas, 51 per cent in Slovakia. (In 1987 the Party claimed that only a fifth of the population were believers, but as it also claimed that twice as many people supported Marxist ideas as were Christians and that Christians were increasingly inactive, its figures must be suspect.) A Czechoslovak expert estimates that 60,000 to 80,000 people are joining the churches each year, and Slovak young people note that a substantial number are from atheistic backgrounds. Twenty-four per cent of people with university backgrounds are involved with the church—a very high figure compared with Western Europeans with a similar cultural background. Even many middle-aged people, who tend to be more cautious than the young, are returning to the churches.

State aggression has backfired; the less aggressive methods used in Hungary might have been more successful. Though there are, as in Hungary, many drop-outs, even Satanists, the traditionally independent, secular elements in society realize that the state, not religion, is the oppressor. Ideological propaganda has spurred thoughtful people—especially the young, who are less haunted by the past—to ask about Christianity. And, as Cardinal Tomášek says, "Our hope lies in the young."

Inevitably Gorbachev's visit in the autumn of 1987 brought back memories of Dubček's reforms twenty years earlier and aroused many hopes. Since the sole legitimacy of the Husák government was Brezhnev's crackdown on the liberalization process in 1968, the hard-liners had been awaiting Gorbachev with some apprehension, determined to see him off again as soon as possible, which they did. They were doubtless immensely relieved by Gorbachev's statement that, in the future, Moscow would not interfere in the domestic affairs of its allies, and by his preoccupation since with internal unrest in Armenia and opposition within the Soviet Communist Party. The hard-liners intend to wait and sit it out, confident in the memory of the debacle of the Prague Spring. To them, Gorbachev is another Dubček, and likely to meet a similar fate.

Husák resigned in December 1987. His 66-year-old successor, Miloš Jakeš, is a party bureaucrat who if anything has been more colorless and more orthodox than Husák. He appears more likely to defend than to modify the orthodox Stalinist political order. One of his first moves as party leader was to dash hopes for any reevaluation of the Prague Spring reforms. He explicitly endorsed the Soviet military intervention, something that both Soviet and moderate Czechoslovak politicians have refrained from doing recently. The government's hard line against opposition groups shows no signs of weakening.

Yet the government did make a few minor concessions to religion in mid-1988. It promised to do something about the shortage of religious literature. And it has allowed 500 young women to enter religious orders in order to care for the elderly sisters. Enrollment for religious education classes will now take place in the church rather than the school. The classes themselves will continue to be held in school, so teachers will still know which pupils are attending them.

Conditions vary widely. In Prague, churchgoers chat with one another after services in a more relaxed way than formerly. A leading Prague priest, Dr. Otto Mádr—unlicensed, a veteran of fifteen years in prison—urged Catholics to conduct themselves as if they lived in a free state, availing themselves of every opportunity and trying to improve the moral climate of the nation. In contrast, a visitor to Moravia was told that it was "like being under Brezhnev again." Believers can take little comfort from the knowledge that state supervision of the church is to be restructured on a regional basis, at considerable expense—a clear indication that the state intends to make supervision ever more thorough than it is already.

In mid-1988, Lubomir Štrougal, then federal premier, told journalists the government wanted to negotiate with the Vatican on church-state matters. He admitted that the government had "committed errors" and said, "We have started on the path toward a solution." Štrougal also criticized

Czechoslovak police for the way in which they broke up a recent assembly of Charter 77 supporters. Štrougal's resignation in October 1988 was considered a setback for the party reformers.

The churches, despite repression, offer authentic values, not only in the religious and moral sphere but also in culture, patriotism, and relations between people—all of which are distorted under Communism. Tensions force the more lively minds, those who have not become slaves to the regime or to hedonism, to mine thoughts through to the end. A Christian intellectual who relished arguing with sincere Marxists complains that he has hardly any left to debate with: "So many of the good ones have become Christians."

Today it is harder to be a committed agnostic in Czechoslovakia than in Western society. Religion has become the banner of dissent, and the underground church is showing that it is indeed an authentic church of the Czechoslovak people. Moral resistance to Communism is best exemplified in the underground church. Through pilgrimages and, in 1988, through a petition signed by more than half a million people, Czechoslovaks have broken through the psychological pall that hung over the land for many years. The spirit that in the past made this nation one of the most talented, individualistic, and creative in Europe has been rekindled by the Christian faith.

6

The German Democratic Republic

THE CHURCHES in the German Democratic Republic are not the typical restricted East European churches. The country teaches Marxism-Leninism more assiduously than any other Warsaw Pact nation and until an amnesty in late 1987 had perhaps two thousand political prisoners and possibly far more—estimates vary considerably. Yet the churches are largely independent of the state: they do not suffer from a state-imposed shortage of clergy, they appoint their own leaders, they have a reasonable supply of religious literature, and few of their buildings have been closed. No one is in prison for religious activities, although before the amnesty there may have been about a hundred imprisoned religious conscientious objectors.

Western Christians, who can visit their German co-religionists fairly freely, bring back an accurate picture of church life. In an efficiently run materialistic society with high living standards—the highest in the Eastern bloc—and with a people who have more in common with the West than the East, church attendance is generally as low as in the secularized West.

The churches contribute visibly to society with their numerous excellent institutions, such as hospitals and homes for the needy, and their publications, which constitute 12 per cent of all East German books. The churches, moreover, almost alone in East Europe, own land (about 500,000 acres), run fifty agricultural enterprises, and employ large numbers of people. The Protestant churches alone employ 15,000 people in social work.

There is some dialogue—slow, painful, frustrating—between the leaders of church and state. There is also outspoken criticism of the state by church leaders, such as is heard also in Poland and Yugoslavia. In recent years church leaders have supported the peace movement and challenged the government's militaristic policies.

The GDR is Eastern Europe's only predominantly Protestant state. Of its population of 16.2 million, about 7.7 million are at least nominally members of the Federation of Evangelical Churches, which consists of eight independent regional churches (*Landeskirchen*) in the Lutheran tradition. (As in other Eastern European countries, membership figures are only approximate; the last official publication of church statistics was in 1964.) Three of these churches belong to the United Evangelical Lutheran Church: (1) the Evangelical Lutheran Provincial Church in Saxony, (2) the Evangelical Lutheran Provincial Church in Mecklenburg, and (3) the Evangelical Lutheran Provincial Church in Thuringia. The other five stress their Evangelical and Reformed heritage and belong to the Evangelical Church of the Union: (4) the Evangelical Church in Berlin-Brandenburg, (5) the Evangelical Church in the Province of Saxony, (6) the Evangelical Provincial Church in Griefswald, (7) the Evangelical Provincial Church in Anhalt, and (8) the Evangelical Church in the District of Görlitz. Church-state relations are generally between the state and this eight-church federation.

The second largest religious body is the Catholic Church, with 1.05 million members. There are also 100,000 New Apostolic Church members, 28,000 Methodists (the largest body of Methodists in Eastern Europe), and 23,000 Baptists. Among other groups are several small sects separated from the Lutherans, 11,000 Adventists, 4,500 Mormons, and 1,000 Old Catholics. The oldest and largest of the Pentecostal communities is not recognized by the government.

Only 450 Jews remain. After the community had gone for twenty-two years without a rabbi, in 1987 Rabbi Isaac Neuman arrived in East Berlin from the United States. This coincided with a suddenly more sympathetic attitude on the part of the government toward giving Judaism a higher profile and restoring synagogues. But after only a few months Rabbi Neuman resigned and returned to the United States. He complained of anti-Semitic tendencies in the GDR press and of differences with the Berlin Jewish community, which for its part complained about his reluctance to spend time on pastoral care for its older members. It appears that despite the GDR's well-publicized attempts to assure world Jewry that all is now well there, anti-Semitism is still present to at least some degree.

The New Apostolic Church, whose chief "apostle" resides in Zurich, took root quickly in Germany. Since one of its principles is allegiance to earthly rulers, it survived the Nazi era well and has been able to come to terms with the Marxist leadership. Many of its churches are new. Its claim to have "living apostles" gives it a certain immediacy. Its person-to-person evangelism is well suited to life in a Marxist state and perhaps accounts for its flourishing condition.

From Nazism to Communism

Prior to the Communist takeover, German Christians were the only ones in Eastern Europe who had experienced life under a totalitarian dictatorship. Lutheranism has a long tradition of accommodation with the state, and under Hitler all the churches were to some extent passive. There were notable exceptions, however. In 1932, for example, the Catholic hierarchy denounced the new myth of race as a violation of the First Commandment. Many members of the Protestant "Confessing Church"—those who refused to comply with Hitler—together with a considerable number of Catholics were imprisoned; some, like Dietrich Bonhoeffer, were martyred. The witness of the men and women who suffered strengthened the German churches and provided a yardstick and inspiration for the future.

The leaders of the Lutheran churches after 1945 were the survivors of that movement. Their new rulers were the same Communists whom they had trusted and with whom they had suffered in the cells of the Gestapo. The leaders refused to retreat into a comfortable pietism, though that was a strong element in their religious tradition. They publicly acknowledged the shortcomings of their churches—the Darnstadt Council of 1947 decried the churches' opposition to needed social change and their failure to meet the Marxist challenge to Christians to work for the poor—and urged renewal through repentance.

The German Communists were efficient and ruthless. Walter Ulbricht did not persecute the churches in the same manner as other Communist leaders, but then he did not expect them to survive. The state in the 1950s was trying hard to eliminate them by administrative means. When the first socialist city of the GDR was founded, Ulbricht boasted, "The only towers which will be built will be ours." He was wrong: a Lutheran and a Catholic church have been erected.

A Practical Theology

While Christians were under considerable pressure, they openly preached a practical and living theology called "critical solidarity." This combines support of the state when its policies are positive with criticism when the state transgresses the moral order. The Lutheran churches' integrity won the grudging respect of the regime, which professes to find them 99 per cent cooperative, even enthusiastic. This description conceals all kinds of difficulties. The relationship has never been comfortable; there has always been conflict if never out-and-out confrontation.

The Federation of Evangelical Churches (the body comprising eight regional Lutheran churches) has had a series of good leaders. While no bishop has been totally hostile to the regime, none has supported it uncondition-ally. The bishops are elected by the churches, and leaders like Albert Schön-herr, a disciple of Bonhoeffer who was bishop of East Berlin until his re-tirement in 1981, and his successors as chairman of the federation, Werner Krusche, Johannes Hempel, and, since 1985, Werner Leich, are men of character and wisdom, experienced politicians ready to exercise a prophetic role when needed. They contend that the church is neither pro- nor anti-Communist but a distinct entity, the Body of Christ, whose duty is to pro-claim and live the Gospel within society, socialist or other. The Lutheran tradition emphasizes the importance of acting according to one's Christian conscience, so Lutheran leaders leave their members free to exercise their conscience. The Methodist approach is similar.

If the churches today enjoy a privileged position and internal freedom, it is because they have earned it in a tough, relentless, continuing battle. When a regulation was introduced (1970-71) requiring that the police receive prior notification of all public gatherings, including church meetings other than worship services, so many clergy ignored the regulation that it was quietly dropped.

A Church Political Party

The GDR has a political party for Christians—the Christian Demo-cratic Union (CDU). It means little, however, for the five hundred members of the People's Chamber meet for only five or six days each year, and the vast majority of seats are held by the Socialist Unity Party—the GDR's name for the Communist Party. A number of seats are allocated to groups that the state openly admits it relies on for support; the CDU has fifty-four.

Church leaders are suspicious of the CDU, which they regard as an agent of government policy. In 1961 the Lutheran bishops refused to follow their chairman, Bishop Moritz Mitzenheim, formerly a staunch opponent of Hitler, who was cooperating with the regime. They disavowed the CDU, re-nounced any obligation to promote socialism, insisted on their right to speak on social issues, and rejected Ulbricht's offer to merge the church's work in human welfare with the Socialist Unity Party's interest in "socialist humanism and proletarian internationalism."

To be fair, some CDU members do use their position to support ends of which most church members would approve. In 1972, in an unprece-dented action, fourteen CDU members voted against legalized abortion, with eight abstaining. In the end, they won for Christian doctors the right to refuse to do abortions.

While Catholics as well as Protestants are represented in the CDU, there is also a special government-sponsored body for Catholics—the Berlin

Conference of European Catholics, one of Moscow's "peace" front organizations. Not a single East German Catholic priest has joined, a testament to a clerical unity within the Catholic Church here not found in the other East European nations.

Not a Martyr Church

East German Christians have never had to face such harsh treatment as Christians elsewhere in Eastern Europe. Two factors profoundly influence GDR policy—the dictates of the USSR, which maintains 400,000 troops for defense and to ensure loyalty, and the existence of the Federal Republic of Germany (FRG). In the early post-war years, the churches were the only major institutions operating across the borders of divided Germany. Any persecution would have been known instantly all over the world. Seventy-two church officials were briefly imprisoned, but no church leader was arrested or forced out of office.

The government tried but failed to instill loyalty to its rule. Before the Berlin Wall went up in 1961, 3.6 million East Germans—over 10 per cent—many of them highly qualified, had fled. Despite massive indoctrination, full employment, a good welfare system, and high living standards, East Germans have only to compare their conditions with those in the FRG—they watch West German television—to know they are prisoners in their own land. (The FRG differs from the GDR not only in its political and economic systems but in being far better endowed with natural resources.) Many are still divided from families and friends.

The state cannot afford to forfeit the good will of the churches. Even less can it afford to forfeit the strong West German currency for which the churches are a continuing pipeline. Over 40 per cent of the Protestant churches' overall costs are met by their wealthy sister churches in the FRG. West German cash therefore undergirds the East German health and social services. The churches also ransom political prisoners with hard cash, a lucrative practice for certain state officials. Although the churches are immensely helped by West German money, support by East German members is quite substantial.

The state's flexible attitude toward the churches is also due to the special relationship between the leaders of the party and the Protestant churches. The bond of their common sufferings under Hitler was strong enough to withstand their ideological differences. In addition, the GDR leadership has had considerable integrity. Moreover, alone among Soviet-bloc states, the GDR government lacks the national identity necessary to build a minimum of popular legitimacy; it has to share its history and nationality with West Germany. Thus it is particularly dependent on the support of the institution most deeply rooted in its German history—the Protestant church. Although the state has opposed the construction of church buildings, it gives generous help towards restoring and maintaining historic cathedrals and churches.

Another significant factor is administrative. Although at the lower levels local officials of the Ministry of the Interior regulate church life, the responsibility at the highest level falls on the Secretary of State for Church Affairs, who is not part of the police structure but is attached to the prime minister's office. The secretary does not—a vital point—intrude in the domestic affairs of the religious communities but serves as the institutional link between the government and the two major churches (Lutheran and Catholic). Until his death in 1979, the secretary was Hans Seigewasser, a tough Marxist whose respect for Christians stemmed from his days in Nazi prisons. He was succeeded by Klaus Gysi.

The Cost of Discipleship Today

Although there is no open persecution, being a Christian in the GDR can still be costly. For a young person, active attendance at church can jeopardize the chances of landing an apprenticeship or entering a university, except for the fields of music and theology. Active church membership also bars promotion to some higher posts. Christians are being eased out of the teaching profession and are virtually excluded from the police force because they lack the right degree of commitment to Marxism.

The churches have been weakened not so much by restrictions as by the pervasive secularism of the society. Materialism has sapped the churches perhaps more than Marxist-Leninist education, to which the population has become impervious. Only about 3 per cent of the total population attend church every Sunday. The normal Lutheran service is staid, dominated by the sermon, with little lay participation. Many churches are nearly empty, and often the atmosphere is depressing.

The social base of the church lies in the former bourgeoisie—many of whom have had to become manual workers because of their Christian allegiance—and some farmers. The church has had little impact among the working class in industrial cities, which provided the basis for the Communist Party, in the vast new housing developments, or, until recently, among the young generation. Only about 10 per cent of church members attend services regularly. Between 1950 and 1980, baptisms fell by 75 per cent, church weddings by 85 per cent, church burials by 33 per cent, and church attendance by 50 per cent.

The church was nevertheless quietly consolidating its role in society when, in the late sixties, the Protestant churches surrendered two tenaciously held positions.

1969: Acknowledging the Divide

In the post-war years, Christians labored to maintain the concept of one Germany despite impenetrable barriers between East and West and despite charges by the government that they acted as a fifth column for the United States. Of particular political significance was the fact that the Evangelical Church of Germany (EKD), a federation that included the Lutheran, Reformed, and United churches, did not divide when the country did. Thus it was seen as the remaining indestructible tie between East and West and a sign that the GDR was not permanent.

But as the years passed, the bitter anti-Communism felt by most Germans in the 1950s, but condemned by far-sighted church leaders, abated to some extent, and people learned to accept the bitter reality of living in a divided Germany. Loss of contact when the Berlin Wall was erected in 1962 made it even more difficult to administer the regional churches that straddled the border.

In 1968, faced with the new GDR constitution that established the concept that state boundaries determine church boundaries, Protestant leaders bowed to reality. On June 10, 1969, the EKD was dissolved, and the eight regional Lutheran churches east of the wall banded together as the Federation of Evangelical Churches in the GDR. The first surrender had taken place.

The initial period was difficult, but in the long run the concession strengthened the churches' credibility and enabled them to focus their energies on working within the GDR, which paved the way for a partial rapprochement with the government in 1978.

The status of the Catholic Church has not been resolved so satisfactorily from the government's point of view. The regime would like the church to establish complete independence from West Germany by establishing full diocesan bishops. Instead, after diplomatic relations with the GDR were resumed in the early 1970s, the Vatican appointed apostolic administrators to the East German parts of the five dioceses that straddle the West German, and in one case Polish, border. In 1976, however, it gave the East German Bishops' Conference autonomous status, making it *de facto* independent. The GDR is the only Warsaw Pact country where the appointment of Catholic bishops does not require formal state approval.

A Second Protestant Concession

A second major issue over which the Protestant churches gave way was the *Jugendweihe* (youth consecration), introduced in 1954. The *Jugendweihe* was set up in the nineteenth century in an attempt to rally the children of humanists and free thinkers against the church. Today's solemn ceremony—"Youth Dedication to Socialism"—is designed to take the place of confirmation, and involves an oath of absolute loyalty to the state. The first loyalty of Christians is to be, of course, to God. At first, the churches forbade their youth to take part in the *Jugendweihe*; in 1964, however, the Protestants, but not the Catholics (officially; many parish priests are non-judgmental), gave in and allowed the young people who participated to be confirmed as well.

It continues to be a bone of contention. Many Protestants are unhappy with the church decision, especially since many active Christians have been discriminated against even though they have taken the oath to the state. In 1984, 97 per cent of the young people participated; but 7,000 fourteen-year-olds had the courage to refuse.

1978: Concessions by the State

By the mid-1970s, the Protestant churches were increasingly expressing dissatisfaction. Shortly after the 1975 conference that produced the Helsinki Accords on human rights, the churches held an ecumenical congress to review its results. Bishop Schönherr, in his April 1976 report as head of the Federation of Evangelical Churches, complained that "freedom of conscience and faith is no longer unequivocally guaranteed for those citizens who cannot embrace the Marxist-Leninist worldview." At this, the government decided to appease the churches, and later that year it promised to respect the equality of all citizens regardless of religious affiliation. The churches were growing in self-confidence. Since 1974 the Lutheran churches have been permitted to hold the traditional *Kirchentage,* or special church assemblies, which were very popular.

But no one was prepared for the historic "summit" between Erich Honecker, the head of state, and Protestant leaders on March 6, 1978, or for the concessions made. The meeting seems to have sprung from the fact that the church had failed to die out. Total church membership was three times as high as Communist Party membership. Christians, moreover, had proved to be a reliable and honest element in national life, a fact that a state beset by corrupt party careerists could not ignore.

The occasion was the only time Communist government leaders and Protestant church leaders have met for mutual help, and some practical results emerged. The state promised fifty new churches—including a few for Catholics—increased radio time, and access, for the first time, to television. It also officially recognized the churches' extensive contribution to social and health services, reaffirmed the equality of all citizens, and promised to end discrimination against young Christians.

Bishop Schönherr, along with many other Christians, was skeptical, and rightly so. Although in the decade since then the churches have enjoyed a higher profile, discrimination has not been eradicated nor equality established, and church construction has progressed at a snail's pace.

On the positive side, the churches did gain somewhat more access to the media. Since 1979, in addition to the brief weekly radio service that the churches had been allowed, there has been a monthly church news program on the radio and six television broadcasts a year. Broadcast sermons are subject to censorship. Thanks to the stimulus of the quincentenary of Luther in 1983, the church is being presented in a positive manner by the media.

If the government expected that a few concessions would tame the church, it was mistaken. The church, having held firm under state hostility, is holding just as firm in its more privileged position. It has refused to accept the Marxist definition of itself as purely "a self-supporting organization of social significance in a socialist society"—Honecker's words—or to be limited in its primary function of preaching the Gospel.

Church Privileges

Today the churches, as institutions, enjoy remarkable freedom, although there are inner tensions over how far to cooperate with the state. Church authorities in the GDR, in contrast to those in most other Warsaw Pact countries, will stand behind individual church members and try to see that justice is done. Regrettably, as this assistance is given through quiet negotiations, many churchgoers with grievances are not aware of their constitutional rights or of the church's readiness to help.

East German churches are in general free to make their own appointments. Clergy and church employees are in a privileged position and are practically immune from discrimination. From their ranks come some of the fortunate few who are allowed to travel to the West. This can cause resentment, which the state likes to encourage, among ordinary church members, who often criticize the clergy for leading a relatively cloistered life, protected from the pressures of the everyday world.

Each of the eight *Landeskirchen* that make up the Federation of Evangelical Churches has its own elected bishop and synod and enjoys considerable autonomy. Although statistics are hard to come by—no official church statistics have been authorized since 1964 because no specific questions on church membership were made in subsequent censuses—the following figures for 1979 are probably fairly accurate. There were 7,400 parishes, 4,000 pastors (including 200 women), 5,000 trained catechists, and 5,000 social workers, nearly 3,000 of whom were deaconesses, the Protestant equivalent of nuns.

The state supports theological faculties at six universities, where 400 students train on state grants. For admittance to a university, a student must, among other things, show a good understanding of Marxist-Leninist theory; being a member of the Christian Democratic Union helps. Side by side, the churches have their own lively seminaries that train about 500 students. As these are not under state control, they tend to be more popular than the universities for theological studies. There is an abundance of both Protestant and Catholic candidates, a healthy sign, especially since being a theological student involves much sacrifice.

Financial support of the churches comes from members, from land, from an annual government subsidy of $6 million, and from the West German churches. Many churches have been coupled with churches in the FRG, an arrangement that has financial advantages and helps reduce the prevalent feeling of isolation.

Church Social Services

The churches make an amazing contribution to social and medical work for the Communist state, caring for half the mentally handicapped and providing 10 per cent of hospital care. Among the institutions operated by the Lutherans are 425 homes for the elderly with 11,000 places, 48 hospitals with 6,520 beds, 89 homes for the mentally and physically handicapped with 6,200 places, 419 rural nursing stations, 330 convalescent homes, 326 children's day-care centers, 23 children's homes, and 6 hospices for the dying. Fifteen hundred people are training for social work.

The Catholic Church runs 107 homes for the elderly, 80 kindergartens, 44 children's homes, 34 hospitals, 15 nursing homes, and other institutions. Much of the work with children is with the handicapped. Since 1975, each year 200 nuns have been allowed to train as nurses in Catholic teaching hospitals, 40 for children's work.

Smaller churches, too, make a strong social contribution. The Methodists, who are strongly committed to social service, run four hospitals, four homes for the elderly, a nursing school, a home for handicapped children, and two other centers of social work. Most of their 125 deaconesses, like the Lutherans, are trained nurses. The Baptists have a number of homes for the elderly and a center for the handicapped.

The state benefits from all of this, using—even exploiting—dedicated Christians to care for the least valued members of society, the elderly, the sick, the handicapped. State care for the elderly is poor. They are the only group allowed to emigrate fairly freely to West Germany. The mentally retarded are made to feel so unwanted that some commit suicide. People obviously prefer the church hospitals and homes, with their staffs' evident human concern and their more modern equipment (thanks to West German churches), to those of the state. The church institutions are a living challenge to the values prevalent in East German society. Indeed, the state recently acknowledged the expertise of the churches in their care of the dying. The state now takes a non-judgmental approach.

The Protestant institutions are facing acute staffing difficulties, for unlike the image of a Catholic nun, the traditional image of a deaconess has little appeal to the younger generation. Some young nurses who feel they are called to the single life in order to respond more fully to their demanding work could form the nucleus of a new type of order.

Religious Literature and Music

By East European standards the church press is in reasonably good shape. The churches publish more than thirty newspapers, magazines, and theological journals. Two periodicals are published jointly by the state and churches. But the church press is expected to limit itself to matters of "pastoral necessities and the care of souls." Although there is no censorship prior to publication, an entire issue can lie fallow if the authorities do not pass it for distribution, as happened during the Polish crisis in the early eighties. As a result, the editors operate their own censorship, and some of the best or most controversial writing never appears. The churches surmount the difficulty by circulating this material in mimeographed form, marked "for internal use only," which is not subject to distribution control. Religious literature can be sold or distributed only by the churches, not through normal retailers.

During April 1988 four church weekly newspapers and the Protestant News Service were not allowed to publish. The reason was that they carried reports on the Berlin-Brandenburg Synod's discussions of problems of travel and emigration, and on the Federation of Evangelical Churches' assertion of the church's right to engage in social activities. The state maintained that issues such as travel and emigration, damage to the environment, refusal to take part in military service, military training in kindergartens and schools, and the use of energy were the responsibility of the state, not the church.

Books are censored, so the churches use their discretion as to what to print. Many shelves in theological libraries are filled only because Western books have been smuggled in. About 20,000 Bibles and Scripture portions are printed annually, but the demand for Bibles is three times higher than the supply. Bibles can also be sent to German communities living abroad, such as to Kazakhstan in the USSR or to Transylvania in Romania.

Church music is encouraged. The Lutherans have five esteemed musical academies. Organ and choral recitals attract larger audiencies than in most other countries, for the great musical tradition of Germany is still very much alive. Proportionately, more church musicians are employed in the GDR than in any other country in the world.

Passing on the Faith

Evangelism is permitted. The Federation of Evangelical Churches employs fifty full-time evangelists, led by the popular Fritz Hoffman of Magdeburg. The small Baptist Church, lively and committed to evangelism, is growing steadily. Religious instruction, though barred from the schools, can be given in church buildings. Christian youth work is not illegal, and is flourishing, for church activity (camps included) outside regular worship is varied and challenging. University chaplains do a good job in general, but some are rather sympathetic to the state.

Young people resent the regimentation and tiresome propaganda of the many state-promoted organizations they are pressured to join. The Party has lost credibility with many youth, particularly since exposure of its large-scale corruption. Today's younger generation has become bored, apathetic, scornful of party hypocrisy.

There are some 80,000 young dropouts who reject the system and live on the fringe of society, managing to avoid open conflict with the authorities. Most feel free to speak out in church clubs, where trustworthy people will listen confidentially to their problems. Since the 1970s, the churches have addressed their concerns and have been able to direct the rebellious spirits of many young people into creative channels. The police visited a successful youth club run by a young Catholic curate, not to close it, but to ask for advice on how to cope with delinquents.

Many adults, ignorant of Christianity, are also groping for something real to believe in. Outsiders usually find the normal Sunday services dull, but churches also sponsor small groups of people who meet to discuss issues and to learn how to pray.

Nevertheless, because of the shortage of clergy and lay workers and the lack of churches in industrial areas, in some places the church plays only a marginal role. Much parish work goes undone: of the 840 parishes of the Evangelical Church in Berlin-Brandenberg, only 125 are filled. Village clergy are often overworked and isolated. A mid-1980s increase in applications for theological training should ease the situation.

Anniversary Kirchentage, 1983 and 1987

East Germany, between the Elbe and the Oder, is the heartland of Luther and the Reformation, and 1983 was the quincentenary of Martin Luther's birth. In celebration of this, 250,000 people attended seven regional *Kirchentage*, church congresses; over 100,000 were at the final assembly.

The state did a volte-face in rehabilitating Luther: it appropriated him as a national hero and reformer, almost supplanting Karl Marx in the process. Both state and church presented imaginative events that attracted thousands of foreign visitors and pilgrims, and millions in hard currency. Opinions were mixed: some church people regarded the whole affair as a meaningless propaganda exercise to promote a picture of cordial state-church relations. But skepticism aside, the Luther year *Kirchentage* were of tremendous value. Participants, including many seekers and fringe members, were confronted with searching questions and discussions on basic issues concerning church and state that would have startled both Marx and Luther. This would hardly have been possible in any other East European country.

The 1987 *Kirchentag* took place in June in East Berlin, to celebrate the 750th anniversary of the church there. East Berlin was the most sensitive location (no *kirchentag* had been held there since the erection of the Berlin Wall), and certain restrictions were imposed by the state. Nevertheless this event confirmed the church's role as the forum for ideas and opinions otherwise taboo. Church authorities successfully defused a splinter group of 1,200 young people who felt that the church was not radical enough for them. Among their criticisms, partly justified, was that the church is stuffy and old-fashioned; that it censors and corrects them; that it is too rigid and bureaucratic; and that it deprives parishes of an active voice in church affairs.

On the other hand, church leaders who find that dealing with independent church groups makes heavy demands on their time and energy have to face criticism from a large part of the laity resentful of the attempts of the young to politicize the church. They nevertheless reiterated their commitment: to be a church for those with questions and for the helpless as well as for believers. How much longer the left-wing radical element will remain under the aegis of the church is an interesting question. Also of interest is the fact that in 1987 Honecker expressed publicly his satisfaction with the course of church-state relations.

The issues of sexuality and the role of women are now surfacing in both Protestant and Catholic circles. Probably because of the East-West link, the churches in the GDR seem to be the first in Eastern Europe to be affected by the liberal attitudes now common in the West.

External Church Contacts

Despite the tight border control, the churches are not cut off from the West. Many Westerners visit the GDR to learn how church and state can coexist satisfactorily under a Communist government. In 1981 the GDR hosted the Central Committee of the World Council of Churches at Dresden.

Not all visitors are made welcome; both Brother Roger of Taizé and

Mother Teresa arrived to a deafening silence from the media. But the church grapevine is very efficient, and both visits became occasions of deep inspiration, especially to the younger generation.

Visits to the West are more carefully controlled. In the 1950s there was a considerable exodus of pastors, largely because of the discrimination practiced against their children. Because of the shortage of clergy in the GDR, Protestant posts in West Germany are, by mutual agreement, open to East German pastors only for exceptional reasons. The Catholic Church, by not preventing the emigration of priests, has had its witness impaired.

Generally, the churches encourage their members to work loyally within socialism, not to flee from it. Church people—in sharp contrast to party members—are the one group who can be relied on not to defect.

Occasionally authorities clamp down on exchanges—for instance, banning church representatives in East and West Germany from attending each other's synods. The number allowed to travel abroad is very limited and is drawn mostly from church leaders and employees, or specially favored individuals. On the twenty-fifth anniversary of the building of the Berlin Wall, Bishop Gottfried Forck of Berlin-Brandenberg pointed out that relaxation of travel restrictions of the kind the churches are advocating would help people feel genuinely at home in the GDR and lessen distress.

It was thanks to Bishop Mitzenheim that since 1962 pensioners had been allowed to travel to the West, but restrictions were so tight that people were often not allowed to visit close relatives until they were at death's door. Half of the GDR's citizens have relatives in West Germany. In 1987 the authorities at last relaxed restrictions, and about a million East Germans under pensionable age were allowed out on a visit (but without any currency, and they had to leave close relatives in the GDR to ensure their return!). How far this concession was due to church pressure is unknown.

Blocked off from travel to the West, some dedicated Christians discovered a new mission of reconciliation with former victims of Nazi occupation; they travel east to aid less favored Eastern-bloc Christians. Czechoslovakia is the one country that East Germans can visit freely. Christians in the GDR are also more aware of and concerned with helping the Third World than most other Eastern-bloc Christians.

The Issue of Militarism

In 1975 the Lutheran, Catholic, and Free (i.e., Methodist, Baptist, Old Catholic, and others) churches of the GDR, alone among Eastern-bloc churches, expressed their disapproval of the United Nations' condemnation of Zionism as a form of racism. Another reflection of concern over Nazi history is the acute sensitivity of Germans—especially Christians—to militarism, particularly since the introduction of conscription in 1962. Germans from both East and West are aware that they would be on the front lines of a future war.

It is impossible to avoid militarism. A 1974 teacher's manual said a goal of school education in the GDR was to teach children to "hate the armies of the FRG and other imperialist countries." In 1978, the year of concessions to the churches, the government introduced compulsory military training during the last two years of obligatory schooling. Lutheran leaders protested immediately, but in vain. They argued that military instruction could lead to an early fixation of the "friend-foe" way of thinking, which trains the young to violence, and which in Germany might involve shooting relatives or friends. It also, said the churchmen, undermines the credibility of the GDR's "peace policy" and the churches' support of it in ecumenical meetings.

Military preparedness is now taught as a separate subject. The courses end with a two-week camp at which both girls and boys are taught to handle arms. Special officers use textbooks unavailable to teachers or parents. The "education in hatred," as it is openly called, reminds the more sensitive of the older generation of the poisonous effect of such training on the Hitler Youth. The churches' offer to help parents who for reasons of conscience refused military education for their children received widespread approval and set in motion demands for a reduction in militarism and the removal of nuclear weapons from German soil.

In the GDR, the Peace People was an amorphous, ill-defined body with no leaders or organization. It included Christian pacifists, anti-nuclear proponents, political dissidents, and young people who, according to Lutheran leader Eberhard Nathe, were "weary of being told that a gun in a worker's hand fights for freedom, whereas a gun in an imperialist's hand means war." It also included people whose real motive was to be thrown out of the country. The Peace People were in essence making a moral protest, not only against nuclear war, but also against certain aspects of the system itself. Their action embodied a struggle for freedom of opinion and for a pluralist society.

The churches took up many of the "peace" issues. They called for less glorification of the military in public life and asked for education for peace rather than for war. In 1982, the annual Lutheran Synod even called on the GDR to disarm unilaterally if necessary. It also demanded better conditions for the *Bausoldaten* ("building soldiers"), the conscientious objectors who since 1964 have been given the option of serving in unarmed construction units, and asked for a further alternative of a "social peace service." The *Bausoldaten* oath contains the following: "I undertake to make an active contribution to the efforts of the National People's Army, at the side of the Soviet Army and at the side of the armies of the Socialist allies, to defend our Socialist State against all enemies and to achieve victory." Obviously, many conscientious objectors could never accept this oath; hence the request for a completely non-military option. The number of conscientious objectors rose to about a hundred annually, and they face longer sentences, up to two years.

The churches' requests were refused. In March 1982, in a stunning move, new laws extended the period during which reservists—including women—can be called up. (Women may refuse to serve in the army, but such a refusal could lead to difficulties elsewhere.)

Promoting Peace

The churches have been successful in countering militarism in other ways. They have set up a variety of peace meetings and classes, and thousands of young people have taken part. The state has responded with its own peace rallies, also well attended.

The churches stopped short of backing all peace campaigners. As Bishop Johannes Hempel explained: "We soon found that peace means different things to different people." Church leaders were far too experienced as politicians to let themselves be drawn into any injudicious action. When two hundred demonstrators slipped through a security net to observe a one-minute silence outside Jena church on December 24, 1982, the regional church there (the Evangelical Lutheran Church in Thuringia) disowned them.

Again, there was some division between the leadership and the common clergy, some of whose younger members are more extreme in their demands. One such is Rainer Eppelman, an East Berlin pastor and co-author in January 1982 with the late Robert Havemann of the "Berlin Appeal." The appeal asked both superpowers to withdraw their forces from divided Germany. Acceding to government pressure, the Berlin-Brandenberg church authorities discouraged people from signing it.

The churches had to back down in 1981 when they adopted the slogan "Swords into Ploughshares." The slogan was combined on badges with a representation of a sculpture presented to the U.N. building by the Soviet government—a case of hoisting the state with its own petard. When the authorities banned the badges and began to persecute some of the thousands of young people who wore them, the churches realized they could not be responsible for all the wearers, particularly those who had no religious affiliation. The churches warned the state, however, that its action could alienate these young citizens. The synod in Saxony also wrote that the government's measures restricted freedom of conscience. The government responded with a typical counterslogan: "Peace must be defended; peace must be armed!"

The churches' qualified support of the peace movement was only a logical step in their practice of "critical solidarity." They played the delicate role of mediator between the state and a grassroots movement, not the role of opposition or political party. Bishop Werner Leich put it succinctly in 1983: "The church is neither a camouflaged government party nor a camouflaged opposition party." Thus it must beware of being saddled with dubious allies. Rather than back all peace demonstrators—including those whose only use for the church was as a weapon in their anti-state activity— it tried to protect those with a genuine commitment to peace. It also used its unique constitutional position to channel potentially explosive situations into the relative safety of its own sphere. Mediators never satisfy everyone, but the fact that church forums were not banned indicated the government's confidence in the church—or perhaps its lack of confidence in the outcome of any confrontation with the church.

By 1984, the peace movement, which had attracted wide Western sympathy, was losing ground with the installation of Soviet missiles a *fait accompli*. Some church pacifists were in prison. By late spring, 20,000 pacifists had settled in West Germany, so many that church leaders appealed to Christians to stay in the GDR in order to maintain a Christian presence there. The peace movement now seems to have lost its impetus.

Meanwhile, at conferences such as the 1984 Budapest Lutheran World Assembly, East German church representatives made notably even-handed, uninhibited contributions on a wide range of issues.

Caution in the Catholic Church

The Catholic Church, much smaller and less powerful than the Lutheran churches, is not indigenous to the GDR. Many of its 1.05 million members (in 1,000 parishes served by 1,300 priests) are post-war refugees from what is now Poland and Czechoslovakia. They are often scattered, sometimes so thinly that they have to share a local Protestant church or receive the sacrament from authorized laymen. The church's resources are quite limited compared with those of the much larger Catholic Church in the FRG, which largely subsidizes it. Yet it makes a substantial contribution to social welfare. It also enjoys considerable freedom. Its 1,800 nuns in 300 convents carry out a variety of callings.

From 1961 to 1979, Catholics were led by the cautious Cardinal Alfred Bengsch. His concern was largely pastoral, and he avoided any church-state confrontation. Despite external pressure from the authorities, the small church achieved an admirable solidarity between clergy and laity through strict internal discipline. Although membership has dropped from 11 per cent of the population to 6.5 per cent, the decline, which occurred mainly in the earlier years of the GDR, is nothing like that of the Protestant churches. Attendance is good, and parish life is impressive.

Because of its insecure historical background and the harsh conditions of daily life, there is little theological questioning. GDR Catholics have to concentrate on fundamental practical problems such as how to survive at work, school, or in the army, and how to face the *Jugendweihe*. The older generation's outlook on faith and morals is solidly traditional, the younger generation's less so.

Aware of its relative vulnerability, the Catholic Church has been far more defensive and inward-looking than the Lutheran churches. Its bishops eschewed political matters because they feared that involvement would make them, like the Protestants, an "establishment" church, subservient rather than serving. Fearing equally the type of religious compromise made in Hungary and Czechoslovakia, they preferred their own brand of quiet resistance to the Marxist-Leninist regime. Thus the ten Catholic bishops were able to exert very little influence on government policy; until 1982 they limited themselves to expressing disapproval of abortion and military training in schools and extolling the role of the family in rearing children in the faith.

A Bolder Catholic Stand

But a significant number of clergy and church members have considerable reservations about the official church line of commitment to socialism. Thus there are strong tensions: church leaders are torn between wanting to secure a reasonable modus vivendi with the state and not wanting to be seen as over-compromising by parishioners and younger clergy.

Notable among the Catholics who have been dissatisfied with the church's non-political stand is the Halle Action Circle, founded in 1969. The priests and laypersons in this group compared the passivity of their bishops with the candor and at times prophetic utterances of the bishops' Lutheran counterparts. In an open letter the Halle Circle complained, "Many Christians can no longer overlook the troubling silence of the Catholic Church in the GDR with respect to the contemporary peace movement."

Signs of change have appeared. In October 1982, when the bishops visited the Vatican, the Pope urged them to cooperate more closely with the Lutheran churches and to become more involved in social issues. In January 1983, the bishops issued a pastoral letter with views similar to the Protestants on the peace question. They had, in fact, issued such a statement in 1978, but it was never disseminated in the GDR. The pastoral touched on several sensitive issues. "Peace with God," it said, "is a prerequisite for peace between men. Thus peace between states and power blocs is not, for the Christian, the highest good. Anyone who closes his eyes to the reality of sin when considering peace is prone to utopian dreams." It also declared that the use of nuclear weapons could never be justified, and criticized other state militaristic policies. Finally it urged people to pray for peace.

There are other signs that the church may be taking a more prominent role in society, moving away from political isolation and towards involvement in social issues, largely as a result of grassroots pressure. An important bishops' letter to priests dated September 8, 1986, indicated a possible new attitude toward coexistence. It emphasized that though the church must not become an extra arm of political and social interests, it has a right and a duty to take a clear stand on vital issues. Christians individually may have to cooperate with Marxists in practical issues where the welfare of individuals or particular communities is at stake, provided it involves no compromise of their loyalty to the Lord. The bishops stressed that they expect equal rights for *all* citizens, irrespective of belief. They also hinted at increasing pressures on the church. Though extremely significant and helpful, the pastoral letter has never actually been published.

The first nationwide Catholic conference, the 1987 Dresden Congress, attracted 80,000 people, 20,000 more than expected. Three thousand people participated in the wide-ranging discussions, mostly in private sessions, though some members complained that politically sensitive matters were not dealt with properly. Cardinal Joachim Meisner pled for the relaxation of travel restrictions that prevent pilgrimages abroad. The church would not allow press coverage of the discussions behind closed doors, because the controversial part would have been cut.

The Catholic approach to ecumenism was long inhibited by various complex factors, and most of the initiative came from the Protestant side. But Protestants' confidence has been undermined by Vatican censuring of Catholic theologians of whom they approve, such as Hans Küng and Leonardo Boff. Future ecumenical development would seem to lie in grassroots initiatives by the younger generation. These have provided encouragement to the churches actively seeking common ground to expound the Gospel in a "godless" society and to help people confront growing social problems, such as high divorce and suicide rates. For instance, Meisner has emphasized to the young that Christian liberty begins with being able to say "no" in certain situations. Closer collaboration may be expected on abortion, against which the stand of Protestant bishops has been as firm and outspoken as that of Catholics.

Both Protestant and Catholic churches have shown penitence on behalf of the whole German nation for the evil days of Hitler. In August 1986, on the twenty-fifth anniversary of the Berlin Wall, both deplored the building of the wall.

The Polish Situation

The tensions between the Polish workers and their government that came to a head in 1980 have had a considerable impact on church-state relations in the GDR. Early in 1980, the Lutheran churches had already spoken out against the Soviet invasion of Afghanistan. After the churches criticized the belligerent Warsaw Pact maneuvers in Poland, Professor Eberhard Poppe accused them of supporting NATO: "The imperialist forces keep trying to affect citizens with religious ties and religious communities in the GDR through anti-Communist agitation and 'Christian' garb and ideological diversion so as to push them into opposition to the socialist state and socialist development."

Unintimidated, the Lutheran churches continued to give the Polish people moral support. In April 1981 the Synod of Berlin-Brandenberg proclaimed its solidarity with Poland, adding for good measure that reciprocal visits between people of the two nations should be resumed. But from 1981 to 1984 private travel to Poland was made all but impossible, frustrating Christians who wanted to take food to the hungry Poles.

In 1980–81 the East German authorities feared the Lutheran churches might serve as a rallying point for opposition in the GDR and conceivably stimulate a movement similar to Poland's. The fear was completely unjustified, for the Protestant churches are not rooted in the working classes— worker protest is almost non-existent—and their tradition does not have the nationalist connotations found in the Polish Catholic Church. Moreover, the GDR regime is far stronger than the Polish one: its economy is relatively sound; the few human-rights dissidents are readily deported. The authorities' attitude may have arisen from Soviet warnings that the government should muzzle its churches or face retaliatory measures.

Certainly since 1982, Catholic leaders under the young Cardinal Meisner have given the authorities increasing cause for concern, and Honecker's visit to the Pope in 1985 was not to enhance his standing but to discuss thorny new issues.

The Zionskirke Incidents

During the summer of 1987 there was a remarkable element of freedom in church life, with the East Berlin *Kirchentag*, the Dresden meeting of Catholics, an opportunity for independent church peace groups to take part in a peace march in September, and the state's acceptance of direct talks with

Protestant church leaders in a set agenda—something the church leaders had been seeking for years.

Then came the blows. On November 17, in the Zionskirke, a rather decrepit East Berlin suburban church used as a meeting place by peace and environmental groups, a congregation of several hundred young people—mainly wearing punk fashions—was attacked by a small, well-organized group described as "skinheads." People were injured. Later, twelve of the assailants were given rather mild sentences for hooliganism. Eyewitnesses reported that the police seemed very reluctant to get involved in the fracas and suspect some kind of silent party approval of paramilitary gangs. Later, however, by heavier sentences of "skinheads" the authorities made it clear that they would firmly oppose any neo-Nazi tendencies.

A week later, on the night of November 24, the church library was raided, photocopies and publications—including a semi-official journal that the state regards as offensive, since atmospheric pollution is a very sensitive issue—were seized, and five arrests were made. (The arrested were subsequently released.) This was the first search of church premises since the 1950s.

In protest, a meeting addressed by Bishop Werner Krusche and a vigil were held; twenty people were arrested but later released. The Zionskirke events had drawn unfavorable publicity for the government, which wanted to end the confrontation. Meanwhile, the important talks scheduled between Protestant leaders and the state were called off, apparently because of a resolution on the Gospel of peace passed at the annual Lutheran Synod in September.

But on March 3, 1988, almost exactly ten years after the historic meeting of 1978, Honecker met Bishop Leich for fairly cordial discussions. Leich stated that the issues causing stress in church-state relations in recent months had arisen from the social sphere and had "no origin within the service of our churches." He also complained of the state's lack of readiness to discuss social problems, particularly emigration and travel.

The Outlook

As for official reaction to Mikhail Gorbachev's *glasnost* reforms: a state official at the 1987 *Kirchentag* was asked whether there were any prospects for democratization in the GDR. There were boos when he answered in the negative. The attitude of the GDR leadership is that since the state is a model of technological efficiency and progress there is no need for *glasnost*. Gorbachev's reforms are hardly reported, and the government made it quite clear that there would be no such discussions. But by early 1988 subtle pressures for reform had begun to arise within the Communist Party, and the resulting debate could influence selection of a successor to the 75-year-old Honecker.

Gorbachev's call for more openness in Communist societies contributed to an increase of strength and boldness in the small but growing dissident movement, which depends heavily on the Protestant churches for meeting space and other logistical support. In early 1988, crowds as large as 2,000 packed Protestant churches in East Berlin and in a dozen other cities to demand the release of some 200 human-rights, peace, and environmental activists arrested in mid-January for attempting to stage an unauthorized demonstration. Many of them had hoped, apparently, to be expelled to the West. By the beginning of February, authorities had released most of the activists, sending over a hundred to West Germany, including Christian activists such as Vera Wollenburger.

These events must be leading to much soul-searching among church members, many of whom have deep reservations about the policy of their leaders. The state, which has been playing on these divisions and the regional ones for years, is obviously trying to split the churches and to force the leadership into dissociating itself from the action groups. Leaders and congregations would do well to make use of the wise guidelines laid down by the Synod of the Provincial Church in Saxony in October 1987, which said in part:

> The statements and views of groups must not contradict the Gospel; members of groups much be prepared to have views discussed critically by the church; groups must show tolerance toward views of church members which are very different from their own; the church must be prepared to make room for unwelcome and uncomfortable viewpoints.

Membership in the churches is unlikely to increase in the near future for various reasons—the secularization of East German society, the discrimination against practicing Christians, and the Lutheran churches' need for liturgical renewal.

There are nevertheless some signs of promise. Lutherans still outnumber the party membership by three to one. (Significantly, in the last five years no fewer than 63,000 party members have been expelled to maintain "the unity and purity of the Party," and another 25,000 have resigned.) There is no shortage of vocations to the ministry. More and more young people are applying for careers in the Protestant churches, so many that half have to be turned away. At present, about 1,000 men and women are being trained as pastors, and about 1,500 in church social work.

About 10 per cent of Lutheran churches and four hundred pastors have responded to the charismatic renewal, and several thousand home Bible-study and prayer groups are expanding rapidly. The young in particular are showing a greater interest in religion. Pastor Theo Lehmann attracts congregations of between five and ten thousand one night a month, a feat seldom matched in other secularized societies.

Discrimination has weeded out the lukewarm: though the number of registered members continues to decline, attendance is on the increase. The caliber of people whom the churches attract is high, for Germans tend to take their faith seriously. The churches provide a vital element in a totalitarian society. They are islands of freedom that offer an invaluable safety valve, for which the state should be grateful.

The churches, indeed, have far more influence than they had forty years ago. According to Bishop Hempel, people are coming to expect Christians to display those virtues that are crumbling in other quarters of life: openness, hope in the future, charity to others. Perhaps the churches' greatest asset is devotion to truth.

As for church-state relations, as long as church leaders continue to challenge the state when its concept of the collective good clashes with the conscience of the individual, their integrity is safe. Neither past repression nor present privilege has caused them to compromise. The government appreciates their integrity—a quality hardly attributable to the government.

Yet despite the promises made in 1978 and Honecker's pledge of good church-state relations given in February 1985, equal rights for Christian citizens have not been forthcoming. Adult Christians are urged to collaborate with the State Security Service. Church leaders admonish them to refuse and warn that any conversations with representatives of State Security will be reported to the relevant church authorities. According to the April 1985 Synod in East Berlin, secret police have been taking children out of their homes to question them on church activities, offering them a university education for spying on members of the churches. Employment and educational discrimination against churchgoing young people continues. Out of forty cases cited by the Saxony church, only one complaint was successfully resolved. The April 1988 bans on editions of the four church newspapers and the news service point to an unsatisfactory situation.

The state, by giving better coverage of religious affairs in the media, is trying to some extent to project a harmonious image, now that its fears over the Polish crisis are in proper perspective. But East German Christians, as individuals, are even more aware of their continuing vulnerability and the state's failure to abide by its promises. While there is much that is humdrum about church attendance in the GDR, what Dietrich Bonhoeffer called the cost of discipleship is still very real to those Christians who take it seriously.

7

Hungary

I N 1956 the Hungarian people inspired the Western world with their
heroic uprising against their Communist rulers. Today there seems to be
little of the heroic left in the nation. János Kádár, the head of the country
from 1956 to 1988, was on the Soviet side in the bloody suppression. He
subsequently won the nation's esteem by obtaining considerable freedom at
home in return for conformity to Soviet policy, a system the Hungarians
call "goulash Communism."

Doctrinaire Marxism takes second place to economic achievement and
the satisfaction of material needs. Political legitimacy and economic success
are closely tied. The economic system combines legal and semi-legal private
enterprise with state socialism, and the standard of living has been fairly
high. Access to Western culture and travel to the West are relatively
unfettered. Hungarians have a sense of the absurd and a considerable capacity
for enjoying themselves.

Yet in recent years it has become clear that "market socialism" is not
working, and economic problems have been worsening. Real incomes have
been falling, with inflation rising to nearly 20 per cent. The foreign debt is
nearly $18 billion. The Party has continued to interfere in industry, dis-
couraging competitiveness.

Since pragmatism and compromise are the order of the day, the many
flaws in the system have been condoned. Some of Kádár's strongest supporters spent years in prison as erstwhile supporters of Imre Nagy—the
moderate premier ousted in 1955—and the revolution. People remember the
wave of arrests and executions following the original Communist takeover
in the late 1940s. They remember too the terrible retribution after the 1956
uprising, when 200,000 Soviet troops in tanks and armored cars attacked
Budapest, and when the lucky hundreds of thousands fled the country to
safety and freedom elsewhere. It was enough. Hungarians have been very
cautious since, and few are in prison for political offenses.

Hungarians are an individualistic people of Finno-Ugrian origin, with a difficult language (Magyar) that few foreigners can grasp. They live surrounded by Germans, Romanians, and Slavs, who admire them greatly for their 1956 heroism but with whom they have little in common otherwise. Hungarian sympathy is concentrated on the four million of their race—the equivalent of over a third of their present population—who, since the dismemberment of the Austro-Hungarian Empire after World War I, have formed substantial minorities in Yugoslavia, Czechoslovakia, and particularly Romania. Hungary itself is a homogeneous state with no awkward national minorities, but the loss of more than a quarter of its people has had an important psychological effect.

In this materialistic state, with caution the watchword, the churches suffer from an excess of worldly wisdom and a lack of fervor. Although church life can be practiced within reason, state restrictions and discrimination do exist. Church leaders are largely in thrall to the government.

The churches do not play as critical a role as they do in East Germany. Nor are there many inspiring examples of protest and heroism in the face of real persecution, as in Czechoslovakia. Church life is sapped by the sickness that has attacked society as a whole: selfishness, envy, and distrust. Apathy and materialism affect people who in other respects are good Christians.

THE CHURCHES TO 1980

As is true in other parts of Eastern Europe, a major cause of the Hungarian churches' weakness in countering state domination can be traced to the past. During the sixteenth and seventeenth centuries Hungarians were busy fighting the invading Turks. In these disturbed circumstances, the Reformation made such headway that at the end of the sixteenth century the archbishop of Esztergom (the see of the primate) lamented that for every Catholic there were a thousand Protestants.

The Counter-Reformation in Hungary went hand in hand with the resettlement of territory devastated by the Turks. As in Czechoslovakia it was backed by the Habsburg emperors and carried out with great thoroughness. By the end of the eighteenth century the Protestant element in Hungary was reduced to one-third of the population. Protestants were given freedom of conscience only in the mid-nineteenth century. This delay weakened both Catholic and Protestant churches and inhibited ecumenism.

The Catholic Church, moreover, was rich. Though not so rich as the Communists claim, it was a major landowner in a poor country, and it had the privilege of being an established church.

There was much need for reform in both church and state. But none of the churches, conservative and strongly nationalistic as they were, was prepared for the social, cultural, and political revolution that followed World War II.

The Communists and the Catholic Church

At the end of World War II, the churches shared the disgrace of the politicians for having led the nation to ruin. Once the political opposition had been destroyed, the Communists tackled the powerful Catholic Church. Its centralized hierarchy was led by the uncompromising primate Cardinal József Mindszenty, who had no illusions about Communism. The Catholic Church was stripped of possessions, institutions, and leaders. The cardinal was arrested in 1948, subjected to a notorious show trial, and sent to prison. Six hundred priests were imprisoned also, and all of the church's 3,150 schools, half the national total, were taken over.

In 1950 the Communists struck again. All but four of the sixty-three religious orders were dissolved. More than 10,000 monks and nuns were thrown out of their convents overnight and subjected to years of humiliation, an irreparable blow to the spiritual life of the church since the religious orders had attracted the best priests. More than 2,000 left the country; many others were imprisoned and tortured. There is no record of the number who died. Only 350 monks were allowed to continue as parish priests, and about 1,000 nuns as nurses.

A group of priests who were in favor of the government "reforms" wanted to show their solidarity with the regime. These "Peace Priests" were soon taken over by the government, though after the Revolution the Bishops' Conference reorganized the group in such a way that it could be recognized by the Vatican, as it was in 1957. It became advisable to join Opus Pacis, and between 80 and 90 per cent of the priests did. All important diocesan posts were filled from their ranks. Although the Peace Priests movement is not popular with the laity, it has never become as unpopular and controversial as Pacem in Terris in Czechoslovakia.

In the face of Communist terror, the bishops signed a concordat. The state guaranteed Catholics full religious freedom and the church freedom of activity. In return, the church was obliged to "recognize and support the political order." The hierarchy pledged—significantly, as it turned out—to "proceed under ecclesiastical law against ecclesiastical persons who may act against the constructive work of the government," a promise they have kept only too well. They also had to accept a decree requiring that the church obtain the approval of the party presidium for all appointments to bishoprics and senior posts. (Since 1971, however, except for the most senior posts, only the permission of the State Church Office has been required.)

All high church appointees have to swear an oath of loyalty to the state.

Key diocesan figures (chancellors and vicars general) are usually chosen from the leading members of the Peace Priests movement; they report on the activities of one another and of the bishops. When the state encouraged these leaders to defy the Vatican after the 1956 uprising, the Pope excommunicated them, but they were later rehabilitated by Rome. In exchange for these concessions, the state granted a subsidy to the church, further tightening its grip.

Cardinal Mindszenty's Uncompromising Stand

Cardinal Mindszenty was released from prison during the 1956 uprising and took refuge in the American embassy when the Soviets marched in. Controversy over his stand will probably never cease. For many, he represented a heroic passive resistance to Communism. He believed that the only way to defend the church was to refuse to show even the slightest sign of weakness.

As his years of self-imposed exile dragged on, the cardinal became an embarrassment to the Vatican, for the Hungarian church could win no concessions while he remained at the embassy. In the end he was sacrificed for what the Vatican felt were the best interests of the church. In September 1971 he was forced into exile, but he refused to resign from the archbishopric of Esztergom. In 1974 Pope Paul VI removed him from office in order to normalize church-state relations. He died, brokenhearted, the following year.

Cardinal Mindszenty has many critics, including the present generation of Hungarian bishops, who dismiss him as a relic of the feudal past and a barrier to progress. Yet many Hungarian Catholics feel that by allowing less dedicated men to fill the vacant posts, the Vatican deprived the faithful of the leadership they expected. Mindszenty supporters—Catholics who refused to compromise—organized small groups of close-knit Christian communities modeled on those of the early persecuted church. Many members of this movement were imprisoned, suffered, and died; some, like Fr. György Bulányi, survived and continue to resist, and their "base groups" flourish today. Although Mindszenty's dismissal may have left the way open for a more normal church life, the state—perhaps correctly—viewed his departure as a great victory.

The Communists and the Protestant Churches

In 1948 the less powerful Reformed Church and Evangelical Lutheran Church, lacking the invaluable experience of working out a theology under persecution that the Confessing Churches of East Germany had had, were forced to sign concordats on similar terms. The leaders who protested were deposed and replaced by more pliant ones. The most notable objector, Lutheran bishop Lajos Ordass, was sent to prison on a fake charge. Restored to leadership during the 1956 uprising, he was removed again in 1958 for refusing to compromise sufficiently. Reformed bishop László Ravasz resigned under pressure in 1948.

After initial persecution, the state handed over to the churches the disciplining of their membership. The 1966 Lutheran General Synod gave the leadership power to discipline clergy for "attitudes" contrary to the political, economic, and social order. The Reformed Church acted similarly, though this was contrary to its form of government. The courageous few who surfaced during the 1956 uprising and accused their leaders of promoting a "servile" rather than a "serving" church were suppressed.

Zoltán Káldy was presiding bishop of the Lutheran Church from 1967 to 1985, and Tibor Bartha was president of the Reformed Church from 1962 to 1986. They both seemed to have come to terms too readily with the government. They were not Marxists, but they were able to argue that the Communist government deserved Christian support because the churches formerly backed reactionary regimes. Both were nurtured in a tradition that deemed cooperation with secular powers a dictate of religion. Bartha even said: "It would be unthinkable to me that anyone should oppose socialism." Their goal was freedom to preach the Gospel and permission for Christians to live and witness under socialism.

Each leader dominated the life of his church and set the pattern for his colleagues. Both were deeply involved in national political life and served in parliament, which also contains Catholic, Free Church (i.e., Baptist and Pentecostalist), and Jewish representatives. All members of parliament are obliged publicly to support the program of the Communist Party, and church leaders who are members are completely trusted by the regime. Bartha and Káldy sat on the foreign relations committee, and Bartha and his successor Gyula Nagy have been members of the country's presidential council. In their defense, some claim that for every clergyman who is an obedient MP, a hundred others are left in peace; but this does not account for the strictness of the internal discipline exercised by the church leaders.

A Policy of Reconciliation

In the 1960s, János Kádár unexpectedly changed his policy to one of national reconciliation. His commitment to Marxism had been shaken years before when he was tortured by his fellow party members. Now, with the party once more firmly in control, he determined that conditions for an uprising should not recur. His regime, moreover, needed a better image abroad. He made the system more humane by allowing Hungarians considerably more ideological diversity.

To assuage the majority (60 per cent) Catholic Church, Kádár allowed a few chosen clergy—who were kept under surveillance—to attend the Vatican Council in 1962. The first agreement between a Communist government and the Vatican was signed in 1964. Five new bishops—men acceptable to the regime—were appointed to the now mostly vacant sees.

The agreement was very limited. During the 1960s arrests and secret trials continued for the "offenses" of evangelism—spreading religious views or literature, or instructing the young. As late as 1971, four priests, seminarians, and a girl student were given sentences of up to five years for evangelism. (One of the priests committed suicide.) The aim was to intimidate, to remove potential troublemakers, yet in such a way as to avoid creating martyrs. Priests' licenses were frequently revoked: in 1965, for instance, 1,000 priests—almost 20 per cent of the total number—were excluded from pastoral activity.

The state continued to clamp down on Christian education. During the late 1950s a vigorous campaign was launched to indoctrinate the young. Through intimidation and secularization, the number of Catholic children registered for religious education fell from a peak of around 90 per cent in 1957 to a mere 6 per cent in 1975.

In 1964 Msgr. Agostino Casaroli, the first Vatican diplomat to travel extensively in Eastern Europe (and Vatican secretary of state since 1979), raised some burning issues: freedom for religious instruction outside school, the rehabilitation of banned bishops and religious orders, and the Peace Priests. The government sidestepped these, instead deliberately—and interminably—haggling with the Vatican over filling vacant bishoprics. By 1974 only four dioceses had diocesan bishops.

In other areas of life—marriage, divorce, contraception, abortion—the state propagated attitudes directly opposed to Catholic teaching. Many of these policies were so disastrous—the birth rate dipped to the lowest in the world—that the government had to revise them. But the revision was instigated by sociologists and demographers, not church leaders. Hungarians ruefully compared the outspoken church leaders of Poland, Yugoslavia, and East Germany with their own silent hierarchy. Nothing was being done to arrest the secularism and materialism of the society. In 1976 Cardinal Koenig of Vienna described the situation of Hungary's Catholic Church: "Feelings of doubt, anguish, disappointment, and despair fill the hearts of the faithful, especially in the cities."

Relations between church and state entered a new phase with Mindszenty's death in 1975. Kádár visited Pope Paul VI in 1976. For the first time in thirty years, canonical bishops were provided in all eleven dioceses, with several auxiliary bishops as well. (As Hungarian Catholics put it: "We'll soon have more bishops than teachers of religion.") In 1977 the bishops were permitted their first *ad limina* visit to the Pope. László Lékai was appointed primate and cardinal-archbishop of Esztergom; he died in 1986. A cautious, stubborn, conservative man, son of a rural tilemaker, Lékai preferred conciliation to confrontation. "We must look not at what divides us but at what unites us," he maintained.

What emerged in the mid-seventies were bishops who, though theologically and pastorally sound, hesitated to deviate from the regime's line. The Vatican *Ostpolitik* succeeded in filling the bishoprics, which it has been unable to do in Czechoslovakia.

CHURCH LIFE IN THE 1980S

Hungary's State Church Office was set up in 1950 to control the churches. Although its legal powers may be less far-reaching than the parallel institutions in Czechoslovakia, Romania, and Poland, it is supported by a department of the state police devoted specifically to church matters. These bodies are entrusted with "caring for" the churches; their high rank and the large numbers they employ indicate their importance.

For many years these bodies kept the churches under constant surveillance and maintained strict control over all their activities. They were helped by a network of informers and collaborators within the churches. The clergy were infiltrated with police agents. State officials were placed in the offices of church leaders to "advise" them, censor communications, and reprimand them if necessary. Diocesan offices were bugged. The resulting isolation of the clergy from their flock had far-flung and damaging effects on church life. Although the situation has eased, the memory of it inhibits the higher clergy.

All the state's measures are geared to give the impression that it does not interfere with the internal affairs of the churches. The historical dependence of the churches on the state, their traditional disunity, and the removal of obstreperous church leaders made it easy for the State Church Office to intervene. Although the pressure on religion is now far less severe than in the 1940s and 1950s, the same system operates and continues to cause deep resentment among rank-and-file believers.

The Catholic Church

Out of Hungary's population of 10.5 million, about 6 million have been baptized in the Catholic Church, but only 1.5 million are active church members. Of these, about one-third (half of whom are over fifty-four) attend church regularly; the proportion is much higher in small villages, about 80 per cent, falling to around 10 per cent in the cities. Secularism is the chief cause of the reduced numbers. By contrast, in the fairly relaxed Hungarian atmosphere, the proportion requesting religious rites of passage is high—over half of the Catholics, for instance, have church weddings.

In 1980 there were 3,600 priests serving about 2,000 Latin Rite and 150 Eastern Rite parishes. By 1984 the number of priests had dropped to 2,525. By comparison, in 1944 there were 5,435 priests. In 1981 there were 267 seminarians; in 1985, only 189. By comparison, in 1948 there were 1,049 seminarians; in 1954, 164.

The majority of Catholics in Hungary are Latin Rite, with eleven dioceses, five seminaries, and a theological academy in Budapest. The number of religious is severely restricted—in 1980, there were 250 religious to run eight church secondary schools. These schools, unique in Eastern Europe, can serve only a tiny minority. In 1984 a further hundred nuns were licensed to form a nursing order.

The Eastern Rite Church, with 230,000 members, is the largest of its kind legally recognized in Eastern Europe and is growing.

The Protestant Churches

Protestants, the Reformed in particular, are most numerous in eastern Hungary, which was occupied by the Turks for over a century and a half and is not so solidly Catholic as the west. Their historic center is Debrecen.

The *Reformed Church,* with 1.8 million members, almost 17 per cent of the population, is divided into 1,250 self-supporting, theoretically independent parishes, with about the same number of ministers plus 250 assistants. The clergy are trained in theological academies at Budapest and Debrecen, which hold 150 students, and in two other institutes. The church is governed by a synod, and all church governing bodies have an equal number of ministers and elders meeting under joint chairmen (clerical and lay). The church runs two secondary schools.

The Reformed Church's longtime leader, Tibor Bartha, retired because of ill health in 1986. His successor as presiding bishop was Károly Tóth, a man acceptable to the authorities and also to church members, with whom his personal relations are good and for whom he has obtained concessions. Since only 5 per cent of Reformed Church young people receive religious instruction, education is a matter of high priority for him. An agreement regulating religious instruction on church premises, similar to that signed by the Catholic Church in 1972, was reached by Tóth and Imre Miklós, the state's minister for religion, in 1987.

The *Evangelical Lutheran Church* has about 350,000 members, or 3 per cent of the population; about 80,000 live in Budapest, and the rest are scattered, with groups of several churches served by one pastor in a "mother" parish. There are approximately 400 pastors, 300 mother parishes, and 1,900 "daughter" parishes. The church is governed by a general assembly. Its theological academy in Budapest has about 50 full-time men and women students and about 50 part-time students who wish to be assistant ministers. It runs homes for the elderly, orphans, and incurables.

The *Baptist Church* has about 440 congregations spread throughout Hungary. Only 95 pastors care for a growing community of 12,000 members and over 50,000 adherents.

Among the smaller churches, there are *Methodists*—split by schism into two separate churches, in part over the question of state control—*Unitarians, Adventists, Pentecostalists,* and *Nazarenes.*

The Orthodox and Jews

In the *Orthodox* community, about 5,000 members are under the Moscow Patriarchate. Another 15,000 belong to various ethnic minorities and come under their own national patriarchates.

In 1941 there were 725,000 *Jews* in Hungary, many of them refugees from Hitler. Adolf Eichmann moved in and sent 600,000 to their deaths. In 1956, 20,000 left, and more have since emigrated to Israel. About 80,000 remain. The Hungarian Jews are the largest and most favored Jewish community in Eastern Europe. They have the only rabbinical seminary in the Communist world, which trains rabbis from other countries, including the Soviet Union. Many of the 100 synagogues are well attended; there are 26 rabbis, a number of secondary schools, a hospital, and two old people's homes. However, young Jews are increasingly marrying non-Jews and show little enthusiasm for preserving their heritage and faith.

Although anti-Semitism is illegal, it is still a powerful factor in society. The government does not exploit it and allowed the topic to be discussed on television in 1987.

Problems of the Clergy

The state has the final say over church appointments, finances, education, and publishing. In 1968, and again in 1980, the state guaranteed aid. In the Catholic Church, for instance, 60 per cent of the income comes from the faithful and 15 per cent from abroad; the other quarter comes from the state. Even when the state appears to relax its control, the effect is the same. When, for example, it renounced its "right" to appoint parish priests, the local party apparatus took over the task.

The state pays the clergy salaries that are so low as to render the clergy vulnerable to offers of promotion in return for cooperation. A typical married minister has no car, telephone, or labor-saving devices. In such discouraging circumstances and such a secularized environment, vocations rapidly declined.

In the Catholic Church, the average age of the clergy in 1976 was sixty-seven. In 1982, nearly a third of the 2,700 active priests were over sixty. Many rural rectories were in a severe state of disrepair, often without electricity or running water, for years. Many older priests, after years of suffering in a climate of distrust, are tired, isolated, and broken, their ministry restricted, their hopes destroyed. Some dioceses have had no vocations for years. A nun commented, "It is a miracle if anyone wants to be a priest nowadays; it takes a saint." In a typical year, 100 priests die and about 40 new ones are ordained.

Difficulties begin in the seminary, where the state-approved rectors can oppose any signs of independence. In 1980 various seminarians were punished for carrying out pastoral work among university students. Some were prevented from organizing study groups on religious matters. When one was refused ordination, fifteen of his friends protested to the Bishops' Conference, an action so unprecedented as to cause a sensation. The seminarian was ordained, but his friends were expelled.

Seminarians are not exempt from military service; in fact, they are deliberately posted to the worst camps along with hardened criminals. Similar treatment is given to enthusiastic young Christians, and some suicides have resulted. Even for non-religious Hungarian young people, military service is so traumatic that very few will talk of it. Yet in a 1984 TV interview, the rector of the Budapest seminary asserted that it was a good way to toughen students. He said nothing about the fact that it was illegal for soldiers in uniform to enter a church during their eighteen months of military service. In a significant concession by authorities reported in 1987, conscripts are now allowed to attend church services.

Young clergy who are more than usually committed may from the start be refused a work permit. Once allowed to work, if they show enterprise and have a flourishing ministry, they may run into the disciplinary measures of their own bishop. One way to dampen spirits is to relegate a successful town priest to a small village. He may be transferred rapidly from parish to parish—one priest, now sixty, had twenty-seven parishes in thirty-six years—or be put in charge of so many parishes that he is grossly overworked. Occasionally, priests have their licenses revoked.

In all this, the bishops are forced to work closely with the State Office, without whose consent clergy cannot be appointed or transferred. Thus the church is not only prevented from making the best use of its limited manpower but also forced to condone the situation. There is bitter resentment, made worse by the lack of communication between upper and ordinary clergy and a deep rift between the conservative majority and the more committed and active minority.

Lay initiatives are also blocked. When in 1979, for instance, an elderly Catholic tried to organize a Mass for the release of American hostages in Teheran, the church authorities refused permission.

The problems of the clergy in Protestant churches are less acute. The shortage of vocations has eased, for since 1981 the churches have allowed women to be both pastors and elders. At one college, two-thirds of the ordinands in training are women.

A Protestant pastor can have a satisfying ministry, within limits. There is even a serious problem of young people entering the church because it offers respectable, assured employment, and there are many clergy who seem to lack a living faith. Most of the conscientious clergy, faced with fighting what they disapprove of or preaching the Gospel, have chosen the latter. The laity on the whole prefer their clergy to be apolitical—neither for nor against the government, but they do resent seeing the best clergy penalized while poor ones are rewarded with good parishes.

Complaints do sometimes surface. In 1978, in a *samizdat* production, a group of Reformed Christians complained about the state's total control over church appointments, organizations, and administration, and spoke of the danger of the annihilation of the church. Six years later, as we shall see, the "servant church" theology of Bishop Káldy, head of the Lutheran Church, came under fire from Pastor Zoltán Dóka.

On the pastoral side, believers strongly object that the clergy have to obtain permission to visit hospital patients. When the point was raised by a retired surgeon in a TV discussion with Imre Miklós, minister for religion, Miklós contended that regular visits disturb the patients.

Church Buildings

Problems concerning church buildings pale in comparison with those experienced in Romania or Czechoslovakia. The state has always helped greatly to restore and care for historic or cultural buildings. But the upkeep of other churches is a crippling financial burden for congregations that, especially in the case of Protestants, are predominantly elderly. State regulations are stringent. A new Catholic church, for instance, cannot be one inch larger than the previous one.

Despite this, 628 new churches have been built since 1948, although only 170—far fewer than are needed—are for Catholics. The Baptists, growing steadily, have 47 new churches; in 1983, for instance, 12 more were under construction, at great sacrifice to the congregations. Overall, for Protestants, enough new buildings have been permitted to keep up with the demands caused by demographic changes, and church members are proud of them.

Religious Education

A major cause of tension between church and state, about which even Cardinal Lékai complained, is the restrictions on religious education in school. It must be requested by the parents (or personally, in the case of secondary pupils) and is limited to two classes a week. The pupils must be divided into only two age groups, 6-10 and 11-18, a wide range that makes teaching difficult. Names of participating children must be reported to the state authorities; this makes it possible to practice discrimination (in housing, careers, and education) against attending parents and children. The pupils are not permitted to have textbooks, take notes, or ask questions.

Since the mid-1970s, the situation has eased somewhat with regard to primary schoolchildren, and about one-fifth of them were receiving religious education in 1982. Among secondary pupils, however, the proportion applying has dropped to about 5 per cent. Wherever the percentage shows signs of rising, local authorities revert to threats and mockery to reduce it. In one place, for example, thirty-six children were enrolled, but after the local officials chose to "enlighten" the parents, only one child was left in the course. In some large urban areas, not a single child is enrolled.

Some clergy have reservations about the hierarchy's attempts to win more generous provision for religious education from the authorities. In their view, what the children receive, given the restrictions, seems hardly worth bothering about. They prefer to risk persecution for teaching unofficially. Some find that taking groups of children to remote villages for holidays, during which they receive solid instruction, is more effective, though the state authorities disapprove and may caution those involved.

In vivid contrast, all schoolchildren must receive three hours a week of Marxism-Leninism. The Catholic bishops, in an excellent critical pastoral letter in 1981, deplored the use of educational facilities for propaganda purposes and complained that children from a religious background were being exposed at an impressionable age to contradictory ideological and moral systems. (In appendix G, two young Christian teachers tell what it is like to teach in an atheistic school system.)

The Catholic bishops are rightly proud of their secondary schools run by religious orders. But there are only eight, and only 2,400 children attend them—including children of some party members who appreciate the excellent education. Graduates of Catholic schools no longer encounter great difficulties in being accepted by a university. Indeed, one such school sees between ten and twenty of its graduates admitted each year to medical schools and faculties, far more than the national average.

Older Protestant children receive instruction in a well-planned pre-Confirmation course. Youth work in the churches is fairly limited (the Catholic Church involves only about 1 per cent of youth), not least because many young people find the churches dull and rigidly traditional. A high proportion of the clergy are elderly, and few have much talent for dealing with young people, many of whom are as trendy and ill disciplined as their Western counterparts.

In 1987 a Hungarian psychologist expressed concern about the number of young people who refuse any positive values and, apparently out of desperation, worship Satan. The only solution, said the psychologist, is to show them real values, which the churches could do. However, she goes on to say, the authorities, afraid of the possible influence of the churches, seem to prefer that these unhappy young people should not be converted. Meanwhile, sadism, violence, and hatred are becoming more widespread among the young.

Bibles and Other Religious Literature

Although the state controls all publishing, Hungary's generally liberal cultural policy assures that restrictions are not nearly so stiff as in most other Eastern-bloc countries. All the main churches publish newspapers and journals as well as religious books.

The state, however, deliberately discriminates in favor of Protestant magazines. The most popular Catholic magazine, *Új Ember*, is allowed to print only a totally inadequate 90,000 copies (until recently only 60,000), whereas the much smaller Reformed Church can print more than 100,000 copies of its weekly paper. The Catholic monthly *Vigilia,* responsible and enlightened under editor Fr. László Zoltán, promotes ecumenism and prints challenging articles. The church press does not carry news of discrimination or persecution. For that, believers have to resort to *samizdat*.

Since 1949 more than 500,000 Bibles have been either legally imported by the Hungarian Bible Council or printed on imported paper. (By contrast, in the Soviet Union 95,000 were legally imported between 1917 and 1980.) Nevertheless, twice as many copies were brought in illegally. The claim of church leaders that this was unnecsssary (Reformed Church president Bartha even used the word "piracy") because believers' needs were being adequately met was palpably false. In 1975 the publication of an entirely new inter-denominational translation aroused tremendous interest. One of the reasons why the State Church Office allowed it to be published may have been the hope that it would drive a wedge between those who welcomed it and those who were antagonized by its modern language. It has become widely accepted.

Catholics have their own new version of the Bible and a simplified version for children. With the improvement in church-state relations in the 1980s, a wider range of Bibles is being produced in far greater numbers than ever before. Government policy recently has favored printing more books on religion.

But because state books are subsidized, books from the church press are more expensive. Moreover, the church press cannot meet the demand for books on religion. Therefore people often turn for information to cheap state books, which are mainly critical of religion. In 1982, only 0.3 per cent of new books were published by the two Catholic publishing houses—a minute proportion considering that Catholics make up 60 per cent of the population. The annual supply of prayer books sells out in about two months.

The first religious bookshop opened in Budapest in 1977. In 1983, religious books were put on sale during Hungarian Book Week, and thousands of Bibles were bought. Although currency restrictions make it difficult for Hungarians to buy books from abroad, those with contacts can receive foreign books freely. But even this additional influx does not meet the demand for religious literature. As recently as 1984 the police confiscated 119 volumes of Catholic *samizdat*, consisting of prayers, theological texts, and reflections produced over several years.

In 1980, in a development unique in Eastern Europe and not common even in the West, the education authorities introduced the Bible as literature in the grammar school curriculum to provide necessary cultural background.

Discrimination Against Believers

Teachers and civil servants are not supposed to be Christian, but many of them are. Since religious discrimination comes largely through local pressures, professional Christians may attend distant churches; one Protestant traveled eighty miles to Budapest each Sunday until he retired. Workers who attend Mass may find their wages lower than the norm. Some couples get married in church secretly. Occasionally, discrimination gets aired, as when the radio carried a complaint by a mother that she had been threatened with the loss of her child-care benefit if her baby were baptized. Many cases, of course, go unreported, especially in villages where churchgoers are at the mercy of local party officials. Such officials frequently behave like their feudal landlord predecessors.

Christians nevertheless have less to fear in Hungary than in most other Eastern-bloc countries. They are not in physical danger. They may lose jobs or promotions; the high proportion of elderly people in church is due in part to the fact that the elderly no longer have a job to lose. But increasingly, younger people risk going to church. Although no party member can be a Christian, there are frequent references in the press to party officials who have been reprimanded for showing up in church on family occasions.

The Churches' Foreign Functions

Miklós (the state's minister for religion) likes to boast about the important contributions the Hungarian churches have made to the World Council of Churches, the Christian Peace Conference (CPC), and the Berlin Conference of Catholic Christians. Men like Bartha (the late head of the Reformed Church), Tóth (his successor), Káldy (the late head of the Lutheran Church), and Károly (president of the Christian Peace Conference) have spent an inordinate amount of time at meetings—such as the state-sponsored peace conferences—at home and abroad. Over a four-year period, Káldy attended 160 conferences abroad and hosted 80 foreign delegations.

The churches' other foreign function is to foster good relations between the Communist states and the Third World, particularly in Africa, with its strong Christian churches. Many African nations, like ravaged Ethiopia, are under Marxist rule. To quote Káldy, "We like to inform the churches in these countries about our experiences, and we exhort them to accept the new social order and serve positively in it."

Discontent Within the Churches

Despite a reasonably adequate church life—at least compared with that in other East European countries—there is dissatisfaction, especially in the larger churches. There is bitterness at the price paid for state concessions and at church leaders for exerting pressure on members at the behest of the regime. Kádár played such an astute political game that it is difficult for an individual or group in a church to reject what amounts to an unwritten compromise between the state and the people. For church leaders, the bait dangled is material advantage.

Critics of the churches cannot understand why their leaders are so afraid to speak out—they would not risk imprisonment. While some government members admit that the early persecution of the church was a mistake, church leaders still avoid any mention of the years of terror. They seem to comply as if no other course were possible, and even search out ways to justify the government.

Discontent within the Protestant churches focused on Bishop Káldy's *diakonia* theology, and in the Catholic Church on Cardinal Lékai's "small steps" policy and the treatment of the base groups.

Bishop Káldy and Diakonia

Tensions in the Lutheran Church came to a head at the Lutheran World Federation (LWF) meeting held in 1984 in Budapest. Although Lutherans represent only about 4 per cent of the Hungarian population, the controversial theology of *diakonia,* or service, proposed by Bishop Káldy has far wider implications, since variations of it have spread to other major churches. In practice, the theology means that the church must support government policies undeviatingly. It puts the church at the service of the state. "There is no 'third way' for travelers between socialism and capitalism," said Káldy. "Our Protestant churches are not neutral; we stand unambiguously on the side of socialism."

It is hardly surprising that Káldy's rise to the position of Lutheran presiding bishop in 1967 coincided with his coining the term *diakonia* to popularize a theology propounded after World War II by a number of Protestant theologians. These theologians reexamined the theological premises of their churches in the light of socialist teachings. Káldy came to prominence in an unsavory episode in 1958 when he replaced Bishop Lajos Ordass and condemned him for opposing state domination of the churches, giving him no chance to defend himself. Resentment against the humiliating treatment of Ordass, who was imprisoned on a fake charge, still exists.

The *diakonia* theology was obligatory for all Lutheran clergy in Hungary. Many complained that a pastor had less intellectual freedom than a student in the university, where obligatory Marxist-Leninist views are enforced far less rigorously.

Whether the theology was anything more than an identification of the social aims of the church with the Party's program was brilliantly analyzed by an eminent Lutheran theologian in the West, Dr. Vilmos Vajta, in a paper written for the 1984 LWF meeting. His constructive paper was attacked as "slandering Hungarian Lutheran leaders." More startling, in a letter issued on the eve of the LWF meeting, Zoltán Dóka, a seasoned pastor and a respected theologian, criticized the theology and the methods of his bishop. (See appendix H.) The letter aroused widespread interest and came at a most inopportune moment for Bishop Káldy: not only was it the first time an LWF meeting had been held in an Eastern-bloc country, but Káldy was a candidate for the LWF presidency.

Under the watchful eyes of the Hungarian Lutheran establishment and the LWF general secretary, Carl Mau, the much needed debate on *diakonia* never took place. Káldy was duly elected LWF president. He referred to the "prejudice and slander" he had suffered but said he forgave his accuser. Shortly after the conference, Dóka was suspended without pay, and church legal proceedings were started against him. But the international publicity embarrassed Káldy, and the charges against Dóka were dropped.

Dóka's point—that the majority lacked confidence in the leadership and subscribed to Káldy's theology out of fear—seems to have been substantiated. His warning that the inner life of the Lutheran Church might collapse and that members might turn to the smaller churches such as Baptist and Pentecostal has had results. The Lutheran Church was subsequently allowed to open an Academic Theology Society—clearly a response to the criticism of Káldy's stranglehold on theology. In April 1986, a nineteen-member Lutheran Reform Group was formed consisting of both pastors and laity. Part of their program was to criticize the *diakonia* theology and to ask for open discussion of problems.

Káldy's Successor

Káldy was incapacitated by a stroke in December 1985 and died in May 1987. His successor as presiding bishop is Gyula Nagy. The Reform Group theologians delivered an open letter to Nagy in 1986 calling for a return to theological pluralism, the election of church leaders "without outside influence," ecclesiastical decentralization, greater lay participation in church life, the reestablishment of a Lutheran grammar school, and the holding of open conferences and forums for dialogue. This led Imre Miklós to step in and warn the church that it could lose much, including an extension to its seminary, if good church-state relations were not maintained. Later that year the state approved plans for a grammar school (church members have to produce the money for it), thus bringing the Lutheran Church into line with the Catholics, the Reformed, and the Jews.

The church leadership has accepted in principle most of the Reform Group's proposals, though not decentralization or open elections. Róbert Frenkl, a moderate and leading member of the Group and a highly respected physician and environmentalist, was nominated unopposed for the highest lay position in the church. But in an election criticized by the Group, Béla Harmati, well known in ecumenical circles, became Káldy's successor as bishop of the southern districts. At the installation of Harmati and Frenkl in the fall of 1987, Miklós praised the late Bishop Káldy warmly, described Harmati as his "helpmate," and cautioned against radical reform—a salutary reminder of how little the basic attitude of the state has changed.

At the installation, Frenkl spoke of a much more open climate within the church but expressed regret that some important topics, particularly an open church press, were still excluded from discussion. This is borne out by the fact that the Reform Group's open letter to Bishop Nagy has never been published. The other churches have the same experience. It is still the *samizdat* press that carries any controversial church material. As sources of alternative ideas, the Hungarian churches are still very weak.

Cardinal Lékai's "Small Steps"

Cardinal Lékai was Catholic primate from 1977 to 1986. During that time tensions revolved around his cautious policy that full cooperation with the government would gradually win small improvements, or, in the words of Miklós, that changes would come about only in "small steps."

The cardinal could indeed point to some positive developments in support of his policy. In 1978 the state allowed the Catholic Church to set up an unprecedented lay training course in theology. The excellent part-time course, run by Professor Tamás Nyeri, has a long waiting list. Thousands initially applied, but the numbers were considerably reduced by the government stipulation that each candidate must have his employer's written permission. The popularity of the course contrasts sharply with the shortage of vocations to the priesthood and suggests that people, though loath to put themselves entirely under church discipline, are eager to study and deepen their faith. The Lutherans began a similar course in 1980.

There is a problem, however. By 1985 half of Nyeri's five hundred or so graduates were women, whose position is not clear. The state has allowed women to teach catechism since 1981, but as of 1985 only one woman had the church's permission to do so.

Nyeri's high hopes that his graduates might function as lay helpers to relieve the hard-pressed parish clergy ran into obstruction from the conservative hierarchy and the state. Late in 1985 an agreement was reached between the Bishops' Conference and the state. After personally discussing the question of lay pastors with Pope John Paul II in Rome, Miklós decided to allow the church to use its trained lay people in pastoral activities, provided they conform to church canons, respect state laws, and support the government's policy. He expected the bishops to enforce the terms.

The development was the most encouraging in years. As Bishop Jószef Cserháti put it: "Without the active assistance of the laity the care of souls will not be possible within ten years." The church, however, seems unsure about how to use the lay graduates and cannot pay them. Also, there is resentment among the clergy at seeing lay people practice parts of their traditional role.

In another concession, religious instruction can now be given in church buildings other than the churches themselves, which in Central Europe are usually unheated. Each case must be decided separately—a proviso probably aimed at keeping out the base groups (which we shall look at later in this chapter).

Lékai worked to increase religious TV and radio time. Since 1977 the churches have been granted half an hour a week at 7:30 A.M.—not exactly prime time, and not long enough for a Mass. Still, the programs attract 2 per cent of the population. This slot is shared by the denominations, the Catholic share totaling nine hours a year.

Lékai also made limited progress toward the reinstatement of religious orders, one of the Pope's dearest wishes. In 1983 a retreat house was opened, run by six elderly Jesuits. There is no likelihood, however, of the reestablishment of the order itself—only enough religious to operate the house are permitted.

Early in 1986, Lékai announced the Vatican's approval of a new order of sisters for Hungary. It is limited to two hundred active nuns—no contemplatives are permitted—and it will be a "national" order, directly responsible to the Hungarian bishops, thus allaying government suspicion about links with Rome. This could represent a way to reestablish religious orders in Eastern Europe. So far, apparently, there has not been a rush of women to join it. The concessions are part of a new government policy of enlisting the churches' help with social problems, rather than a sign of any relaxation in its hostility to religious orders.

One surprisingly enlightened step taken by Lékai was the introduction of special monthly Masses for remarried divorcees, although they are not permitted to receive the sacrament. Lékai felt it was vital for them to know that the church still cared for them. He was deeply concerned for family life and described the family as "the pillar of society . . . which prepares children for life." He strongly criticized atheistic teachings that portray the family as "some kind of revolting cancerous growth," and that make parents into "objects of contempt to their children." Lékai also joined Bishop Cserháti, the official spokesman for the bishops, in protesting discrimination against believers.

Criticism of the Cardinal

There was nevertheless considerable feeling both inside and outside Hungary that Cardinal Lékai, who died in June 1986, did not take a strong enough line, and some Catholics criticized him for failing to obey papal directives. (Asked when a papal visit to Hungary might take place, the Pope reportedly answered, "When the cardinal has learned to bang his fist on the table.") Lékai was appointed at a time when Vatican policy sought to patch up the division caused by Mindszenty's strong line. Pope John Paul II is of course only too aware of the precarious situation of the church under a

Communist regime, but he would prefer a less subdued Hungarian hierarchy.

During the bishops' visit to him in 1982, the Pope made it clear that the most critical problem was the lack of proper catechetical instruction. Lékai—possibly obeying government orders—nevertheless rejected the modern catechism approved by the rest of the bishops. He seemed suspicious of anything not firmly under official church control.

Cardinal Lékai should not be judged too harshly. He operated under considerable unpublicized pressure. If he failed to toe the line on a given issue, the authorities threatened to withdraw a specific "concession." Moreover, the Hungarian element in Lékai's policy should not be underestimated. In essence, present church-state relations are only a continuation of what pertained under Habsburg rule. The idea of an alliance of "throne and altar" that Lékai apparently accepted is based more on ancient tradition than on a convinced acceptance of Marxist ideology; the cardinal used this same tradition to justify the preservation of his church's character and limited autonomy *vis-à-vis* Rome.

Cserháti, the bishops' spokesman, criticized the Vatican condemnation of liberation theology in 1985. His distinction between what he considers positive and negative aspects of Marxism does not endear him to most Catholics.

Cardinal Lékai was succeeded by Archbishop László Paskai of Kalocsa, at 59 one of the youngest and fittest of the bishops. Paskai was the favored candidate of the state, which felt, no doubt, that his greater sophistication and political adaptability would enable him to present a more credible face to Catholic opinion both in Hungary and abroad. As head of Opus Pacis he had been identified with rallying the clergy behind government foreign policy. His basic approach and concerns are similar to those of his predecessor: Paskai is deeply committed to the re-evangelization of Hungary, a daunting task. With one in seven parishes without a priest, he is eager to see lay pastors fulfilling a role similar to that of the licensed lay leaders who contributed much to the resurgence of Catholicism during the Counter-Reformation.

During 1987 the Vatican and the Hungarian government reached an agreement on the appointment of much needed new bishops to succeed a mostly elderly and ailing hierarchy.

Support for Hungarians in Romania

Until 1986 church leaders were silent, no doubt under state instructions, about the oppression of their fellow Hungarians—some two million—in Romania, although some church members were deeply concerned and gave quiet help. By late 1986 the situation had deteriorated so much, and so much effective propaganda had been mounted on their behalf in Hungary by exiles and the unofficial opposition, that protests were sanctioned.

First, an unofficial, interdenominational Committee for Reconciliation launched a remarkable appeal to the WCC, the Pope, the USSR, and Western human-rights activists, to draw attention to flagrant abuses of religious liberty in the Romanian region of Transylvania. While acknowledging the past responsibility of their churches for fomenting nationalism and religious hatred, the committee expressed a vision of a Transylvania where Orthodox, Catholic, Reformed, Lutheran, and Baptist would mutually enrich one another. In response to this, a joint Christmas message from Hungarian church leaders (including the Catholic Bishops' Conference) called for a radical improvement of the situation of Hungarians in Romania. Both statements were markedly stronger than any made previously by Hungarian leaders.

By May 1988 there were approximately 60,000 refugees from Ceausescu's wretched Romania in Hungary, many in desperate need of food, shelter, and employment. All three major churches—Catholic, Reformed, and Lutheran—were operating busy refugee centers. The aid campaign involves all denominations and has resulted in remarkable cooperation between Hungarians and Romanians both in exile and in Romania. Catholic bishop Endre Gyulay urged the Hungarian government to enlist the help of the United Nations and its Soviet allies in persuading the Romanian government to respect the human rights of the minority in Transylvania. He advised that refuges with near relatives, i.e., spouses or children, and those whose work positively contributes to the cultivation of the Hungarian language or national culture, should be persuaded to return to Romania, as a number have.

A Low Level of Ecumenism

For Christians living in a secular society, ecumenism should be an imperative; but in Hungary it hardly exists except by chance. The formal political ecumenism promoted by the state goes only skin-deep. Matters are not helped by such episodes as the sudden withdrawal of the Catholic Church from a major ecumenical service with Protestants and Orthodox in December 1980, and, on the Protestant side, the excommunication of three church members who married Catholics.

Exceptions do exist—the Lutheran Church and the Reformed Church have good relations—but they are rare. The widening scope of Ecumenical Council projects is promising. Some of the most fruitful contacts between Catholics and Protestants are made within the base groups, most of which are Catholic, a few Protestant, but some genuinely ecumenical.

Tensions in the Jewish Community

The opposing forces of secularization and revival are evident elsewhere. Some young Jews are taking their heritage much more seriously, in a way that could lead to a reassertion of the central place of religious life in Judaism, as has happened in the Soviet Union.

On the other hand, many Jews are fast integrating into Hungarian society. Some of the revival Jews, members of the Shalom Independent Jewry Peace Group, blame the official leaders for this. They feel that if the leaders do not reverse their "servile loyalty" to the state and their failure to speak out about Soviet Jews and other such issues, the Jewish community in Hungary will disappear within twenty years. The "establishment" brand them as reactionary and point to the tolerance and support Hungarian Jews have received from the state.

In 1987 Budapest hosted the World Jewish Congress—the first time it had been held in a Soviet-bloc country, and a tribute from world Jewry to the enlightened approach of the Hungarian government.

THE BASE GROUPS

Base groups or communities are part of a worldwide phenomenon that has sprung up in the Catholic Church mostly since Vatican II. They vary tremendously from one part of the world to another, from being concerned primarily with spiritual renewal to fostering political revolution. In Hungary, much of the official church has not really come to terms with them. One group in particular, the "Bush," led by Piarist Fr. György Bulányi, has become the center of deep controversy within the church. Yet Marxist sociologist Miklós Tomka asserts that without such Christ-centered groups, Hungarian society would rapidly disintegrate.

There are between 4,000 and 6,000 base groups in Hungary, mainly in urban areas, involving from 60,000 to 100,000 persons. A high proportion of the members are adolescents and young families, either students or graduates, although the groups do attract a cross-section of society.

Since the Communist regime has abolished all but party-controlled organizations, the sense of community has broken down. The breakdown is enhanced by the prevailing materialism and by the move away from the country to the city. Base communities have sprung up as a challenge to the trend and also as a reaction to the official churches' subordination to the state. An additional factor was the dissolution of the religious orders, which threw thousands of community-minded people into the world and greatly diminished the opportunities for religious education of children. It was natural that some Catholic families that wanted to carry on a close, private religious life should turn to the base groups. (See appendix I for some typical views of participants.)

The Four Types

Base groups can be divided broadly into four categories: (1) charismatics, (2) independents, and (3) "Regnum Marianum" (Regnumists), all of which are accepted by the church, and (4) the Bush, which is not.

The base-group movement is not really new. The Regnumists and the Bush are rooted in pre-war agrarian-reform groups. The Regnumists began in the 1940s as a movement of priests and lay people who were concerned with community life and also with religious education for young people.

Many of those who became spiritual leaders of the base groups had been imprisoned during the early 1950s. Father Bulányi, then a student chaplain involved in organizing small underground religious groups, received a life sentence in 1952, was freed in 1956, was sentenced again, and was released in the general amnesty in 1960. The state would not, however, accept him as a parish priest, and he worked as a heavy-goods loader by day while organizing groups in the evenings.

Like many who have suffered for their faith, Bulányi has found it difficult to accept leaders who appear to betray the faith, especially when they associate with the very people who have persecuted the church. Openly critical of the institutional church, he accuses church leaders of having compromised shamefully with an atheistic government for limited ends, while ignoring the devastation wreaked upon the church in the past. Christians, he argued, should not be bound by worldly considerations but should re-Christianize the secular world. Moreover, he received Mindszenty's blessing and follows his principle that party secretaries can never determine the task of the church. Now in his seventies, Bulányi is a vigorous man, a powerful, charismatic leader, and a superb organizer. It is a tragedy that a person of such uncomprising integrity, a rarity in Hungary today, should have become the focus of a debilitating conflict in the church.

By 1972, there were about 4,000 church groups of one kind or another. Many of them were simply unofficial Bible-study or music groups and not controversial. Most originated around a priest, but with the scarcity of priests, they are increasingly lay-centered. Until they were recognized legally in 1976, the authorities entrusted the bishops with the unenviable task of bringing them under church discipline. The bishops divided them into two categories: those that followed episcopal directives and those that did not.

The Regnumists fit into the first category: they adhere strictly to church rules. They follow Vatican II and are open to the Holy Spirit and ecumenism. They concentrate on religious education, and their groups are normally led by priests. Such eminent figures as Bishop Cserháti, András Szennay (abbot of Pannonhalma, a renowned Benedictine abbey school), and Professor Nyeri have described these base groups as the best hope for the survival of the church, the seed of renewal of religious life. Cserháti has gone so far as to recommend that his priests participate in them. The more conservative clergy remain suspicious, given the introduction of contemporary features such as rock Masses into worship.

The Unacceptable "Bush"

The Bush, on the other hand, is unacceptable to the hierarchy. With 5,000 members and about 150 groups, it is by nature potentially schismatic because of the members' appeal to the individual conscience. They combine a radical return to New Testament Christian life, as interpreted by themselves, with an uncompromising stand on conservative Catholic principles. The state sees in the Bush—correctly—the quintessential Catholic resistance to atheism. The Bush members' insistence that the spiritual values of Christianity transcend political and temporal expediencies marks them as the true heirs of Mindszenty.

They oppose abortion, divorce, and secular materialism. They are pacifists and teetotalers. They tend to have large families, and mothers stay at home with their children, though a second income is almost essential to maintain ordinary living standards all over Eastern Europe. Bush communities that have a surplus distribute to those in need.

The crucial issue that has made the Bush unacceptable is its pacifism. The authorities believe the Bush poses a threat to the national sovereignty, which requires compulsory military service, and therefore they have put presure on the church to discipline it. Whereas the authorities have officially exempted minor denominations—the Nazarenes and Adventists, most of whom refuse it—from military service since 1978, conscientious objection within the majority church is quite another matter. Military service is so unpopular among the young that the state fears a mass exploitation of conscientious objection.

The prolonged conflict has dominated church affairs. The state has cleverly used those elements in the church best fitted for reviving religious life to generate a divisive crisis. Both state and church authorities have overreacted to a movement that requires such intensive commitment that it will never affect more than a few thousand good, peaceful people.

State and Church vs. Bulányi

In 1977 the State Church Office presented the bishops with a list of priests whom it considered "destructive." They were transferred or warned to conform. Six times Miklós asked Bulányi's Piarist superior in Rome to recall him; six times the request was refused. Hidden pressure on the church intensified when eight of Bulányi's followers chose prison over military service. The cardinal tried to get Bulányi declared a heretic by sending samples of his writing to Rome, but Rome found nothing in them contrary to church teaching. In September 1981 Lékai preached a sermon at Esztergom in which he spoke of the dangers of Bulányi's influence and drew attention to famous Hungarians who had defended their country by armed force.

Later that autumn the boom fell: Lékai suspended two of Bulányi's most respected followers for six months for preaching pacifism. Since then, nearly half of the movement's approximately forty priests have been suspended, pensioned off, or banished to remote parishes. The clergy were told not to offer their rectories to the Bush communities for their obligatory retreats. Seminarians who joined the Bush were refused ordination until they left, and lay members were refused admission to the new part-time theology courses. This increasing isolation of Bush members from the mainstream of church life harms both the church and the Bush

The controversy has caused bitterness and aroused sympathy. It has hurt the image of the church among non-Christians and the growing number of pacifists.

The event that triggered Bulányi's own suspension in June 1982 was the annual meeting of the base communities, at which the cardinal presided. He refused to have Bulányi as one of his concelebrant priests. In protest, many of the pilgrims left the church and went outside to pray with Father Bulányi. The church authorities could hardly tolerate such an open act of defiance. Bulányi was accused of spreading erroneous teachings and of wanting to impose a new church discipline. He refused to retract. Instead he compared his present treatment unfavorably with that inflicted on him by the secret police in 1952. He was placed under *suspensio a divinis,* a strict form of punishment, pending a final decision by Rome.

The Vatican and Bulányi

The Vatican did not come down unequivocally on either side, although it tended to back the cardinal. In its report in May 1983, the Holy See did not condemn Bulányi as a heretic, but it did criticize his followers for disobedience. The Pope tried to pour oil on troubled waters and avoid alienating the government, from which he hoped to gain further concessions. For the same reason he did not condemn or excommunicate the Hungarian Peace Priests.

Finally, in 1987, the Vatican issued its decision on Father Bulányi's teaching and writing. It expressed reservations about some of his views that deviate from official church teaching and seem to have more in common with congregationalism than with Catholicism, but it stopped short of condemnation and left him the opportunity for further clarification. Significantly, it made no reference to his pacifism. The Vatican was obviously not bowing to pressure from the Hungarian authorities. However, Bulányi's controversy with the Hungarian bishops remains unresolved, and he resents the fact that he has never been allowed to defend his views in the official media.

In 1985 the Vatican rejected the appeal of three priests whose bishop had threatened to transfer them to remote parishes. They are members of the Dignitatis Humanae Committee, formed in 1980 by priests who oppose the disciplinary acts of bishops against base groups. One of the three, Gyula Havasi, held base-group retreats in his rectory and was told by the cardinal that he must get permission for such activity. He refused. In 1985, before the Vatican rejection of the appeal, the committee pointed out how damaging such a rejection would be to the image of the Vatican: "If the Vatican made political concessions in the interest of the well-being of the Hungarian church by allowing these priests to be dealt with in accordance with the demands of the atheistic authority, is not such an action worthy of Caiaphas rather than of Rome? (John 11:50)."

Pacifists in Prison

By 1986, nineteen young members of the Bush had been sentenced to prison for up to three years for their pacifist stance. Late in 1985 twenty-four priests informed the minister of defense that they would perform no military service and expressed their solidarity with those of like mind. Pacifism is a burning issue among Hungary's intellectuals, and the fate of the 150 who are serving sentences for conscientious objection has evoked numerous protests in *samizdat* literature. In March 1988 Bulányi said there were twenty-five members of base groups in prison.

In an open letter to the European Cultural Forum in Budapest in 1985, Catholic pacifist Károly Kiszely, imprisoned in 1979, claimed that pacifists had been intimidated into signing confessions, obliged to accept conniving lawyers, and treated like criminals. Pacifist prisoners are forbidden to read religious literature and on release cannot enter a college or university. He said that the state is particularly hard on Catholics, citing the case of two young Catholics who were condemned to solitary confinement.

In 1987, under government pressure, Kiszely emigrated to the West. The pacifist movement thus lost its leading spokesman. According to Kiszely, of the 150 or so Hungarian pacifists in prison, 120–30 are Jehovah's Witnesses and 8 are Catholics. Sentences have been lengthened to three years. However, by 1988 there were indications that the state might be reconsidering its tough policy, and that the issue would be discussed by parliament later in the year.

In a West German TV interview, Cserháti, the bishops' spokesman, after claiming that Bush priests were "among our best," went on to criticize base groups for undermining the bishops' authority and for accepting the Protestant principle of appealing to conscience in the final analysis. He said that Catholic pacifists were on weak ground because Vatican II enjoined citizens to obey state laws. However, Hungarian Catholic pacifists compare the stance of their own bishops unfavorably with that of the Polish and West German bishops.

New Opportunities for the Churches

Faced with pressing social problems, the state has turned to the churches to bail it out. Marxism-Leninism has failed to win the heart and soul of the nation. Most Hungarians tend to regard all ideologies with indifference and cynicism. After forty years of socialism, society is less caring, more amoral and hedonistic, than ever before. There is a widening gap between the haves and the have-nots, especially large families and the elderly. Ten per cent of the people are now living below subsistence level, and the standard of living is falling. The housing problem is so acute that the average wait is ten years. Some couples move in with old people and gain the right of tenancy on condition that they look after the elderly people until they die—an invidious situation.

Myriad serious social ills testify to a malaise in the society that could endanger the political stability painstakingly built by Kádár. A plummeting birth rate, currently the lowest in the world (at 11.96 per thousand), manifests a lack of confidence in the future. Nearly half the marriages break up, usually fairly quickly. Juvenile delinquency is up, as are alcoholism and drug abuse. Hungary has the highest suicide rate in the world (48 per 100,000).

In 1987 the interdenominational Committee of Reconciliation along with leading Hungarian intellectuals took part in an ecumenical conference on the fate of the Hungarian people. The focus was on the social, political, and spiritual causes of their demographic decline, both in Hungary and in adjacent countries (Romania, Czechoslovakia, Austria, Yugoslavia, and the USSR). One speaker, Reformed pastor Géza Németh, claimed there was a link between the decline of Christian values and the apparent lack of a will to live on the part of the Hungarian people collectively.

The Catholic Bishops' Conference unanimously backed the government's austerity program announced in the fall of 1987, but the primate asked that members of parliament speak out on behalf of large families, which would be especially badly hit by the measure.

New Opportunities

The government, shaken by the nation's social crisis, has come to realize that the church is not an anachronism but a social necessity. Kádár intended to maintain national unity, even if it involved sacrificing his atheistic principles. He realized that a healthy society needs a solid moral basis and a vigorous family life; this the churches, with all their shortcomings, can offer. This change seemed to vindicate Lékai's policy and his emphasis on family life, and Káldy's *diakonia*, but probably the quiet witness of thousands of good Christian families and the challenge of the base communities have been more effective.

In the past, the churches were allowed to minister only to the least valued in society, such as the mentally handicapped. Now, in view of the nation's social crisis, they are allowed to undertake pioneer projects with problem groups, although—particularly since the abolition of the Catholic orders—they lack the necessary pool of trained specialists to rise to the challenge.

Pioneering schemes have been launched by the Ecumenical Council. A Wayward Youth Mission was set up to rescue and train "drifters." The Protestant churches have contributed in various ways to the campaign against drug abuse. The Reformed Church started a telephone counseling service in Budapest in 1984 and has opened a home for alcoholic and delinquent youths. The successful work of the Free Churches (Baptists and Pentecostalists) in evangelizing Gypsies and the impressive changes in the Gypsies' way of life have attracted favorable media coverage.

The media are increasingly open to the views of Christians. In 1983 a ninety-minute color documentary was made in cooperation with the churches; entitled "A Better Way," it showed the positive developments in church-state relations. Less biased coverage is given to the part played by the churches in national history. Miklós himself made an unprecedented one-hour television appearance to answer frank questions on religion from the audience. (He reiterated that no party member could be a Christian.) Even non-Christians feel more time should be given to such discussions. In 1987 there was a radio series of readings from the Bible followed by discussion. It was, however, aired at the same time as a popular TV public-affairs program.

A resurgence of interest in religion has affected all segments of the population, especially the young and the better educated. Although not on a large scale, it is sufficiently significant for Miklós himself to admit that Communism has been unable to provide a compelling alternative to religion. An upsurge in church attendance since 1978 is reflected in a rise in vocations to the ministry. According to a Hungarian weekly, between 44 and 59 per cent of adults still believe in God, and a third of Hungarians attend church on special occasions. Nevertheless, the movement back to church is limited. Only about 12 per cent of Catholics attend church regularly, and in 1987 the number of Reformed Church congregations had declined, with funerals outnumbering baptisms by two to one.

Beyond the base groups and the interest of the young, certain churches are growing, deepening their spiritual life, and becoming more confident. The 230,000-member Eastern Rite Church now has its own seminary and—in contrast to the rest of the Catholic Church—has no shortage of vocations. Its married clergy are no longer regarded as inferior to the Latin Rite priests. Vatican II led to a reversal of the previous trend of Romanization, encouraging Eastern Rite members to worship at their own churches. As the church under Bishop Imre Timko shows increasing confidence in its Eastern heritage, it tries to develop better relations with the Orthodox and could well serve as a model for Rome's dealings with its other Eastern Rite churches.

The Baptists and Pentecostalists are a source of real growth in Hungarian church life. They attract people who find the historic churches too accommodating, too conservative, and spiritually unhelpful. They also make converts among the unchurched, not least through the charismatic movement. High moral standards and a strong sense of community add to their appeal.

New buildings continue to rise, and Baptist statistics showed 330 baptisms in 1984, the highest in ten years. On his 1985 trip to Hungary, Billy Graham preached to 13,000 in Budapest and 10,000 at Pećs; the latter meeting, at Bishop Cserháti's invitation, included both Catholics and Protestants—an ecumenical milestone in Hungary. Baptists are looking forward to 1989, when the European Baptist Federation will be in Hungary for its first meeting in a Communist state. The Hungarian Baptists hope that discussion will not be inhibited, as it was at the 1984 Lutheran World Federation meeting.

An interesting development is the emergence of the Free Christians, a Methodist breakaway group. Although it has only about 2,000 members, hundreds of non-members are attracted to its "days of silent communion," where excellent sermons are preached. The group is flexible, charismatic, and ecumenical.

Pilgrimages are a popular feature of church life. Eighty thousand pilgrims, including Protestants and Orthodox, attend the annual pilgrimage to the Eastern Rite Catholic shrine at Mariapócs. Pannonhalma, the famous Benedictine abbey and school, attracts pilgrims and guests, including Protestants, all year round and has for years been a beacon of Hungarian spiritual life. The base groups have their own pilgrimages.

Finally, there is a growing interest in the Bible, which has transformed the lives of whole communities. At Debrecen, a Bible-study group drew 300 people instead of the anticipated 50. Many people, even some atheists, are taking Bible study seriously for the first time.

Some Church Gains

A heartening improvement in church-state relations has led to some positive developments in church life. These are not primarily due to the strength of the churches; the majority of Hungarians have long since stopped actively practicing their religion. There has been a resurgence of interest, especially among the young and educated, but often these persons bypass mainstream churches and join smaller ones (or even way-out sects). On the whole, the positive changes have come despite the churches' lack of initiative.

As we have seen, among the government concessions that have made the churches' lot more tolerable in recent years are: a limited step toward reinstating religious orders, a Catholic retreat house, theological courses for laypersons, more trainees for the ministry, more open discussions, less discrimination at the local level, new buildings where needed, expanding facilities for the sale of Bibles and religious books, increased church access to the media, the projected opening of a Lutheran grammar school, the agreement on religious instruction of Reformed Church children, and permission for conscripts to attend church services.

Miklós has said that he wants people to view the State Church Office not as an opponent but as a bridge between church and state. But although some progress has been made, church life still suffers greatly from: discrimination against believers, particularly in regard to religious education; continuing limitations on religious orders, the point most worrying to the Vatican; and a considerable number of petty restrictions inappropriate to the overall tolerance within Hungarian society today. The list of regulations stipulating what the churches can and cannot do has actually grown in recent years.

Asked about the revival of religion and whether Communism is really dangerous for the faith, a refugee from Hungary described the situation this way in 1985: "It is astonishing how deeply many church groups live their faith today, even though they must live completely or at least half underground. They pray a lot. Christian solidarity leaves its mark on daily life.

Nevertheless, man living under Communism is in danger right down to the very roots of his personality, because he lives under the constant pressure of atheistic propaganda. Communism destroys the human values on which religious values are built. Confronted by an all-powerful state, man becomes insecure, loses hope, and finally gives up thinking for himself."

In the fall of 1987, *Beszélö,* an influential *samizdat* journal, called for new laws to guarantee the rights of believers and end state interference in church affairs. Its list, part of a sixty-page "Social Contract: The Conditions for Development," makes a good summary of restrictions in force. It urges the government to grant teachers the right to worship regularly, to allow religious conscientious objectors the right to perform some alternative to military service, and to end the distinction between "recognized" and "unrecognized" religious groups. (Until 1974, independent groups of any kind were illegal. They still need state approval to function unhampered. By 1988 there were signs that the law might be modified.) It claims that most daily violations of believers' rights result from an incomplete separation of church and state as seen in the state's practice of patronage regarding church appointments, the financial dependence of the churches on the state, close state supervision of unofficial religious gatherings, and restrictions on publication.

A similar call for religious freedom by dissidents, mainly young urban professionals, in the *samizdat* publication *A Demokrata* urged a review of the legal status and role of the State Church Office, an end to the monopoly position of atheistic education, and permission for religious communities to pursue profitable economic activities.

Miklós's views on freedom of religion do not coincide with those of Christians. They exclude, for instance, religious communities free of state control. The state's insistence on the "political usefulness" of the churches has had harmful effects and hinders the churches' basic mission. Meanwhile, party leaders, faced with increasing complaints from left-wing members that the Party's alliance with major churches is politically dangerous and ideologically subversive, reiterate that the struggle against religion is to continue.

Developments in 1988

Early in 1988, Imre Markoja, then justice minister, announced that the government would propose new laws regarding religious affairs to parliament in the near future, though only after the competent authorities for creating legislation have been redefined in the constitution. The government apparently plans to bring the activities of the State Church Office under the closer supervision of parliament. Heretofore, laws regarding church-state relations have taken the form of decrees issued by government ministers and state secretaries, not laws sanctioned by parliament.

The reform of church-state relations has acquired an influential advocate in Imre Pozsgay, general secretary of the Patriotic People's Front, who said the time had arrived to stop thinking in terms of limiting church activity. Such a change would, he maintained, help to create a new national consensus, reflecting the views of millions of Hungarian believers. In church circles there is considerable hope that the new laws will improve the status of the churches, though there is still a strong conservative element within the government for the reformers to overcome.

Meanwhile the Catholic bishops made their boldest requests so far, declaring that the government program has the support of the church, and that government policy in many respects corresponds to recent papal teachings. The gist of their argument was that the church would be better able to help the government solve the country's social problems if it were able to work without restrictions. *Új Ember* stated in an editorial that the bishops are looking for a new system of institutions for church-state relations rather than an update of the old one. The bishops asked for a new agreement to replace the existing one, which they signed under duress in 1950.

In March 1988 Bishop József Szendi of Veszprem presented the bishops' demands at a meeting with the Prime Minister Károly Grosz, who two months later was named Kádár's successor: freedom for the church to operate off church premises, a free hand with young people, an end to bureaucratic interference in religious instruction, the rehabilitation of religious orders, expansion of the eight church schools to meet the demand for places, access to radio and television and the right to reply to false anti-church allegations, the right of priests to visit hospitals, prisons, and schools, and the right to establish youth groups. Bishop Szendi also made an unprecedented attack on the Peace Priests movement, which he said was a waste of time and money. The primate, László Paskai, asked the government to reconsider its attitude toward Catholic conscientious objectors. The government is considering an alternative form of service.

After this meeting, Father Bulányi said in an interview, "The *modus vivendi* devised for the church by the Stalinists is nearing its end." The move to allow an alternative to military service "surpassed our wildest dreams," he said. Bulányi cautioned, however, that the bishops could not adequately represent Jesus Christ so long as greater freedom for the church was dependent upon concessions by the state.

The Hungarian state appears to be willing to listen to church demands for greater freedom. At the same time, more Hungarian church members are showing a responsible and caring attitude toward persecuted believers in

Czechoslovakia and Romania, including refugees from the latter, and their interest is not limited to Hungarians.

Perhaps the biggest problem for the churches is their own leaders, who have long since forfeited their prophetic role. It is small comfort that, owing to illness and death, the controversial leaders of the three main churches have been replaced since 1986, since their successors had to meet with state approval.

The Outlook

The churches are of course benefiting from the renewed interest in religion and from the concessions the state has made. But are they making full use of the greater freedom they possess? Are they setting their sights too low? Will they be able to meet the reawakened need for God—to which state media testify—that is apparent in Hungary today? These difficult questions have to be answered in the context of an ideologically hostile state that until recently, at least, has expanded and contracted the freedom of the churches according to the dictates of political and social expediency.

A confidential Politburo policy document that leaked to the West in 1987 exploded the concept of a liberalizing regime. It revealed an elite still using the jargon of the Stalinist era, and making no distinction between "enemy" and "opposition" in its relations with the considerable and stimulating unofficial opposition.

But the replacement of the 76-year-old Kádár in May 1988 seemed a clear signal of the possibility of economic and political reforms. His successor, Károly Grosz, 57, leads a new Politburo and Central Committee purged of many of Kádár's longtime allies and seemingly shifted toward proponents of change. Among the six new Politburo members are two of the country's best-known advocates of reform: Imre Pozsgay, leader of the Patriotic People's Front, and Rezso Nyers, architect of the economic reforms of the 1960s. Grosz himself appears to be an energetic and pragmatic politician who has adopted Gorbachev's open style. "We have faced critically the errors committed earlier," he told Hungarian television. "A new approach is needed in public life, in production, in human sectors, and other fields."

In the fall of 1988, this "new approach" seemed to be leading toward an unprecedented end: the parliament was said to be considering legalizing non-Communist parties and other dissident organizations. The Hungarian Democratic Forum, legalized in September, was close to declaring itself a party. The Forum is a reincarnation of the left-of-center Peasant and Smallholders' parties, which won two-thirds of the popular vote in Hungary's last free election in 1945. More startling was the prospect of a split in the

Communist Party itself, with Prime Minister Grosz heading the conservative bloc and Pozsgay a progressive faction. The reformers, though not
officially registered, were calling themselves the Reform Party and had
adopted the slogan "Let's make the turn irreversible."

Whether it is nor not remains to be seen, of course. But once again
there is hope.

8

Poland

Grażyna Sikorska

POLAND IS a country of paradoxes. Atheism is an integral part of the political program of the ruling Communist Party, but only 15 per cent of party members are atheists. Of the other 85 per cent, the majority have a religious background, and a substantial number are probably practicing believers.

Since 1970 the Party's official line has been that it is permissible to combine party and church membership. But in practice few "Communist" believers would dare manifest their faith openly. Some believers who joined the Party did so for material benefit; some joined in the hope of changing it from within. But most, especially the vulnerable young, joined because of psychological blackmail.

Despite its official atheism, Poland has remained a deeply Christian nation, with Catholicism almost a national ideology at variance with the ruling state ideology. Poland is today one of the most Catholic countries in the world. More than 90 per cent of its people are proud members of the church. By contrast, fewer than 10 per cent—3 million in 35 million (1980)—are members of the Communist Party. Although 55 per cent of the people are now urban, 40 per cent are still private landowners—more than four-fifths of the agricultural land reverted to private ownership when the Party failed to impose collectivization.

A census on religious affiliation conducted between 1969 and 1979 covered 1,534 young people between fifteen and nineteen. Of these, 86 per cent considered themselves religious, 72 per cent regularly attended Sunday Mass, and 70 per cent went to confession at least once a year. Over half said they would sacrifice their lives in defense of their faith. "Socialist ideas" came at the bottom of a scale of values.

THE CHURCHES TO 1945

The Catholic Church has proved a steady, unifying force since Poland's inception as a state in A.D. 966, when Prince Mieszko's subjects were baptized following his conversion to Christianity. Up to the twelfth century only the higher ranks of society embraced Christianity. The numbers grew over the next three hundred years as the church expanded. The Franciscan and Dominican orders helped consolidate the worship of Christ and the Virgin Mary and brought out the profoundly humanitarian qualities of Christianity. Fear and coercion in matters of faith never gained as much ground in Poland as elsewhere during the Counter-Reformation. The slow and peaceful Christianization of local folklore paralleled a folklorization of Christianity. The fruit of this age-old process is a powerful, popular Christianity.

The consolidation of the young state was closely related to its Christianization. The strong link between the state and the church was reflected in the proximity to the cathedral of the royal castle in Kraków (residence of the Polish kings from approximately 1300 to 1600) and in the primate of Poland's position as *interrex,* the person who ruled between the death of one monarch and the coronation of the next.

Despite this strong bond, the Catholic Church never became either subordinate to the secular authorities or part of the state as did the Orthodox Church in Russia. The moral dimension of the struggles between church and state is epitomized in the case of St. Stanisław, bishop of Kraków, who like an Old Testament prophet rebuked the king for abducting a peasant girl. The bishop lost his life in 1078, but the king lost his throne. Stanisław became the patron saint of Poland.

The Orthodox Church did not appear in Polish territory until the second half of the fourteenth century, when Poland occupied the duchies of Halicz and Włodzimierz, where Ruthenians professed the Byzantine rite. In the fifteenth century, after Poland and Lithuania were united, ten dioceses in the new monarchy fell under jurisdiction of the patriarchate of Constantinople.

The Arrival of Protestantism

In the sixteenth century Protestantism spread to Poland, first the Lutherans and later the Calvinists. Reformation movements took root among the townfolk of German origin, the aristocracy, and the rich gentry. For a brief period, advocates of the Reformation had a considerable majority in the Sejm (parliament), made up exclusively of the gentry, but Catholicism continued to be the dominant religion in Poland.

The country's exemplary tolerance allowed Protestant churches to flourish. A law passed by the Sejm in 1573 guaranteed Catholics and Protestants equal freedom of faith. At a time when Europe was being shattered by civil wars over religion, the great chancellor Jan Zamoyski said in the Polish senate: "I would give half of my life if those who have abandoned the Catholic Church would voluntarily return to its fold; but I would give my whole life rather than suffer anyone to be constrained to do so."

Late in the sixteenth century the interdenominational contest ended with a victory for the Catholic Church. In the following centuries the Protestant churches dwindled both because they failed to win the support of the peasantry and because Protestantism was divided—theologically, socially, and ethnically.

The country's decline from the seventeenth century on, exacerbated by ruinous wars, plagues, and the collapse of town life, affected religion as well. The wars Poland had to fight against Islamic, Orthodox, and Protestant powers cemented the centrality of Catholicism in the Polish nation.

Partitioning and Reunification

The greatest threat to Polish Catholicism came at the end of the eighteenth century, when Poland was partitioned among its three neighbors—Austria, Russia, and Prussia. For 123 years the Polish state disappeared from the maps of Europe. During the years of captivity, a unique combination of religious faith and patriotism took root in the popular mind. The leading intellectuals—priests and poets—were largely prophets and visionaries. Significantly, in 1846, two years before the Communist Manifesto was issued, the exiled Polish poet Zygmunt Krasiński warned: "Maybe a Communist society is the highest goal toward which the history of the world inclines, but for it not to become the most terrible irony, the most lunatic despotism, it must come about at a time when the light of Christ turns everyone into a saint."

During the years of partition, Germanization and Russification accompanied the attempts forcibly to convert Poles to Lutheranism or Orthodoxy. Largely in consequence, today Polish Catholics view Protestantism and Orthodoxy as foreign imports. In the Russian zone of partition, the church was additionally persecuted for its support of the Polish uprisings in 1830 and 1863.

In the second half of the nineteenth century, various free-church movements began to spread throughout partitioned Poland. The Baptists, Pentecostals, and Church of Christ became especially vigorous after World War I.

In 1918 Poland regained its independence. Within its new borders only 64 per cent of the population belonged to the Latin Rite Catholic Church; Catholics of the Byzantine (Eastern) Rite constituted 10.4 per cent, Orthodox 11.8 per cent, Protestants 2.6 per cent, and Jews 9.8 per cent. Under the constitution of March 1921 all churches were given equal rights, although the Catholic Church occupied a position that reflected its numbers and historical role.

None of the new denominations formed after World War I as yet had legal status. A religious denomination, moreover, that had not been legalized by any one of the former partitioning powers had no right—with minor exceptions—to spread its activities to the territory of another former zone of partition.

The Horrors of World War II

On September 1, 1939, Hitler invaded Poland. Two weeks later the Soviet army attacked Poland from the east, in line with the Molotov-Ribbentrop Pact of August 1939. Poland was partitioned again, this time between two totalitarian powers.

The fate of the Poles in the following six years is comparable in many ways to that of the Jews, a fact that is frequently overlooked. Between 1939 and 1945 the population of the former Polish republic was reduced by over 6 million, including some 2.9 million Polish Jews. About 644,000 Polish citizens lost their lives as a direct result of the war, while 5.3 million were executed in acts of "pacification" and above all in concentration camps.

The church shared the tragic fate of its people at the hands of both Germans and Russians. According to church historians, 3,646 Catholic priests were sent to concentration camps where 1,996 priests, four bishops, 238 nuns, 170 monks, and 113 seminarians perished. Many church buildings were destroyed. The Protestant churches, especially the Lutheran church, shared in the nation's tragedy. The Lutheran presiding bishop, Julius Bursche, who stoutly resisted, was taken away to camps in September 1939 with thirty-four other prominent clergymen; he died in a camp in 1942. The fate of the 1.5 million Poles who were deported from the Soviet-occupied part of Poland to Siberia and the Asian republics in the south in September 1939 is still largely unknown, but by 1941 almost half of them were already dead.

The Communist Takeover

Having fought on the side of the Allies, Poland was theoretically victorious at the end of World War II. In reality, its allies abandoned it, and it became part of the Soviet sphere of influence. According to the Potsdam Agreement, a free election in post-war Poland would decide its political future; but the election was rigged, and the Polish Communist Party took power. Marxist doctrine demanded the repudiation of religion. The Communist leaders had every reason to declare war on the Catholic Church—and good reason to keep that war a cold one.

The post-war border changes along with the German extermination of nearly three million Polish Jews made Poland, for the first time in centuries, an almost homogeneous Catholic country in which non-Catholics made up less than 3 per cent of the population. At the Teheran meeting in 1943, the Big Three agreed that the 1920 Curzon line would form the basis for Poland's eastern frontier. This meant that the Polish lands annexed by the Soviet Union in 1939, where the majority of Poland's non-Catholics lived, would remain in Soviet hands. Two years later, at Yalta, Poland's right to the lands annexed from eastern Germany was recognized, but without being defined. At Potsdam in 1945, the new Polish-German frontier, 220 miles west of the former one, was fixed, and Germans were expelled from Poland, Czechoslovakia, and Hungary.

The Catholic Church, with a structure equal to the Communist Party's and a wide social base that the Communists lacked—the Party had only 40,000 members when the Red Army arrived—was a worthy adversary. The church represented great power, with over 90 per cent of the people united in faith.

The Polish peasants, at first attracted by the Communists' agrarian reforms, soon understood their real intent. Persecuted for their opposition to collectivization, they are still the church's strongest allies. The workers, in whose name the Communists claimed to have seized power, became disillusioned by the ineffective economic policies of the new regime. The majority of the intelligentsia—mainly the former landed gentry—were naturally opposed to the new proletarian government, whose only claim to power rested on Stalin's will. Attending Sunday Mass was the only way—even for the irreligious—to express openly their disapproval of the Communist government.

THE RELIGIOUS MAKEUP

It is sometimes said that religious liberty is greater under the Communists than under the pre-war Polish government. For instance, Dr. Zahariasz Lyko, editor of an Adventist paper, said in an address to the First World Congress on Religious Liberty in 1977 that although before World War II Poland had a Christian government, not all Christian churches enjoyed religious liberty. Some churches obtained freedom only, he said, under the Communists: the Methodists, the Reformed Church, the Mariavite Church, the Polish Catholic Church (a minority body not in communion with Rome), the Seventh-Day Adventists, and the Baptists.

This assertion is misleading. The Polish Second Republic had only two decades (1918-1939) in which to reunite itself, politically and economically as well as legally. All religious denominations that had been established before partition were granted legal status. Because of the differing religious policies of the three partitioning powers, it took several years—even in the case of the Catholic Church—for the final decree to be issued. By 1938, the positions of various churches had been regularized: the Catholic Church, the Orthodox Church, the (Lutheran) Evangelical Church of the Augsburg Confession, the Muslim Religious Union, and the Karaite Religious Union. Of the old pre-partition churches, only the Reformed Church did not have a regulated legal position; it had not sought a new agreement because it considered its pre-partition treaty with the state still valid. The Eastern Rite Catholic Church shared the rights of the Latin Rite Catholic Church.

Contrary to life under Communism, in pre-war Poland these churches were free to choose their hierarchy and to manage their material assets. The government helped them with their building projects. Moreover, religious instruction in schools (now forbidden) not only was permitted for all denominations but was legally obligatory. None of the non-recognized denominations on Dr. Lyko's list suffered any religious persecution during the years of the republic; all could carry out their mission freely.

The Catholic Church

Today the Roman Catholic Church enjoys more freedom in Poland than anywhere else in Central and Eastern Europe. Expediency, not government good will, is the reason. The church—strong and independent—has far greater authority than the government with the population. To survive politically, the Polish Communist regime needs the support of the church.

Institutionally, the church is much stronger than at any time during the past 150 years. It has grown considerably since the advent of Communism. The figures for 1987 with the comparable 1937 figures in parentheses are: 27 dioceses (20), 8,224 parishes (5,170), 15,340 churches and chapels (7,257), 23,432 diocesan and monastic priests (11,239), and more than 30,000 nuns (17,000)—all despite appalling wartime losses. In 1987 membership reached 33.5 million; 95 per cent of all Polish children are baptized in the church. The primate, three other cardinals (one resides permanently in Rome), and eighty-seven bishops exercise an authority that sometimes extends beyond the church.

In 1987, 9,030 seminarians were preparing for the priesthood in forty-six diocesan and monastic seminaries. While churches almost everywhere bewail the decline in vocations, ordinations in Poland are two or three times the pre-war figure. The church even has a surplus of priests and exports some to the Third World. Priests and religious have much to do. Nuns, expelled from the hospitals in the 1950s, were allowed back only in Solidarity times. But without interruption they have been allowed to care for the handicapped in homes run by the state-controlled Caritas organization. Monks are permitted to work in a few hospitals. Hospital chaplains can visit patients who request a priest; but as for saying Mass and visiting patients informally, the situation varies from hospital to hospital and according to the temper of the authorities.

Although the church can no longer teach religion in schools, it manages to teach the majority of children, with the help of nuns, in the 20,000 catechetical centers set up for the purpose. University students participate in a wide range of church-sponsored activities. The Catholic University of Lublin, created in 1918—the only independent university in the whole of Eastern Europe—is financed by the church with the help of the church in the West. In addition, there are the Catholic Academy of Theology, a state-financed institution whose degrees must be verified individually by the church, and the Papal Theological Institutes. Since the various Papal Institutes are not properly acknowledged by the authorities, their 4,600 students face a bleak employment prospect.

Access to the media has long been a bone of contention between church and state. Only since 1980 has a Mass been broadcast every Sunday. The religious press, greatly revived after August 1980, has 89 journals and newspapers, of which only 33 are recognized by the hierarchy. These represent only a minute fraction of the official total of 2,766 periodicals currently published in Poland. The threat of closure of a paper is often used to bring the church to heel. Under the stringent regulations, religious material is exempt from censorship, but the definition of "religious" rests with the censors, and the government admits that 43 per cent of all censored items are from Catholic publications. Although there are 56 daily papers, none is Catholic in inspiration.

In 1977 the bishops complained that only 300,000 copies of the catechism had been published that year. This number would be a bonanza anywhere else in Eastern Europe, but in Poland it meant only one copy for each twenty-six children.

The church may complain bitterly—and justifiably—of harassment and restrictions, but it carries out pastoral work and imaginative projects on a scale unknown to other East European churches. The Communists, while resenting the church—even during the short periods of church-state rapprochement—have over the years come to realize that they cannot destroy it. What they do instead is work constantly to limit or subordinate it.

The Polish authorities take pains to attempt to persuade the West that tension between the Catholic Church and the state stems from the "politicizing" of the church. They refer to their harmonious relations with non-Catholic churches as proof of their religious good will. Leaders of the minority churches publicly support the assertion, even claiming that their churches do indeed have greater freedom under Communism than before. But they have no illusions: they are well aware of the authorities' desire to offset the influence of the Catholic Church. The state is willing to support any religious group that might undermine the allegiance of Catholics to their church.

The concessions that Catholics win from the state are generally shared by all non-Catholic churches. The Solidarity era made this quite clear. The denominational churches, some of whose leaders later criticized Solidarity for being too Catholic, benefited from the concern for religion shown by the movement. For instance, one of the demands of the Lenin Shipyard workers was that the churches have access to the media. Since January 1982, the eight denominations in the Polish Ecumenical Council have broadcast services twice a month and on Christian festivals. The sudden increase in permits for church buildings has helped Catholics and non-Catholics alike. All religions, moreover, can more easily import, print, and sell Bibles and other religious literature.

The minority denominations have benefited from being overshadowed by the Catholic Church. The Polish authorities, always eager to undercut the power of the majority church, never hesitate to blazon their "protection" of minority churches.

The Orthodox Church

Although it lost 30 per cent of its followers in the border changes at the end of the war, the Polish Autocephalous Orthodox Church is still the largest non-Catholic group. It has some 200 priests and six bishops serving 850,000 members in four dioceses and 218 parishes; there are more than 300 churches and chapels and six monastic houses. The priests are trained at a seminary in Warsaw and the interchurch Christian Theological Academy. The church has been publishing a Russian journal since 1954 and a Polish quarterly since 1971.

Historically, Polish-Russian relations—and hence Catholic-Orthodox relations—have put the church in a difficult position. Poles identify Orthodoxy with Russification; the Orthodox believers for their part have not forgotten the closing and destruction of hundreds of their churches in 1938–39.

The Orthodox Church of Poland was formed out of several dioceses of the Moscow Patriarchate that were in the territory of the newly independent Polish republic in 1918. The dioceses consisted of more than five million

Ukrainian and Byelorussian Orthodox believers. Over protests from the Russian patriarch, the patriarchate of Constantinople granted them autocephaly in 1924 at the request of the Polish government. In 1951 the canonical situation was finally resolved when the Council of Bishops elected a metropolitan from among themselves. The internal statute of the church was accepted by the head of the government's Office for Religious Affairs in 1970.

According to the *Ukrainian Quarterly,* the Polish government manipulates the church at will, demoralizing it from within and keeping it on the brink of disaster. Many priests, who are arbitrarily selected, have low moral standards, as witness their eagerness to cooperate with the state security apparatus. Since 1970, the church has been under the spiritual leadership of Metropolitan Bazyli, a weak man subservient to the state.

In the 1980s an Orthodox renewal, under the direction of Bishop Sawa, sprang up among the young, giving the church some hope for the future.

The Eastern Rite Catholic Church

The only significant minority church that, for political reasons, has been denied legal status in post-war Poland is the Eastern Rite Catholic Church. The (Ukrainian) Eastern Rite Church traces its origins to the Uniate church (Orthodox in liturgy but in communion with Rome) formed in 1595–96 by Ukrainian and Byelorussian Orthodox hierarchy who transferred their allegiance from Constantinople to Rome.

After the partition of Poland, most of the area populated by the Byelorussians and some Ukrainian territories were taken over by Russia, which abolished the Eastern Rite Church. Most of the Ukrainians came under the rule of Austria, where they were known as "Greek Catholics" and enjoyed government support, despite pressure to assimilate with the mostly Polish Latin Rite Catholic Church. Then, after World War II, the majority of Ukrainian "Greek Catholics" came under Soviet rule, although up to 100,000 remain in Czechoslovakia and a quarter to half a million in western Poland, where they were resettled by force in the late 1940s.

Their church was never formally abolished in Poland, but its hierarchy has not been restored, and the government has refused to allow Eastern Rite Catholic parishes. After 1956, the Polish authorities granted *de facto* recognition to an arrangement of the previous decade whereby some fifty Eastern Rite Catholic priests were installed to assist Latin Rite Catholic parishes that have large number of Ukrainians. At present, the church is administered by two vicars general who are responsible directly to the primate of the Catholic Church.

In June 1984, Archbishop Myroslav S. Marusyn, secretary of the Vatican Congregation for the Eastern Churches, visited Poland by invitation of the primate and as representative of the Pope, the first such visit since World War II. Many Ukrainians interpreted the visit as a major step toward legal recognition of the Eastern Rite Church in Poland.

The Jewish Remnant

Controversy obscures the history of the Jewish community in Poland during the twentieth century. The frequent articles on Polish anti-Semitism seldom mention that there were 3.2 million Jews living in Poland at the outbreak of World War II. Their legal position had been recognized in 1927. During the six years of war, some 2.9 million were killed by the Nazis, and a large proportion of the survivors emigrated to Israel, some voluntarily, others driven out by the Marxist government.

The Polish Communist authorities have made Jews scapegoats in every post-war crisis—1956, 1968 (a particularly brutal purge), 1976, and 1980–81. The Jewish problem resurfaced in the Solidarity era. In an influential weekly a group of twenty-one Polish intellectuals called on the government to combat anti-Semitism. But an anti-Semitic campaign—organized at the top levels of the government—had already gotten under way. It aimed to discredit Solidarity as a Jewish-inspired undertaking. The slogan "Wałęsa is a Jew" appeared all over Poland, and trade-union leaders were denigrated as Zionists.

Polish intellectuals and Solidarity leaders were indignant over the resurgence of anti-Semitism. After martial law was declared, the anti-Semitic campaign escalated. A certain Professor Józef Kostecki stated that "only the Russians stand as a barrier against Jewish chauvinism and its plans to conquer the world."

At present there are only about 5,000 Jews in the whole of Poland; the Union of Religious Congregations has eighteen affiliated local congregations with 1,739 believers. There are few local leaders, no religious education for children, and, since 1965, no rabbis. A weekly Yiddish-Polish paper *Folks-Styme* (The people's voice) has a circulation of about 3,000, and a Yiddish theater attracts large audiences.

Protestant and Other Minority Churches

The Protestant churches constitute a tiny minority of about 100,000 Christians. The Lutherans are the largest body with about 74,000 members. Today most Protestant churches are members of the Polish Ecumenical Council (PEC), which was created in 1945 to coordinate the activities of the country's non–Roman-Catholic Christians. It includes, in addition to the Polish Autocephalous Orthodox Church, the following seven churches:

(1) the Lutheran *Evangelical Church of the Augsburg Confession,* whose 1946 membership of 270,000 fell by more than two-thirds through deportation and emigration of Lutherans of German origin, 73,818 members in 121 parishes, 331 churches and chapels and 177 preaching centers, 89 pastors, 37 deaconesses; (2) the *Reformed Church,* 4,500 members in 8 parishes, 5 branches, 12 churches and chapels, 4 pastors, 32 lay workers; (3) the *Polish Christian Baptist Church,* a result of Baptist activity that began in 1858, 5,925 members, 58 churches, 59 pastors; (4) the *Methodist Church,* established by missionaries of the American Methodist Church in the 1920s, 4,040 members, 60 parishes and branches, 56 churches and chapels, 36 pastors, 31 lay workers; (5) the *United Evangelical Church,* a federation (achieved in 1947) of autonomous churches including Pentecostals and Evangelical Christians, 13,907 members, 114 parishes, 129 churches and prayer houses, 248 pastors; (6) the *Polish Catholic Church,* an autonomous church formerly part of the Polish National Catholic Church of America (which began in the United States late in the nineteenth century), 33,700 members, 92 churches and chapels, 121 priests, 7 bishops; and (7) the *Old Catholic Church of Mariavite,* with 24,850 members, 55 churches and chapels, 29 priests, 3 bishops. (There is also a Catholic Church of Mariavite, not part of the Ecumenical Council; the Mariavite Church split in two in 1935.)

Contact Among Minority Churches

All the minority churches are members of one or more of the various international church bodies, such as the World Council of Churches (WCC), the Christian Peace Conference (CPC), and the Conference of European Churches. These contacts give them a higher profile than their numbers might warrant.

The Polish Ecumenical Council (PEC), which is associated with the World Council of Churches, provides a basis for limited cooperation. But its greatest significance is in its international contacts: very small churches represent all Polish Christians at international gatherings. Originally the PEC had a provisional statute but no legal status. From 1950 to 1956 its activities were suspended, but in 1958 the Polish Ecumenical Council finally received legal status.

The major weakness of Polish Protestantism is its fragmentation. Even in the cities, where several Protestant denominations maintain small, struggling churches, there is litle fellowship, and in some cases—e.g., between Pentecostals and Baptists—there are even tensions. Reformed and Lutheran churches have shown the most promise; in 1970 they had a shared ministry, intercommunion, and a mutually recognized baptism. (Intercommunion and a shared ministry are also found in the Polish Catholic and Mariavite churches.)

Cooperation among the churches has been most effective in theological education. The Christian Theological Academy was set up in 1954 with two sections, Evangelical (i.e., Protestant) and Old Catholic. A third was added in 1957, when the Orthodox Church joined.

Other Recognized Church Bodies

Apart from the Catholic Church and the PEC, the state has recognized three other groups of religious bodies.

Four religious bodies are recognized by an act of law: the *Catholic Church of Mariavite*, the *Karaite Religious Union* (the Karaites are a Jewish sect that rejects the Talmud in favor of the Bible as the source of authority), the *Eastern Old Rite Church*, and the *Muslim Religious Union*.

About 2,300 Muslims live in six communities in Poland, descendants of Tartar prisoners of war. In pre-war Poland, in the region of Wilno alone, there were sixteen mosques; today there are only two mosques in the whole country. The Tartar Association was abolished after the war.

During the 1960s and 1970s, the regime thought that Muslims could help to further contacts with oil-rich Arab countries. Funds were accepted from Islamic countries to aid in rebuilding mosques. In 1969 the first post-war Polish Muslim congress was allowed to take place, and two years later the Office for Religious Affairs introduced legislation regarding religious activity among the dwindling Tartar population.

Although the situation of the Tartars has not really improved, the government propagandizes its benevolent attitude toward Polish Muslims. A Polish translation of the Koran, published in Sarajevo and paid for by the Moroccan government, was distributed free of charge in 1981. In July 1983, during the Salat al Fitr-u holy days, a ceremony was staged in Warsaw mainly to impress the several thousand foreign Muslim students studying in Poland.

A second group of religious bodies, those legally recognized by the Ministry of Public Administration, includes the *Seventh-Day Adventist Church*. From small beginnings, the Adventists spread throughout Poland in the late nineteenth century, mostly in the Prussian zone. The clergy were mainly of foreign nationalities until the turn of the century, when Poles entered the ministry. In 1979 there were 6,794 believers in 120 congregations, with 68 clergy.

The third category of churches, the *registered associations,* includes the Jews as well as a dozen small Christian or near-Christian groups, with memberships ranging from twelve to just over two thousand.

The Catholic Church and Other Churches

Relations between the Catholic Church and other churches have improved in recent years. In 1978 the Catholic primate, Cardinal Wyszyński, urged Catholics to work with the Orthodox and Protestants to form a common front against an "ideology which imprisons man in a cocoon of his egoism." Since 1974, a Joint Commission of the Polish Ecumenical Council (PEC) and the Commission of the Episcopate for Ecumenical Work has been operating. The commission attaches special importance to an annual week of prayer for Christian unity and to dialogue on theological matters. A subcommission for dialogue meets twice a year.

The present primate, Cardinal Józef Glemp, has given a new impetus to ecumenism in Poland. In September 1981, on the day after his entrance into Warsaw Cathedral attended by representatives of the Polish Ecumenical Council, Cardinal Glemp received at his residence a joint delegation from the PEC, the Christian Theological Academy, and the Bible Society. Two months later he visited PEC headquarters. Another landmark came in January 1982 when Cardinal Glemp preached in the Orthodox cathedral in Warsaw. A few months later, Bishop Zdzisław Tranda remarked that the Catholic Church in Poland allows other denominations to use its buildings for their services.

Also in 1982, the Catholic Theological Academy of Warsaw organized two symposiums for Catholic and Protestant theologians to discuss Martin Luther's thought as an ecumenical reflection. In June 1983 there was another first: a joint delegation from the PEC, the Union of Religious Congregations (Jewish), the Muslim Religious Union, the Christian Theological Academy, and the Bible Society met Pope John Paul II during his second homecoming.

Even so, the times have not been free of tensions. An Anglican, Brian Cooper, after talking to Protestant leaders in Poland, wrote: "Since the election of Cardinal Wojtyła of Kraków, John Paul II, Polish Catholicism has gone far beyond justifiable pride. It has become triumphalist, arrogant, anti-ecumenical, and intolerant."

During the Solidarity era, the PEC spoke of its unhappiness with what it called "recent tendencies in Catholic society in Poland." It pointed to the close ties between the Catholic Church and Solidarity as evidence of the church's exclusive claims to represent the Polish people. (But visitors to Poland reported Solidarity's disappointment when non-Catholic representatives declined invitations to attend their events.) People such as United Evangelical pastor Andrzej Bajeński said they would be afraid to live in a country governed by Solidarity. Later, under martial law, Andrzej

Wojtowicz, press officer of the PEC, accused Solidarity of wanting to take power and abolish the Party and faulted the Catholic Church for not showing Solidarity "the right way."

The numerical and institutional strength of the Catholic Church coupled with attempts by the authorities to set the denominations against one another have slowed down ecumenism in Poland. Many Catholics, moreover, regard other Christians as too subservient to the state. Indeed, minority churches enjoying the support of the authorities have little reason for complaint. But the Catholic Church is able to criticize or even condemn the regime from the relative safety of numbers. For small Protestant churches, any act of open disobedience could be suicidal.

For Protestants, perhaps the biggest block to Protestant-Catholic ecumenism is Polish Catholics' devotion to the Virgin Mary. On the positive side, developments in Catholic life such as Sacrosong—in which foreign as well as Polish Protestants participate—the Oasis retreats, and the Light-Life movement have spurred interest among Western Christians. (More will be said of these movements later.)

Bible Production

Today Protestants and Catholics share a hunger for the Bible. Historically, Catholics were discouraged from studying Scripture for fear of "private interpretation." In part because of Vatican II but more through the Light-Life movement, Catholic Bible reading caught on in the 1970s. After years of struggle, the government in 1965 allowed a new translation, the Millennium Bible, in Catholic and Protestant editions. By 1980, the Protestant version had sold 130,000 copies. Since then a Protestant New Testament has proved so popular that its entire third edition of 20,000 sold out within a week of publication, even though the price was about $16. Catholic publishing houses currently print about as many Bibles as Protestants; they cannot meet the Catholic demand.

The United Bible Societies' shop in Warsaw used to sell Bibles mainly to Protestants and to customers from other East European countries. It stocks Bibles in sixty-seven languages and has a large mail-order business. Since 1981, the rocketing demand from Polish Catholics as well as Protestants has made it the busiest Bible shop in the world.

THE CHURCHES 1945–80

From 1945 to 1947, the new government, confronted with the task of reconstructing a devastated country, was too weak to risk a major confrontation with the church. The state helped rebuild churches destroyed in the war and allowed the Catholic University of Lublin and a number of seminaries to reopen. The church was permitted to retain its pre-war land holdings, and religious instruction in all schools was compulsory. Great state events began with Mass in the cathedral.

But conflict was inevitable. On September 12, 1945, the Polish government unilaterally renounced the Concordat of 1925, the Vatican-state agreement on the regulation of church affairs. The official reason was the Vatican's refusal to recognize Poland's post-war frontiers by appointing diocesan bishops to the Oder-Neisse territory taken from Germany. (The Vatican also continued to recognize the Polish government-in-exile instead of the Warsaw government.) Although the Vatican appointed titular bishops to the territory in 1967 to placate the state, those dioceses were not fully integrated into the Polish church until West Germany acknowledged the Polish frontiers in May 1972.

The Assault on the Church

Following its "victory" in the 1947 election, the party was ready to declare war on the church. During 1947-56 the church struggled for survival against a government determined to gain total control. Part of the credit for the Communists' failure to do this must go to Cardinal Stefan Wyszyński, the best-known church leader in Eastern Europe prior to the election of Cardinal Wojtyła as pope.

Born in 1901, Wyszyński was transferred to the primatial see of Gniezno and Warsaw in 1948. Thus began his epic leadership of the Polish church. He was made cardinal in 1952. Cardinal Wyszyński had an intimate knowledge of Soviet Communism and was therefore under no illusions about the system. He understood Communist psychology and tactics thoroughly enough to keep his adversaries off balance. He was a fearless and superb diplomat and statesman who knew when to attack and when to retreat. At first the Vatican criticized him for compromising, not understanding his tactic of gaining time for subsequent advances. When he chose his ground, he was never satisfied with anything less than he asked for.

On the surface Cardinal Wyszyński seemed full of contradictions. A pre-war "progressive" and a champion of human rights, he was also an autocrat and was cautious about introducing both Vatican II church reforms and the new theological trends that were popular in the West. He was convinced that only a united church, strictly disciplined, could withstand Communism and secularism.

As primate, he had to act autocratically to preserve the Polish church. He was an expert in Polish history and a patriot with a unique awareness of the nation's *raison d' être,* which explains why he backed the regime in moments of crisis. In him, more than in any other church leader in the Soviet orbit, the Communists met their match. Christians of whatever denomination and country who were ground down by Marxist dictatorships looked up to Cardinal Wyszyński as an unrivaled leader.

In 1947 the Pax movement was founded by the authorities to undermine or destroy the reputation of the hierarchy and to create a bloc of "Catholic" opinion that would capitulate to the state. During the Stalinist era, Pax was almost more Stalinist than the Party, and in the 1960s it was in the forefront of the campaign against writers and students who were agitating against censorship. In 1964 Cardinal Wyszyński denounced Pax as a Communist-front organization. In the mid-1970s, it had about 4,000 members; there are far fewer today.

The Decrees of 1949

The papal decree of 1949 that threatened to excommunicate Catholics who belonged to or supported the Communist Party was received with mixed feelings in Poland. It was difficult to accept the idea that holding a government post necessarily meant rejecting the Catholic religion. Poles also thought the decree unjust since the political system had been imposed on Poland from outside.

The Council of Ministers reacted with a decree of its own in August 1949. The decree purported to guarantee freedom of conscience and religious belief, but, as with similar documents in the Soviet bloc, it gave the regime wide powers to deal with alleged abuses of religious freedom, especially when they conflicted with the interest of the state.

In 1950 the state declared Catholic schools illegal, along with Catholic Action and other church associations, and took over about a thousand of the church's educational and charitable institutions. This included Caritas, whose name was retained, to the confusion of Poles who assumed it was part of the worldwide Catholic charitable movement of the same name. In 1950, "patriotic priests' circles" attached to Caritas were formed to fight against the hierarchy. The church press was banned, and church property, except for church buildings and churchyards, was confiscated. In March 1950, Bishop Kowalski was arrested. A number of monks and priests were already in prison.

The 1950 Accord

Against this background the Catholic hierarchy signed a nineteen-point accord with the state in April 1950—not a legal agreement but a kind of *modus vivendi*. (See appendix J.) The supremacy of the pope in matters of faith and ecclesiastical jurisdiction was recognized. Worship outside church buildings, such as pilgrimages, was allowed, as were monastic orders. The church could also give religious instruction in schools, minister in hospitals and prisons, publish journals, maintain the Catholic University, and retain control over seminaries and church appointments.

The church, in its turn, was forced to recognize the new social order and the right of the Marxist regime to govern. The church also agreed to urge the faithful to work harder for reconstruction, to oppose "activities hostile to the Polish People's Republic," not to oppose the development of agricultural cooperatives, to condemn any act against the state, and to punish clergy guilty of such an act.

The agreement was seen as part of the strategy of Cardinal Wyszyński, the new Polish primate, to "buy time" in the life-and-death struggle. But the cardinal's concessions met with serious reservations in the Vatican. In the 1950s, the Curia's and the cardinal's policy on dealing with Communism were at opposite poles, and Wyszyński's independence combined with his diplomatic flexibility gained him many critics.

Throughout the post-war years, the cardinal never let the Curia dictate his political policy. When in 1961 party head Wladysław Gomułka accused the Polish church of troublemaking, Wyszyński could retort in all honesty that during his tenure the Vatican had never instructed the Polish hierarchy in Polish church affairs. His independence from the Vatican contributed largely to the strong position of the church *vis-à-vis* the state.

Had the church not signed the 1950 agreement, it would have had no official recognition in a situation where contact between church and state was unavoidable. The authorities interpreted the agreement as the first step in the church's capitulation.

Further Steps Against the Church

Soon after the agreement was signed, the Office for Religious Affairs was set up to limit the church's activity and independence. Religious instruction was slowly being strangled. By the mid-1950s, more than a thousand schools were run by the Association of the Friends of Children, which brought children up "in the spirit of socialism." Parents, threatened with the loss of jobs, were often forced to send their children to these schools.

In 1951 Bishop Czesław Kaczmarek was arrested. A year later the new constitution proclaimed the separation of church and state (though the church had never been legally attached to the state) and subordinated the church to the state. Catholic journals were closed one by one. All institutes of religious knowledge and all junior seminaries were liquidated. The "patriotic priests" sprang into action, openly criticizing various bishops and demanding Wyszyński's resignation.

In May 1953, the head of the Council of Ministers ordered the implementation of a February 9 decree giving the state the right to appoint and dismiss not only priests but bishops. All priests and bishops were to take an oath of loyalty to the Polish People's Republic. The decree was in contravention of the constitution, canon law, and the agreement of 1950. It amounted to nationalizing the church.

"Non Possumus"

The Polish episcopate met in plenary session in Kraków and issued a memorandum—including the famous *non possumus* ("we cannot")—that was signed by Cardinal Wyszyński and sent to President Bolesław Beirut. (See appendix K.) While restating their desire for an agreement and a reconciliation with the state, the bishops declared their determination to defend the church against destruction. They listed all the church's grievances—the confiscations, arrests, expulsions, and destruction—and made it clear they would prefer to leave church positions vacant "rather than place the spiritual rule of souls in the hands of unworthy individuals." This document stands as proud proof that Poland continued to have a genuinely independent Catholic Church when all others in the Soviet bloc were being subordinated to the state.

The authorities described the memorandum as an attack by the bishops on the constitution—high treason—and on September 26, 1953, Cardinal Wyszyński was arrested and confined to a convent. By the end of the year, eight other bishops and nine hundred priests had been imprisoned and the remaining hierarchy pressured into taking an oath of loyalty to the state. All church appointments were subject to state approval. The number of seminarians fell from ninety to twenty, the theological faculties were closed, Catholic University activities were curtailed, punitive taxes were levied on the church, and, in 1955, religious instruction in schools was forbidden.

By then some two thousand bishops, priests, and lay Catholic activists were in prison.

1956: A Brief Lull

In February 1956, Khrushchev's attack on Stalinism precipitated a crisis. The workers in Poznań rioted in June under banners demanding "Bread and Freedom" and "Russians Go Home." During two days of fighting, fifty-three men died. A pattern appeared that would be repeated in 1968, 1970, 1976, 1980, and 1981: The Party changed its leadership and asked the church to help appease the populace. In return, the church was offered concessions—which the authorities forgot as soon as the crisis had passed.

In 1956, Władysław Gomułka became party secretary. He asked Primate Wyszyński to return to Warsaw from the convent to which he had been exiled and calm the people. And so in 1956, as he would also do in 1970, 1976, and 1980, with Soviet intervention waiting in the wings, Cardinal Wyszyński, the "uncrowned king of Poland," restrained the people from violent confrontation with the Communist authorities. A political realist, he had learned from the Allies' betrayal that the Polish people could count only on themselves in their struggle for a democratic and Christian Poland.

In return the party promised that Bishop Kaczmarek and all imprisoned priests would be released. The decree of February 1953 was revoked. A new agreement signed in December 1956 gave the state the right to approve or veto, but not to appoint, clergy.

The church also secured other concessions—religious instruction in schools, a reinstated Catholic press, pastoral care in hospitals and prisons, the return of the monastic orders recently expelled and of the bishops removed from their sees. The party allowed five Catholic intellectual clubs and a Catholic parliamentary grouping called Znak. As a gesture of support for the new regime, the cardinal voted in the January 1957 election.

The cardinal, it was believed, had struck a good bargain—the church was bound to respect the law, but the state recognized the church's right to administer its own affairs.

1957: Resumption of the Attack

By the end of 1957, the new agreement had proved to be one more instance of Communist treachery. As the political scene stabilized, the struggle with the church resumed. For the next thirteen years the state used every means it could muster to try to confine the church to the sacristy. Gomułka spelled it out at the Third Party Congress in March 1959: the church must limit itself strictly to matters of faith; it must remain within the church's four walls.

In April 1957, draconian new tax laws were introduced that, if obeyed, would have meant total bankruptcy for the church within months. They were somewhat softened in August. Many publications were banned, thousands of books were destroyed, and strict censorship was resumed.

While insisting that the church was separate from the state, the authorities constantly intruded in its internal affairs. By 1960, religious instruction had again been removed from schools, and nuns, the core of the catechetical program, were forbidden to teach religion. The church categorically rejected the order. The authorities even tried to interfere with the content of religious instruction: they asked the church to leave out the history of the church and all discussion of moral problems.

An offensive was mounted to control the seminaries. In defiance of laws and agreements, the decrees of 1961 and 1965 subordinated the seminaries to the Ministry of Education. The fundamental right of the church to train its pastors was being infringed. The hierarchy shot back with another *non possumus,* and the authorities slowly backed down.

No new parishes were allowed in the expanding industrial areas, and building permits for new churches were severely restricted. Nowa Huta, for example, was originally conceived as the first model Polish socialist town: a statue of Lenin would replace the church. It took eleven years to obtain permission to build a church; then bureaucratic tactics delayed completion for another ten years. By then, it had to serve 200,000 inhabitants.

The observance of religious feasts, pilgrimages, and processions ran into state-generated difficulties, and the government offered counterattractions—secular festivals and school outings. Attempts were made to create a national Catholic Church, totally subservient to the state, and the state-sponsored Pax movement was given increased support.

The Church's Response

The authorities hoped that the church would slowly die. Cardinal Wyszyński thought otherwise. When religion was excluded from schools, the church created catechetical centers and refused to register catechists and children. When Catholic papers were confiscated, the clergy worked all the harder to teach the faithful. Heavy taxation was met by the enormous generosity of parishioners. Building restrictions fired the will to fight for permits and to defend illegally built churches against demolition.

The most important factor in the survival of the church, however, was Cardinal Wyszyński's pastoral program. Confined within four walls, deprived of the right to form Catholic associations, prevented from teaching children unhindered, lacking access to the media, the church turned to popular religion to transmit the gospel message. These traditional forms were deeply rooted in the devotion to Mary that for centuries has characterized Polish Catholicism. Marian services in May and October, devotions in honor of the Virgin, and pilgrimages to Marian shrines were essential to Wyszyński's pastoral strategy.

In 1957, the cardinal initiated a remarkable nine-year spiritual renewal— the "Great Novena"—to culminate in the 1966 celebrations marking a thousand years of Christianity in Poland. The entire Catholic population would renew the vows of loyalty to God and the Virgin Mary that King Kazimierz took in 1656 after a few Polish noblemen had successfully defended the monastery of Częstochowa against overwhelming Swedish forces. Polish bishops would dedicate Poland to the Virgin Mary for the freedom of the church both in Poland and throughout the world. The sacred icon of Our

Lady of Częstochowa, known as the Black Madonna and revered by Catholic Poles as the Queen of Poland, would visit all parishes.

The authorities did everything conceivable to impede the novena and the millennial celebration. When the church announced the theme "Faithfulness to God, the Cross, and the Gospel," the authorities responded by removing crucifixes from the schools; in answer to the church's "defense of the life of soul and body," they passed more liberal abortion laws. The icon of the Black Madonna was "arrested" several times and finally "confined" indefinitely to the shrine of Jasna Góra in Częstochowa—only the empty frame arrived in many parishes.

1965: The Bishops' Open Letter

The biggest clash came in 1965 when the Polish bishops sent an open letter of reconciliation to the German episcopate—at a time when Polish–West German relations were non-existent—with the famous words, "We forgive you and ask your forgiveness." The letter threw the government completely off balance—the church was taking control of foreign policy! The government withdrew Cardinal Wyszyński's passport and denied a visa to Pope Paul VI, who wished to join in the millennial celebrations.

The Polish media ridiculed the primate for his alleged religious obscurantism, ultraconservatism, and use of primitive folklore. Rumors flew about that even some bishops, including Cardinal Karol Wojtyła, wished he would adopt a more conciliatory attitude toward the state. In March 1966 the Polish bishops laid the rumors to rest by signing, *en masse,* an open declaration of loyalty to Cardinal Wyszyński.

Throughout the 1960s, the Party found unexpected allies among Polish intellectuals. Wyszyński's pastoral program—especially the Great Novena with its strong Marian overtones—was criticized for its "conservatism" and "traditionalism." During Vatican II, the cardinal was further accused of impeding the implementation of the council's decisions. Many Catholic intellectuals were interested in dialogue with Marxists and in Western theological developments.

The cardinal was not vindicated until the late 1970s, when the "religious folklore" and "festivals of faith" were recognized as having put the church firmly at the center of a Polish society ruled by a new spirit of unity.

The Vatican hierarchy continued to try to normalize relations between church and state. But from the start Cardinal Wyszyński made it quite clear to the Vatican that, unlike the Hungarian church, the Polish church was going to dictate the conditions of "normalization." His incredible goal was full normalization—the recognition of the church as a legal entity. And, as usual, he would settle for nothing less.

In 1968, after students and intellectuals revolted against the party's totalitarianism, the pattern begun in 1956 was repeated—the harsh press campaign against the cardinal suddenly eased and repressive measures against the church were lifted. Revisionists were expelled from the party. (Also at that time, a massive government-engineered anti-Zionist campaign forced unwanted Jews to emigrate.)

The 1970 Crisis and Its Aftermath

Two years later, after a drastic increase in the price of basic foods, the workers on the Baltic coast went on strike and were crushed by force. How many people were killed by the ZOMO (armed police recruited largely from the worst elements of the society) in December 1970 is still not known. Poland's outrage forced Gomułka to resign. The Poles had defeated their government a second time.

Gomułka was replaced by Edward Gierek, who revealed a significant shift in policy in his inaugural speech. In contrast to the Stalinism and nationalistic rhetoric of Gomułka, he portrayed himself as a pragmatist and technocrat and pledged a new deal for Poland: working within the *status quo,* he would seek an economy of private consumption. In line with his predecessors, Gierek promised rapprochement with the church.

As in past crises, Cardinal Wyszyński called for prudence, forgiveness, and responsibility. Yet the bishops' pastoral letter issued on New Year's Day read like a charter of rights. They demanded: (1) freedom of conscience and of religious practice, (2) free access to Christian culture, (3) social justice, (4) freedom of expression and of information, and (5) the right to decent living conditions. By the end of 1971 the great majority of the Polish people had joined in the five demands.

In June, the bishops issued another document that included a general outline of normalization. The totalitarian authorities found it completely unacceptable.

Yet church-state relations were somewhat more relaxed in 1971-72. The government made a show of participating in a constructive dialogue. A March 1971 meeting between the prime minister and the cardinal was advertised by the government and Pax papers, which praised both sides for their good intentions. In 1971 the government formally acknowledged the church's ownership of thousands of church buildings. In 1972 it freed the church of having to submit annual accounts and inventories of its possessions. The Vatican at last agreed to appoint residential bishops to the Oder-Neisse dioceses that were formerly part of Germany, and the embassy of the Polish government-in-exile at the Vatican was closed.

But the situation was still far from satisfactory. In 1973 the bishops accused the authorities of abusing the law with their aggressive secularization and atheistic propaganda. Two years later, the bishops called on the authorities to ease the media's "cultural terror"—the official anti-religious and materialistic ideology that went unchallenged.

That same year, 1975, the government announced amendments to the Polish constitution, including "the principle of the leading role of the Communist Party" and the "unbreakable bond" with the Soviet Union. The bishops sent a letter of protest to the parliament. Many Polish intellectuals also opposed the proposed amendments, and some 40,000 people signed a protest. As a result, the proposals were not adopted in their original form. Once again, strong, united opposition was able to move the government.

The 1970s—Defiance and Renewal

During the 1970s, belief in the official ideology plunged, and Christianity emerged as the only alternative. Thousands of people flocked to hear Cardinal Wyszyński's sermons, in which he accused the regime of "banning the church from public life," of "making Catholics second-class citizens," of exacting "slave labor" on Sundays, and of destroying the church and persecuting priests. Against the absolute claims to power by the Communist authorities, he appealed to higher laws and God-given morality. He mobilized the people and fought against compromise and hopelessness. Throughout the 1970s, the spirit of defiance spread across the nation.

In the diocese of Przemyśl, more than one hundred churches were built without state permission. There were several clashes with the police; whole areas were cordoned off and electricity and water supplies cut. Parish priests were heavily fined, but the bishop, Ignacy Tokarczuk, encouraged them to defy the authorities and would often himself come at night to consecrate a new church.

Tokarczuk is reputed to be the most outspoken of the bishops. In a 1976 sermon he summed up Poland's situation: Polish citizens, he said, had to live with lies; they had "elections," but only to confirm the Party's candidates; they were all equal, but some were more equal than others. State capitalism was the worst type, he said: workers were forbidden to strike, and the employer controlled the unions and the courts—in short, everything.

As the spirit of defiance spread, so did the spirit of religious renewal. Since 1969 a festival of religious song, Sacrosong, has attracted large crowds. In the early 1970s the Light-Life movement, a synthesis of general renewal movements in the church, developed rapidly, largely under the direction of Fr. Franciszek Blachnicki. By the early 1970s, summer Oasis retreat camps, aimed at specific groups—students, young workers, adults, priests—were organizing thousands in a disciplined year-round program. In the late 1970s, the Light-Life movement introduced a renewal program to educate Christians, and a non-violent Polish-style liberation theology evolved, which was to have far-reaching effects. (Appendix L is a 1980 declaration of the movement's principles.)

Over the last fifteen years, more than 300,000 young people have been spiritually formed within the Light-Life movement, which provides 40 per cent of all religious vocations. Various attempts have been made to infiltrate the movement, to restrict and even to destroy it. The Light-Life movement was put under the protection of the hierarchy—since 1970 Cardinal Wojtyła, among others, had been promoting and participating in it—and a special agreement was signed by church and state authorities on the Oasis camps. Pressure against the movement nevertheless continued.

The State Courts the Vatican

The authorities decided to bring the Polish church to heel by a direct agreement with the Vatican. In November 1973, Poland's foreign minister was received by Pope Paul VI. The following February the Vatican sent Archbishop Casaroli to pay a formal visit to the Polish government. Soon the Vatican was being praised for its policy of détente and for supporting the Soviet-sponsored European Security Conference. But Cardinal Wyszyński still insisted that there could be no concordat, no Poland-Vatican normalization, prior to church-state normalization in Poland itself. The church's conditions were restated.

The government's view of normalization was expressed in May 1976 by Kazimierz Kąkol, the minister for religious affairs. The church, he asserted, "has the right to carry out its services within the limits of the sanctuary, or shall we say the sacristy. . . but we are never going to allow evangelization outside the church. We shall never allow the church any influence on cultural and social life." He explained that the government would not use violent measures against the church, which would only make it more popular. The regime's tactics, he said, were to create a consumer society "in which we shall have conditions similar to those in the West, which will hasten the day when the church dwindles away."

The Late 1970s: Dissidence Grows

The "economic miracle" Gierek had promised when he came to power in 1970 was heading toward a dramatic collapse. The first alarm bells rang in June 1976, when the government introduced a drastic increase in food prices. The workers at Radom, Płock, and Ursus went on strike. The government was forced to back down, but severe reprisals followed. The striking workers were fired, beaten up, imprisoned. The church came to their defense. It was soon joined by a small committee of intellectuals (KOR) who provided legal help for the accused, publicized their plight, and collected money for their families.

A powerful dissident movement grew despite police harassment. Irrespective of their political preferences, all the opposition groups agreed with the church that social disintegration had to be resisted through moral revival.

In June 1977, a number of Catholics staged a hunger strike in St. Martin's Church, Warsaw, to protest the imprisonment of five demonstrating workers. Meanwhile, peasants were setting up their own grassroots committees. The Christian Association of Workers in Nowa Huta pledged to "deepen the workers' spiritual and religious life, to spread Christian ideals and principles, to defend and strengthen workers' awareness of human rights, and to struggle for official recognition of the Polish Christian heritage."

In January 1978, a group of intellectuals set up the Society for Academic Courses—the "Flying University." It challenged the party monopoly over education by giving lectures in private apartments. Cardinal Wojtyła, bishop of Kraków, had allowed the use of the academic chaplaincy and monastery for public lectures as early as November 1977. By autumn 1978, most of the lectures were taking place in churches. (In appendix M, Cardinal Wyszyński explains to the state minister of religion why the "Flying University" was needed.)

The convergence of the opposition and the church alarmed the authorities. In a worsening economic climate and after the ratification of the 1975 Helsinki Accords on human rights, the government could deal with dissidents only if the church remained neutral.

1978: A Polish Pope

On October 16, 1978, Cardinal Karol Wojtyła of Kraków was elected pope, taking the name of John Paul II. The impact of his election on Eastern Europe cannot be overestimated. It was seen by Catholic Poles as God's reward to the Polish nation for its faithfulness to Christ and his Church, symbolizing the victory of Christ over the evils of totalitarianism. The psychological barrier between believers and non-believers broke down— thousands of people began to return to the fold, including former party members. One party member, for instance, told how, while watching the installation of the Pope on television, he and his wife and daughter suddenly dropped to their knees. "I, a member of the Communist Party, who had not been inside a church for perhaps fifteen years, was now crossing myself! It was a victory for this man, a victory for our cardinal and the church, and it was also my own victory."

The Pope's pilgrimage to his native land in June 1979 united the whole nation despite the authorities' obstructionist tactics. Teachers were told to hold classes during the visit, and anyone absent from school or work could be dismissed or incur a "disciplinary transfer." To prevent his reaching large crowds of workers, the Pope was barred from visiting the famous Marian shrine of Piekary Śląskie in the Silesian region. Rumors spread of possible street disturbances, and coffins were stored in the Warsaw Theater to scare people off.

Undeterred, millions of Poles greeted the Pope, peacefully and with dignity, in an outburst of faith. Communists were nowhere to be seen. To many in Poland at the time, it seemed as if the whole system were collapsing. Certainly government officials would never have allowed the visit had they foreseen the results.

The Polish Pope's speeches to his countrymen stressed human dignity, derived from man's unique relationship with God—a direct challenge to Marxism. He urged the Polish hierarchy to continue the dialogue between church and state, but with the understanding that normalization must involve human rights. He reminded the workers that "Christ will never accept that man should be seen or see himself as a mere means of mass production. He hung on the Cross to protest against any degradation of man, including degradation of work." The Pope left his countrymen with a clear message: "The future of Poland depends on how many people are mature enough to be nonconformist."

While the Poles were cherishing a new confidence and unity—vocations to the priesthood doubled—the authorities were plotting against the church. At the end of 1979, for example, they hatched the idea of building a new highway that would separate the monastery of Jasna Góra from the town of Częstochowa. The authorities were determined that the scenes of June 1979, when tens of thousands came daily to meet John Paul II, should not be repeated. The bishop of Częstochowa denounced the plan as "a sharp attack on the heart of Polish Catholicism" and alerted the whole of Poland. Within four months, the authorities had backed down.

THE CHURCHES IN THE 1980S

In August 1980, ten million Polish workers united to form the trade-union movement Solidarność. Many observers who saw banners with pictures of the Madonna and the Pope on the gates of the Gdańsk shipyard, or the workers in overalls kneeling in the open to receive Holy Communion, could make no sense of it at all. The Polish workers' revolution cannot in fact be explained exclusively in economic or even political terms, for Solidarity was in essence a spiritual revolution, a reaction in a Christian spirit to violations of human dignity and human rights. The spiritual value of truth was at the center of the protest. The Solidarity revolution was a fight against falsehood—the total untruthfulness of the Communist system. The struggling masses had the deeply rooted, if not always clearly formulated, conviction that a person is free when he bears witness to the truth. The Soviet system of enslavement is based above all on lies. The yearning for liberation through the truth had become so strong that the example of the Gdańsk shipworkers propelled the entire nation to break through the barriers of fear—which along with falsehood is the chief support of the Soviet system.

At the core of this Polish revolution was another value, expressed symbolically by the Cross: that there is meaning in suffering, even unto death, for the truth; a victorious resurrection can be achieved only through the Cross. The Cross conveyed another essential concept—that those involved in a struggle for liberation must be free of hatred and violence and ready to forgive. On countless occasions, the Polish workers refused to be provoked into bloody confrontations. The leaders of Solidarity persistently warned against violence and spoke of their readiness to forgive in response to signs of good will.

It is extraordinary that in the sixteen tense and passionate months of Solidarity's sway, no one was killed. Solidarity, if not a peace movement, was unquestionably peaceful. Its leader, Lech Wałęsa, explained how the hatred in society had been harnessed when he said, "If I did not believe in God I would become a very dangerous man."

With Solidarity, the Roman Catholic Church entered a golden age. Religion, which had been suppressed for so many years, bubbled up in joyful and spontaneous ways. Images and statues of St. Barbara, the patroness of miners, were brought back to the coal mines at the insistence of the miners. Crucifixes were raised in offices, factories, and schools. Many factories placed especially blessed religious banners in their Solidarity offices. In towns, Catholic Intellectuals' Clubs (KIKs) mushroomed.

A joint government-episcopate commission was suddenly reactivated at the insistence of the government and met for the first time since 1960 in September 1980. In short order the commission won some important concessions for the church. Religious material was no longer censored, and five Catholic journals were started up. Children in state-organized summer camps could attend Mass on Sunday, and state supervision of religious instruction—unsuccessfully promoted for years—was unofficially abolished. Permission was granted for pastoral work in prisons, reformatories, hospitals, and welfare homes. Thanks to the demands of the Gdańsk workers, Sunday Mass was broadcast over the radio.

In November 1980, Jerzy Ozdowski, a member of the Catholic parliamentary Neo-Znak group, was appointed one of the seven deputy prime ministers. The state hoped to give the impression, mostly to the West, that Catholics were no longer second-class citizens.

The Government Gathers Its Strength

While Western observers were heralding the improved relations between the Catholic Church and the atheistic state, the Polish church remained skeptical. Poles understood that the concessions were a ploy to gain time while authorities scrambled to find the best way to return to the dark pre-Solidarity days.

The government's real intentions burst out sporadically. The head of the Łódź party committee, for example, demanded that only atheists be employed as teachers and lecturers to ensure "proper ideological formation of Polish youth." In Leszno, a branch of Solidarity reported that "unknown persons" had destroyed a large amount of religious literature—some five thousand copies of children's prayer books were found in a roadside ditch.

The most important evidence came to light in the summer of 1981 when a four-page leaflet published by Solidarity in Krosno reached the West. The text, called "How to Destroy Solidarity," was based on official pronouncements at sessions of Poland's Central Committee of the Communist Party and on information disclosed to Solidarity by former high-level officials of the Party, the security organs, and the old trade unions. The leaflet contained a section on the "new" approach toward the Catholic Church as called for by, among others, the minister of religious affairs:

"Activities of the joint government-episcopate commission should be diverted to social problems such as the family, children, alcoholism. Whenever possible, attention should be directed to any positive approach by the church to the Party. . . . Distribution of books and films emphasizing the role played by the Pope in advancing peace and discreetly showing similarity between his opinions and those of Soviet representatives is a good idea. Our aims should be to calm the country through the church. . . . Give full support to Mr. Ozdowski and Catholic members of Parliament, using their official pronouncements for the good of the Party." Limited "cooperation" with the church was permissible, but real cooperation between the church and Solidarity would not be tolerated. Priests sympathetic to Solidarity should be arrested for minor traffic infractions. As a scare tactic, hooligans should be encouraged to attack priests and rectories.

"The church must not be allowed to expand its presence on radio and television; on the contrary, in time even the Sunday Mass should be stopped. Neither must expansion of catechizing be allowed, nor the return of religious orders to schools, nurseries, or hospitals. Church publications must be impeded, but it must look as though technical problems . . . are to blame for this. Every effort should be made to prevent the church from obtaining paper and presses from abroad."

1981: Death of Wyszyński, Birth of Martial Law

In 1981, Cardinal Wyszyński died, and with him an era of church-state relations. In September of that year Archbishop Józef Glemp, the newly appointed primate, celebrated Mass at the First Solidarity Congress. The church's symbolic presence was marked by a cross hung prominently next to a national emblem in the hall.

Then, on December 13, 1981, the government struck. Martial law was declared. The Solidarity union, with more than ten million members, was suspended overnight, as were all social, charitable, and religious associations. Thousands of Solidarity activists and sympathizers were detained. The church was spared any direct attack since the authorities badly needed its help to pacify the people. Some priests were picked up but shortly released; the only priest put on trial was released in the custody of his bishop.

Although all public meetings were banned, the churches could operate freely. The church was allowed to run legal advisory centers for people awaiting trial and to distribute the massive material aid from the West. The episcopate-government commission met frequently to give the impression that the church was supporting government attempts to restore political stability. Indeed, the church and especially Cardinal Glemp were praised by the Polish media for cooperating with the authorities in averting a national catastrophe—Soviet intervention.

Since December 1981, the church has been struggling to discover how best to lead the Polish people, who have been dealt an almost unbearable moral blow. The church realizes that the whole political and economic system has been rejected by the people. Independent culture flourishes: classes, lectures, and even workers' universities strive to correct the disinformation propagated by state education. There is a vast clandestine publishing network—1,350 titles produced since January 1982.

Cardinal Glemp's Difficult Role

The people of Poland still look to the church for political guidance as well as spiritual sustenance. The government, for its part, continually reminds the church of the hovering presence just across the Soviet border. The Polish Communists have gladly passed on to the church the responsibility for averting this grim solution.

Cardinal Glemp, relatively young and inexperienced compared with his predecessor, has been criticized in Poland and abroad as an appeaser. In December 1982, he was subjected to a barrage of criticism by some three hundred priests in the Warsaw diocese. He had transferred popular priests, barred the outspoken Fr. Stanisław Małkowski from preaching, and apportioned the blame for the crisis in Poland equally between the people and the authorities. Such moves could contribute to a split in the church and undermine its moral authority.

Many also complained about his lack of finesse. When the pupils' protests against the removal of crucifixes from schools (which had been placed there during Solidarity days) began in 1984, the cardinal was in Rome. When Fr. Jerzy Popiełuszko was abducted in 1984 and the whole country anxiously stood watch, Glemp was on his way to East Germany. Later, on a lengthy tour of Brazil and Argentina, the cardinal described the Solidarity movement as "a mixed bag, including opposition Marxists, Trotskyists, careerists, and party members," and said that Wałęsa had "lost control and allowed himself to be manipulated."

Even the cardinal's critics admit, however, that the social and political conditions of the 1980s are far more complex and difficult than anything faced by Cardinal Wyszyński. Primate Glemp is in a sense harvesting the fruits of Wyszyński's pastoral strategy—a society that expressly opts for a Christian and democratic nation. Since no substantial domestic change is possible without major developments on the international level, Glemp hopes to find a way to "social peace and reconciliation."

The task was given to the Social Council, a body of various experts set up in November 1981 to advise the primate. The council's first document, in April 1982, sought a compromise acceptable to both sides. It called for the reinstatement of Solidarity while accepting the limitations of Poland's international position within the Soviet bloc and the legitimacy of the Polish Communist regime. The goal—self-government—was to be achieved by "little steps."

1983: Further Moves Against the Church

In October 1983, the thirteenth ideological plenum of the Central Committee openly called for confrontation with the Catholic Church in order to overcome "hostile and alien orientations." The Party would "cooperate" with the church but only in an attempt to uphold internal peace and improve the working ethos. "Normalization" could come about only on the government's terms. Any criticism or "clerical militancy" would not be tolerated.

Moves against the church had begun some time before the plenum. There were numerous attempts to split the hierarchy and the clergy between "bad" and "good." Pressure was put on Cardinal Glemp to "pacify" the first group: about sixty people were named.

The Pope's second homecoming had been postponed from August 1982 to 1983 to give the authorities more bargaining power. In May, shortly before the Pope's arrival, twenty men in civilian clothes broke into a convent near St. Martin's Church in Warsaw and beat up voluntary workers who belonged to the Primate's Aid Committee, set up to help the families of the interned. Six people were injured; four men were driven to an outlying forest and abandoned.

The ideological war with the church has been pursued on all fronts. For the first time since the 1960s, attacks on the church have spilled over from atheistic journals into the national press. In February 1985, Warsaw Radio quoted Foreign Minister Mieczyław Rakowski as suggesting that the monopoly of the church as a moral force must be counteracted. "Ideological verification," by which people are required to sign a pledge condemning Solidarity and endorsing party policies, has also been toughened up, especially in schools and universities.

In November 1985, seventy-nine academics were purged. Jan Rem (a pseudonym used by Jerzy Urban, a government spokesman) attacked radical priests in an article. He claimed that the unpatriotic outpourings of "political agitators in soutanes" made it seem that Poles were an ignorant mass of "anachronistic fanatics." Also in 1985, the remaining crucifixes put up by pupils in classrooms were removed.

Since September 1986, the curriculum in a limited number of secondary schools has included classes on comparative religion and church-state relations. The syllabus bears a strongly atheistic bias and could more aptly be entitled "The Marxist Theory of Religion." Barring a public outcry, the course could become compulsory in Polish schools.

Attacks on Priests

The authorities have tried various methods to silence the most courageous priests. In 1982, Frs. Tadeusz Kurach and Jan Borkowski were arrested for "hooliganism," found guilty in a staged trial, and sentenced to three years' imprisonment plus two years without civic rights. A number of priests have been beaten up by "unknown assailants." In May 1984, the car of Archbishop Henryk Gulbinowicz of Wrocław, a fearless critic of the authorities and staunch supporter of Solidarity, was blown up—again by "persons unknown." Some priests, like Fr. Tomasz Aleksiewicz, have received death threats. A few have died in mysterious accidents, like Bishop Kazimierz Kluz (1982) and Fr. Honoriusz Kowalczyk (1983).

Father Kowalczyk, a Dominican chaplain in Poznań, was immensely popular with young people, active in charitable works, and closely connected with Solidarity. His typewritten *Anchor*, founded in 1970, was probably the first *samizdat* magazine in Poland. Solidarity meetings at the Poznań chaplaincy continued even after the union was outlawed. A TV camera was installed outside the chaplaincy to frighten people away. Only a few days before his fatal car accident, Father Kowalczyk was warned of what might happen if he did not sever his links with Solidarity and tone down his sermons.

Fr. Tadeusz Zaleski is particularly vulnerable. A promising poet in delicate health, he helped organize a branch of the French L'Arche movement, a community for the handicapped. He was closely linked with workers' Christian associations, and with aid to the families of the victims of martial law. The church tried to send him to Rome, ostensibly to pursue further studies, but he was refused a passport because of "vital national interests."

Early in 1985, "unknown assailants" hurled a stone through the front windshield of the car in which he and a pro-Solidarity priest were traveling. In April of that year, Father Zaleski suffered second-degree burns when unidentified men poured a chemical substance over his face and body, set his anorak on fire, and left him unconscious. In December, he was again attacked; this time he was beaten up and a wire was tied around his neck. It is commonly believed that these assaults were intended to stop Father Zaleski from collecting evidence on various fatal "accidents" suffered by Solidarity activists in which the secret police are suspected of having a hand.

A number of other priests have had similar experiences, but except in the case of Fr. Jerzy Popiełuszko, the authorities have not felt compelled to investigate or to put the guilty on trial.

Father Popiełuszko was neither learned nor endowed with a dynamic personality, but he evoked a special kind of love and loyalty. He was a courageous priest who imparted the message of peace and truth to his dedicated flock. In 1984, at the age of thirty-seven, he was killed in a vicious planned attack by the security police. The execution was virtually public. The shocked outrage in Poland and abroad forced the authorities to pass severe sentences on three security men found guilty of his murder. Physical assaults on other priests nevertheless continue.

Social Problems

Many Poles are physically and psychologically exhausted. Their everyday problems would daunt most Westerners. Food prices are exorbitant: in 1985 pensioners and families with several children had to spend 60 per cent of their income on food. Most basic drugs are in short supply, and medical care is deteriorating. Illnesses long forgotten in the West, like tuberculosis, have returned, and life expectancy has fallen. More than half a million Poles, mostly young professional couples, have emigrated. The church is trying to discourage the exodus. The government has appeared to support emigration and since 1983 has steadily liberalized passport and travel regulations, but it too now seems concerned about brain drain.

In 1987, after six years of negotiation with the state, the church finally won approval for a scaled-down version of a project it initiated in 1981 to stimulate private-sector agriculture. The original proposal had included a pledge of $28 million to the church's agricultural fund by Western churches and governments. The authorities stifled the plan because it would have strengthened individual farmers—one of the few economically independent groups—and further increased the prestige of the church. The scaled-down version will be funded by a $10 million appropriation by the U.S. government. Whether it will be allowed to become self-perpetuating or will end after the current funds are used up remains to be seen.

In Eastern Europe, only Hungary has an alcoholic problem comparable to Poland's. About 10 per cent of young Poles are showing various signs of demoralization: delinquency, drinking, drug use. Corruption and disregard for honest work are widespread.

The previously high rate of abortion has been dramatically reduced, thanks to a massive church effort. But the church campaign incurred the severe displeasure of the government.

Hope for the Future

Yet hopeful signs proliferate. For all the criticism leveled at Cardinal Glemp, the church has made no deal with the regime at the expense of the people. Although the church has all but abandoned its fight for Solidarity as an organization, it still struggles for trade-union pluralism and other rights. Janusz Onyszkiewicz, Solidarity's official spokesman in 1980-81, aptly summarized the situation: "Today the church fights issues: the plight of political prisoners, the need to modify repressive laws, and the need of the people to participate in the government."

Since 1987 the Polish authorities have displayed a new resolve to normalize relations between church and state and between the state and the Vatican. Such a gesture would further enhance the prestige of "liberal" General Wojciech Jaruzelski and prove that *glasnost* thrives also in Poland. Hardly a month passes without a meeting between at least two of the three parties involved: the Vatican, the Polish church, and the Polish government. No doubt the government would have liked to finalize a church-state-Vatican agreement before October 1988, the tenth anniversary of the Polish Pope, but this did not happen. As much as the church would have liked to present the Pope with this anniversary gift, it has made absolutely plain the fact that it will not agree to anything less than full legalization of its status.

In a new law effective September 1988, the Polish government made an important concession to the political opposition by creating the Warsaw Pact's first alternative to military service for conscientious objectors. The law requires objectors to perform three years of community service in lieu of the two-year military term.

Other welcome developments in mid-1988 were an amnesty for conscientious objectors, in which dozens were released from prison, and a revision of the military oath, excluding a reference to the "brotherly alliance with the Soviet Army" and replacing a pledge of loyalty to the Communist government with a promise to serve "the nation and homeland."

The Light-Life movement is growing in strength and transforming parishes; in 1985, 60,000 young people joined in Oasis summer retreats. Children and young people defended crucifixes in their schools against the authorities' attempts to remove them.

The Christian maturity of young Poles was especially noticeable during the Pope's second homecoming. Many Western observers reported that large groups of youngsters marching to meetings with John Paul II shouted at fully armed ZOMO riot police—"Throw away your batons and come with us; we forgive you!" The spirit matches the growing nonconformism. In the "ideological verification" pursued throughout 1985, many preferred to lose their jobs rather than renounce their ideals.

The number of people going on pilgrimages is also increasing. Most famous is the annual pilgrimage to Częstochowa, when thousands of pilgrims (51,000 in 1981) leave Warsaw on August 6 to walk 150 miles in just over a week. They stop at night in villages and sleep in barns, tents, or sleeping bags. En route their ranks are swollen so that some 300,000 to 400,000 arrive at the shrine on August 14, ready to join in the celebration of the Assumption of the Blessed Virgin Mary the next day. In 1985, 600 pilgrims from the north walked nearly 400 miles to reach Częstochowa.

While the authorities were jockeying with the church, a new theology of inner freedom was taking root in Poland. Between February 1982 and September 1984, thousands of people from all over the country came to the church of St. Stanisław Kostka in Warsaw on the last Sunday of every month to attend a Mass offered for Poland. During Mass they would listen to a young priest, Fr. Jerzy Popiełuszko, urging them—as Pope John Paul II had done during his visits to Poland—to meet violence with nonviolence, evil with good, hatred with love, and to build the solidarity of hearts.

Today, even more pilgrims come to Popiełuszko's grave at St. Stanisław Kostka, which has become one of the most popular national shrines.

Poles talk of St. Stanisław's church as a fragment of a "truly free Poland." More people than ever attend the two Masses offered for the country on the nineteenth of every month—the day Father Popiełuszko was kidnapped. He has given the Poles and the world an example of the final sacrifice that those who truly believe in the value of Christian civilization must be prepared to make.

9

Romania

I N MANY WAYS, Romania is an enigma; ambiguities and contradictions abound. The people—dark-complexioned, charming, emotional—regard themselves as the descendants of Roman colonists who intermarried with local tribes, Dacians and Getae, and they speak a predominantly Romance language. Although their country is a Latin island in a Slavic sea, their national church is Orthodox.

Almost half of Romania's 23 million people are peasants for whom religion is an integral part of daily life. Orthodox parish churches are crowded on Sundays and rarely empty during the week. People of all ages and classes drop into church to venerate an icon or to engage in a few moments of reflection—for many the church building is their second home. In several respects Romania is Orthodoxy's Poland, although evangelical Protestant churches too are packed with enthusiastic worshippers.

The flourishing state of religion owes nothing to President Nicolae Ceauşescu, who has played a gigantic confidence trick on Westerners for years. The impression of religious liberty has been indispensable to persuading Western governments that his country is independent of Moscow along liberal lines; it has, for example, since 1975 won for Romania Most Favored Nation (MFN) trade status (which it renounced in 1988) from the United States.

The visible piety of the people makes it difficult for Western visitors to believe that church institutions (and all others) are rigidly controlled by the state. Some Western leaders, however, have stopped accepting the glib assurances of Romanian church spokesmen that there is no religious persecution. When the American ambassador to Bucharest, David Funderburk, resigned in 1985, he reported an economy—in a fertile land that was once the breadbasket of Europe—brought to almost total collapse, with the people on the brink of starvation. Romanians now have the lowest living standard in the Soviet bloc.

Ceauşescu—party chief, head of state, commander-in-chief of the army, chairman of the Economic Council, head of the Security Services, chairman

199

of the Political Academy—is the most hated ruler in Eastern Europe. When he took charge in 1965, he inherited a country emerging from years of brutal tyranny. Although he permitted some relaxation, the Securitate (secret police) still employ various methods to terrorize their victims, and repression in general is more savage than anywhere else in the Soviet bloc.

Ceauşescu appeared to move toward some independence from the Soviet Union in order to foster national pride and support at home and to attract Western credit abroad. In doing so, he was following the policy of his predecessor, Gheorghe Gheorghiu-Dej. When Romania signed a trade agreement with the United States in 1964, the government declared its right to conduct its affairs free from Soviet interference and adopted a new constitution. The MFN status it received has had an impact on the fate of individual Christians and on the nation as a whole.

Ceauşescu's charade succeeded. Because he did not take part in the invasion of Czechoslovakia and has never allowed Warsaw Pact maneuvers on Romanian soil, Western governments believed he was a liberal who dared to stray from the Soviet line. Several facts were overlooked: according to some sources, he retracted his condemnation of the invasion of Czechoslovakia within forty-eight hours after a sharp reproof from the Soviets; Soviet chiefs of staff have regularly taken part in Romanian maneuvers, and Romanian high officers regularly take part in Warsaw Pact maneuvers on other Soviet allies' soil; and since Romania is peripheral to Warsaw Pact strategy, Ceauşescu's stance has never greatly worried the Soviet Union. He also has condemned Solidarity, backed the Soviet invasion of Afghanistan (though he criticized it in some speeches), and runs the most Stalinist regime in the Eastern Bloc.

The Short-Lived SLOMR and ALRC

Ceauşescu's economic policy, fruitful at first, soon turned to disaster. Much of the foreign aid was squandered on the huge Securitate, the party *nomenklatura* and top hierarchy, and, first and foremost, Ceauşescu's thirty-eight relatives, who occupy most of the high government posts. Widespread strikes in the coal mines in 1977 were brutally suppressed—some mine leaders even died from their "treatment" in psychiatric hospitals.

A free trade-union movement, SLOMR, founded in March 1978—some time before Poland's Solidarity—was ruthlessly crushed; Romanians were far too cowed by years of repression to respond as the Poles later did. The population is divided in that there are large national minorities of probably 1.7 million Hungarians and about 350,000 Germans. Because the churches were also divided—by nationality as well as denomination, but mostly by the state's divisive manipulation—they were unable to lead the opposition.

ALRC, a religious-rights movement also founded in 1978, was also speedily dismantled by the state.

In 1980–81 the names of between forty and fifty Christian prisoners were disclosed. Many were merely hostages, for almost all were released after pressure by U.S. congressmen. Ceauşescu's apparent leniency was clearly timed to fake an acceptable human-rights record and preserve Romania's MFN status. Year after year, until he renounced MFN status in 1988 in order not to be subject to the emigration requirements attached to it, he found it useful to keep several important figures on hand to whom he granted amnesty in the summer when the annual MFN status review occurred. For a month or so prior to that, Romania used to relax pressure on the more active Christians; then it was back to business as usual.

Some informed Westerners—many of them Christians aware of the plight of their co-religionists—had long wished to stop subsidizing Ceauşescu. Those who argued that this would drive Romania back into the arms of the Soviets overlooked the fact that today Romania is more dependent than ever on Soviet oil. While the Soviet leadership may have been uneasy at Ceauşescu's posturing in the past, it has known all along it can call him to heel. There is little need for Soviet intervention; the Soviets are already in Romania and in control of much that goes on. Thousands of Romanians work on the Siberian gas pipeline, and Romania regularly transfers technology obtained from the West to the Soviet Union.

Certainly the plight of the ordinary Romanian could hardly become worse. During most of the 1980s, enforced austerity has drastically reduced food and medical supplies and sharply limited energy consumption. Reportedly, thousands die each year from hypothermia in the winter and diseases related to malnutrition all year round.

THE CHURCHES TO 1948

Romania's varied church life is rooted in its past. The original Dacians and Getae, conquered by Rome in the second century, intermarried with the Roman soldiers. Thus Christianity probably first reached the Romanians' land from Rome, as did their language. The Romanians became essentially Orthodox through Byzantine, Bulgarian, and Greek dominance from the ninth to the eleventh centuries. A bulwark of Christendom against successive waves of barbarians from the East, Romanians later fell prey to the Ottoman, Austro-Hungarian, and Russian empires.

Orthodoxy was thoroughly integrated into Romanian life; it kept the heart of the nation alive under Turkish rule, although it could not escape the accompanying corruption. Unlike other Balkan peoples, the Romanian principalities of Moldavia and Wallachia, though Turkish vassal states, retained considerable independence, and there was no need to convert to Islam to escape second-class citzenship. Today, despite Communist harassment, the Romanian Orthodox Church is one of the largest—15.5 million members—and most active in the world.

1859–1918: United Principalities and Independence

In 1859 the two principalities Wallachia and Moldavia joined to become a state, almost entirely Orthodox in religion. And in 1877, under the leadership of Catholic-born Charles of Hohenzollern, Romania became an independent state.

The third major region of modern Romania, Transylvania,which joined the state in 1918, is far more complex religiously than Wallachia and Moldavia. First occupied by Romanians, with its rich soil it attracted large numbers of Hungarian settlers during the Middle Ages. From the twelfth century on, the Hungarian kings installed rulers in Transylvania from what is now Germany to help defend them against the Turks, and Transylvania became a dependency of Hungary. The Hungarians were Catholic, as were the Germans, but substantial numbers later joined the Lutheran, Reformed, and Unitarian churches.

When Austria liberated Transylvania from the Turks in the late seventeenth century, Leopold II wanted to reestablish Catholicism, but by then Protestantism was too deeply entrenched among the Hungarians and Germans. Turning to the Romanian peasantry of Transylvania, whose Orthodox faith had long been threatened by Protestants, he offered them equal rights, their own services, and recognition of their traditional custom of a married priesthood if they would acknowledge papal supremacy and adopt the *filioque* clause in the Nicene Creed. (The *filioque*—"and from the son"—clause, describing the procession of the Holy Spirit from God the Father and from the Son, is a principal point of division between Catholics and Orthodox.) This was much more palatable than an alien Calvinism, and in 1698 the Romanian Eastern Rite Catholic Church came into being.

Most of the Orthodox, about 200,000, joined the new church; they had little alternative (though most reverted to Orthodoxy in the ensuing years). The seminarians who went to study in Rome came to realize how much their language and culture owed to the ancient Latin heritage. The result was not a Romanized church but a Romanian church that helped bring about the rebirth of national consciousness. Orthodox and Catholic, united in the struggle for independence, had almost identical services in Romanian. The Eastern Rite Church became thoroughly integrated into national life and did pioneering work in education and culture.

1918: Birth of Today's Romania

In 1918, Transylvania seceded from the Austro-Hungarian Empire and joined with the independent state of Romania, a kingdom after 1881, to create modern Romania. With Transylvania came a significant number of non-Romanian Catholics and Protestants.

Between the world wars, the *Orthodox Church,* autocephalous since 1885, enjoyed a privileged position as Romania's national church, with about 85 per cent of the population. Its bishops had considerable social and political influence, as did the parish clergy in local affairs, and there was little conflict between the church and the organs of secular government. Although officially the state had the final say in appointments, in practice the church was unhampered.

The *Latin Rite Catholic Church* was divided by language and nationality: 75 per cent Hungarian, 21 per cent German, and only a tiny minority Romanian. The various groups had little contact and little in common, a factor skillfully exploited by the Communists after 1948. They numbered about 1.2 million in 683 parishes.

The *Eastern Rite Catholic Church* (1.5 million) was stronger, more compact (concentrated in Transylvania), and homogeneous (completely Romanian). Romanians generally held the Eastern Rite Church second only to the Orthodox Church—mixed marriages were normal. The harmony exists today at the grassroots level, despite Communist interference and despite the 1948 betrayal of the Eastern Rite Catholics by the Orthodox hierarchy.

Both Catholic churches had a large number of monks and nuns, most of whom, apart from their charitable works, staffed the many religious schools. All the churches had flourishing presses.

Growth of Evangelical Movements

Meanwhile, the Hungarian and German Protestant churches of Transylvania, finding themselves in a "foreign" state, became even more closely linked with their own national cultures. With the arrival of missions from abroad, new forms of Protestantism gained a foothold. An increasing number of Romanians became attracted to more evangelical forms of worship, and two interesting developments emerged.

First, Pentecostalists, Adventists, and particularly Baptists began to flourish. The Baptists grew from a few hundred in the early twentieth century to 58,000 by 1935. Probably because they attracted many ethnic Romanians, they underwent periods of persecution when all their churches were closed. The year after the arrival of the Communists in 1947, most evangelical Protestant churches received legal status.

The other development was an evangelical revival movement within the Orthodox Church, known as the Lord's Army. It grew in the 1920s and 1930s around Iosif Trifa, an Orthodox priest from Transylvania, although it was essentially a lay-centered movement to counter the inroads being made by the evangelical Protestants. These "soldiers of Christ" promoted Bible study, gave stirring sermons, and evangelized actively. In the heyday of the Lord's Army, the mid-1930s through the 1940s, more than 300,000 Orthodox, including priests and religious, took part in its varied activities.

Not surprisingly, the movement ran into trouble with the Orthodox hierarchy, most of whom looked askance at its "Protestant" practices. Although Trifa was defrocked in 1935, he and most of the Lord's Army remained faithful to their mother church and provided it with a reservoir of enthusiasm. (Another group did break away from the mother church and, amalgamating with Brethren groups, became today's Brethren movement in Romania.)

During much of the inter-war period, Romania was badly governed, and it was easy prey for Hitler. When the Nazis occupied the country, northern Bukovina and Bessarabia, which Romania had acquired after World War I, were ceded to the Soviet Union, then Hitler's ally, while Hungary took over part of Transylvania, which still had a large minority of settlers of Hungarian descent. At the end of the war Romania regained Transylvania. Larger than Hungary in area, it remains a bone of contention between Hungary and Romania, but since both governments are part of the Soviet bloc, open hostilities are impossible.

THE CHURCHES 1948–80

After two years of maneuvering in a coalition government, the Communist Party, aided by the Soviet Union, came to power in late 1947. The Communists took over a deeply religious but backward country: 23 per cent of the population was illiterate.

At first there was coexistence between church and state, though the state wielded strict control. As a precondition to legal recognition, the state demanded a charter from all religious bodies. Fourteen were recognized, including Jews and Muslims, but not those that refused to accept the government's terms—the Catholic Church, the Lord's Army, and some small Protestant and Orthodox groups.

The state revoked the 1927 Concordat with the Vatican and tried, unsuccessfully, to force the Catholic Church to break with Rome, a precondition for recognition. At present, though the church lacks the legal status of the other "cults," it is protected because of its large numbers of Hungarian and German members, whose governments the Communists are afraid of antagonizing.

Romanian law, promulgated in 1948 and reaffirmed in the new constitution of 1965, guarantees freedom of conscience and religious belief. But that freedom has always been interpreted in a unique way, best summed up by a statement of Ceauşescu in 1979: "Religious freedom is for those cults recognized by the law, but the cults have to respect the laws of the country and help build a socialist state. Romanians cannot close their eyes to any infringement of the law under the pretext of Christianity." State recognition of a religious body may be withdrawn for what the state considers "good and sufficient reasons."

The law has also decreed that "assemblies other than for worship . . . may be convened only with the approval of the authorities," a measure that has been used to prevent, for instance, the convocation of Baptist central congresses. Pastoral letters and other church circulars are censored. All church budgets are subject to state control, which has led to much falsification. Religious instruction in schools is forbidden, and the only religious schools allowed are those that train the clergy. Overall, Romanian religious legislation reflects that of the Soviet Union.

The Attempt to Destroy Two Churches

Two major churches, the Eastern Rite Catholic and the Lord's Army, have officially ceased to exist. This means that in a country claiming religious freedom, 10 per cent of the people belong to churches that have been banned. Both churches were Byzantine in ritual and Romanian in membership; one was suspect for its allegiance to Rome, and the other posed a threat to the complete state control of the national Orthodox Church. Their betrayal, the vicious persecution suffered by thousands of their members in prison, and their resilience have earned them the respect of other Romanians.

1. The *Eastern Rite Catholic Church.* Stalin ultimately sealed the fate of the Eastern Rite Catholic Church, as he had its Ukrainian counterpart in the USSR. He insisted that Romania emphasize its Slavic origins at the expense of its Latin elements. In February 1948, the Romanian Communist Party chief obediently declared that the sole obstacle to democracy in Romania was the imperialist Catholic Church.

Tragically, the suppression of the Romanian church—as in the case of the Ukrainian church—required the complicity of the Orthodox hierarchy, and the new patriarch Justinian complied. He argued that Eastern Rite Catholics were the victims of a forced conversion and should be reintegrated with the mother church. Justinian set a precedent of compromise that damaged the credibility of the Orthodox hierarchy among the people.

Stalin's policy—as in the Ukraine—was doomed to failure. On October 1, 1948, despite threats, deceit, torture, and blackmail, only 430 out of 1,800 Eastern Rite priests were represented by the symbolic thirty-eight delegates (the same number that had signed the original Act of Union with Rome) at a completely invalid synod held in Cluj. The delegates were literally held underground, and several later recanted. On October 3, the Latin Rite bishops, whose church was also under attack, joined their colleagues in protest: "Three million citizens are being treated as if they were enemies of the people." Later that month, the patriarch and all the Orthodox bishops met in Alba Iulia and signed a "synodical declaration" confirming the end of the union with Rome.

A church with 1.5 million members had officially ceased to exist. At the time, there were five dioceses, about 2,500 church buildings, 1,800 parishes, and numerous seminaries, religious houses, schools, and charitable institutions. All six bishops were arrested, and about 600 of the church's 1,800 priests as well as many members were thrown into prison. Half of the priests and five of the bishops died. Some courageous Orthodox priests who spoke out against the "reunion" were also imprisoned.

Resistance to the takeover was almost universal, but tyranny overcame the resistance. More than a thousand married priests joined the Orthodox Church rather than see their families starve. The more resolute parishioners faced a similar threat. Soon most Eastern Rite Catholics were attending the same churches, many with the same priests—but now officially Orthodox. They conformed on the tacit understanding that, if given the chance, they would revert to Rome.

Meanwhile, the papal envoy in Bucharest, Archbishop Gerald O'Hara, tried to ensure that there would be bishops for both branches of the Catholic Church, even if forced underground. He secretly consecrated an ample supply and drew up lists of possible replacements should any be imprisoned—as they all were. O'Hara was expelled in 1950 as a *persona non grata*.

The Latin Rite Catholic Church was allowed to exist, but it was in effect cut off from Rome. About two hundred of its priests were imprisoned, and all its bishops were tried and condemned in 1951. Fr. Petru Mareş said that his bishop, Anton Durcovici, was thrown naked into a crowded cell. No one recognized him until he said, "Sorry, brothers, I'm your bishop." He was removed, dying of starvation, and never seen again. A priest passing along a prison corridor heard the words "Antonius moribundus" from a cell and, through the locked door, spoke the words of the Last Rites.

2. The *Lord's Army*. In 1947 the Lord's Army asked the government to recognize it as part of the Orthodox Church or, failing that, as an independent denomination. In reply, a full-scale attack was launched against it in

1948, with the apparent approval of the Orthodox hierarchy. It went underground, and its leaders were arrested and freed in 1952. Then in 1958 five hundred prominent members were reimprisoned; many were not released until 1964. The Lord's Army continued to meet despite the danger. After 1965, members caught worshiping were fined rather than imprisoned.

Romania's Dreaded Prisons

To suppress the churches, the Communists unleashed a reign of terror and sentenced thousands of innocent Christians of all denominations to camps and prisons. That these are probably the worst in Eastern Europe is attested to by Lutheran pastor Richard Wurmbrand—who horrified the West with his disclosures after his amnesty and exile in 1965—and many others, Orthodox, Catholics, Lord's Army, traditional Protestants, and evangelicals. An Orthodox group has an incomplete list of the clergy—seventeen metropolitans and bishops and sixty-four priests—who have died in prisons, in camps, or in exile. Four thousand clergy passed through the prisons and camps. Members of families lost contact for years, often forever.

Every Romanian knows about Piteşti, the Romanian prison selected by the Soviet Union for the ultimate in dehumanizing experiments under Communism. Between 1948 and 1952 a thousand teenagers, the elite of their generation, were so terribly brainwashed that only two did not break. Three committed suicide; the rest became robots, ready to torture others mercilessly.

A young medical student named Gheorghe Calciu-Dumitreasa regained his willpower and vowed to become a priest should God bring about his release. Twelve years later, in 1963, he was freed, and he did become a priest. We shall hear much more of Father Calciu and his subsequent fearless criticism of the regime.

For most Romanians, however, the reign of terror left them ready to comply with unsatisfactory religious arrangements. They themselves are only too aware that courage is not a Romanian characteristic. They prefer to be docile and submissive and avoid trouble. "After so many years of physical and moral maltreatment," wrote an Eastern Rite Catholic priest, "fear has become an integral part of our nature." Calciu estimates that two million people have been imprisoned under Communism, and over 200,000 executed.

The Orthodox Church Under Persecution

Ten years after the Orthodox hierarchy betrayed the Eastern Rite Catholic Church and the Lord's Army, the Orthodox Church was itself facing a hostile government, by now deeply influenced by the Soviet Union.

Between 1958 and 1963, about 500 priests, monks, and laypersons were arrested.

The persecution was mainly directed against the monasteries. At the time of the Communist takeover, there were about 10,000 religious, and monasticism was flourishing, providing a reservoir of spiritual vitality for the whole church.

Under government orders, the church removed all but the elderly from the monasteries. Justin Moeiscu, later (in 1979) to become patriarch, was made responsible for implementing measures that reduced the number of monasteries from 200 to just above 100 and the number of religious from 7,000 to 2,000. Many religious were put in prison, many others into psychiatric hospitals, where at least two nuns are known to have died under drug treatment. Fr. Dumitru Zamiznicu, who with others had tried to maintain the monastic life in secret and was condemned to a psychiatric hospital (he died in 1974), reported that the state was obstinate in believing that the monasteries were hives of political opposition.

The Orthodox Church: Patriarch Justinian

When they took power, the Communists lacked the popular support that only the Orthodox Church could provide. The church was autocephalous and had no foreign ties. It had produced in Justinian an outstanding leader and organizer, a man whose poor origins gave him genuine socialist convictions. He believed in the new order and wished to help reconstruct his impoverished nation. He is said to have sheltered Romania's new leader, Gheorghiu-Dej, when the latter was on the run from police in the pre-war days.

Aided by Gheorghiu-Dej, Justinian's career rocketed up with unseemly haste. In 1947, then a village priest, he was promoted to metropolitan. Early the following year Patriarch Nicodemus died, and Justinian became patriarch. He had an unlikely ally in Petru Groza, a leading Communist who was a lay member of the Orthodox Synod and remained a Christian until his death in 1958.

At first Justinian wrote enthusiastically about socialism and Christianity. But somewhere in the mid-1950s, foreseeing the persecution of his own church, he changed and tried to do all in his power to defend it. As Fr. Gheorghe Calciu put it, his predicament was that of a Romanian Thomas à Becket. He remains a controversial figure. His admirers point to the continuing strength of the Orthodox Church compared to the fate that befell the Russian Orthodox Church after the 1917 Revolution. Later Justinian (in contrast to his successor, Justin) prevented Ceauşescu from closing any churches. The Orthodox Church is still virtually an established church; its commitment to nationalism is irrefutable. Its belief that it is the spiritual and moral soul of the nation causes some resentment among other Christians.

At his death in 1977, Justinian left 10,000 parishes adequately staffed and two or three applicants for each place at the seminary. He had improved the educational standards of the clergy far beyond the average in Orthodox countries. He was especially concerned that priest and parish should become more collectively involved in social work, despite the government's restrictions on such activity.

The prestige of the church abroad was ensured by the high quality of the church's theological scholarship, and enhanced when it became a member of the World Council of Churches in 1962. Romania, with a people of Latin origin and Slav forms of worship, forms a vital link between Western and Eastern spirituality. From the state's point of view, the church served as a good propaganda outlet through its membership in the world body and its other contacts abroad.

There is a darker side of the picture. Justinian was the epitome of the enigmatic and complex Romanian character, with its astonishing—and to outsiders, infuriating—capacity to ignore, even to transcend, contradictions, a characteristic typical of the church today. He was not, in the end, able to prevent the persecution of his own church between 1958 and 1963. Many Orthodox believers say that he led the church into a fatal subservience to the state and that he betrayed hundreds of thousands of his fellow Christians, some to unimaginable suffering and death. Such a man, they maintain, could hardly prevent the cancer of corruption that pervades the nation's life from spreading throughout the institutions of the church.

It would be misleading, however, to single out the Orthodox Church for such criticism. Every other recognized church and almost all Romanians compromise and live a "double life" in order to survive.

Mid-Sixties and Early Seventies: A Lull

A general amnesty in 1964 brought the release of 12,000 "political" prisoners who had survived up to eighteen years of imprisonment, including many leaders from the various churches. Imprisonment continued but fell sharply, and church life became more normal—if the Romanian situation can ever be described as normal. Some Orthodox religious were able to return to monastic life. But the seeds of unrest were germinating.

The general movement toward human rights in Eastern Europe reached Romania toward the end of the 1970s, along with a growing unease within certain churches—particularly the evangelical Protestant churches—at the subservience of their leaders. These churches had gained legal status in 1948, but the Department of Cults put them in a false position regarding freedom and evangelization. When the reaction set in, it hit the Baptist congregations particularly hard.

The Baptist Church

The Baptist Union was formed in 1920. In 1951 a statute regulating its activities was agreed upon, and in 1954 the state began to interfere. The government presented church president Ioan Dan with restrictive regulations that he refused to sign. The government immediately forced upon reluctant church leaders the "election" of a new president and other new church officials.

The new leaders circulated the regulations Dan had refused to sign. More rules followed, further stifling the life of the church. In 1959 there were 540 active pastors; five years later, 400 had lost their licenses for failure to comply with the new rules. In the early 1960s, under government pressure, the Baptist Union closed 300 "redundant" churches.

In the 1960s, a new generation of Baptist leaders was emerging, well educated and impatient of restrictions, such as the gifted pastor and preacher Iosif Ţon. Between 1969 and 1972, Ţon was granted the rare concession of studying in Oxford, perhaps in the hope that further exposure to modernist theology would undermine his faith, as it had once done. Whatever the reason, it was a mistake. On his return, Ţon fearlessly exposed the state's method of controlling his church, "a major deviation from Baptist doctrine." He was the first Romanian to articulate the case for internal freedom in church life. Ţon also questioned whether atheism was necessary to socialism. Communism's goal—the new man, unselfish and incorrupt—was, he said, to be found in the committed Christian.

Ţon's writings expressed the dilemma of the confessing Christian in an atheistic state with a significance that went beyond his own denomination or country. In Romania his writings had a profound effect. They infuriated the Baptist leadership because Ţon implicitly accused them of betraying Baptist principles. But they inspired the younger pastors, who saw they must dare more, demand more, and live their faith more fully.

Growth of Religious Dissent

By the early 1970s, a revival had begun in the Baptist and other evangelical Protestant churches, spurred on by Ţon's views. The Baptist Union—which was now completely Romanian in character—was growing at an annual rate of 13 per cent. It drew most of its converts from the Orthodox Church, many of whose members were disillusioned with their hierarchy. Leading Baptist evangelists were prepared to take risks for their faith. The persecution they suffered as a result only helped to unite them.

In February 1977, a remarkable Baptist Congress was held. The 2,000 Romanian Baptists who attended engaged in frank discussion, forcing the older, cowed leadership on the defensive. Among matters discussed was the fining of Baptists under the same article of the criminal code as vandals and anarchists. The new Baptist leadership was still too divided to stand up to the government. Never before, however, had a church dared speak so openly in Communist Romania, and the other churches were emboldened by the example.

Also in 1977, a secular human-rights group led by the writer Paul Goma issued a Romanian version of the Czechoslovak Charter 77. And following the Baptist Congress, two important documents were circulated by a small group of evangelical Protestants. They exposed the discrimination against evangelicals and called on believers to cast off fear and to trust utterly in God's care. (See appendix N.)

In March 1977 a catastrophic earthquake shook the nation. Among the many victims were church leaders and some of the staff and students of the Orthodox and Baptist seminaries in Bucharest. Many Romanians felt it was a divine judgment. Thousands of lapsed Orthodox returned to their faith, while new faces appeared in the crammed evangelical churches.

In April, rights activist Goma and five of the protesting evangelicals, Ton included, were arrested. Since large numbers of foreign journalists were in the country following the earthquake, Goma and other secular dissidents were allowed to emigrate. The evangelicals were also released, but—in a subtle move—they were handed over to the Baptist Union's Central Council for punishment.

1978: SLOMR and ALRC

General unrest continued in 1978. In March 1978 SLOMR, a free trade union, was formed. Ton's younger friends, too, felt that believers should promote human rights, and a religious-rights group called ALRC sprang up, founded by nine Baptists. In July 1978, twenty-five Baptists, one Pentecostalist, and an Orthodox economist issued demands that included legal recognition of the Lord's Army and the Catholic Church and the reestablishment of the Eastern Rite Catholic Church. They also called for an end to interference in church matters by the Department of Cults. They charged that state intimidation had created a deep gulf between Christians and the state: "Our ideal is a free church in a free state that would allow dialogue and co-operation between the two."

ALRC became a focus for the grievances of all the churches, with a wider ecumenical basis than any other East European human-rights movement. Protests began to pour out from other denominations, though few were signed, an indication of the still prevalent terror. The similarity of the complaints among the various churches only increased their credibility. (A comprehensive list of the churches' needs compiled by the ALRC appears in appendix O.)

Some protests were hard-hitting indeed. Certain Romanian Christians, having felt Communism's attempts to crush man's spirit and faith, see relations between church and state as a battle between good and evil, God and the Devil. In their suffering, they have experienced a deepening and purifying of their faith: compromisers get short shrift.

ALRC began providing documentation on abuses. Pavel Nicolescu, a friend of Țon, became a spokesman. Although it disclaimed political or economic aims, ALRC was threatening Ceaușescu's reputation as a "liberal." The group began to attract some Orthodox, who revealed abuses in their own church. Orthodox priests who tried to "snatch a little spiritual oxygen from the grasp of the totalitarian regime," as ALRC put it, were punished not only by the government but also by patriarchate officials and their bishops. Fr. Ștefan Gavrilă, because of his pastoral success, particularly with young people, was suspended for three years and reinstated only after his case was broadcast on Radio Free Europe. Later he was defrocked and spent time in a "psychiatric" hospital. (As of 1986, he and his family had been refused permission to emigrate and reduced to near starvation; the authorities were threatening to take away his eight children, two of whom had nearly been killed in "accidents.")

The Case of Father Calciu

Father Gheorghe Calciu, a member of the Lord's Army, emerged as a man with the integrity, courage, and spiritual stature to renew the Orthodox Church; the whole basis of its relationship with the state was challenged. Father Calciu was also closely connected with SLOMR and was concerned about all persecuted Christians, whatever their denomination or nationality.

Calciu had come out of prison in 1963 after sixteen years, having withstood the horrors of Pitești. A committed Christian, he was a living reproach to the regime. He was ordained a priest and in 1973 was appointed profesor of New Testament theology in the Bucharest seminary. He became the spiritual father of the seminarians, inspiring them with their church's history and the highest ideals of the priesthood.

Inevitably he clashed with the head of the seminary and alienated the authorities. Preaching in the patriarchal cathedral, he condemned atheism as "a philosophy of despair" and taught that there was only one subject for sermons—Jesus Christ. An 84-year-old priest who shared these views wrote to Ceauşescu and the party Central Committee in 1979 requesting the reinstatement of religious instruction in schools. He was sentenced to six years in prison, where he died of ill treatment.

During Lent 1978, Calciu preached seven sermons specifically addressed to the young that drew an unusually large number of people, up to five hundred, including students and non-Christians. When the seminarians were locked in their rooms to keep them from attending, they climbed out of the windows.

These sermons were a high point in the history of preaching Christianity under Communism. Copies were secretly circulated throughout Romania. Calciu urged his hearers to turn to Christ and to adopt religious ethics based on the uniqueness of each person in place of Communism's ethical relativism that repudiates the value of the individual. Calciu's bold preaching was living testimony of the ultimate powerlessness of evil.

Calciu finally overstepped when he denounced the deliberate destruction of historic churches, personally ordered by Elena Ceauşescu, the president's wife and a dangerous and vindictive woman. At first he was only transferred from his seminary post, but the Securitate net was closing round him. In March 1979 he was arrested; after being tortured and suffering appalling treatment, he was given a ten-year sentence in closed court. A fellow Romanian said that his real crime was articulating what the majority of Christians and Romanians thought but dared not say. "Plain speaking," he said, "is not the Romanian way. With notable exceptions, we are not a heroic people; we carry an internal cross."

The Orthodox bishops and senior clergy forfeited what little credibility they had left in the Calciu case. Not only did they fail to speak on Calciu's behalf, but some even repeated the government's slanders. Had Calciu recanted and asked Ceauşescu's pardon, he would have been freed—and would thereby have denied all that he was.

Suppression of ALRC

The government did not rest; it stifled what was left of the human-rights movement. Two leaders of SLOMR who were friends of Calciu, Ionel Cană and Gheorghe Braşoveanu, were given long sentences. During 1979 ALRC lost almost all its original membership, including the indefatigable spokesman Pavel Nicolescu, as a result of the government's physical and psychological terror campaign. Some were imprisoned, some "treated" on an "outpatient" basis—beaten regularly, given truth drugs, threatened with death. This method, the stock-in-trade of the Securitate, rarely fails. Ioan Teodosiu, an ALRC member, told how his eyes were kept forcibly open during a sixty-hour interrogation in which he had to remain standing, with no food or water; he went temporarily insane. After release, harassment continues to such an extent that the victims have little choice but to beg to emigrate.

Although Iosif Ţon and Aurel Popescu, a leading Baptist lay preacher, were in general sympathy with the aims of ALRC, they refused to join it. After much soul-searching, they decided that evangelization was of primary importance and that campaigning for human rights would jeopardize their work in the church. (Ţon personally found ALRC too ecumenical.)

In a way Ţon was correct, for the authorities moved against ALRC members, while he was able to build one of the most flourishing churches in Europe before being pressured into exile himself. But his silence when Nicolescu and other friends were expelled from the Baptist Union, and when three other friends were arrested, seemed inadequate, a betrayal, compared to Calciu's protests. The ALRC members were expelled from the Baptist Union on the grounds that they were taking part in an illegal political group that had damaged the prestige of the Baptist church and the "trust which it must enjoy before the state." Ţon got off with a warning. Nevertheless, the Protestant evangelicals set a vital precedent. Throughout the following decade evangelicals have been, in effect, the most courageous opponents of the regime, actively challenging its dishonest maneuvers.

THE CHURCHES IN THE 1980S

With most of its original members driven into exile, ALRC has virtually disappeared. The few members left operate anonymously, occasionally producing documents. The impetus in Romanian religious life passed from protest to pastoral work. But in the mid-eighties, even the pastoral work has brought its proponents into conflict with both church and state authorities.

Since it cannot wipe out religion, the Communist government makes life as unpleasant as possible for believers, particularly those who protest or evangelize. The Romanian Department of Cults watches the churches with an eagle eye, and it works closely with the Securitate. Together they infiltrate and corrupt the churches, exploiting differences and preventing them from becoming centers of dissent. The effects are somewhat neutralized by the unsecularized nature of society and the innately religious character of the people. (A report on repressions suffered by Christians of various denominations during 1981 appears in appendix P.)

Controlling the Clergy

Church appointments and transfers depend on the Department of Cults. This has led to continual conflict with some evangelical Protestant churches whose congregations traditionally appoint their own pastors; in other churches, the situation is grudgingly accepted. The department tries to use church leaders to police the rest of the clergy, causing deep resentment among ordinary clergy and laity, especially in the Orthodox Church.

The clergy have to file routine reports on all their activities. They are required, for example, to report whether there were any visitors in church and, in the case of evangelical Protestants, any conversions. The clergy may also have their houses bugged. In the early 1980s, some Baptists reported that the ratio of informers had risen from one in ten to one in three. Many clergy are compromised through fear. The handful who speak with foreigners either have official approval or are already in trouble and have nothing to lose.

Meetings of clergy are held in the presence of department officials, who are adept at fomenting distrust so that most churches cannot present a common front. There are exceptions: the Romanian Catholic priests of Moldavia and the German and Hungarian Lutherans are more united than most. The department also interferes, illegally, in church elections to keep the central bodies under control.

There are strict limitations on pastoral ministry; services or activities beyond the normal worship routine are seldom allowed. The banned churches—the Lord's Army and the Eastern Rite Catholics—have to hold clandestine services, and many evangelical Protestant congregations cannot get registration or permission to meet and have no church buildings.

Open-air services are extremely popular among evangelicals and the Lord's Army, though at the risk of fines amounting to about two weeks of the average person's pay or, for those who cannot pay, confiscation of some possessions or worse. Meetings may be broken up by violent police assaults; in January 1979, for instance, children and old people were beaten with rubber truncheons at a Pentecostal rally at Alba Iulia.

The churches' financial dependence on the state, with state-subsidized clergy stipends, allows the state to manipulate personnel and policies. Churches must submit their accounts to the Department of Cults, whose officials may then alter the figures if they wish to accuse any active clergy or layperson of embezzlement. A document smuggled out in 1979 claims that local officials expect hefty bribes from Orthodox clergy who wish to be appointed to a parish.

Building and Repairing Churches

The state has deliberately destroyed many churches. Far too much time, effort, and money—which could help relieve the destitute—are spent trying to keep a roof over a congregation's head. Many worship in difficult conditions, crammed into houses or forced to stand outside. Obtaining a permit to build or repair a church of any denomination can take years. The disastrous earthquake of 1977, the proliferation of evangelical Protestant organizations, and the high birth rate of many evangelicals and of Moldavian Catholics aggravate a difficult situation.

Some congregations take matters into their own hands and build or buy without a permit—but they rarely win. As soon as the unauthorized church is built, the bulldozers arrive.

Theological Training

Despite the difficulties, there is no shortage of vocations in most denominations—a tribute to the strength of the faith of the Romanian people. Yet state intrusion is at its worst in theological training.

There is, for example, a limit on the number of clergy and seminarians each church is allowed. Even the Orthodox Church is facing cuts, and the very future of some churches is threatened. The Orthodox seminary at Sibiu, which is the largest theological college in Europe, had had 700 students in the 1970s, when it was allowed to expand. But there were cuts in 1980 and again in 1984, when the Synod passed a resolution limiting admissions. At present there are 830 seminary and 500 academy students. Theological training is closely supervised by the Department of Cults, and students are frequently interrogated by the police. A few of the best are expelled.

The department has considerable influence over staff appointments, though less so in the Catholic and Protestant seminaries for Hungarians and Germans. The Orthodox and Baptist seminaries in Bucharest have particularly bad reputations. In 1978 Orthodox students described their seminary as "a concentration camp for spiritual mutilation"; the high standards set by Patriarch Justinian seem to have been abandoned. Father Calciu tried to revive them and was fired. So was Iosif Ţon, the Baptist theologian, who tried to maintain high standards for Baptist seminarians.

Baptists and Catholic complain about drastic limitations on the importing of basic teaching materials. The Baptist seminary has no textbooks or Bible commentaries. In the late 1970s, only four out of 170 Baptist pastors were university trained; another thirty had secondary education. Baptist leaders feared that the lack of adequately trained clergy could lead to losing converts, who are increasingly sophisticated and in need of modern theological instruction.

Bibles and the Religious Press

The Orthodox patriarchate's press has been operating for three hundred years. The first complete Romanian Bible appeared in 1688; the most recent translation was made in 1968. The patriarchate, using paper supplied by the United Bible Societies, is sometimes allowed to print Bibles for other churches, though not for Catholics. The supply for the smaller churches is strictly rationed.

Since 1968, according to official figures, the total number of Bibles printed or imported was roughly 800,000, or about one for every twenty church members. Probably only a fraction reach the ordinary people. Many copies printed in Romania are presented to foreign visitors or sent to Romanian Orthodox parishes abroad. There is evidence that the authorities have recycled some of the Reformed Church's Hungarian-language Bibles for toilet paper, an item in scarce supply; occasional fragments still bear legible verses. Reportedly, only 200 out of a promised 200,000 Bibles reached their destination. Since 1974, circulating unauthorized printing material—including Bibles—has been a punishable offense, and trying to supply or obtain Bibles from unofficial sources is dangerous.

The patriarchate prints periodicals of high theological quality. The international reputation of Romanian theological scholarship hardly compensates, however, for the tremendous shortage of popular religious reading material. Romanian *samizdat* is for foreign consumption only. The risk is too great for there to be any regular *samizdat* magazines.

All recognized churches may own a press and produce journals, but the censorship is strict and the production limited. As a result, Romanian Christians are segregated from the rest of the Christian world; most Romanian Catholics, for example, know of Mother Teresa only by hearsay and from foreign radio broadcasts.

The Orthodox Church

The Orthodox Church remains dominant—15.5 million members, about 80 per cent of the population—and far better supplied than its counterpart in the Soviet Union. There are 24 bishops, about 8,100 parishes served by 8,500 priests, two academies, six seminaries, and 122 religious houses. Church attendance is regular and open and spans all ages. Communism has been unable to crush the familiarity with religion that is inherent in the Romanian people. Popular faith erupts at Easter into nationwide celebration.

Priests are kept busy with regular services, officiating at domestic ceremonies, and ministering to the sick and the dying. Formal religious instruction of the young has been forbidden since 1948, but in Romania the mother traditionally teaches the child. A good priest can also teach through his sermons, and the liturgy teaches through its chants, psalms, Bible readings, and prayers.

Priests are paid on the same salary scale as secular school teachers. The government, of course, expects a return for the church's semi-established status, and uses it as a branch of the civil service. Some congregations have complained that the sermons sound like party speeches. Many Orthodox believers, disenchanted with priests who perform the rites mechanically, have turned to the Lord's Army, to evangelical Protestant groups, or to the Catholic Church.

Officially, the highest authority in the church is the Holy Synod, but in 1948, as a result of state pressure and contrary to Orthodox tradition, the power was vested in the patriarch. This left the church open to manipulation from the Department of Cults.

Approval for a new parish is given only if there are at least five hundred Orthodox families in an urban area, or four hundred in a rural one. In practice, permits for repairs or new building are hard to come by, and it is almost impossible to get permission to build in new housing areas. Nevertheless, 308 new churches were built between 1975 and 1986, if patriarchate figures are to be believed!

Orthodox Monasticism

In 1988, the 122 (other sources say 103–130) religious houses had 2,700 monks and nuns. The houses are thriving and, because of the state limit on numbers, have long waiting lists. The government has not closed them for various reasons—to assuage popular feeling, to impress foreign delegations, and to earn hard cash from tourists. Some of the more attractive or historic monasteries—a few of which are little more than showpieces—have been preserved with state assistance, but others, less well known, have fallen into ruin.

In 1986 a census of religious aroused fears of a campaign of expulsion, as in 1959. But the most immediate problem has been the destruction of irreplaceable monastic buildings in Bucharest to make way for Ceauşescu's Victory of Socialism Boulevard (more on this later).

Thanks to Justinian, the government integrated many of the monasteries into the national economy, but forced them to become collectives. Nuns in general are exploited as cheap labor, and the Romanian ones are particularly overworked, for they must fulfill state quotas as well as their monastic rule. Many of the women's monasteries are virtually villages, with adjacent farmland on which local peasants and young aspirants to the religious life share the work.

The monasteries are also places of pilgrimage. Thousands stream to them for feast days or longer visits. The people share meals and memories and attend services while they generally enjoy themselves and seek their roots in the traditional way of life. According to Father Calciu, the monasteries also play a vital role for people who, though they have adopted a Communist mentality, still want to pray or confess and dare not be seen in their local church.

The monasteries' spiritual influence is all the more amazing in view of the intense pressure to which religious have been subjected and the way some seminary authorities disparage their life, calling the monks "immoral, uneducated egotists." Many of the older monks and nuns have survived a persecution so terrible they will not speak of it. The fear is compounded by the Securitate, who make frequent checks and intimidate some into becoming informers; plainclothesmen check visitors and chase away unauthorized foreigners. Monks who attract too many "spiritual children" are harassed and are liable to sudden transfer to the remotest monasteries.

Yet there are still plenty of vocations. A rigid discipline, an exhausting work schedule, and appalling psychological pressures do not deter the young people.

The Orthodox Hierarchy

Justin was patriarch from 1977 until his death in 1986. Under him, the hierarchy remained submissive. His successor, elected in 1986, is the able Teoctist Arăpaş. Arăpaş is reputed to be an ambitious man who had long set his sights on the patriarchal throne; he can be expected to follow the pattern set by his predecessor.

Several bishops and senior church officials, particularly Metropolitan Antonie Plămădeală of Transylvania, though accepted by the West, have bad reputations in Romania. Clever and persuasive, Antonie was described by Calciu as "the most dangerous of all." The department relies on these men to discipline any priests who challenge the carefully constructed façade of church-state relations.

The government, by a law passed in 1947, can dismiss a bishop for other than religious reasons; as a result, bishops are drawn from clergy acceptable to the state. The bishops, though originally monks, are wealthy men and live accordingly, but the faithful nonetheless retain their traditional deep respect for the office. A foreign visitor witnessed a weeping peasant woman, who had approached one of the bishops, being received with the utmost courtesy.

As in the Soviet Union, none of the bishops is a completely free agent. Bishop Gherasim Cocosel, who refused to compromise, was "retired" to a monastery. No one else has dared speak up. There seems to be a common understanding that docile public utterance is an inescapable element in Romanian life. Some, however, quietly do what they can for their flock.

Priests Who Resist

There are some excellent priests, like Fr. Bejan Dumitru, who, according to a 1980 ALRC document, spent twelve years under house arrest for being "too spiritual." Father Calciu has had a profound effect on younger priests. One priest, for example, wrote to the patriarch to ask that the hierarchy stop participating in pro-regime activities, and that lay people (meaning state agents) not be allowed to staff the metropolitanates and bishoprics. In 1981, five young disciples of Calciu drew up a similar list in a "Testimony" addressed to the patriarch. All were suspended and vilified and have since emigrated to the United States.

In 1985 and early 1986, several more priests, some of them associated with the "Testimony" and all engaged in successful ministries, were threatened, and most were defrocked. Fr. Radu Pamfil, for instance, was accused by an ecclesiastical court of "occult practices." In 1986 Fr. Alexandru Pop sent an open letter to Radio Free Europe protesting religious persecution. He said that other priests "continue to carry the same message of Christianity" as Father Calciu and wanted to add their signatures to his, but "for the time being" he was signing alone. Father Pop was forced into exile.

The rights requested would be thought no more than elementary in several other East European countries, but they are little short of radical in the Romanian context. That these religious rights do not exist in a country where the church is numerically strong shows how little the hierarchy has achieved through submissiveness. "Romanian Democratic Action," an unofficial movement claiming Christian roots that was started in 1985, regards the hierarchy as "the chief obstacle to a rebirth of Christian spirituality prepared to tackle social and political problems," and proposes "the reorganization of the church on democratic lines."

The Lord's Army

Described in an ALRC document as "a limb of the Orthodox Church that goes on bleeding," and regarded by many Romanians as its conscience, the Lord's Army continues in strength despite arrests and the hierarchy's disowning of it. With up to 450,000 members, three-quarters of them young people, it attracts those who are looking for a personal commitment and greater vitality in church life. Its members are mostly ordinary working people, and it is particularly strong in rural areas and in Transylvania, where some Eastern Rite Catholics have joined. Many of the more active parish priests belong to or sympathize with it.

The authorities lump the Lord's Army and the evangelicals together as a "sect," a derogatory term. According to its leader, the vulnerable Traian

Dorz, the main strength of the Lord's Army is that it has remained within the Orthodox Church, but with an emphasis on Bible reading, lay training, and public commitment. Members use public events like weddings and funerals to attract converts. Usually they meet in house groups, keep a low profile, and gain new members through personal contacts. Some groups have been infiltrated, and there were a number of misunderstandings among the leaders in the late 1970s, but the Lord's Army remains vigorous. Its fresh approach could become a salutary pattern for other Orthodox churches.

The Eastern Rite Catholic Church

The other major banned church survives in secret and maintains a basic network of church life, though its contact with Rome is all but severed. Estimates of its strength vary from under a million to 1.5 million. New bishops are consecrated clandestinely to replace those who die. The only bishop to survive the prison camps of the 1950s, Julius Hossu, who died in 1970, was made a cardinal *in pectore* (i.e., named by the Pope in secret), the first in the history of the Romanian church. His tomb in Bucharest attracts many pilgrims, not all of them Catholic. About 300 of the original priests who remained Catholic when the church's union with Rome was dissolved in 1948 are alive, and new priests are secretly trained and ordained—perhaps 600 priests in all, representing all classes. Since their identity is usually known to the Securitate, they are subject to harassment and their families suffer discrimination. Reportedly no arrests have been made since 1974.

Despite the laws against "assisting at private Masses conducted by priests following another profession" and "developing any form of social activity which could intensify religious life," retreats are arranged, and tiny secret groups of nuns instruct the young. There is no *samizdat* press, however, and such literature as there is has to be smuggled in.

The overall situation is very complex. There are about twenty "Orthodox" churches whose congregations are staunchly Catholic. When vacancies arise, the Orthodox bishops, on state instructions, appoint priests considered hostile to Rome, though some are secretly friendly.

Some Eastern Rite Catholics attend only clandestine Masses said in private houses. As long as only the family and friends of the celebrant are present at these gatherings, local authorities tend to ignore them. Since the Vatican in 1969 gave them a dispensation to receive Orthodox sacraments, Eastern Rite Catholics can be baptized and married in Orthodox services. Many are content with this, since the services are almost identical.

At a local level, friendship and intermarriage between Orthodox and Eastern Rite Catholics continues. In the 1970s the Eastern Rite bishops, unrecognized by the state, and all survivors of long prison sentences, formed a committee to press for the restoration of the church and addressed over a hundred appeals to the government. Three appealed to the 1980 Madrid Conference (a follow-up on the Helsinki Accords), comparing their plight in a traditionally Christian nation with that of the Muslims, who are a recognized religious body.

On January 2, 1982, the Pope gave public support to the Romanian church and appointed émigré Traian Crişan as archbishop and secretary of the Vatican's Sacred Congregation for the Cause of Saints. The Romanian Orthodox hierarchy reacted sharply: the Pope's statement, they said, was "an intrusion in the internal affairs of the Romanian church." The government could not understand that Crişan's job had nothing to do with political activity. Relations between Romanian authorities and the Vatican over the Eastern Rite Church remain at a stalemate.

In Vienna in 1987 Patriarch Teoctist claimed that Romania had solved the problem of "Uniates," "once and for all." Nevertheless, the church now has five unrecognized bishops, it is attracting more members, and its credibility and reputation are higher than ever. The upsurge of Catholics in the neighboring Ukraine with whom it has close relations should increase its self-confidence.

The Non-Romanian Churches

The majority of members of the Latin Rite Catholic Church and the traditional Protestant churches are either Hungarian or German. Neither nationality is generally popular with Romanians, with whom they have little in common. They mostly live in distinct geographical areas: about 90 per cent of Hungarians live in Transylvania, where they form a minority of almost 30 per cent; the rest have moved to Bucharest. The Germans are also mostly in Transylvania and the Banat, the middle Danube plains, but their numbers have dwindled since 1975, when emigration became not only permitted but encouraged.

There is not much cooperation between either national group and Romanians, although three of the signatories of the key ALRC document had Hungarian names. Their closest spiritual links are with their compatriots outside Romania, on whom they depend for material aid in times of crisis and for culture and spiritual nurture. Not surprisingly, some feel little loyalty to Ceauşescu's Romania, especially now that their culture and identity are under threat.

Non-Romanian Churches: Traditional Protestant

The three main denominations are Reformed (Hungarian-speaking), Lutheran (German- or Hungarian-speaking), and Unitarian (Hungarian-speaking). These churches keep a low profile. Their religious life reflects their communities—law-abiding, cohesive, conservative. Until the recent anti-Hungarian campaign, they had slightly more leeway than Romanian churches because the government was aware of possible repercussions from Hungary and West Germany. The usual subsidies for church life, literature excepted, are provided.

The dramatic decline in churchgoing in Hungary and East Germany is not so apparent in Romania, a less secularized society. The church is still very much the center of the local community, and those in the more remote villages have retained distinctive ancient customs that have vanished elsewhere. For people whose ancestors who have been there for eight centuries, the church is the center of their cultural life and the pastor their unquestioned leader.

These churches have the weaknesses as well as the strengths of "folk" churches. Many people attend out of habit rather than conviction. These churches tend to lose their hold on young people, who gravitate to the cities. They are not likely to do anything that falls afoul of the law.

The *Reformed Church* probably has more than 715,000 members, 734 "mother" churches, and nearly 1,600 congregations; it has two bishops, neither noted for his courage *vis-à-vis* the government, and 714 pastors, an inadequate number. Attendance at church varies from about 15 to 30 per cent of the membership. The Reformed Church has not been permitted to build enough churches to provide for its members, though in general more church activities are allowed than is usual in Romania.

The *Lutherans* are divided into two churches, German and Hungarian, each with a bishop. In 1986 there were 169,000 members, 137,000 Germans and 32,000 Hungarians in a total of 250 parishes with about 190 clergy. Neither group wants to compromise with the state. The Lutherans boast that not a single church has been closed and that no compromised candidate is allowed in their seminary.

The German churches, however—Catholic as well as Lutheran—are facing great internal strains and might even vanish, because for the last twelve years or so, around 11,000 Germans annually have found the money to buy themselves out of Romania and emigrate to West Germany. Eventually only the old or those too poor to buy their freedom will be left. Pastors and congregations are accusing each other of "desertion." The clergy were down from 220 in 1981 to 148 in 1987. The laity are ill equipped to fill the gap.

The *Unitarian Church*, dating back to 1568, is the largest of its kind in Eastern Europe. It has about 70,000 members under one bishop, in 121 congregations served by 111 pastors. Its decline from a high of 400 congregations in the sixteenth century was mainly the result of Habsburg persecution.

The State and Traditional Protestants

Like all other religious groups, the Protestants suffer from state intrusion. In the Hungarian Reformed Church, whose bishops are rather weak, a successful pastor may be transferred to a remote parish. In 1983, for instance, Ferenc Wisky was thought to be attracting too many young people and was forced by his bishop to retire. Wisky's son, Andras, has suffered considerable harassment, probably as much for the Hungarian poems he has written as for his evangelical activities. In 1987 religious literature was confiscated during raids on the homes of two Reformed clergy.

Despite often daily interrogations and pressure to become informers, the students and staff at the joint Lutheran/Reformed seminary have maintained their integrity and high academic standards. But the government has cut their numbers drastically. In the fall of 1987 only eight or ten out of eighty-two seminary applicants were accepted, despite the need for a minimum of fifty trained clergy to maintain the current level.

Overall, Hungarians probably have been less badly treated under Romanian Communism than Romanians—many of the original Communists were Hungarian. In recent years, as a result of Ceauşescu's nationalist policies, the Hungarians' language and culture have come under attack. The resulting upsurge in Hungarian nationalism has led to further repression. Thanks to émigré Hungarians, the plight of the Hungarians in Romania has received attention abroad. In 1986, two strong protests were mounted by interdenominational church bodies in Hungary over abuses of religious liberty in Transylvania. These statements were markedly stronger than any made previously by Hungarian church leaders. They drew a heated response from Metropolitan Antonie Plămădeală of Transylvania, who asserted—probably correctly—that no Hungarian locality in Romania was "without a church or pastor [or] religious services in Hungarian." By spring 1987 the leaders of both states had joined the fray with a barrage of accusations and counter-accusations.

The Hungarians in Romania rightly feel that the government's squeeze on teaching and publishing in Hungarian is an attempt to destroy their nationality. It is also an act of historic reprisal for centuries when Romanian peasants in Transylvania were termed "robbers, thieves, and vagabonds" by their Hungarian and otherwise alien rulers. But it must not be forgotten that *Romanian* culture, too, is under attack. Christianity, which is an integral part of it, has been under attack for forty years.

Christians have clashed with the authorities over the suppression of the nationalities. In 1979 Otto Kugler, an active Protestant of mixed Hungarian and German origin, was sentenced to twenty years in prison for treason. He and his wife had erected a system to help would-be emigrants and had sent letters to Radio Free Europe. He was released in 1986.

In 1983 Sandor Denes, a former Reformed seminarian, received his second prison sentence for complaining about the destruction of Hungarian culture—a sign of the worsening situation for the national minorities, as Ceauşescu looks for scapegoats.

Non-Romanian Churches: Latin Rite Catholic

The Latin Rite Catholic Church, the second largest church in Romania with about 1.4 million members, has no charter, no official status, no basic privileges. Yet it is as much under the control of the Department of Cults as any other church. Because it has been isolated from Rome, many Catholics in the West are unaware that there is a strong Catholic Church in Romania.

In 1948 the number of dioceses was arbitrarily reduced from five to two, and for twenty-two years only one bishop functioned. That bishop, Aaron Marton, was a good, uncorruptible man who had spent some years in prison. The archdiocese of Bucharest was administered by Francisc Augustin, who, with the blessing of the state, exercised jurisdiction from 1954 until his death in 1983. Though accepted by the Holy See, he was not fully trusted and was never consecrated. In recent years, former dioceses have been reconstituted, with "interim" bishops chosen by the Pope, and work has begun again on a charter.

When Augustin died, the priests of the archdiocese courageously designated a successor, Msgr. Ioan Robu, an ethnic Romanian from Moldavia who has studied in Rome. Unlike Augustin, Robu refused to take a seat on the Grand National Assembly, citing the Vatican instruction against priests' taking part in politics. When Jerome of Wallachia was beatified in 1983, Catholics were allowed to make a pilgrimage to Rome for the first time since the war.

The Catholic Church's Problems

The church's tremendous difficulties have been aired through the rare *samizdat* appeals that reach the West and occasional reports from visitors. These are sometimes, and understandably, controversial and contradictory, especially concerning prominent clergy. Bits of information seep out, such as the fact that priests may teach the catechism but may not use a blackboard, and that children may not take notes.

There are the inevitable building troubles, especially in Moldavia. Judicious bribes to local authorities, a risky business, can speed up building. In

1980 an elderly Jesuit, Fr. Michael Godo, was given a six-year sentence for collecting money for a new church. Thanks to pressure, he was released in 1981.

The ban on Catholic orders causes great resentment, especially since Orthodox orders are allowed. Hundreds of women are willing to enter the convent, but the clergy dare not organize secret communities. Many women form little groups, living together in twos and threes, attending church, and giving their surplus earnings to the poor.

The church is denied a press. It took years for Vatican II documents to reach Romania. Until 1976 there were no prayer books or catechisms—and then only in completely inadequate numbers. Until 1980 there were no New Testaments; then a mere 10,000 were allowed in. There have been no imports of Bibles.

A Divided Church

Because they are divided into three major national groups, Catholics have been unable to present a unified front against the state, which foments disunity by seeming to favor first one group and then another. Membership has shifted in recent years. The Hungarians, who used to form 80 per cent, are no longer so dominant, with roughly 800,000 out of 1.3 million members. The Germans, who used to form 21 per cent, have declined by emigration to 200,000 and have been overtaken by the Romanians, who now have at least 300,000 members, partly as a result of their higher birth rate. By 1978 the Romanian Catholics were claiming that 97 priests and 80 parishes were inadequate. They also objected that they were being treated more harshly than their Hungarian counterparts, and that when they had to move out of Moldavia to find work, they had to attend Mass in a foreign language. Romanian Masses were however permitted after 1978, as part of the government's anti-Hungarian policy, and Hungarians now claim they are being forced to provide Romanian Masses to satisfy former Eastern Rite Catholics at the expense of their own services!

The state's anti-Hungarian trend has given rise to increasing harassment of conscientious priests and of parents and children, and to a series of brutal attacks on Hungarian priests. A popular priest, Fr. Ion Ecsy, was murdered under mysterious circumstances in 1982. In December 1983, Fr. Géza Palfi, a healthy young man, protested that Christmas had not been declared a public holiday. He was arrested and beaten up "within an inch of death," and died in a hospital two months later from liver damage. (The "official" cause of death was cancer. His case was hushed up by both the U.S. State Department, desirous of maintaining MFN status for Romania, and the Vatican, fearful lest the improved status of the church might be jeopardized if it protested.) Fr. Imre Tempfli, transferred from his parish because of his pastoral work with young people, dropped out of sight in December 1987 and was thought to have been murdered by the Securitate. But in March 1988 he was back in his parish. If Hungarian (and even Romanian) Catholics start revering these priests as martyrs, the Securitate has only itself to blame.

Signs of Health

Despite such harassment, the Catholic Church is healthy; more people than ever—around 80 per cent—attend Mass. The simple faith of Catholics in Romania has been tested and deepened by forty years of adversity.

The church's isolation from the West has protected it from becoming secularized. The standard of preaching is high, and people often take notes on the sermons. Many Orthodox and Eastern Rite Catholics in Transylvania have been attracted to Latin Rite services partly because of the sermons, and some Orthodox intellectuals have actually become Catholics. Indeed, the survival of the church owes a great deal to the caliber of the priests and their preaching. The ratio of priests to people is second only to that of Poland, in Eastern Europe.

The seminarians have been little short of heroic. Despite government attempts to infiltrate and divide staff and students, despite their almost complete lack (until 1981) of basic textbooks, and despite, in the seminary at Alba Iulia, appalling overcrowding and the worst physical conditions of any Catholic seminary in Europe, the seminaries have sent out dedicated young priests.

The number of priests has fallen drastically in the years since 1948, but from 1976 to 1982 the seminaries were allowed to accept as many applicants as they could hold—about 250. Since 1982 they have been allowed only thirty a year, and some students already in have been ejected.

The Baptist Union

Romanian Baptists are the most militant and fastest-growing Baptist church in all Europe. With a membership of about 160,000 (government figures of 75,000 are very misleading) growing at a rate of approximately 3,600 a year, the Baptist Union is probably the most important Protestant group in Romania. (An attraction for some converts is that thanks to Western church pressures, it has become easier for Baptists to emigrate.) Visitors testify to its dynamism. The enthusiasm, warmth, and practical generosity of its members—even outside their own denomination—and the challenge of their demands on personal behavior, act as a magnet in a society where standards are declining in every sphere of life. Their sermons focus on the

Gospel, and their relief network shields them to some extent from economic hardships.

Some Baptist churches, full to overflowing, are open every night. Groups of up to five hundred, including many young people, meet for Bible study. The atmosphere has a vitality seldom experienced elsewhere in Romania. A good congregation will proliferate; the laity study theology in order to preach and evangelize, and young evangelists hold nationwide rallies and conduct week-long crusades.

That all this can go on in Romania is a tribute to the power of a faith that is clearly preached and backed by love, especially in the face of interference by the Department of Cults and discouragement from Baptist leaders. With the appointment in 1977 of a leadership under the sway of the government, and, a year or two later, the expulsion of ALRC members from the Baptist Union, state authorities felt they had gained control of the church. In 1982, however, 66 pastors (out of 160) wrote to Ceauşescu outlining their major grievances. In response, the signatories were interrogated and pressed to withdraw their names, some with threats, others with promises; about ten succumbed. The triennial Baptist Congress, already postponed, was put off again, and representatives freely elected by local areas were, under state pressure, not ratified by the Central Committee. Because of the postponements, some compromised leaders stayed in office long after their mandates had expired.

The Department of Cults finally permitted the congress to meet in 1984, but for one day instead of three. Attendees were limited to a few hundred, and no foreign observers were allowed. The congress elected as president Mihai Huşan, a man who, though more popular than his predecessor, proved to be somewhat cautious and compromising. As secretary it chose Vasile Talpoş, current president of the European Baptist Federation; he is not at all popular in Romania. Huşan took some steps to restore church unity, but did not, however, manage to ease the shortage of pastors in either of two possible ways—by persuading the government to increase the number of seminarians, or by facilitating the licensing of qualified laymen who have no formal training.

The most important proposal scheduled for discussion at the 1984 Congress concerned a change in the Baptist Union's constitution to allow the central leadership to have a hand in placing pastors in local churches. This would have gone against the Baptist principle of local autonomy and would have opened the door even further to state machinations. The proposal never came up for discussion.

The next Baptist Congress, due in April 1987, was postponed because of the failure of Baptist electors to produce candidates acceptable to the Department of Cults. In the preliminary elections, Huşan came close to losing the presidency, and Talpoş was not returned as secretary. (Though president of the European Baptist Federation, he had also been turned down in every vacant charge he had applied for during the last two years; no congregation was willing to have him.) Elsewhere, too, respected "independents" carried the day.

State-Created Shortage of Pastors

The Baptist church suffers for lack of pastors—only 160 (out of a state limit of 170), of whom more than a hundred will reach retirement age by 1990, for a thousand or so churches. In 1959, with many fewer Baptists, there were 540 pastors. At present, some look after ten to fifteen congregations. In 1982, ten seminary students were rejected by the authorities as "surplus." Although there was room for eighty in the seminary, only five were in training. The seminary itself is in danger of being demolished. Protests from abroad helped get the number of students up to ten in 1984, but a great deal of pastoral work has to be done by men with no formal training.

Smear tactics are used against outstanding pastors and evangelists. Baptists are denigrated in the media as "shakers" or "repenters" and are blamed for violent crimes, described as "cult sacrifices" or "ritual murders."

Permits to build, enlarge, or repair churches are always hard to come by, and some buildings have been deliberately destroyed. A reporter who saw the remains of Bistriţa Church, razed in 1984, said he had seen nothing like it since the earthquake. Every piece had been so battered that none could be reused. Members of Blaj Church, badly damaged by floods, were promised permission to rebuild if they helped with the harvest in 1985. They worked hard, but the promise was broken.

There is much provocation. The most widely publicized case concerns the Mihai Bravu Church, the liveliest congregation in Bucharest, which has been at odds with the state for years. When Pavel Nicolescu, who served as a spokesman for the ALRC (and still does, from exile in the United States), was the pastor there, seminarians were forbidden to enter. Its current and also very good pastor, Vasile Taloş (not to be confused with the unpopular former denominational executive named Talpoş), has pursued a quiet, consistent course. In September 1983, after years of threats, the church was pulled down. The congregation now worships in an enlarged house.

Harassment of Baptist Pastors

The two main "test cases" between church and state in the last three years concerned pairs of successful pastors who, the Department of Cults contended, were not properly licensed. In both cases, the congregations had decided to employ their pastors directly instead of through official channels, in order not to have state employees for pastors.

At Mediaş, under department pressure, the Baptist Union withdrew the licenses of pastors Ioan Ştef and his son-in-law Beniamin Cocar, a fearless young man. The unofficial charge: they had baptized children. Their real crime: the congregation had doubled under their ministry. In 1983, Ştef and Cocar were threatened with prison if they continued to preach. To protect them, members of the congregation slept in their yards.

The harassment continued. Whenever Cocar was interrogated, his wife was left to wonder whether he would be tortured, and whether she would ever see him again. Phone callers threatened their son with an accident. Ştef's wife, hospitalized for heart surgery, was forced to answer a barrage of questions from a woman informer. And yet the church continued to expand, with about sixty baptisms a month.

Cocar's brother, Bunian, another unlicensed pastor, was also affected. Bunian Cocar and an elder, Ioan Cojocărescu, were arrested. The latter was hung by his wrists for twenty-four hours and beaten on the stomach.

Ştef and the Cocars applied for emigration, which was speedily granted. They were seen off at the airport by a thousand supporters. Their churches are making plans to use other unlicensed pastors, and further trouble is expected.

The pastors at Iosif Ţon's old church at Oradea, the fastest-growing congregation in Romania, have had no theological training. Dr. Nicolae Gheorghiţă and Dr. Paul Negruţ gave up lucrative careers, the former as an internationally recognized endocrinologist, the latter as a clinical psychologist, to become pastors. Ţon had discovered that men could be ordained into the ministry by a contractual arrangement with the local church without formal recognition or seminary training. The government was chagrined that such eminent men should leave their professions to become pastors; it has tried to persuade them to return to their secular employment. After three years of waiting, both pastors received licenses from the Baptist Union (April 1985), a significant breakthrough that sets a precedent, since at least six other ministers are in the same position. Emulation, however, may prove more difficult for less publicized congregations.

Significantly, the election of Gheorghiţă as president of the Oradea Area Baptist Association was confirmed in the elections that were to precede the 1987 Baptist Congress, which was postponed, yet again, to 1988. Gheorghiţă is now well known in the West as well as popular at home. However, a young, well-qualified engineer, Duru Popa, chosen as pastor of the 2,000-strong Arad church (second largest in the country) by a 98 per cent majority, was expelled by the Baptist Union in the fall of 1987. This followed an angry confrontation between two denominational representatives and the congregation, which was backed by other Baptist pastors.

By the spring of 1988, five of the six area associations were reported to be in support of Gheorghiţă as next president of the Baptist Union, and the long postponed Congress was scheduled for April. The Department of Cults threatened to remove Gheorghiţă 's license (perhaps just temporarily) so that he would be unable to stand, meanwhile trying to force the election of Talpoş, which was invalid, according to Baptist Union rules. At an informal meeting, so as to avoid a head-on confrontation between church and state, both Gheorghiţă and Talpoş agreed not to stand.

At the Congress, held in April 1988, the Baptists avoided appointing to leadership posts persons who were controversial either to the authorities or to believers. The unpopular secretary Vasile Talpoş was given the less influential post of principal of the seminary. The Baptists passed a resolution asking that 300 unregistered local churches have their status regularized by becoming "daughter churches" of nearby existing congregations. This would short-circuit the long process of applying for individual registration and enable the churches to operate within the law. The future looks bright for the Baptist Union.

The Visit of Billy Graham

How much the church benefited from Billy Graham's visit in 1985 is open to question. Nearly 150,000 people attended his meetings, some of which suffered from judicious state interference. The people were, of course, happy to hear such a distinguished foreign preacher, though many felt that evangelization was already being successfully carried out by Romanians.

Graham did not endear himself to the Romanian people by expressing his "gratitude to the leadership of their country, which gives full and genuine freedom to all religious denominations." His remarks in Transylvania about "harmonious relations" between Romanians and Hungarians were equally naïve. Host congregations, moreover, were heavily charged by the state for each visit, even though the Graham organization had already paid all the expenses. (An account by a Romanian Baptist who followed Graham's visit appears in appendix Q.)

Visiting preachers are warmly welcomed by congregations, but a "new law" (presumably an internal Department of Cults ruling) states that in the future no foreigner will be allowed to preach without special permission.

The Pentecostal Church

In recent years, Pentecostals have shared in the growth of the evangelical Protestant churches. They have also shared in the harassment of congregations whose activities become too public. In 1978, for instance, the Gypsy pastor Ioan Samu was sentenced to six years in prison; he had too speedily built a Gypsy church of around four hundred members. (Evangelical Protestants have converted a number of Gypsies.) Upon his release, broken by the appalling treatment, Samu emigrated with his family.

Since the church deemphasizes politics, the Pentecostal leadership, which has remained unchanged since 1962, has generally been on good terms with the state. About eleven new churches have been built in various cities since the late 1970s, and in 1976 the state allowed a small Bible school for pastors. Membership is estimated to be between 200,000 and 250,000 and is increasing rapidly, especially since families with fifteen or sixteen children are not uncommon among members. In addition, Pentecostals tend to poach from other denominations, which is resented by other Christians. Charismatics, as in the West, prove a key growth element, yet are divisive.

Of the 140 pastors, 70 per cent are well over retirement age, and only about 100 are active. Since they have over a thousand churches to supervise, pastoral problems are acute. Many churches rely on lay leadership, which, though claiming to be inspired, is often undisciplined and ignorant of Christian doctrine. State restrictions have led to an acute lack of even the most basic religious literature, and this accentuates existing problems. Services, often held in houses, are frequently overcrowded. Some of the churches are to all intents and purposes independent. A number of Pentecostals have managed to emigrate.

The Brethren, or Union of Evangelical Churches

The Brethren have 40,000–50,000 members in 380 congregations with 80 local leaders. Though still small, they have been growing significantly over the last twenty years. The church is far more a homegrown product than other East European Brethren churches; only a third of its membership has come through Western missions. Unlike the other Protestant churches, it does not train clergy; services are organized by its members.

A clampdown and several arrests since 1984 suggest that the Department of Cults is worried over the Brethren's expansion. Three leaders were fired in 1984 and replaced by department-approved men. Two noteworthy cases occurred in 1985. Elisei Rusu, editor of the denominational magazine, was convicted with three others of distributing Christian literature and sentenced to a year's "labor under prison conditions"—living at home and working for little or no wages. In the other case, Ilie Neamţu, a foreman, held small evangelical meetings at work. Under duress he confessed to embezzling funds, a patently false charge.

The Seventh-Day Adventists

The Adventists, with 50,000 members, 524 congregations, and 143 pastors, have been in constant trouble with the regime, particularly over their pacifism and their refusal to work on Saturdays. They have been mocked and brutally treated. Some have died in prison. The largest Adventist church in Bucharest was demolished in 1986, despite a sit-in protest by 200 members.

Dorel Cataramă was sentenced to ten years in 1982 on unfounded charges of embezzlement. The real reason: he had worked with a church youth club and had distributed Bibles, and his brother and father had defected on a visit to the United States. After fasting in prison he was released in 1986.

Life is difficult for Adventists in Romania. A sizable number have refused to join the state-registered Adventist body. One of ALRC's demands was the lifting of regulations to allow a reintegration of all Adventists.

Non-Christian Groups

Muslims and Jews, numbering about 50,000 and about 22,000 respectively, are officially recognized in Romania and are permitted their own languages, culture, and faith. Neither group is large enough to cause the government much concern.

The Muslims inhabit the Dobrogea, a region south of the Danube delta. There are about eighty communities, Turks or Tatars, and they have seventy mosques and about sixty imams. Politically loyal and generally diligent, they enjoy reasonable freedom of religion and a good relationship with the government.

Romania has also treated Jews reasonably well, a factor that helped it to obtain MFN status from the United States. It is the only East European country with good diplomatic relations with Israel; the Israeli embassy in Bucharest benefits Moscow, which does not have one. The Jews, half of whom live in Bucharest, play an important part in national life. They are the remnant of a much larger community that was cut in half in 1941 when Romania ceded northern Bukovina and Bessarabia to the USSR and upper Transylvania to Hungary. Since the war about 300,000 Jews have emigrated to Israel.

The Jews have 130 synagogues and 68 local communities, many of which retain distinctive cultural features. Unfortunately, there are only three rabbis and no rabbinical seminary, though there are 20 religious-instruction schools for the young.

Some recent signs are disturbing, however. In 1984 and again in 1987

Dr. Moses Rosen, chief rabbi, and other leading Jews protested against a number of virulently anti-Semitic writings. The anti-Semitism seems to have been officially promoted; Ceauşescu may be picking the Jews, as well as the minority nationals, as scapegoats for his failures.

Younger Jews, who can often afford hard-currency visas, are leaving at a rate of about a thousand a year. They may see in Ceauşescu's threat to demolish three synagogues and the center of Bucharest's Jewish area a sign of things to come. Like the German community, the Jews may well all but disappear.

Imprisonment of Believers

Romania's record of imprisonment for religious and political reasons is an affront to all civilized nations. Estimates of political prisoners in 1987 ranged as high as several thousand. In January 1988 Ceauşescu announced on his seventieth birthday the most important amnesty since he came to power in 1965: all prisoners serving up to ten years were freed. No credit is due the regime for granting amnesty to prisoners who were unjustly condemned in the first place. Nor does amnesty necessarily bring freedom, as Father Calciu can attest; and granting an exit visa after inflicting severe hardship can hardly be seen as an act of compassion.

Sentences have always been given not for religious but for (trumped up) "criminal" offenses, since there is no specifically anti-religious legislation. But as the government's record in the 1980s makes clear, only the longer sentences are reported. No one knows how many Christians have been incarcerated for a few months. Nor does the record include the several hundred mostly unknown people who, Calciu has revealed, are sent to psychiatric hospitals, many never to be heard of again.

Since the disbanding of ALRC, many cases have gone unreported. The visible cases are the tip of the iceberg. People sometimes simply disappear; some are murdered. Sabin Teodosiu, brother of the well-known ALRC prisoner Ioan Teodosiu, was "accidentally" electrocuted following death threats.

A 25-year-old Baptist, Traian Bogdan, who at nineteen had been the youngest founder of ALRC, met a tragic death in December 1983. He and his wife Elena had been campaigning on behalf of the persecuted by getting information out to the West. Discovered and threatened, they went underground and prepared to flee the country. Elena managed to cross the Danube. Traian, who was planning to follow, went out one evening to make a phone call and didn't come back. His body was found hanging in the house a month later; the official verdict—suicide.

Arrests are normally followed by beatings or drug treatment (standard in pre-trial examination). The apparent aim is to discredit those arrested, to frighten others engaged in similar practices, and to ensure a supply of "hostages" who can be released at strategic moments.

As a gesture to the 1980 Madrid Conference, the Orthodox SLOMR leaders Ionel Cană and Gheorghe Braşoveanu were given amnesty, while the Jesuit Father Godo was released in 1981. In August of that year, as the annual MFN review came up, five Brethren of German origin, sentenced for taking Bibles across the Soviet border, were also amnestied. But in the same year a Bible distributor was beaten to death, and another, Ioan Clipa, father of seven, committed suicide after having betrayed his colleagues under drug treatment.

Eleven evangelicals, including two young Lord's Army sisters condemned to six years' imprisonment for smuggling 600,000 Bibles, were amnestied just before the MFN review of 1982. Meanwhile eight more evangelicals had been sentenced to up to six years for the same offense. Perhaps the case that aroused the most widespread concern among Romanian Christians was the 1982 sentencing of 75-year-old Traian Dorz, a Lord's Army leader, to two years for importing copies of children's hymn books. Dorz, a much revered poet and hymn writer, was in poor health, having previously served seventeen years in prison. As a result of protests he was released after a few months.

The list goes on and on. By the end of 1984, most religious prisoners known in the West, with the exception of Calciu, had been released. But new cases in the last two years have been travesties of justice, even by Romanian standards. By 1986 it was nevertheless evident that world public opinion was proving effective and many victims were being released. A visitor was told that outside the well-known towns, "the law of the jungle reigns."

The "Freedom" of Father Calciu

For five years and five months, Father Calciu disappeared in prison. At times his very life was in doubt. He was held in a damp, subterranean cell, wearing shirt and underpants, forced to sit upright for over sixteen hours a day, and starved; he almost went blind, and almost died. At one time he was put in a cell with two hardened criminals in the hope they would kill him. Within two weeks they were on their knees, saying, "Father, let *them* do it; that's what they're paid for."

Apart from keeping him out of circulation, the authorities had no clear plan for him after he refused to recant. He has since traced his most brutal treatment to times when Ceauşescu was being feted by Western politicians, his better moments to times when international protests were loudest.

To countless Romanians Father Calciu became a living martyr, a symbol of spiritual freedom, a reminder that Romania's Stalinist past has never been exorcised. One of his defenders, Professor Doina Cornea (an Eastern Rite Catholic), suggested that the failure of Romanians to speak out against injustice was to blame for the country's distress, and that nothing would improve if they continued in cowardice. She was sacked and (briefly) arrested.

On August 20, 1984, just in time for the MFN review, Ceauşescu apparently accepted Calciu's terms (no forced emigration, placement in a parish, a university education for his son), and he was freed—in theory. In practice, as he wrote, "I knew that after my release my family and I would find ourselves in a larger, more subtle, and perhaps more effective prison."

Three Securitate cars were stationed day and night near his apartment. Uniformed militia were continuously on duty inside and outside his home and turned away all visitors except relatives and a few close friends. Foreign visitors, whether official or private, were not allowed. Whenever he and his wife and son ventured out, at least six policemen kept them apart from others; despite this they were assaulted and beaten up in the street by police. (Appendix R is Father Calciu's account of his imprisonment and his "freedom.")

In prison, he had been able to conduct services for other prisoners and had been recognized as a priest; now, on orders from the Securitate, he was defrocked by his church. With no hope of a parish or any priestly work, he gave in and asked to be allowed to leave Romania. His request was granted in time for the 1985 MFN review. From the West, Father Calciu continues to expose the evils of Ceauşescu's regime, although he is still in danger from the secret police.

In 1987, both the U.S. House and the U.S. Senate voted to suspend Romania's MFN status. In the House-Senate conference process, the suspension—attached to a trade bill—was deleted. In spring 1988, however, Romania renounced MFN status. The Jackson-Vanik Amendment ties MFN status to emigration policy, and Romania did not want to be pressured on this matter.

Living Conditions: From Bad to Worse

Living standards have deteriorated badly and are the worst in the Soviet bloc. They are far worse than those in Poland, which has received massive aid. The Western media took a belated interest in Romania only after the terrible winter of 1984–85.

Part of the trouble was caused by the huge foreign debt. Ceauşescu, in his pride, decided that the debt must be reduced by 40 per cent within two years, no matter the consequences. The choicest food is routinely exported to the USSR, and now much of the remainder was exported to earn money. The whole nation, with the exception of Ceauşescu's elite, was brought to the brink of famine.

The most basic foods are rationed. Each month an average family receives less than a pint of cooking oil, a few slices of meat, a pound of sugar, and six pounds of flour. Soap, toothpaste, and toilet paper are almost unobtainable for long periods, as are rice, butter, margarine, cheese, coffee, chocolate, citrus fruit, and other basic foods. Peasants who grow food are little better off than townsfolk, and large numbers have now been forcibly resettled in shoddy apartment blocks so as to make police supervision easier. The shortage of foodstuff was so acute that in some cases peasants had to buy chickens and pigs to hand over to the state, which has owned all the land since 1974. Peasants have been put to death on Ceauşescu's orders for stealing food off what, until 1974, was their own land.

Conditions became desperate during the winter of 1984–85. Acute fuel shortages led to repeated power cuts. Street lights were out. Gas pressure was so low that it was all but impossible to light an oven, and a kettle could take an hour to boil. People crowded into one room and slept fully dressed, huddled together for warmth. Communal heating was turned off at night and for most of the day, while temperatures fell below zero.

The death rate soared. Probably no one will ever know how many people, particularly babies, died of hypothermia. (Births are not registered for the first four months, to conceal infant mortality rates.) Hospital patients dependent on electrical equipment also died. Ceauşescu personally ordered incubators to be turned off to economize on fuel. For the elderly it was a case of survival of the fittest.

The following winters showed little improvement. "Give us this day our daily bread" took on real meaning for Romanians. A great deal of sharing has taken place. Romanians are very generous people, and some churches, the Baptists in particular, organize unofficial practical help to those in particular need.

However, almost everyone in Romania is involved to some extent in what might be termed corrupt practices. Throughout the Communist world corruption is rife, but in Romania, which already had a bad record before the Communist takeover, it has become worse than anywhere else. It is now almost impossible to get the simplest thing done without rewarding the person who makes it possible. This applies even in church life. Even evangelicals with their strict moral code may, for example, have to give bribes to get building materials for essential repairs.

Standards are falling in every sphere of life, particularly in education and health services. Forced labor has been reintroduced. Perhaps the most degrading measure of all was passed in 1984–85. To reverse the rapid decline in population, women were told to produce four children or face heavy taxation; they are examined each month to insure that pregnancies are carried through. Previously, abortion, though contrary to church teaching, had become common, for women were unwilling to bring children into the world they knew.

The government is also moving against the elderly, who are denigrated as "consumers who produce nothing, passing their time waiting in lines in front of shops, whining about the price of medication and talking nonsense." Plans are afoot to move old people to rural areas and to refuse them medical treatment.

In 1986, reduced to desperation, peasants rioted, raided government grain stores, and refused to reap the harvest. Troops were brought in. Some peasants fled over the border into Yugoslavia, as have increasing numbers of Romanians since, even at the risk of being drowned in the Danube or shot in the process. Charges against Christians nowadays are often connected with their trying to escape, or helping others to escape. A few people even dared vote against official candidates. A converted Baptist lawyer, Nelu Prodan, defended two teachers sacked because of their faith, the first such case in the history of Communist Romania. He was briefly arrested in December 1987, later nearly killed in a car "accident."

By late 1987 there were glimmers of organized opposition, though in a country where every typewriter's script has to be checked by police twice annually, there is virtually no *samizdat*. Increasingly, people feel they have nothing to lose and are manifesting their feelings openly, with pamphlets, posters, and protests, even though they face almost certain discovery and years in prison. Professor Doina Cornea declared that with Romania dying spiritually, socially, culturally, and economically, its people cowed into untruth and degradation, people must refuse to render to Caesar what is due only to God, and live in the truth. She and her son were arrested briefly, and she is still under judicial inquiry. Romania's economic situation had deteriorated even further. Each winter was awaited with dread. There were ominous signs of alcoholism, previously not a problem, as people already suffering from malnutrition turned to drink. Rations were reduced, wages cut (until December, when Ceauşescu granted a token rise), new austerity measures imposed on fuel consumption, light, and heating. Unemployment was so widespread that people were paying bribes to get jobs.

The situation was as bad as in the severe winter of 1984–85. In some places, even such staples as bread, potatoes, sugar, milk, and cooking oil were unavailable. On November 15 thousands shouting "Down with the dictator!" rioted and clashed with the police in Braşov, the second-largest city, in the biggest demonstration since the coal miners' strikes of 1977. There and in Timişoara and other places, protests were ruthlessly suppressed.

Naturally, Gorbachev is very concerned. Ceauşescu has made his antipathy to *glasnost* clear, and there has been no mention of it in the Romanian press. Relations between the two men during Gorbachev's 1987 visit were manifestly strained. During Ceauşescu's visit to Moscow in October 1988, Gorbachev made it clear that he is disturbed by economic mismanagement and human-rights violations in Romania. But the visiting dictator made it just as clear that he intends to continue along his solitary path. "One should always bear in mind that the revolutionary process is unfolding in each country in different conditions," he responded. Ceauşescu, aware of Romania's increasing economic dependence on the Soviet Union, is certainly also aware that the Soviets might intervene to promote a successor more amenable to their way of thinking. Yet Gorbachev appears to feel that any type of intervention would damage his credibility; he appears to have no policy other than to outwait Ceauşescu and hope for a coup after his death.

Ceauşescu himself, 70, is aging rapidly. Although nepotism is practiced on a grand scale, neither his playboy son, Nicu, nor his vindictive second-in-command wife, Deputy Premier Elena, is considered a likely successor. But he has ruthlessly eliminated any possible successors from outside his family.

Destroying a Nation's Heritage

Although his country is on the verge of collapse, Ceauşescu is still trying to establish a dynasty, for he believes that a "man like me is born only once in every five hundred years." To perpetuate his own memory, he began in 1984 to tear out the heart of old Bucharest to make way for a grandiose government and party headquarters, framed by an immense quarter-mile-wide Victory of Socialism Boulevard. This entails destroying churches and monasteries of immense cultural and architectural value.

Ceauşescu has already demolished some of the most historic churches, monasteries, and synagogues in the country. To show his contempt for religion, he chose Palm Sunday to dynamite the Spirea church and Văcăreşti Orthodox monastery, second largest in southeast Europe (though it had not been used as a religious establishment for more than a century). All this has provoked a degree of hostility remarkable in law-abiding people. In some cases, demolition workers have refused to carry out orders, and troops or convict labor have been brought in. In a very few cases the public authorities bowed to public pressure, and a few buildings have been saved.

But by spring 1988 Bucharest looked like a blitzed, ravaged city. More than twenty Orthodox churches and a fifth of Old Bucharest had been demolished. Some 40,000 people had been moved out to the suburbs, often at only a few hours' notice, in an orgy of destruction that observers are now comparing with the bombing of Dresden. Even the patriarchal cathedral is now under threat, as well as sixty other churches. While one of Europe's finest cities is being wiped out at the whim of a megalomaniac, the psychological damage to the Romanian people is incalculable. They are seeing their past crumble irretrievably before their eyes. People light candles and weep helplessly as one old church after another is bulldozed. Neither the patriarch nor one Orthodox bishop has publicly raised his voice in protest, while leading Western cultural personalities denounce the wanton destruction.

Ceauşescu's demolition policy is not confined to Bucharest: a similar policy is planned for towns throughout Romania. Cultural, religious, and historic buildings will disappear forever, replaced by blocks of apartments, the better to supervise the populace. It was announced in March 1988 that half of the country's 14,000 villages would be razed by the year 2000. Peasants would be moved into apartment buildings, individual farms eliminated in order to "systemize" agriculture more fully. The campaign would destroy the homes and cultural identity of many of the country's Hungarians and Germans.

Significantly, no foreign clerics were invited to the 1987 centenary celebrations of the autocephaly of the Romanian Orthodox Church, as they had been to the ninetieth anniversary ten years earlier. Some of the authorities were too ashamed to let foreigners see what was happening to the nation's heritage.

The Outlook

The brightest light in Romania is the faith of the people. Observers note that the churches are still packed. Cynics might say that religion is all the people have left. But religion in Romania not only has survived persecution but has ventured into renewal. The contrast with neighboring Bulgaria is striking.

All the churches face daunting problems. Swift urbanization has taken its toll. With its weak leadership, the national church cannot retain its hold on the industrial population as the Catholic Church has in Poland.

There is little likelihood of further large-scale arrests of religious activists such as took place in the early 1980s, but the system is such that Christians here and there will still be imprisoned for their activities. For example, Victor Opriş, a young Pentecostalist pastor responsible for eleven unofficial church communities, was given a nine-year sentence in 1987, though he was freed after a year in Ceauşescu's seventieth-birthday amnesty. Gabriel Tărlescu, an Orthodox activist who was a member of the now disbanded ALRC, Pavel Dragu, a Baptist, and two others, all engaged in distributing Bibles from abroad, were given ten-month sentences for trying to cross into Yugoslavia illegally. A Baptist film editor, Nestor Popescu, said to have written a novel about life in today's Romania, was arrested partly for "carrying out religious propaganda" at his place of work and disappeared into a psychiatric hospital.

Even without using imprisonment, the Securitate are adept at making life intolerable for individual congregations and believers who step out of line. For instance, some church members are being denied work or are made to do forced labor on reduced wages, either of which, under present Romanian conditions, condemns them and their families to near starvation. The teenage daughter of an outstanding active evangelical pastor, Titus Mihet, suffered a severe nervous breakdown, worn down by terror and threats from her teacher.

Particularly damaging for all churches is the recent deliberate reduction of seminaries, which puts the churches' long-term pastoral care in jeopardy. The Department of Cults, moreover, continues to use any means whatsoever to create divisions between and within the churches, especially between Orthodox and evangelicals, and between Catholics of Hungarian and of Romanian origin. Many of the best Christians have emigrated, some forced to do so, others choosing to do so out of sheer exhaustion. The drain of leaders and active Christians during the last decade has been very costly.

Harassment and terrorism continue. For instance, late in 1986 an overhead cable was brought into contact with part of the home of psychologist-turned-Baptist-pastor Paul Negruţ, making it "live." A year later he was warned during an interrogation to "remember what happened to the Polish priest"—presumably Fr. Jerzy Popiełuszko, killed in an attack by the Polish security police in 1984.

There are nevertheless grounds for encouragement. One is the spontaneous, grassroots ecumenism that has grown out of common adversity and the defense of common values. The basic divisions are national rather than denominational. In general, there is more flexibility than is normal in Eastern Europe, much coming and going among different churches, and a deep interest in the rights and tribulations of members of other denominations. Those who tend to be unecumenical are the church leaders, particularly the Orthodox *vis-à-vis* the Eastern Rite Catholics.

Revival, previously restricted to the evangelical churches, has now entered the Orthodox Church. Religious faith is proving more resilient than the state realized. "No one can remove God from the Romanian soul," says Father Pop. He points out that, after forty years of the regime's "fight against faith and conscience," a schoolchild will still reply in an official questionnaire (designed to spy on both child and family): "I have only one God." (An excerpt from such a questionnaire, and an 11-year-old girl's reaction, appears in appendix S.) He adds that "there has never been and can never be a distinction between what is religious and what is Romanian."

In recent years, according to Father Pop, people—particularly the young—have been returning to church. Father Calciu saw far more young people in church after his release in 1984 than before his arrest in 1978. Government sources substantiate these claims—the policy of atheistic indoctrination of the younger generation has fallen far short of expectations. Indeed, to some extent it has been counterproductive, serving to increase the young people's interest in religion.

Ceauşescu's Romania represents Communism in the hands of a plausible madman. Intent on molding a nation in the image of socialism to his own glory, he has placed that nation on what one commentator called a "forced march toward the Middle Ages." Only Christianity gives hope in such an apparently hopeless situation.

10

Yugoslavia

YUGOSLAVIA IS the only East European nation, aside from Albania, that is not a member of the Warsaw Pact and is not dominated by the Soviet Union. It is able to pursue a policy free of Moscow's dictates.

Josip Broz Tito emerged as undisputed leader after the internecine struggles of World War II. He had been a faithful ally of the Soviet Union but was far different from the rather faceless leaders of the neighboring Communist states. A man with flair, charm, and an assertive personality, he used his gifts to woo and win over Western leaders. In 1948 complex differences between Stalin and him came to a head, and Stalin expelled him from the Cominform.

After Stalin's death, Yugoslavia resumed a somewhat ambiguous relationship with Moscow. The country is more closely tied to the USSR than many Westerners realize. The two are linked by their common ideology, one that demands absolute power for the state, even though Tito challenged the ideology with some heterodox views (as, for instance, in applying a local variant of Communism, "self-management socialism"; Yugoslav Marxism became a permanent irritant and challenge to Soviet Marxism). By establishing Yugoslavia as a "non-aligned nation," Tito was doing a vital job for the USSR—using his charisma to get the Third World nations to join his "non-aligned" bloc and thus to back Communist policies in general. The USSR still exerts a stranglehold on Yugoslavia's economy.

Yugoslavia and to a lesser extent Albania occupy a strategically vulnerable position because together they deny the Soviets access to the Adriatic. A Yugoslavia under Soviet control would drive a wedge between Western NATO countries and their allies, Greece and Turkey. The Yugoslav government has skillfully played on the West's fear of Soviet influence to extract recognition and some economic aid.

Openness to the Free World

Yugoslavia's relative openness to the West—unique in Eastern Europe—not only has moderated its policy toward religion but also has freed the churches, and the population as a whole, from the psychological block of isolation. When in the early 1950s his country was on the brink of collapse, Tito turned to the West. This gave the Christian churches some protection from persecution. Later, in the 1970s, when seeking closer relations with the oil-rich Arab states, he allowed his large Muslim minority to open contacts abroad—with unforeseen consequences.

Economically, Yugoslavia shares the vulnerability of Western economies. Over a million of its people are unemployed, and inflation in 1987 soared to over 175 per cent. As a safety valve, and to bring in Western currency, Yugoslavs are allowed to seek work in other countries. One-tenth of its 22 million citizens are or have been employed in the West, mainly in West Germany.

Tourists from the West flock to Yugoslavia for its scenic beauty, historical buildings, and beaches. The influences of the West—its profusion of goods and its democratic freedoms—have accentuated the problems inherent in the complex national structure of Yugoslavia.

Internal Divisions

Yugoslavia is not one nation but a conglomeration of several nations, each with its own history and religious affiliation. More than any other European country, it is an artificial creation. Its six constituent republics are Serbia, Croatia, Slovenia, Bosnia-Herzegovina, Macedonia, and Montenegro. Nationalism is, not surprisingly, an ever present problem for the central government.

During the last war the country was torn by an intricate and destructive civil war that tragically involved the churches. The government's attitude toward the churches is colored more by the fear that they may support breakaway nationalist movements than by any anti-religious ideology, which is not to say that persecution and the ideological element do not exist. The situation is further complicated by the open divergences within the ruling Communist Party.

It is estimated that 40 per cent of the people are nominally Orthodox and 32 per cent Catholic. The single most important factor in the matter of national cohesiveness is probably the relationship between the Orthodox Serbs and the Catholic Croats. The recent rise of Muslim influence has added a new factor; Muslims now make up 18 per cent of the population.

The country's nine million Serbs (40 per cent of the population) and five million Croats (23 per cent) speak variants of the same language that are about as different as American and English, though Serbian is written in Cyrillic, Croatian in the Latin alphabet. Of the smaller Slav nationalities, the Slovenes (8 per cent) are predominantly Catholic, the Bosnians (6 per cent) are mixed Muslim, Orthodox, and Catholic, while the Macedonians (6 per cent) and Montenegrins are mostly Orthodox, though Macedonia has a growing Muslim minority. The Macedonians are not considered a separate nationality by most Serbs, but, like the Slovenes, they have their own language; to Serbo-Croats, Macedonian and Slovenian sound as foreign as other Slav languages such as Czech and Polish. As for the Muslims, half of their four million adherents are Serb or Croat, half Albanian or Macedonian. (Others of the two million Albanians in Yugoslavia are Catholic.) Yugoslavia contains several other nationalities—Hungarians, Slovaks, Romanians, Greeks, Turks, and Vlachs, the 600,000 Hungarians being the largest group. None of these smaller groups has threatened to disrupt national unity. Everyone has to learn Serbo-Croat at school.

THE BACKGROUND: TO 1941

In 1919, in the breakup of the Austro-Hungarian and Ottoman empires, the dream of a new nation uniting southern Slavs came true—the Kingdom of the Serbs, Croats, and Slovenes. The name was changed in 1929 to "Yugoslavia." In a sense the new Slavic state was a re-creation, for from the twelfth to the fourteenth century the major southern Slavic people, the Serbs, ruled a large empire whose heartland was the province of Kossovo, now an autonomous region in the south of Serbia. Kossovo, with its historic monuments, particularly its monasteries, represented a high point in Byzantine civilization, and it is greatly treasured by Serbs, a factor of considerable importance in understanding current troubles in the region. Balkan peoples have incredibly long memories.

After the Turks defeated the Serbs at the battle of Kossovo (1389), the Ottomans ruled for five centuries; only the Montenegrins in their rocky fastness regained independence by the eighteenth century. The subject peoples were cut off from the mainstream of European civilization. During the late seventeenth century many Serbs migrated north to help defend the Austro-Hungarian emperor against the Turks, and, according to Serbs, the Turks encouraged Muslim Albanians to move into the vacated Kossovo regions. Other sources claim Kossovo was already Albanian.

The Ottoman Empire was tolerant toward religions, although people who adopted Islam had considerable privileges. The Orthodox Church became the guardian of Serbian nationhood, and as the empire weakened and the ideal of the southern Slav state—an equal union of Serbs, Croats, and Slovenes—took shape, the Serbs and their clergy led the struggle.

Having gained independence and experienced parliamentary and democratic government during the nineteenth century, the Serbs regarded the new Yugoslavia of 1919, under the rule of their royal family, as simply an extension of their former control. Serbian dominance of Yugoslavia in the inter-war years led to resentment among the other peoples, exacerbated by their different religions and cultural ethos.

Although the Croats were from the same stock as the Serbs, they settled further west, converted to Latin Christianity, and formed an independent kingdom in the tenth century. In 1102 they were linked politically with Hungary, which eventually brought them into the Habsburg Empire. In the nineteenth century, as Ottoman power waned, this Catholic empire began to extend southward. Some Catholics began to proselytize vigorously among the Orthodox, whom they regarded as schismatics. This and the resentment against Serb rule were the roots of the tension today between Serb and Croat.

Politically and geographically the Croats were closer to Western civilization than the Serbs, and religiously they were close to the Catholic churches of Italy and Austria.

In 1929, King Alexander set up a dictatorship, and the Serbs became even more powerful. Since then, Croats and Slovenes have been suspicious of every central government in Belgrade. The Serbian Orthodox Church saw itself as the national church. Alexander was assassinated while abroad in 1934 by a fringe group of Croatian extremists, the Ustashe, led by Ante Pavelić and trained in Fascist Italy.

When in 1935 the government discussed the possibility of a concordat with the Vatican, the Orthodox raised such opposition that it backed down, leaving the Catholics very resentful. The acute poverty of much of Yugoslavia and the ineffectiveness of the government added to the general social unrest. Yet the various national and religious groups coexisted peacefully if not always harmoniously. Few people could have foreseen the coming holocaust and the ensuing bitterness.

FROM 1941 TO 1980

In 1941 Yugoslavia fell to the invading German forces and was parceled out among Germany, Italy, Hungary, and Bulgaria. By playing on the communal divisions, the Germans set Yugoslav against Yugoslav, encouraging cruelties worse than what they inflicted themselves. Tragically, Pavelić and the Ustashe, whose aim was to set up a militant Catholic Croatia, became rulers of a Fascist puppet state in Croatia and Bosnia. A brutal civil war followed in which the contenders seemed more intent on eliminating one another than in fighting the Nazis.

There were two main groups resisting the Nazi invaders: an army led by the Communist Field Marshall Tito, and Serbian Četniks led by Draža Mihajlović. The Allies were persuaded by Tito and left-wing infiltrators of the British Intelligence Service to back the Communists.

The Ustashe Reign of Terror

The country, the only Eastern-bloc member to provide guerrilla resistance against the Nazis, suffered appalling losses during the war; 10 per cent of the population, between one and two million people, died, of whom only 305,000 were soldiers. A large number were victims of the Ustashe, who were determined to eliminate all Jews, Gypsies, and any Serbs who refused to become Catholics—but Muslims were left alone. The alliance of Catholic and Muslim has been a significant factor in the religious life of Croatia and Bosnia.

Even the Germans were shocked at what happened. The Croat Catholic bishops at first welcomed Ustashe rule but were soon repelled. Bishop Mišić reported from Bosnia: "Men are captured like animals, slaughtered. Six truckloads of mothers, young girls, and children . . . were led up to the mountains and thrown alive off the precipices. This [massacre] can benefit neither the Croatian nor the Catholic cause."

Nazi-style concentration camps were also established. Of about two million Serbs in Ustashe-governed territory, approximately 350,000 Orthodox were killed, 250,000 were forcibly converted, and 300,000 were deported or fled to what remained of Serbia. The Orthodox Church has yet to recover. Some 60,000 of the 76,000 Jews died in concentration camps, as did large numbers of Gypsies.

The killing horrified many Catholics and Muslims, but most were too terrified to intervene. Thousands of Croats were slaughtered in a vicious and indiscriminate backlash.

Archbishop Stepinac and the Massacres

Bishop Mišić's report was sent to the Archbishop of Zagreb, Alojzije Stepinac, who in 1934 at the age of thirty-six had unwillingly become the world's youngest archbishop. More impassioned controversy has raged around Stepinac than any other East European church leader. He was vilified and tried as a war criminal; yet he became a cardinal of his church, is adulated by Catholics in general and Croats in particular, and has been proposed for beatification.

Almost certainly, no church leader could have prevented the Ustashe killings. Stepinac was first and foremost a Catholic, a holy man devoted to his church but limited in vision. He felt forced conversions were invalid and was appalled at the massacres.

At first he protested to the government in private, but later he spoke out publicly in his sermons. His efforts on behalf of Jews and "schismatics" were nevertheless timid compared to the exemplary courage he later displayed in defense of the Catholic Church against Communism and during his trial in 1946.

The Communist Takeover

Tito became premier in 1945. Lacking power, the non-Communist members of the government resigned and were arrested. National elections—from which the opposition abstained—resulted in victory for the government.

Tito and the LCY, the League of Communists of Yugoslavia, summarily settled accounts with their opponents. These included Catholics and Orthodox, not because of their religions, but because of their political activities as Ustashe and Četniks. According to émigré sources, the Communists were also responsible for the merciless extermination of thousands of potential opponents; thousands more were put into concentration camps, including many former inmates of Dachau and Belsen, and Albanians were massacred if they refused to cooperate. This was hushed up in Yugoslavia until recently, although Četnik and Ustashe atrocities—damaging to religion—have been given full publicity.

Tito wanted the Vatican to recall Stepinac so as to avoid a head-on confrontation with the church. The Vatican refused, and Stepinac was brought to trial for supporting the Ustashe, for the forced conversion of Serbs, and for Fascist leanings. Unlike other East Europeans tried by new Communist governments, he was not broken beforehand, and he managed to make a classic defense speech in which he indicted the authorities. Sentenced to sixteen years, Stepinac spent five in prison and the rest in his village under constant surveillance until his death in 1960.

To some extent the trial misfired. Although Stepinac became a convenient symbol for branding the entire Croat church Fascist whenever it suited Tito, as a result of the government's action a rather ordinary bishop was transformed into a Croat national hero.

Tito's Yugoslavia—Six Republics

Fulfilling his wartime promises, Tito reorganized Yugoslavia into a federation of six self-governing national republics. (Tito, himself a Croat, showed no partiality toward any national group and was equally tough with troublemakers of any nationality.) The major lesser nationalities were given their own republics, with one crucial exception, the Albanians. Of the six,

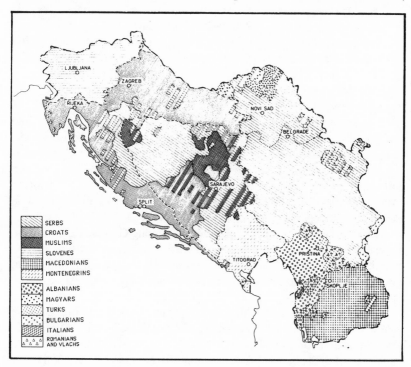

ETHNIC DISTRIBUTION OF THE POPULATION, 1948

only two can be called homogeneous: Slovenia, in the north, and Montenegro, adjacent to Albania. The others—Serbia, Croatia, Macedonia, and Bosnia-Herzegovina, are ethnically mixed. The "frontier" between Latin and Byzantine Christendom runs right across Yugoslavia, roughly along the divide between the Austrian and Ottoman empires.

Serbia is the largest republic and has two autonomous regions— Vojvodina to the north and Kossovo to the south. Its capital, Belgrade, is also the federal capital, but Tito ensured against its regaining its former dominance. There are 600,000 Hungarians, mostly Catholic or Protestant, in Vojvodina, and Albanians increasingly dominate the Kossovo region.

The Albanians of Yugoslavia, a non-Slavic people, make up about 6 per cent of the population, but they are increasing and are now the third largest of the seven nationalities, after the Serbs and Croats. They are intensely proud, wild, and primitive, with a per capita income half the national average. They were grossly neglected by the central government until the late 1960s. Their society is tribal and basically Muslim. The Law of Lek still carries much force, and some clan blood feuds continue. Kossovo is Yugoslavia's most intractable long-term problem.

The population of Vojvodina—a fertile, relatively prosperous region north of the Danube—is fragmented among Orthodox, Catholic, and Protestant. The proportion of active churchgoers is rather low and that of atheists relatively high, and this region has seen a number of clashes between religious activists and local LCY members.

The second largest republic, *Croatia*, is the most industrialized and prosperous area of the country. Tourism along the Adriatic coast is important to its economy. Its capital, Zagreb, is the cultural center of Yugoslavia.

In pre-war Yugoslavia, the Macedonians were regarded as southern Serbs, and Serbian bishops administered their dioceses. In another effort to keep the Serbs in line, Tito made *Macedonia* a distinct national republic and promoted a separate Macedonian Orthodox Church.

The Macedonians are currently divided among Greece, Bulgaria, and Yugoslavia. Although they disliked the Serbs, their bitter wartime experience in Bulgaria turned them even more against Bulgarians. Another of Tito's reasons for fostering a separate Macedonian nationality was to counteract Greek and Bulgarian claims to their territory.

Thus favored, the Macedonians are enthusiastically building a nation with Communism only an incidental ingredient. Only 71 per cent Macedonian, the region contains Greeks, Vlachs (a mountain people who speak a Latin language), Turks, and Albanians, mostly but not all Muslim. Skopje, the capital, was the birthplace of Ganxha Bojhaxiu, better known as Mother Teresa, whose parents were Albanians.

Bosnia-Herzegovina, with its capital at Sarajevo, is the most mixed of the six republics: 40 per cent Muslim Slav, 32 per cent Orthodox Serb, and 18 per cent Catholic Croat.

Neither *Montenegro* nor *Slovenia* poses any threat to Yugoslav unity. Montenegrins, a mere 2 per cent of the population of the nation, are basically a Serbian people who are traditionally Orthodox, part of the Serbian Orthodox Church.

The Slovenes are a small nation accustomed to looking to a large one for protection. They are homogeneous, industrious, and strongly Catholic, and have much in common with the more advanced Central European Slav peoples. Slovenia has been sensibly governed by moderate Communists, and the church has been guided by far-sighted clergy. Their relations with other Yugoslavs, Serbs included, are reasonable.

Tito's Religious Policy

No one can deny Tito's ruthlessness, but he did succeed in reconstructing and modernizing Yugoslavia. A Marxist, he was also a politician in the devious, Byzantine mold; he could be pragmatic, and at times openly critical of the Soviet Union. In foreign affairs he lifted his backward, war-torn country to a prestigious position as a non-aligned state, a key factor in the delicate balance of East-West politics.

Yet the reality is not quite what some Western politicians imagine. They often equate Tito's independent stance with liberalism. The truth is that Yugoslavia is basically as repressive a police state as most others in Eastern Europe, only less predictably so. The world war and civil war left Yugoslavia a shattered country. With his ambitious social, economic, and educational programs, and with no certain support from either East or West, Tito needed the cooperation of the entire population. An all-out attack on religion would have been disastrous. Furthermore, Tito's mother was a devout Catholic, and he realized how deep the roots of religion went. Once he had dealt with his political opponents and any obstacles to national unity, he relaxed the pressure on the churches and became far more tolerant than many of his fellow Communists.

After some early imprisonments and confiscations, the churches were given legal status as "persons" and thus permitted to own property. The 1953 constitution guaranteed liberty of conscience and religion as well as separation of church and state—guarantees that have actually been respected, unlike the practice in other East European countries. There is no "ministry of religious affairs," but there are Commissions for Relations with Religious Communities attached to federal, provincial, and communal assemblies, to monitor church activities and to communicate between church and state. They are less tightly organized and intrusive and less obviously connected with security agencies than elsewhere. The churches have freedom in "ecclesiastical matters," although the definition of what these actually are has caused difficulties. Most important for a country as divided as Yugoslavia, the churches have equal legal status.

The Serbian Orthodox Church

The war was a total disaster for the Serbian Orthodox Church. From its prominence as almost the established church, it was plunged into suffering and persecution, at the hand of foreign invaders as well as Croats. After the war, it was too weak to stand up to the Communist state. Of its 4,200 churches and 220 monasteries, almost a quarter had been destroyed, and another half had been damaged. Six bishops and about seven hundred priests, almost a fifth, had been killed; the loss among the laity was perhaps half a million. The once proud church was physically and psychologically in disarray. It had to devote all its energies to reconstruction.

The early years—before Tito's hand lightened—left it all but bankrupt, almost all its lands and assets confiscated, often unable to pay its clergy. Unlike the Catholic Church, the autocephalous Orthodox Church had no outside sources of material and spiritual support.

The state, however, saw a use for it. It could, for instance, help the state maintain contact with other Communist countries that had prominent Orthodox churches—the USSR, Romania, and Bulgaria. And so Patriarch Gavrilo, who had been sent to Dachau by the Nazis, was invited to return as head of the church.

Against all odds, the Orthodox had by 1980 restored 841 churches and built 220 new ones, reestablished seminary education, and reopened a church press, although they are still far behind the Catholics.

Neither Tito nor his succesors found relationships with the Orthodox leadership straightforward, for having preached submission to the state in pre-war Yugoslavia and having been more flexible in response to pressure than the Catholics, they were expert prevaricators and infuriatingly devious. They tended to look at things from the perspective of eternity, prepared to wait it out.

Resisting the Macedonian Church

The Serbian Orthodox Church put up a stubborn resistance on central issues, such as when the unity of the church was threatened by Macedonian separatism. It had already suffered one schism when some of its parishes in Europe and North America seceded to form a church loyal to the exiled royal family. (Peter II, son of the assassinated Alexander, formed a government in exile in London after the German invasion in 1941.) In 1958, much against their will, the bishops granted a form of autonomy to the three Macedonian dioceses. But when the Macedonians uncanonically declared their autocephaly in 1967, the church tried to get other Orthodox churches to boycott them. This, ironically, pushed the Macedonian Orthodox Church into seeking help from the Vatican, with which it retains good relations.

The Serbian Orthodox Church strongly resented the LCY for supporting the creation of the Macedonian Church for its own purposes—to strengthen Macedonian national consciousness. It questioned the viability of such a small church. For the sake of the faithful, however, it stopped short of excommunication; clergy and laity of the two churches remain in touch. The Serbian Church believes that the issue should await the decision of an ecumenical council.

The Catholic Church

Orthodox and Catholics face similar problems. As in other Communist states, the government sponsored left-wing priests' associations, but they have not proved very divisive. The clergy who join (83 per cent of the Orthodox, only 17 per cent of the Catholic) do so largely for reasons of pension and insurance. These associations cannot be compared with the Peace Priests elsewhere in the Communist world. "Peace" is definitely not a Yugoslav specialty, and "peace" conferences do not happen.

In the aftermath of the war, the Croatian church bore the brunt of the backlash against Catholics, but the Slovenian church suffered, too, with many of its priests imprisoned. Under the wise leadership of Bishop Vovk, however, sensible and fairly good relations have become a continuing feature of Slovene church life. Priests, who before the war had held parliamentary office, renounced their past involvement in politics.

Persecution in Croatia was mainly directed against those who had been politically inolved, and while Stepinac lived, relations between church and state were strained. A series of events brought about a rapprochement—the death of Stepinac in 1960, the reestablishment during the late 1960s of relations with the Vatican, which had been severed in 1953, the progressive decrees of Vatican II, and the enforced adjustment of church life to a modern secular Yugoslavia. The able Cardinal Franjo Šeper negotiated for free church activities. In 1963 Archbishop Alfred Pichler admitted the church's past offenses in his Christmas message. Many of his clergy refused to read it out, for Catholics found it difficult to revise their attitudes toward the state and toward other churches.

In 1966 the Vatican and the Yugoslav government signed a protocol—the first time the Vatican recognized a "socialist" regime. It was the outstanding achievement of Pope Paul VI's *Ostpolitik*, but a bitter pill for the church to swallow. Agreement was reached without consulting the Yugoslav hierarchy, and one of the clauses of the protocol—a reference to possible "terrorist" activities of priests—causes offense.

In the protocol, the state recognized the Vatican's jurisdiction over the spiritual and ecclesiastical matters of the church, and in return the Vatican agreed that the Catholic clergy would not interfere in the country's political life. This ensured, for instance, that bishops could be appointed freely and keep open contact with Rome.

The snag is that the government can define "politics." It may brand an informal church activity or a church pronouncement on secular affairs, no matter how relevant to church life, as a foray into politics. Nevertheless, the churches in Yugoslavia—for the same principle is applied to them all—have a degree of internal autonomy unknown anywhere else in the Eastern bloc except East Germany.

By 1970 full diplomatic relations had been restored between Rome and Yugoslavia—the first Communist country to recognize the Vatican. Tito himself visited Pope Paul in 1971, as one head of state to another. With state encouragement, high-level relations between the Catholic and Orthodox churches also improved considerably during the 1960s.

Catholic life recovered much more quickly than the Orthodox or Muslim. It had the advantage of a far better educated and disciplined body of clergy and religious, an adequate number of vocations, and some outstanding leaders, like Franjo Šeper of Zagreb, created cardinal in 1965 and assigned to Rome in 1967 as prefect of the Congregation for Doctrine and Faith.

An important development in the late 1960s was a genuine dialogue between Catholics and academic Marxists. The Catholic press attracted intellectuals involved in reexamining Marxism, whose shortcomings were particularly glaring in the confused Yugoslav setup. The "dialogues," in which more than 3,000 students participated, aroused considerable interest. Sociological studies of religion became fashionable and often indirectly marshalled appreciation for the churches.

Deterioration of Relations

The church-state situation deteriorated in the 1970s, largely because of the government's reaction to the "Croat Spring." In 1970–71, in an atmosphere of new confidence and prosperity, there was an upsurge of Croatian national fervor that united Croats behind their intellectuals and church leaders. Tito, shaken by the strength of the revival of what he called "national euphoria," struck back with a wholesale purge of the leaders of the Communist Party in Croatia and also in the other republics, replacing them with hard-liners. He also purged academic and cultural circles of their liberal or nationalist elements.

The Catholic Church was left in the invidious—though not entirely unwelcome—position of sole champion of Croatian national aspirations. The authorities accused the church of excessive nationalism; priests were, and still are, actively engaged in Croat nationalist groups. The Croat Spring was also a period of religious revival, especially among the young. The church, by opening numerous youth centers to attract young people, filled a genuine need in society. But since the youth centers were also, potentially, breeding grounds for nationalism, they have been periodically stamped on by the government. The authorities sniped at the churches and at individual leaders but refrained from an outright attack on religious belief. The churches did not suffer any more than other segments of society.

At the same time the Catholic Church in Slovenia was asserting itself. In 1973, some of the clergy claimed the right of the church to become a "self-managing organization." They also focused on human rights and demanded the right of religious education.

The Catholic-Marxist dialogue halted. In Zagreb several issues of *Glas Koncila,* the popular and excellent Catholic paper, were banned for alleged nationalistic propaganda; its editor, Fr. Živko Kustić, and a woman journalist were given prison sentences, though Father Kustić did not serve his.

Not surprisingly, the Croat upsurge produced a Serbian reaction, which Tito also dealt with. In 1972 a Serbian Orthodox bishop, Vasilije of Žiča, was given thirty days for "hostile propaganda" when he preached an "indiscreet" sermon; he was the first bishop to be imprisoned since 1954.

Tito's last ten years were difficult for the churches. Discrimination against church members, always a sore point, was more widely enforced. Tito and his advisors were preoccupied with ensuring that Yugoslav unity would hold after his death and bristled at the faintest whiff of nationalism.

THE RELIGIOUS MAKEUP IN THE 1980s

The prosperity of the 1970s has given way to unemployment and inflation, exacerbated by the migration of workers from the backward south to the more affluent north. Liberal elements have also become disillusioned with the enforcement of an ideology hardly anyone believes in, with the tight security, and with the rough police methods in this relatively free society.

The strongest potential opposition comes from educated liberal Slovenes, Croats, and Serbs who share a desire for a more democratic society and who look to the West for their values. A number of Christians, particularly Catholics, are involved. The arrest and subsequent mysterious death in 1984 of one of twenty-eight intellectuals who met to hear leading dissident Milovan Djilas was a revelation to Westerners who regard the regime as liberal. However, the last recorded murder of a believer by the police was in 1956.

In the uncertain atmosphere, any expression from the churches that could be interpreted as nationalism has been pounced upon. The government fears not only Croatian and Albanian nationalism but a Serbian backlash. The continued honoring of Stepinac and the reported appearances of the Virgin at Medjugorje in 1981 have caused nervous authorities to overreact by imposing prison sentences on various Christians and Muslims. Self-interest is built into the political system. The old guard may be dying off, in church and state alike, but its successors do not want to lose power through compromise.

Tito, the first and last president, had fostered a personality cult. Before his death in 1980 there was speculation that for lack of a strong leader Yugoslavia would disintegrate before separatist tendencies of the different nationalities. Tito was replaced by a prime minister whose office—and those

RELIGIOUS DISTRIBUTION OF THE POPULATION
(Approximate, 1979)

at all levels of the central administration—rotates annually among representatives of the six republics and two provinces. This is to prevent any republic or nationality from becoming overtly dominant. The position of prime minister is not given prominence; many Yugoslavs do not even know who the current incumbent is.

Yet the de facto federalism of church and state continues to stimulate regional nationalism, and has been accentuated by a very real lack of communication between the republics. It has also been aggravated by the rise of

Islamic self-consciousness and by Albanians' aggressive reaction to their suppression in the riots in Kossovo in 1981.

The Serbian Orthodox Church, though with about 7 million members the largest religious body in Yugoslavia, is all too conscious of its post-war vulnerability. The morale of the Catholic Church, with 6.9 million members in 1981 and enthusiastic support from Croats and Slovenes, is far higher. The church is well endowed with personnel, institutions, and literature. It has had, for ten years, a Slav as pope, and it can maintain close contact with Rome and the rest of the world.

The Orthodox Churches

The *Serbian Orthodox Church,* which is much more traditional than the Catholic Church, is less well equipped to meet the challenges of modern life; its support depends on a deep emotional attachment rather than on regular church attendance. It has 22 dioceses and 2,400 parishes, but only about 1,400 priests. The acute shortage of clergy and churches reflects not only the church's wartime losses but its meager vocations. Congregations are predominantly elderly. Government surveys show that in a traditional Orthodox area only 3 per cent of young people are religious, while 90 per cent claim a positive aversion to religion. This contrasts with surveys in some Catholic areas where one-third of the youth attend church regularly, one-third are passive believers or uncertain, and only one-third are atheists. Even so, there are about 600 students at the five Orthodox seminaries, with more than 400 more studying at the theological faculty at Belgrade.

Repairing damaged churches and getting permits from the state to build new ones poses more of a problem to the Orthodox than to other churches, partly because local LCYs (the Communist leagues) are reluctant to grant them permits, but also because they refuse to modify the traditional, expensive Byzantine-cross building plan. The state has helped restore monasteries of artistic or historic significance.

The Orthodox press, with only ten journals, is less varied, less modern, and more nationalistic than the Catholic press, and its circulation is considerably lower.

Male religious life, which suffered badly under the Turks, is at a low ebb. Many of the 220 pre-war monasteries were destroyed; 48 have been repaired, and 8 new ones have been built. As a symbol of Serbian resistance, the monasteries attract many pilgrims and visitors. Vocations are few, though increasing in the women's orders. There are about 200 monks. The 750 nuns—of high caliber—are traditionally enclosed and support themselves largely by farming. Handicapped by being regarded as inferior to men, they have much untapped potential. While Catholic orders are Westernized,

Orthodox religious seem to belong to another world. They nevertheless play a vital role in preserving Serb consciousness.

The *Macedonian Orthodox Church,* favored by the state, has an impressive new metropolitanate and a seminary at Skopje. It purports (the figures have been challenged) to have about 250 clergy serving between 600,000 and one million members in 225 scattered parishes. The Macedonians, who have had a raw deal since their heyday in the eleventh century, regard themselves as the true heirs of the influential Slav saints Clement and Naum of Ohrid. In 1984 the Pope received a Macedonian delegation, thus arousing Serb suspicions that Rome's aim is to establish the church as an Eastern Rite body under its own control.

The Catholic Church

The Catholic Church has eight archbishoprics, fourteen bishoprics, and two apostolic administrations. Its 2,782 parishes are served by about 2,700 secular priests (i.e., those not in priest's orders, not living in monasteries) and 400 religious. In 1979, the two theological faculties had 760 students, and the eight major seminaries had 560 students, all of whom go on to the theological faculties. A decline in vocations, for which materialism is blamed, seems to be continuing. The only state restriction is that all seminarians must complete their military service.

Rebuilding has proceeded more vigorously than in the Orthodox Church. By 1970 in Croatia alone, 1,250 churches had been extensively repaired, 273 new ones had been built, and another 89 were under construction.

Religious orders were discouraged in the early days of Communism. In Slovenia, women's orders were actually disbanded, but when the party needed trained nurses to run its "priority" hospitals, they were restored. They are now accepted and make a considerable impact on church life.

There are about 9,000 Catholic religious, approximately 2,500 male, of whom 1,400 are in priest's orders. A third of the church's 4,000 priests, therefore, are members of orders. The most popular—and, because of its links with Croat nationalism, the most controversial—is the Franciscan order.

Most of the parish priests in Bosnia used to be Franciscans. Their influence in Bosnia stems from the Turkish invasion, when, unlike the secular clergy, the friars did not desert their parishes. As a result the Franciscans were granted papal permission to act as parish priests, a privilege they have only recently been forced to relinquish. To placate the authorities, the Vatican has been appointing secular bishops, untainted by wartime excesses, to the dioceses, and is backing these bishops' attempts to replace the

Franciscans (who are answerable only to their superior) with secular priests. This has aroused fury among the parishioners. For twenty years there has been continuous friction between the bishops of Sarajevo and Mostar on the one side and the Franciscans and the laity on the other, which has made the Medjugorje appearances (in Mostar diocese) even more controversial and divisive.

The Franciscans have also suffered at the hand of the state. In 1983 the police arrested two novices, Franjo Vidović and Ivan Turudić, charging that a pro-Croatian poem and Croatian flags had been found in their possession. The bishops complained strongly. Turudić, who was sent to the punishment cells several times, came close to a breakdown; Vidović had to work as a smelter despite a weak heart.

The nuns, about 6,400 in 400 convents, are not permitted to teach in schools but otherwise can exercise a varied ministry, both in the church, where they are responsible for catechetical work, and in public life, where they do charitable work, especially where the state cannot cope with the needs.

There is a small *Eastern Rite Catholic Church*, numbering 65,000, with its own bishop. Most are Ruthenes from the Ukraine, but about 20 per cent are Croats or Macedonians.

The Muslims

Yugoslavia's four million Muslims, 18 per cent of the population, have only within the last decade or so had any political impact or been potentially divisive. Although there are Muslims in every republic, the majority are either Slavs living in Bosnia (where Muslims make up 40 per cent of the population) or Albanians living in the autonomous region of Kossovo. There are also many Turks—128,000 in 1971, 109,000 of them in Macedonia. There are also half a million Muslims in Macedonia, where they make up a quarter of the population.

Muslims are the descendants of those who conformed under Ottoman rule, but rarely out of any deep conviction. In the Middle Ages many of the Bosnians were Bogomils, a heretical sect whose adherents saw Islam as a way of improving their social status at the expense of Christians. The Albanians were extremely primitive, and though many became nominal Muslims, they clung to their tribal beliefs; the result was often syncretistic— part Muslim, part Christian, part pagan.

Coming from primitive regions and relegated to an inferior status in pre-war Yugoslavia, Muslims at first took a back seat in Tito's Yugoslavia. They had no national identity: the 18 per cent Croats in Bosnia claimed the Muslims there as fellow Croats and the 32 per cent Serbs claimed them as

Serbs, while everyone ignored the poverty-stricken and feud-ridden Albanians.

Establishing Muslim Nationhood

By the 1960s devolution was beginning at the local level, and in the 1961 census people were allowed to state "Muslim" as their nationality. A total of 843,247 did so, and in 1968 their separate nationhood was confirmed, providing a counterweight to the Serbs and the Croats in Bosnia. There are now 1.85 million Muslims in Bosnia.

Muslim nationhood also fitted in with Tito's policy of building a closer relationship with the Muslim world. Men with Muslim names were used in diplomatic and economic negotiations. Although those chosen for this were usually members of the LCY and tepid, if not lapsed, Muslims, many who were sent abroad returned feeling much closer to the worldwide Muslim community; some even returned as fanatic converts to Islam. Meanwhile, thousands of young Muslims were allowed to visit Mecca or go to Cairo to study the Koran.

At the time, no one realized the danger of resurgent Muslim nationalism. In trying to resolve one problem, Tito unwittingly fostered a greater one. In Bosnia the Muslims emerged as the largest single nationality and began to demand that Bosnia be declared a Muslim republic. Justifiable discontent was also mounting in Kossovo, although there Albanian rather than Muslim nationality is the key factor.

Islam in Yugoslavia is far stronger today than during the days of the Ottoman Empire, partly because of the religious revival and partly from generous funding by wealthy Muslim countries. Educational standards, previously very low, have been raised at every level. This includes a madrasah (theological school) that was opened in 1977 in Sarajevo (Bosnia) and has 250 students. In addition, Sarajevo has a faculty of Islamic theology and, remarkably, a madrasah for girls. There are also madrasahs in Kossovo and Macedonia.

There are 3,000 mosques, many built since 1966, and about 1,600 imams. Muslims are organized, as a religion, into four seniorates. The largest is in Sarajevo, where the head of the Islamic community, the Reis-ul-Ulema, lived until he moved to Belgrade in 1987. There is also a small but growing Islamic press.

The Protestant Churches

Protestantism has made little headway in Yugoslavia; the total membership is less than 1 per cent of the population. Since the churches are so few and have no political or nationalist stance, the government generally approves of them. Seventh Day Adventists complain, however, that they have been mistakenly classified with Jehovah's Witnesses as proselytizers and lawbreakers.

In the north are four long established Protestant churches, all members of the Lutheran World Federation, that are a direct legacy of the Reformation in Europe: the Slovak church (51,000), the Slovene church (20,000), and two Hungarian churches, one Calvinist and one Lutheran. The newer churches—Baptists (3,500), Pentecostalists (11,300), Seventh Day Adventists (10,600), Methodists (4,000), and a few Brethren—are distributed among the various republics.

Since 1975 a Protestant theological faculty in Zagreb has been open to all Protestant churches. Together with the interdenominational Cooperative Council, founded in 1980, it has helped bring together the previously noncooperative churches.

A seminar on evangelism in 1983, attended by fifty people from seven denominations, as well as by Protestants from Hungary and Bulgaria, launched courses on urban evangelism. Protestants are making small but significant contributions to Yugoslav church life.

The Jews

In the past, Yugoslavia had long-established communities of Jews. Sephardic Jews, fleeing from the Spanish Inquisition, settled in Serbia, where they were given equal citizenship under the 1888 constitution. Before the war the Yugoslav Jewish community numbered 70,000.

Of the 16,000 Jews who survived the concentration camps during the war, 10,000 left for Israel. The remainder are organized into thirty-five communities. The communities run secular activities, such as youth camps, that attract Jews from other parts of Eastern Europe. With no rabbis or older laymen carrying out rabbinical functions, religious life is hard to maintain. Press allegations in 1984 that they were a fifth column for Israel have increased the Jews' insecurity.

Legal Position of the Churches

The LCY contains more divergence of opinion than any other East European Communist Party. In matters of religion there seem to be three main groups. The first consists of doctrinaire orthodox Marxists—the "old guard" who saw the worst effects of religious nationalism during the war—who see no future for religion. Although gradually losing influence and numbers, they still get media coverage when church events give them a pretext for attack. The second or majority group believes that stiff anti-religious measures are counterproductive; this group prefers to allow the churches free play so long as they avoid a public or political stand. The third group—found chiefly among the Marxist sociologists of Zagreb, Ljubljana, and Sarajevo, and supported by younger party members—advocates active dialogue with the churches. It considers repression outmoded and detrimental and appreciates the social contribution the churches make.

Party policy tends to support the third group in times of peace and prosperity but switches to the first group when things are unsettled, as they have been for some years.

Religious bodies are more secure in Yugoslavia than in any other Communist country since its constitutional guarantees are generally upheld, but their position is complicated by differing laws in the six republics. In general, all new congregations have to register with the state. Although all religious groups are allowed their own press, access to the secular media is denied, despite protests by the Catholic hierarchy. In theory, clergy are allowed to visit old people's homes, hospitals, and sanatoriums, but not prisons or the army. In Split (Croatia) in 1985, however, Fr. Albert Prebeg was sent to prison for fifty days for visiting the sick and the dying without permission. The local authorities had ruled that clergy can visit only if specifically invited by the patient, even if he is too ill to ask. In 1987, Sava Nedeljković, an Orthodox monk, was sentenced to twenty days for giving communion to a dying parishioner. Protests came not only from Orthodox but also from the secular press and *Glas Koncila*.

Church social work was banned, but thanks to determined protest, the ban is not applied to the charitable work of religious orders. "Out of hours" clubs—such as church-sponsored discos and sports events—have been prohibited, but the ban is ineffectively enforced.

Family religious activities are permitted, as are religious rites in cemeteries, provided political matter is not introduced, as in the singing of nationalistic songs.

Clergy must be licensed by the state, but there is no interference with their training and selection. The names of new bishops must be made known to the authorities before the appointment is announced. So far, there has been no veto.

Religious education of the young is permitted if consent is given by both parents. It must be on church premises after school hours, and it cannot interfere with school activities—which are sometimes arranged deliberately to clash.

Penalties for purely religious offenses are relatively mild, but the abuse of religion for political ends, or spreading religious or national intolerance, can be punished by sentences of up to ten years.

Still a Police State

Yugoslav life is full of contradictions. Outwardly it is more free and easy than in the Soviet bloc. Daily life is more relaxed, with fewer restraints. Western rock music and soft porn are in evidence. There is little propaganda and less pretense concerning belief in Marxism. Open discussion, even in the press, is allowed, and people even joke against the system.

But beneath the surface lies a very unpleasant police state. Prying foreigners, particularly in Kossovo, are not welcome, and few Yugoslavs speak freely to visitors. There are also more political prisoners in Yugoslavia than in most other East European countries and the USSR. According to Amnesty International, in the 1980s an average of more than 500 people have been arrested yearly for opinions expressed in private writing or in conversation; there are now thought to be between 2,000 and 8,000 political prisoners.

Among the more enlightened population, the extent of brutality is increasingly unacceptable. Groups like the Yugoslav Writers' Conference are working for human rights, and appeals to the West are made, many successfully, against blatant injustices.

Two Croats, both believers in equal rights for Serbs, were sentenced primarily as political prisoners with church connections. Professor Marko Veselica, a former Communist, now a Christian and democrat, was given a seven-year sentence in a 1970s clamp-down for helping students articulate their views, and was sent back to prison after Tito's death. Nineteen-year-old Dobroslav Paraga (who will appear again later in this chapter) was sentenced to four years in 1980 for collecting signatures asking for the release of all political prisoners.

THE STATE AND THE ORTHODOX CHURCH

The Orthodox pose fewer problems to the authorities than the Catholics, but friction does exist. The main cause, of course, is nationalism. As recently as 1982 the government was accusing the Serbs of propagating "an ideology of blood and soil" and of trying to resurrect "darkness and a state of dangerous religious segregation," accusations not totally misplaced.

The Orthodox Church was for years as much a political as a religious organization. To expect it voluntarily to relinquish its historic role as guardian of the Serb nation, as the LCY demands, is wishful thinking. Not only extremist elements but even ordinary Serbs—who are defiant, if pessimistic—could quickly be roused to violent action. The Serb minorities in Croatia, Bosnia, and Kossovo are potentially troublesome.

The nervous authorities overreact to any church activity that even suggests nationalism. Most of the arrests have, significantly, taken place in Bosnia, the most hard-line republic. There in 1980 two priests and three guests at a baptism were given sentences ranging from four to six years for singing nationalistic songs.

It was also in Bosnia that the government clamped down on a genuine renewal movement in 1981 by arresting several priests and prominent laymen who were members of the Bogomolci, a spiritual renewal group. The movement was founded after World War I by Bishop Nikolaj Velimirović, an outstanding preacher, theologian, and pastor. The regime faulted him for emigrating to the United States (after emerging from a Nazi prison), where he became known as an articulate anti-Soviet, pro-Serb bishop—"a national chauvinist," according to the Yugoslav press. Particularly strong in Bosnia, the Bogomolci fulfill their Christian duties scrupulously. The Orthodox hierarchy strongly protested the sentences that the Bogomolci priests and laymen received, and the sentences were reduced considerably. The general opinion was that only in Bosnia would such activities have called forth sentences.

Patriarchal Restraint

The three post-war heads of the church—Gavrilo, Vikentije, and German, the present octogenarian patriarch—have generally shown restraint and good sense in their relations with the government. Unlike the Catholics, they have not riled the state on social matters, for their strong conservatism does not encourage such outreach.

Now, however, a growing number of priests see the need to "compete" with the Catholics. Younger priests especially are organizing a wide range of cultural and sporting activities for Serbian youth, while trained laity expound the position of the church within the present social structure.

Although the patriarch deliberately keeps a low profile, the feeling persists that the state, in its preoccupation with nationalistic problems, pays attention to the Catholic Church while ignoring Orthodox complaints.

Stating the Complaints

In 1982, not only the patriarch but the Bishops' Assembly and even the government-backed Association of Serbian Orthodox Priests complained about, among other matters, the unresolved "schism" of the Macdeonian Church, the treatment of Serbs in Kossovo, problems with religious instruction, and the difficulty of getting permits to build or repair churches. They also defended the Bogomolci as a non-political group open to all, and made the point that since Velimirović (its founder) had never been condemned, they had never pressed for his rehabilitation—a snide dig at the Stepinac controversy. The association said that the church was an essential element of the national identity, conscience, and honor of the Serbian people but that it was not political, and that there was no political purpose behind the statement.

The authorities' response was surprisingly moderate. They expressed gratification that church moderates had prevailed and admitted to some irregularities in the matters of building permits and religious instruction. As a result, the building of the Cathedral of St. Sava, patron of Serbia, long delayed because the authorities saw it as a grandiose manifestation of Serbian nationalism, was begun in Belgrade in 1985. It will be the largest Orthodox church in Europe.

Despite this favorable sign, state hostility toward perfectly normal church ceremonies and the lack of response to complaints, particularly at a local level, suggest no appreciable improvement in the situation. The Orthodox Synod responded in 1985 by declaring Radovan Samardžić, secretary of the government Commission for Relations with Religious Communities, *persona non grata* because of his attitude toward the churches. He has described them as prisoners of the past who, unable to learn the lessons of history, wish to impose their prejudices on society.

In 1986 Dragan Stepković, the son of a very popular Orthodox priest, was released after serving twenty-two months for having criticized the state and its church policy during bar and barrack-room conversations while he was in the army.

In 1987 Samardžić complained that national opponents of the system have been looking for shelter in the church. This may be a response to the more frequent gatherings of clergy with leading figures of the Serbian dissident intelligentsia, whether believers or non-believers.

THE STATE AND THE CATHOLIC CHURCH

Within the Catholic Church there are divisions other than the obvious national ones. The church is rather feudal in structure and prone to rivalries and factions. There is a major personality clash between Franjo Kuharić, chairman of the Bishops' Conference since 1970 and cardinal since 1983, and Frane Franić, archbishop of Split, the senior see. While both are ecclesiastically conservative, Franić is the more so; yet it is Franić who cooperates with the state and is sympathetic to socialism, whereas Kuharić regards the authorities with suspicion and contempt.

Both men are resistant to Vatican II ideas. Neither adult education nor ecumenism appeals to them, as they do to Archbishop Alojzije Šuštar of

Ljubljana, whose studies abroad and experience as secretary of the European Bishops' Conference give him a broader perspective. For Franić, democratization of the church is the "heresy of the age, more dangerous than Protestantism in its time."

Yet Franić has written: "It is our opinion that dialectical-historical materialism will [play] . . . a positive role with respect to Christianity" by forcing it to "purify itself and renew itself spiritually." Kuharić, however, sees no point in pursuing Christian-Marxist dialogue: "The Marxists are bent on making our society atheist." Kuharić, a good, likable person, has emerged as an outstanding defender of human rights who respects the views of his clergy; Franić has been far harder on those of his clergy who do not toe the church's line. Their lack of rapport has provided the state with opportunities to sow dissension. So has the unedifying clash of the bishops of Bosnia with the Franciscans and their parishioners.

TDKS

In addition, there is the problem of TDKS (Theological Society of the Christian Present), a group of forward-looking theologians—mostly but not all Catholic—that in 1977 drew the wrath of the bishops by accepting the status of "self-managing unit" (to gain tax exemption) without first consulting them. In 1982 it fell under the interdict of the Vatican.

The bishops accused TDKS of being under party control, a charge strongly denied by its members, who are independent-minded priests rather than stooges. The bishops nevertheless decided that members could not hold any official position in the church or in theological faculties, and that no further members should be recruited. Franić banned TDKS from his diocese, but Kuharić left things as they were.

This attitude has done the church a disservice, for although (given the Yugoslav situation) TDKS is not likely to attract wide support, it has tried to encourage Catholics to think for themselves in a constructive fashion. Moreover, the church's most eminent theologian, Dr. Tomislav Šagi-Bunić, is its leader. As a publishing house, however, TDKS has gone from strength to strength, and with official approval has extended its range to films, cassettes, and records.

The Stepinac Affair

The internal divisions within the state and the church have exacerbated an already complex situation. The election of a Slav pope took place while the church was celebrating the thirteenth centenary of the arrival of Catholic Christianity in Croatia and its unbroken loyalty to the papacy. Archbishop Kuharić's annual sermons on the anniversary of Cardinal Stepinac's death became more impassioned, and though the secular press ignored them, the Catholic press gave them full coverage.

In 1981, the twenty-first anniversary of Stepinac's death, the church pressed hard for his rehabilitation to clear the way for his beatification. People were flocking to his tomb, whose epitaph read: "Love the truth and hate falsehood; that is my principle. But in love of the Croatian people I yield to no one."

Since the purges of 1971, the Croatian government had been run by the hard-line element in the Party. Aware of their unpopularity, they worried about the liberal rumblings elsewhere in the country. The push for rehabilitation of Stepinac gave them an ideal opening for a sweeping attack on the church. It was led by Stepinac's prosecutor, Jakov Blazević, a leader in the Croatian government. The notoriously brusque Blazević has often been repudiated by the press, but on this occasion his colleagues supported him. One newspaper claimed that Stepinac "knew hundreds of priests who were in the Ustashe" but that no one can "find a document in which Stepinac excommunicated any priest for collaboration with the occupiers and the enemies."

The church was obviously being accused of trying to become the focus of political opposition, something the hierarchy wanted to avoid at all costs. The government onslaught went to ludicrous extremes. In the recently built church at Stražeman, one of the saints in a mosaic looked like Stepinac; the artist and the priest were jailed for two months each and the mosaic was removed. A government spokesman made the understatement of the year when he said in 1982: "We believe that the beatification would not exert a positive influence on the development of our relations."

The bishops, in a public statement, expressed regret that their religious activity was being misrepresented as political. Nevertheless, quite undeterred, the church continued: "The appropriate investigations are proceeding."

The Medjugorje Appearance

Just when it seemed that the excitement over Stepinac was dying down, the air was filled with reports that the Virgin had appeared in June 1981 to two boys and four girls, ages eleven to eighteen, in Medjugorje, a remote mountain village in Bosnia. Laying the ghost of Stepinac was one thing; an apparition of the Virgin, who had no business appearing in a Communist country at all, was quite another matter. On top of the troubled economic and nationalistic situation, the last thing the government needed was a Yugoslav Lourdes or Fatima. But the people thought otherwise. Soon crowds of up to 50,000—Catholics, Orthodox, Muslims, atheists, even LCY members—from home and abroad were flocking to Medjugorje.

The reaction of the Bosnian authorities was predictably hostile. Party members who went to Medjugorje were expelled or disciplined. Meetings were held throughout the republic to "unmask" the fabrication that had been conceived to deceive simple people. The six children were interrogated by the police and turned over to psychiatrists, who were impressed by their wholesomeness.

Strong pressure was put on the bishop of Medjugorje, Pavao Žanić, to dissociate the church from the apparition. Žanić was no friend of the Franciscan parish clergy, and the priest at Medjugorje, Fr. Jozo Zovko, was a Franciscan. But the bishop put out a wise and guarded statement: though there was no evidence that the priests had manipulated the children, the church was always most careful before accepting any vision or miracle. He finished with a quotation from Acts 5:38–39, "If this counsel be of God, you cannot overthrow it"—a verdict that, seven years later, seems amply justified.

The authorities arrested the parish priest and two other Franciscans. Father Zovko, who had at first been skeptical about the appearance, said that during Mass one day he too had seen the Virgin. From then on, he said, his preaching had taken on an entirely new dimension.

At his trial Father Zovko was accused of, among other things, having called on the people to rise against Communism. He had preached on Psalm 95 with its mention of forty years of wandering in the wilderness; this, the prosecution said, was a clear allusion to the forty years since the 1941 partisan uprising. Zovko was sentenced to three and a half years in prison. The other two Franciscans, Frs. Ferdo Vlašić and Jozo Križić, were sentenced to eight and five and a half years respectively for being on the staff of a magazine that had publicized the apparition. The protests were such— 40,000 letters from Italy alone—that two were freed within three years. The third, Father Vlašić, was released in 1986.

In matters such as alleged miracles, Rome wisely moves very slowly. In 1982 the bishop appointed a commission to investigate the apparition. Although it has not yet reached any definite conclusions, it issued a report in 1984 in which it commended the gatherings for prayer and the local spiritual improvement that had occurred in the region since the event but expressed reservations about pilgrimages and uncritical publicity.

Medjugorje now attracts pilgrims from many parts of the world. However, locally it is still a source of division. In July 1987 Žanić banned visiting priests from celebrating Mass in his diocese. However, his superior, Archbishop Franić, and the Croatian section of the Yugoslav Bishops Conference produced a sensible directive in September. It said that although the church had not yet made a final judgment on the validity of the apparition, it had the obligation to provide spiritual service for the thousands of pilgrims. The pilgrimages must not be official. No one should use the altar either to speak about or to attack the apparition.

As for the secular authorities, they seemed to have accepted Medjugorje. With the building of local accommodations at last in 1987 by company enterprises (permitted under Yugoslavia's self-management brand of socialism), there are signs that Yugoslavs realize they can cash in on the apparition.

In 1987 Bosnian authorities closed a Catholic institute in Mostar, the capital of Herzegovina, on the grounds that it was offering courses for lay people and thus breaking the law, which provides solely for the training of priests. The Mostar institute is modeled on similar ones in Slovenia and Croatia (at Zagreb, Split, Ljubljana, and Maribor), where the attitude of the authorities toward religion is less strict.

Other Causes of Friction

An area of tension between church and state is the authorities' arresting of priests on the flimsiest provocation. In 1983 as many as ten Catholic priests were in prison. Father Prcela, a Franciscan, was sentenced in 1980 to five years (later reduced to three) for criticizing the LCY in sermons and objecting to a cartoon in a student publication that pictured Mary taking contraceptive pills and Jesus smoking pot. Bosnian Franciscan Fr. Emanuel Jurić got thirty days for slandering Tito in the confessional in 1985, while another priest got six months for a similar offense. These involved a betrayal of confidence and may have been deliberate traps. Such arrests erode church confidence in the regime. The practice of reducing long sentences after protest suggests an admission that they were unjustly imposed in the first place.

Cardinal Kuharić has meanwhile followed the example of the late Archbishop Jože Pogačnik of Ljubljana, a Slovene, as a champion of human rights. Other religious leaders are equally concerned. In 1980, for example, forty-three Catholic intellectuals and clergy, including Archbishop Pogačnik, signed a petition demanding amnesty for all political prisoners; and in 1982 the Catholic theological institute in Zagreb defied the regime by hosting an international conference on human rights.

Several priests have been imprisoned in connection with Croatian nationalism and the Stepinac case. In 1986, for example, Fr. Filip Lukenda was accused, apparently without justification, of mixing the Gospel with nationalism and was sentenced to four years in prison. His bishop was particularly incensed at the way he was attacked in the press before his conviction. He was released in 1987.

Neither the state nor the church has acted in the best interests of the Croatian nation. An objective biography of Stepinac might help. Vekoslav Grmič, former auxiliary bishop of Maribor, has spoken of the need for penance for past crimes and has criticized attempts to rehabilitate people who "have done things they should not have done." He is very much a lone voice in the hierarchy. Because he is the nearest thing in the church to a friend of the regime, his views carry less weight than perhaps they deserve.

Tensions in Slovenia

Even in the relatively liberal republic of Slovenia, with little national antagonism and an advanced Christian-Marxist dialogue, relations between the state and the Catholic Church have been marred by bad personal experiences. Archbishop Šuštar of Ljubljana, like his predecessor, has complained numerous times. In 1984 he pointed out that the LCY's lack of confidence in the Slovene church had neither historical nor theoretical grounds.

The estrangement of the two sides was apparent when Fr. Josef Krašovec, a writer and lecturer at the Ljubljana theological faculty, was sentenced in 1984 to a month in prison for objecting to the anti-religious slogans of militant atheists.

A further source of friction comes from the recent influx of impoverished Muslim and Orthodox immigrants in search of jobs, who have complained of Slovenian chauvinism. Church officials are trying to counter the hostility toward the immigrants, but whether the laity will follow them is another matter.

During the last three years a strong separatist tendency has developed. Slovenes see their future with the European Economic Community rather than with Yugoslavia. No violence would be involved; the Slovenes are realists, aware of their vulnerability.

In 1987 Slovene intellectuals produced the most carefully worked out challenge to the LCY monopoly so far. In July the Slovenian bishops' conference issued a major declaration demanding greater democratization, pluralism, decentralization, and civil liberties. The bishops cited abolition of the article in the code concerning imprisonment for verbal offenses, thus backing the intellectuals, but also added issues of special concern for believers. These included the right of prisoners to have religious literature in prison, receive pastoral visits from priests, and have access to the sacraments. Some of these issues had been raised before, by certain church leaders, in particular Cardinal Kuharić. But the formulation of all of them in a single document addressed to the public at large was a significant event in church-state relations. The excellent Catholic bi-monthly Glas Koncila gave the declaration considerable prominence.

Attitude to the Papacy

The authorities in general have a positive view of Pope John Paul II. The liberal wing of the LCY regards him as socially and politically progressive, if doctrinally intolerant. When, however, it was proposed that the Pope visit Yugoslavia for the closing celebrations of the Eucharistic Congress at Marija Bistrica in 1984, the idea was turned down. Opposition came not only from hard-line party members but from the Serbian church, which insisted he make the Croat bishops apologize for past atrocities. The LCY, for its part, would have demanded that he lay a wreath at Tito's tomb. The government decision was probably a wise one.

The situation subsequently improved, and Kuharić was able to issue an invitation to the Pope for 1988.

THE STATE AND THE GROWTH OF ISLAM

Until 1983, far fewer Muslims that Christians had been arrested, because Yugoslav Muslims can rely on outside support and also, probably, because of tacit sympathy from some local officials. Yugoslavia's economic situation is so dire that it cannot afford to offend its Muslim allies. Nevertheless, in August 1983, thirteen Muslims were accused of trying to set up a fundamentalist Muslim republic and were put on trial in Sarajevo. Hamdija Pozderac, a Communist party leader in Bosnia, complained that Muslim intellectuals had too much influence in the press and in the universities. Of the thirteen on trial, only one was not university educated; one was a professor, and several were teachers and lawyers. Two of the thirteen were women. Muslims denied plotting any nationalist or religious uprising, saying they only wanted more civil liberties and greater freedom of religious expression. Bosnian Muslims are Sunni, not Shi'ites, and some are not fundamentalists but modernizers.

According to a knowledgeable non-Muslim émigré, the thirteen brought to trial could in no way be called extremist. But Bosnia has a tough and illiberal leadership, and the sentences totaled ninety years. The judge denied that it was an attack on religion. The defendants, he said, violated "brotherhood and unity," the code words for the government's nationality policy. Amnesty International adopted the thirteen as prisoners of conscience, and later their sentences were drastically reduced. By 1988 only three were still in prison.

The trial was probably a warning shot fired at any incipient Muslim nationalism. It was also an example of Yugoslavia's "even-handed" policy, for the same leaders had already come down hard on Orthodox and Catholics.

The official Islamic community has on the whole cooperated with the state. In 1983, it affirmed its historic role as an integral part of Yugoslav, and particularly Bosnian, society. The Slavonic Muslims in Yugoslavia enjoy a greater freedom than Muslims anywhere else under Communism and have traditionally lived amicably with their fellow Slavs. Influential people like Dr. Ahmed Smajlović, a member of Sarajevo's Islamic faculty, are trying to promote good relations with Christians. Muslim and Christian leaders appear together at major official occasions, and until recently coexistence seemed a reasonable possibility—except for the situation in Kossovo, which continued to worsen in 1988 and might be the powder keg that blows the unity of Yugoslavia to pieces.

A Fundamentalist Resurgence

There seems to be a resurgence of a more fundamentalist type of Islam, especially among the young, in Bosnia, Montenegro, and Macedonia, and it is causing the LCY increasing concern. In May 1983 a religious teacher, Hussein Smajić, was sentenced to five years' imprisonment for inciting national hatred and spreading anti-state propaganda. He had "justified the actions of war-criminal Stepinac" and "spoken against mixed marriages and donating blood for, or accepting blood from, Serbs"—signs of the traditional Catholic-Muslim "alliance" against the Serbs.

According to the Bosnian government, there is "an underground organization of Muslims working energetically along the lines of creating an ethnically pure Bosnia"; the group reportedly has links to the Mladi Muslimani (Young Muslims), a pre-war organization. Another group, the Muslim Unity Organization, has appealed to "dear Muslim brothers" throughout the world, complaining of "endless humiliations," especially a new law that all Yugoslav girls must do military service. The LCY has tried, unsuccessfully, to persuade the Ulema (the Muslim hierarchy) to consider itself no more than a liturgical association. In 1987 there were complaints that Bosnia had become a bastion of Islam.

Central among the concerns of fundamentalist Muslims are issues of intermarriage and food; there have been conflicts over pork in schools and in the army. In 1982 they announced a twenty-point struggle against non-Islamic customs.

In 1987 at a trial in Sarajevo, three Muslims were sentenced to five, four, and two years for "propagating Muslim nationalism, demanding the setting up of a purely Muslim state, and inciting Jihad" (holy war). In Bosnia, the younger generation was described as fanatical. In Montenegro, it was said that "ideology has been taken over by the imams, while party members watch with folded arms."

In Macedonia, where a quarter of the population is now Muslim, a significant proportion of them Albanian, the imams are taking an increasingly aggressive line, especially about religious education. Ninety per cent of Albanian Muslim girls there do not go beyond the compulsory eight years of primary school.

The Macedonian government, concerned because Muslims were withdrawing their children from state schools as early as possible, tried to ban all religious education for those under eighteen. The Catholic paper *Glas Koncila* leaked the story, which aroused such an outcry that the proposal was dropped. In 1987 party members discussed the Macedonian problem but turned down a suggestion that religious education should be allowed only to young people over fifteen, on the grounds, interestingly, that Yugoslavia is not an atheistic country. The Albanian Muslims of Macedonia and Kossovo have been accused of Muslim irredentism, charges rejected by the Supreme Council of Islam as "the crudest attacks against Muslims and an assault on basic human rights."

As usual in Yugoslavia, it is almost impossible to arrive at the truth. Certainly there has been some over-reaction among the authorities. But as they see more and more Muslim children (the Albanian birth rate is three times the national average) and more and more mosques being built (700 since the war, as against 500 new Catholic and only 220 new Orthodox churches), their fears are not groundless. In Zagreb, where there are 30,000 Muslims, what is probably the third-largest mosque in Europe has just been opened after twenty-five years of campaigning and a prolonged court case. It was opposed both by the local authorities and by the Catholic majority. The new mosque turned out to be two and a half times as large as what the original plan showed!

The 50,000 Dervishes, or Bektashi, a charismatic, peaceable type of Muslim, exert an influence well beyond their numbers, but the Muslim establishment disapproves of them and has tried to close their fifty monasteries. The government recognizes them as a separate religious group under the leadership of Dzhemel Shehu.

THE KOSSOVO TROUBLES

The political decentralization in the 1960s brought many improvements to Kossovo, one of two autonomous regions in Serbia. In 1970 the University of Prishtina was established; the first literate generation of Yugoslav Albanians is now emerging. Although much money was invested in Kossovo, it was misdirected and failed to cope with unemployment, currently running at 28 per cent. The highest birth rate in Europe (32 per 1,000) increases the problems. About 10 per cent of Albanian men in Kossovo have had to leave home to search for jobs.

There is considerable validity to the Albanian demand that Kossovo, which contains 42 per cent of Balkan Albanians, be made a seventh national republic, since Albanians are now the third largest of the seven nationalities. Basically the Albanians are going through the same development of national self-awareness that the Serbs, Croats, and Slovenes experienced a century ago. But against it is the deep attachment of Serbs to what they claim was their original heartland and the possibility that a republic of Kossovo might try to link up with Albania. The university seems to have spawned a generation of Albanians who look toward Tirana (capital of Albania) as their mecca and the late Enver Hoxha as their prophet.

The 1981 Riots

The riots of 1981 originated at the university. Directed at first against the Kossovan authorities, they soon involved the Serbian population. The government stepped in quickly and ruthlessly; thirty-eight Albanians were killed, and a thousand were later sentenced for "counter-revolutionary activities." Between 1981 and 1986, the police questioned some 56,000 people.

Much antagonism, more nationalistic than Muslim, has been directed against the Serbian Orthodox Church. In the early 1980s, monasteries and shrines were attacked; part of the patriarchate at Peć was set on fire in 1981; graves were desecrated, women raped, cattle blinded, children bullied. Attacks continue sporadically despite military suppression. The Orthodox patriarch, German, has objected to the authorities but quietly, for fear of a vicious Serbian backlash. Serbs and Montenegrins—fearful, vulnerable, vengeful— are leaving Kossovo in droves, 120,000 in the last ten years. The Albanian proportion of the population has increased from 71 per cent in 1971 to well over 80 per cent in the mid-1980s.

By 1987 the situation had deteriorated considerably. Serbs and Montenegrins were in retreat and threatening revenge, the grip of the police was still tight, and Albanian Kossovans were attracting wider attention to what they claim as appalling injustices in an area that could become a Balkan Ulster.

At the 1987 annual Synod of the Orthodox Church, held at Peć, Patriarch German underlined that he and the entire episcopate had come to express sympathy with local Serbs, whose sufferings represent "an open wound for the Serbian Orthodox Church." The bishops spoke up on behalf of the Serbs, giving details of villages vacated, churches and graveyards profaned, and children attacked. When, in the fall, Ecumenical Patriarch

Demetrios during his world tour visited Yugoslavia (the first visit to the country by an ecumenical patriarch of Constantinople), he was taken to Peć.

Muslim and Catholic Albanians

About 90 per cent of Kossovo's Albanians are nominally Muslim, but some of the religion, Islam or Christianity, practiced in this remote province is corrupt and mixed with paganism. The schools and Prishtina University are very anti-religious, and people exposed to modern education often lapse into atheism.

Some Muslims take part in Catholic pilgrimages and share a deep devotion to the Virgin Mary. And some Laramanni, crypto-Christians who are afraid to identify themselves, are also living among Muslims. The basic tensions are not so much between Muslims, even of the more fundamentalist sort, and Christians as between Albanians and Serbs, who are identified with the hostile political establishment.

In an area where extremist nationalistic passions are becoming more inflammatory, there may be an upsurge of fundamentalism. The imams tend not to support the nationalist movement vocally. They are in an ambivalent position, because of the possibility of Kossovo's breaking away and joining Albania, in which case they would find themselves in a militantly anti-religious state. However, the Albanian Kossovan population, assured of its numerical superiority, is spilling over into adjacent parts of Montenegro, Serbia, and Macedonia. In Macedonia something of a Muslim revival seems to be taking place, and a quarter of the population is Muslim.

In 1987 Baptist pastor Simo Ralević of Peć was given an eight-month sentence in an obviously fabricated charge, probably because of his successful ministry among Muslims. In 1988 he won his appeal against it. Despite all the complaints of the Kossovan Albanians, they still control much of the local government.

Catholic Albanians have a small church of twenty-five parishes; yet under wise leadership they are an influential and committed religious community. Aided by priests and nuns from other areas, the church is flourishing and expanding. Vocations are booming, chiefly among the first literate generation. The diocese of Skopje-Prizren has the highest number of vocations in Yugoslavia.

The excellent Catholic press publishes modern-language New Testaments (plans for a whole Bible have been set aside) and a bi-monthly magazine called *Drita*. It has produced a biography of Mother Teresa with details of her Albanian background. She herself has visited Kossovo on the several trips she has made to Yugoslavia, where the state welcomes her with pride as a famous Yugoslavian.

CHURCH LIFE IN THE 1980S

While academicians talk of cooperation and dialogue, discrimination against believers, a problem common to all Communist states, shows no signs of disappearing. Although the Catholic bishops have failed in their attempts to get anti-discriminatory laws into the legal system, they speak out boldly, as do the church media, whenever human rights are infringed.

This has not endeared them to the state. The outspoken Kuharić has agitated for the right of prisoners—whether criminal, religious, or political—to fair treatment and the pastoral care of the church. He also guarantees protection for any of his priests who is threatened in any way—a far cry from prelates in neighboring Hungary. Yugoslav believers may not always obtain satisfaction, but their legal position is better than elsewhere in the Communist world.

As usual, senior posts in most fields are closed to believers (but equally to non-party members). Although believers can theoretically be teachers, many have been fired. Parents have been discriminated against for requesting baptism or religious instruction for their children, and children are sometimes asked by their teachers if they believe in God or attend religious instruction—and ridiculed if they do. In a 1986 school questionnaire for teachers in Zagreb, religious activities were still branded as anti-social, in the same category as stealing and promiscuity.

In an article in 1987, Kuharić pointed out that, paradoxically, lay believers are more liable to suffer discrimination than priests or religious. Many people still have to receive the sacraments secretly, for fear of losing their jobs. He said that attacks against the church have increased: "It's as if we were back in the years immediately after the war." The church does not try "to substitute for states, or threaten them," he said; "it only wants relationships to be as human as possible, in justice and liberty." Kuharić expressed satisfaction that the government had dropped the cases of three priests, Lukenda, Martinić, and Fr. Peter Šolić, a Split theology lecturer, very popular with young people, who had been sentenced to six months for preaching against atheism.

Party Members and Religion

Discrimination against LCY members on religious grounds is a burning issue in Yugoslavia. Despite assertions that atheism is not synonymous with Communism, the LCY tries—to a ludicrous extent—to remain untainted by religion. Two teachers, for example, were expelled from the Party for attending a concert of one of their pupils, which was held in a church. In Vojvodina (like Kossovo an autonomous region of Serbia) the

LCY has demanded that young Communists leave the party if they marry believers. Such rules are hard to enforce. The Yugoslavs are convivial and have strong family ties; party members are hard put not to attend family celebrations, which often have religious trappings. Religious influence often goes deep. A 1987 survey of party members in the Zagreb region (admittedly an area where the proportion of Catholic believers is high) revealed that 7.7 per cent were believers, and 12.5 per cent actually sent their children for religious instruction.

The Serbian Socialist Youth Federation said in 1986 that young believers could become members. While some LCY groups take a hard line, the official position, legally and publicly, is to respect the rights of believers. In 1983 the media commented unfavorably on the removal of wooden crosses from coffins after a pit disaster: "At such a time, why should the feelings of believers be less important than those of atheists?"

In 1985 an objective film on mysticism and religion featuring Medjugorje was shown on television throughout the country—except in Bosnia, where Medjugorje is located. Inconsistency is still the overriding feature of the attitude of the LCY toward religion—not surprising, because since Tito's death the gulf between the republics has widened.

Speaking Out

Believers are less easily intimidated than formerly. Dobroslav Paraga, a Croat Catholic former theology student, was nineteen years old when sentenced to four years in 1980 for collecting signatures asking for the release of all political prisoners. He tried to sue the state for damages suffered to his health after he was kept for two months, half naked, in a subterranean, unheated, unlit cell in the dead of winter. Because he was drawing attention to appalling prison conditions, in 1987 he was tried for "circulating false rumors causing dissatisfaction and alarm." He was given a six-month sentence, suspended for three years. His thirteen witnesses were not allowed to appear. The trial attracted wide attention, and Kuharić pled for him without actually naming him.

Although Paraga is silenced for three years, his revelations and demands have already spurred Serb journalists and Slovene party officials to investigate prisons. Yugoslav prisoners may give interviews, which do appear in the press. Three years in prison is as much as anyone can take without permanent damage to his health.

Issues of believers and military service became more important in the mid-1980s. Church leaders, primarily Kuharić, have insisted that believing conscripts and soldiers should not be prevented from attending church. Also, the question of imprisonment of believers for conscientious objection aroused concern in local peace groups. Ten thousand Nazarenes petitioned the government to accept only one sentencing—as laid down by Tito in 1960—not repeated sentences to the age of thirty, which had become the rule. Pacifists sent protests to the International Court at the Hague against the repeated imprisonments of Jehovah's Witnesses, Nazarenes, and Adventists. In 1987 a group of Jehovah's Witnesses tried unsuccessfully to declare compulsory military service as unconstitutional.

In 1986 the Socialist Alliance of Working Peoples of Yugoslavia reserved places for believers, clerical and lay—a sensible step forward.

Contacts Abroad

The Yugoslavs, alone in Eastern Europe, can travel to the West without restrictions, and entertain foreign visitors at home (though possibly observed by police). The churches are also allowed to minister to the many Yugoslavs working abroad. The Catholic Church has about 400 priests and 1,000 nuns abroad, mostly in West Germany, either working with migrants or studying.

The authorities are suspicious, sometimes justifiably so, of traveling Yugoslavs who contact émigré groups, especially Catholic Croat nationalists or Orthodox Četniks. Christians and Muslims have been tried for alleged contacts with hostile groups abroad. Yugoslavia's government seems more afraid of its émigrés than any other East European government; it tops Bulgaria's record of the political murder of such persons. Émigré Yugoslavs on visits home have on occasion been detained, had their passports confiscated, and even been arrested. A stone mason resident in Germany, Milan Vidaković, was given a twelve-year sentence in 1982 allegedly for links with émigré church groups. In 1987 Fr. Šimum Ćorić-Sito, a Croatian leader of a Bern (Switzerland) mission, was detained for at least two months while on a visit home after he complained about the treatment of Croat émigrés. An Orthodox bishop was humiliated by being stripped naked in a body search upon his return from abroad.

Although the Orthodox do not have the level of international support that the Catholic Church enjoys, they maintain close relations with the Russian and East European Orthodox churches. Muslim connections abroad have grown greatly in the last decade.

The Churches and the Secular Press

In Yugoslavia matters of common concern can be discussed in a manner undreamed of in most other East European countries. *Glasnost* has been around for a long time. A fairly broad range of opinion can be expressed through the varied secular and church press, the academic publications, and wide-ranging symposiums and courses, and there is a considerable divergence of opinion within the LCY itself. Yet at the grassroots level, interplay between the party and the church is fraught with difficulty.

The churches resent the continuing disregard of the law by certain journalists (obviously with hard-line LCY backing) who attack religious personalities at will. The victims can only justify themselves in the church press—which leaps to their defense but whose circulation is more limited than the daily press and may even be banned.

The churches, particularly the Catholic Church, have pled in vain for regular access to television and radio. In 1985 Protestants were given a series on TV; this unusual concession was probably allowed because they are not regarded as trouble-makers. In 1986, for the first time, Archbishop Šuštar of Ljubljana and Patriarch German were allowed to broadcast Christmas messages on Slovene and Belgrade radio, respectively. In 1987 Slovenes were officially informed that they would not get into trouble if they took Christmas day off as a holiday. Christmas as a religious holiday was the most widely discussed religious issue in the press that year!

The Church Press

The legal and independent church press in Yugoslavia is unique in Eastern Europe. Yugoslavia alone has done away with preliminary censorship, although occasionally the government will ban a particular controversial issue and take reprisals against authors and editors. The church press is also remarkable in its extent. Between 1970 and 1980 there were five times as many religious as Marxist publications, a situation that still prevails. There are no limitations on the number of copies.

The Catholic press, with sixty-seven publications, including diocesan newspapers for the different language groups, is ahead of that of the other churches. The best-known Catholic paper is *Glas Koncila* (Voice of the council), originally an information bulletin on Vatican II. It developed into a first-class bi-monthly with a circulation of about 120,000. The paper takes an independent stance that may differ from the bishops' rather conservative line; its news coverage is excellent.

The church press is attacked, especially in Bosnia, for numerous sins, such as resembling the secular press and being clericalist and nationalist. *Glas Koncila* justifiably claims that it is continually being made a scapegoat. Criticism of the Serbian Orthodox press on the grounds of nationalism is well justified.

Bible reading is not widespread and, Protestants excepted, was only recently encouraged by the churches. In 1976 only 6 per cent of the population owned a Bible; today, with modern-language translations, the figure should be higher. Because of the economic crisis, no Bibles have been imported since 1985, though with foreign financial help Bibles are being printed within the country. Although the state puts no difficulties in the way of Bible production, the Yugoslav Bible Society frequently has no stock because of problems obtaining distribution licenses.

Church Social Outreach

The churches' growing confidence, demonstrated in their stand against discrimination, has spilled over into their organizations, especially those involving young people. These are going from strength to strength, involving Orthodox as well as Catholics. The Party is anxious about the number of previously non-religious young people—even members of the Party— who are participating. Aware of how effectively the churches use such things as films, sports, and music to attract young people, the Party does its utmost to restrict priests and religious to purely liturgical matters.

Yet there is a grudging admiration in the secular press for the efficiency, imagination, and care the churches show in dealing with social problems. The Croat LCY decided to build a center for young drug addicts only after it discovered that priests were already befriending the youngsters. What impresses outsiders is that the work is not an indirect form of evangelism but springs from genuine concern. The churches run nursery schools (very much a bone of contention) and social and educational programs for the young, raise funds for the poor and the unemployed, and look after unmarried mothers, the disabled, the mentally handicapped, the elderly, and the homeless.

Ecumenism: Difficult Amid Divisions

Ecumenism has a hard time in a country deeply divided by chauvinistic drives, where the national groups are closely identified with religion. Such ecumenical advances as the Catholic Church has made to the Orthodox are usually misinterpreted as attempts to turn them into Uniate churches—the same charge leveled at the cordial relations between Rome and the Macedonian Orthodox Church. Catholics have had little enthusiasm for Vatican II directives on ecumenism; therefore in a message to young Croat Catholics in 1985, the Pope exhorted them to develop closer interconfessional relationships. Ecumenism has made little headway among Serbs, who are usually hostile toward those who are not Serbian and Orthodox.

There are exceptions. At a joint conference of Catholics, Protestants, and moderate Muslims in Bosnia, Islamic professor Ahmed Smajlović spoke highly of Catholic documents on Islam and urged Catholic seminarians in Bosnia to continue their good relations with Islamic students after ordination. In 1987 a new interconfessional paper backed by Orthodox,

Catholics, and Muslims appeared in Sarajevo. Theologians of different groups are meeting together more frequently. And when religious leaders appear jointly at state occasions with state officials they may discuss problems. Dr. Peter Kuzmić, a key figure in interchurch endeavors, is director of the Pentecostalist Biblical Institute at Zagreb and known internationally as a spokesman for the Protestant churches. Catholic archbishops Šuštar and Alojz Turk (recently retired) are notably ecumenical. Unfortunately, the most ecumenical group in the Catholic Church, TDKS, is generally unpopular with Catholics.

Occasionally ecumenism is evident at the grassroots level. A whole community turned out for the funeral of a Catholic priest who died on the mountains searching for some lost people.

All this amounts to very little, however. A radio program on Christian-Marxist dialogue made a telling criticism: "Ecumenical prayer, now a regular practice . . . among Catholics and Protestants in Germany, is unacceptable and unobtainable between the religious communities of Yugoslavia."

The main hope lies with the younger generation. Generally more tolerant, they think of themselves as Yugoslav first and their own nationality second. By the 1970s, one-third of the marriages were of mixed nationalities, though a 1987 survey showed that many young Muslims still had reservations about marrying someone of a different religion and culture. More and more young people are going their own way—breaking with tradition and family. This can lead either to secularism or to faith. During a pilgrimage to Aquileia in northern Italy in 1987, Catholic leaders tried to give guidance to young Slovenes in the face of the social, secularizing, and cultural crisis affecting their nation. Many young people, of course, are involved in the pervasive rock culture and its indifference to religion.

Pilgrimages in the past have tended to accentuate national and religious disparities. Two events in 1984 could have, but did not, become the focus of nationalist demonstrations. One was the consecration of a rebuilt Orthodox church at Jasenovac—formerly a concentration camp—in the middle of Croatia, commemorating the thousands of Serbs who perished at the hands of the Ustashe. The authorities reportedly gave permission from a desire to see a permanent indictment of Croats and their church. The consecration, which was attended by a Croat Catholic bishop, went peacefully. The second event was the celebration of 1,300 years of Christianity in Croatia at Marija Bistrica, "Yugoslavia's Częstochowa," attended by 300,000 pilgrims. The prevailing mood was one of peace, joy, and devotion, and official representatives of both the Orthodox patriarchate and the Muslim community were present. Thanks to the church's new educational programs, the pilgrims were well prepared.

Orthodox Metropolitan Jovan said that these events were the start of better Orthodox-Catholic relations. A meeting in May 1985 between Patriarch German and Cardinal Kuharić was also promising, although it aroused more enthusiasm in enlightened LCY circles than among churchgoers. The hierarchies, which have shown courage and wisdom in dealing with the state, have not been able to persuade their flocks to follow their example in interchurch dialogue.

An important ecumenical event in 1987 was the first ever Taizé international meeting (Taizé is an interfaith community in France) in Eastern Europe, held at Ljubljana. Some 1,000 visitors joined 4,000 young Yugoslavs, from all the different republics and a wide variety of confessions. For most of the Yugoslavs, it was like being in a foreign country, and the first chance to meet fellow Christians of different churches and nationalities. Such encounters are very important for Yugoslav Christians, who need to meet as individuals to break down the barriers that divide them.

Christian-Marxist Dialogue

The dialogue that was interrupted in the 1970s has been reopened. In Ljubljana in 1984, for instance, a conference on "Science and Faith" was attended by Marxist and Christian sociologists, scientists, and theologians. To hear Marxists speak openly about the church with well-informed and sympathetic Christians was an illuminating experience.

Various views were publicly expressed, among them: atheism is not an essential element of socialism; the forces of socialism should find ways of incorporating the positive aspects of religion; religion, which is growing everywhere, even in the USSR, has deep roots and should not be obstructed.

Christian-Marxist dialogue is still limited to Catholics: the Orthodox do not seem interested.

Religious Revival?

Reports conflict concerning a revival of religion. Certainly a number of religious buildings are going up. Medjugorje has stimulated self-examination and revival within the Catholic Church, and promoted a message of peace, repentance, and reconciliation in an area that had been the scene of bitter strife. The church has been touched by the charismatic movement (strong at Medjugorje), which has the potential to overcome national and denominational barriers. Evangelical Protestants also report a new spiritual climate. Many people, especially the young, are waking from apathy and showing a thirst for God. The Seventh Day Adventists in Niš, Serbia, for instance, are gaining members from the conversion of nominal Orthodox.

Titograd—a large new industrial center in Montenegro, a republic not noted for religious devotion—presents an interesting case. In an article attacking the churches, the city's party newspaper reported that the churches were attempting to attract young people through "2,000 forms of organized activity, which involve around 30,000 young people." It went on: "More and more children are being baptized, quite often children of Communist parents. Seven friars and two nuns have shown great skill in gathering together young people, sparing no expense. Five thousand Orthodox calendars have been sold. Many people are absent from work on religious holidays, and local [state] organizations hardly react at all."

That revival is certainly strong in Croatia is clear from press comments. It is qualitative as well as quantitative—through Franjo Batovac, secretary of Young Communists in Croatia, wonders how far it is due to the lack of alternatives available. Twenty trainloads of youngsters from Split went to a youth congress in Rome. In New Zagreb, where no permits were given to build churches and there are 70,000 people, Catholic churches have been started in apartments.

Revival is undeniably present, but a sociological study imposes caution, for figures vary considerably. A survey in predominantly Orthodox Belgrade showed that only 9 per cent of 1,000 young people went to church for purely religious reasons. In Catholic Zagreb, a remarkably high 45 per cent of those questioned called themselves believers, 19 per cent were undecided, 18 per cent had no interest, and a further 18 per cent (a drop of 6 per cent from a previous survey) said they were atheists.

Social cohesiveness, based on the family, is still fairly strong. This acts as a guard against secularism, the Western form of atheism, which Archbishop Franić rightly believes is far more insidious than the government's atheism. In any case, much of Yugoslavia's "religious" adherence is traditional and ethnic. It is weakest in Orthodox areas, stronger in Catholic republics, strongest of all among Muslims. Religious affiliation is to be declared in the 1991 census, a practice discontinued in 1953. There is a growing feeling that statistics to monitor religious trends are needed, but naturally the news has aroused concern among some believers.

The Outlook

On the whole, church-state relations are better in Yugoslavia than in any other Communist country. The authorities generally prefer not to antagonize religious sensibilities, thanks partly to the good sense and political sensitivity of church leaders. Periodic crackdowns are motivated more by political considerations than by anti-religious ideology. The danger comes from zealots, whether religious, nationalist, or Communist.

The churches have had both a positive and a negative impact on Yugoslav life. Most of their leaders have begun to put nationalism aside as their chief concern—thanks to the harsh measures of the state—but they still have to search their souls and erase any lingering political ambitions. This will be difficult, and for the new Muslim fundamentalists perhaps impossible, though tolerant Slavonic Islam should hold them in check.

A land where Catholic Croat and Orthodox Serb reside in complete harmony and where the churches stand up unequivocally on behalf of religious liberty is still far in the future, even though the younger generation shows signs of wanting to shed the dead weight of the past. It is unfortunate that Yugoslav believers are divided rather than united by their religious convictions. The churches are learning that they can be politically relevant without being political organizations. The various LCYs, for their part, must accept the fact that the churches can make positive contributions to the well-being of the people.

The Catholic Church in particular seems to be shifting ground from nationalism to service and the promotion of truth and justice. The Serbian Orthodox Church remains largely a nationalistic institution, though loyal in its way, and that is a hindrance to the development of the church. That church is, moreover, weakened internally by divisions; there is tension between bishops and parish clergy, bishops and priests' trade unions, clergy and parishioners. Serbs tend to be proud, argumentative, and easily offended. The Macedonian Orthodox Church presents no problem to the government. Islam, at least in the past, has demonstrated a remarkable capacity for co-existing in Communist states. In its new, aggressive, fundamentalist guise, however, it poses a potential threat to Yugoslav unity, fragile as it is.

In 1987, the Yugoslav authorities issued guidelines on religious gatherings. Only those faiths that have communities in Yugoslavia may organize gatherings, and these must be devoted to religious matters and must not be "conducive to bloc rivalry and confrontation." Only if they conform to the Yugoslav constitution and other laws can such meetings deal with socio-political and international matters. With regard to religious practice, the government has finally accepted such devotions as those at Marija Bistrica and Medjugorje.

All this, however, has been overshadowed by the economic crisis. By the end of 1987, it was very bad, with soaring inflation, widespread (but uncoordinated) strikes, the devaluation of the dinar, and huge, state-imposed price rises. Unemployment benefits do not exist, and the overall attitude is one of despondency and fear. The need for massive Western credit is even greater, so Yugoslavia is very sensitive to adverse Western publicity on religion. The LCY is divided and seems to lack the will to move decisively; despite its draconian methods, its power base is weak.

Some educated Yugoslavs believe that the failure of Marxism and the barrenness of atheism have left a spiritual vacuum that may be filled by regression into a primitive ethnic chauvinism, of which "religion" would be an ingredient. It is generally agreed that the LCY has been fomenting the nationalism it so loudly decries as an excuse to maintain its illiberal controls. Lack of democracy prevents representative members of the nationalities from trying to work out peaceful solutions to their problems. Moreover, by accusing the churches of "nationalist activity," it makes them convenient scapegoats for its own failures.

The nationalities could still get out of hand, although the majority of Yugoslavs have sufficient sense to realize that their brand of "socialism" is preferable to other East European varieties. Serbian nationalistic feeling, aggravated by the turmoil in Kossovo, is running high. As for the Albanian extremists, anything could happen.

The uneasy mix that is Yugoslavia makes it the most unpredictable country in Eastern Europe, and the churches—the only organized communities outside the Communist Party—are in the same rocking boat.

11

Summing Up:
Problems and Prospects

A STUDY OF the East European countries makes it strikingly clear that Communism remains an alien system, one that shows little understanding of or identity with normal human society. The various governments have no real legitimacy, and most attempts to reform and humanize them from within have been crushed.

The promotion of secularism and the attempted destruction of religious faith have begotten social problems all too familiar to the West—an increase in alcoholism, drug abuse, family breakup, and juvenile delinquency. Communism not only has failed to solve but has exacerbated the problems of national minorities, notably the Hungarians in Romania, the Turks in Bulgaria, and the Albanians in Yugoslavia. And it has also failed to provide material well-being. Living standards are falling as economies struggle and debts mount.

Ideologically, Marxism-Leninism has shown it is unable to provide answers to the problems of modern life. By subordinating everything to a deterministic philosophy with little relevance to local conditions, the ruling ideologists have lost sight of truth as an absolute value.

Few people believe in the imposed ideology. A random survey taken in Budapest revealed that the average Hungarian, after years of indoctrination, had little interest in and very confused ideas about Marx and Lenin. The whole way of life is based on hypocrisy. People at every level of society conform outwardly, but inwardly they despise the system.

Recent statistics highlight the general malaise: most East European populations are declining or only just maintaining themselves; infant mortality is increasing (twice as high as the rest of Europe); and life expectancy has actually fallen since 1978. The deterioration in Eastern Europe is unparalleled in the rest of the developing world.

Demographic expert Jean-Claude Chesnais cites various factors in the decline. Education, housing, and health have all suffered because of the disproportionate amount of national income spent on armaments. Rigid central planning hinders productivity and leads to shortages. Food shortages, inadequate heating caused by fuel shortages, drug shortages, and deteriorating medical services and hygiene lower life expectancy. Noxious chemical pollution and industrial accidents (of which Chernobyl is only a dramatic example) take their toll, as does widespread chronic alcoholism. The habitual use of abortion as a means of birth control leads to lower fertility and higher infant mortality.

The Churches' Revised Role

Most churches have come to realize that direct confrontation with the state and its ideology is not possible; they have been forced to modify their original hostility. Many have come round to the view that no social system is inherently "Christian" and that religion must operate within whatever system it finds itself in. Apart from the Catholic Church's links with Rome, the churches have had to sever those institutional ties to the West that made them suspect. They no longer wield their former worldly wealth and political power. Some feel that regaining the poverty and humility of the apostolic church—becoming once again a "servant" or "pilgrim" church—is a blessing.

The Orthodox and the more pietistic Protestant churches tend to act indifferent to the system. For them, survival demands flexibility, silence in the political arena, and a determination to preserve the worship and structure of the church. The Orthodox have given uncritical support to two particularly tough Eastern-bloc regimes—Bulgaria and Romania. This has yielded some immediate practical fruits but has damaged the church in the long run.

The most fruitful option has been critical support. In the more tolerant countries, the churches have spoken out critically on such social concerns as divorce and abortion, on which the Marxist approach is purely pragmatic (witness Romania, where liberal abortion laws have been reversed to counteract the falling birth rate). Unfortunately, in most states criticism of any sort is utterly unacceptable to the government, even in the *glasnost* era. They are slow to follow Gorbachev's new lead.

Some Marxists have reconsidered their attitude toward religion. They recognize that it is too deeply rooted to eradicate, and that believers are a stabilizing element in society—islands of honesty and reliability in a sea of corruption and sloth. The churches can also be islands of love and care, qualities in short supply in materialistic societies. Some Marxists now admit that churches can relieve social problems before which Marxism, with its weak ethics, has proved helpless. Many Yugoslav sociologists approve of the Catholic Church's social concern. Facing a breakdown in society, the Hungarian government is allowing the churches wider scope.

In Poland the Catholic Church has been strong enough to enlarge its sphere of influence. The hierarchy has adroitly balanced support for and criticism of the government. The East German Protestant churches have also justified their position by responsibly exercising their moral authority. They too have perceived the political mood of the country and what is right or wrong for the people as a whole, atheists included.

In Poland, the GDR, and Yugoslavia, some churches have moved beyond their allotted spheres and have spoken out in defense of not only religious rights but also broader human rights—to the governments' evident displeasure. The Catholic Church's central role in providing the ideological basis for Solidarity—the largest mass movement in Polish history—was the high-water mark of the political and social influence of a church under Communism.

There have been promising glimpses of possible improvements in church-state relations. Wherever there has been genuine cooperation, whether at the national level or at the local level, the *modus vivendi* has markedly improved.

Religious Ferment

What has been occurring since the early 1970s in some countries is not so much a religious revival as a ferment—profound stirrings that pervade not only religion but other areas of life as well. It has political, social, ideological, economic, nationalistic, and religious overtones. It is a symptom both of the collapse of Communist ideology and of the lack of acceptance by the people of their bondage to the Soviet Union.

Ferment within Eastern Europe cannot be dissociated from the religious revival in the Soviet Union, particularly in the Baltic states (notably the Catholic Church in Lithuania), the Ukraine (Orthodox, Protestants, and the banned Eastern Rite Catholics), and Soviet Moldavia (with 3.5 million Romanians). Even before the election of the Polish Pope, the Soviet rulers were convinced that the Vatican had designated the Polish church as the vanguard of the "re-Christianization" of Eastern Europe and the Soviet Union. Communists have always regarded the Catholic Church as a major political power. Hence their extreme measures—including almost certainly even the attempted assassination of the present Pope.

East Europeans have gained great hope from the election to the papacy of one of their own and his subsequent support of believers of all faiths. In addition, the Poles' struggle for freedom, in which the people and the church joined as one, sent shock waves throughout Eastern Europe, further alarming the Communist authorities.

The religious ferment is not universal. Albania, still suffering the most dire oppression, reveals no signs of it, though even there, according to an internal Catholic source, there has been a "purification" of the faith. Bulgaria has not been affected apart from charismatic murmurings within some tiny Protestant churches, and any progress has quickly been stifled.

Ferment seems to be concentrated in the predominantly Catholic areas—Poland, Czechoslovakia, and Croatia in Yugoslavia—and to a more limited extent in the GDR, Hungary, and Romania, most notably among the evangelicals.

Contrary Factors

On the practical level, there seems to be little motivation for people to join the church or to take religion seriously in these societies where Christians are ridiculed and discriminated against and even persecuted. The young have been taught to despise religion and are often totally ignorant of it. Most churches are unable to provide any extra amenities for their people, such as clubs and comfortable facilities that help people to know one another. Communist governments are suspicious of any groups.

Believers are daily confronted with difficult moral choices—conflicts between their duty to God and their duty to the state. At times of crisis, the tension can become almost unbearable. Reinforced by nationalist and anti-Soviet sentiments, some have turned against the government, as happened in the national uprisings in the GDR, in Hungary back in the 1950s, and, on several occasions and more recently, in Poland. Others compromise.

Constructive Conservatism

Because of their isolation, most East European Christians have remained ignorant of the main trends in Western theology and, until recently, of liturgical reform. This has spared them the watering down of the Gospel and the ensuing crisis of faith that has afflicted the West. People who have suffered for their beliefs are in any case far less likely to dilute them. Conservatism of this kind is a source of strength and attracts people searching for stability and unchanging values.

Within the Catholic Church the Pope's conservative theological outlook has reinforced the innate traditionalism of many East European Christians, while his openness on most human-rights and social problems has encouraged Catholic renewal groups and fostered the ferment. The 1986 papal encyclical *Humanae Vitae,* though, which reaffirmed the church's teaching about birth control, has not been a help to young couples facing life together. In Poland they may have to wait twenty years for an apartment. Almost everywhere, shortage of accommodations, low wages, high prices, deteriorating medical services, and, now, inflation, put immense strains on family life.

For the Orthodox churches, conservatism is part of their ethos and liturgical reform is anathema. Their worship is probably richer and more inspiring than that of any other churches. Their profound theology and spirituality could be more fully realized in an encouraging environment. Nevertheless, the Orthodox believer is convinced that the gates of hell will not prevail against the church and is consoled for his present trials by his belief in the eternal.

The upsurge of evangelical Protestantism in Eastern Europe is comparable to that in the Soviet Union. The evangelicals have attracted people from every level of society, from highly qualified professionals to the Gypsies, who are numerous in most countries and universally disliked. In Romania, where the evangelical movement is particularly strong, the authorities have resorted to terror to combat it. A Yugoslav Pentecostalist, theologian Peter Kuzmić, has described the evangelical upsurge as "marked by a theology of the cross. Their Christian life has a depth of commitment and spirit of sacrifice going far beyond . . . the 'cheap grace' or 'prosperity theology' popular in some segments of Western evangelism." Kuzmić has also criticized the movement, particularly for an "escapist eschatology," a view that the present is unimportant because Christ's return to earth is imminent, which he attributes to a lack of systematic theological training.

In a paradoxical way, the conservatism of the church—the clear, constant faith in a transcendent and unchanging God as against the anti-religious and the variable—has contributed to the religious ferment.

Other Contributing Factors

The young and the lapsed are returning to the churches in increasing numbers. The prime reason, of course, is to worship God, to bring eternity into their lives. But there are many other reasons. Some attend church in order to escape, for a few hours, from the drab monotony of life under socialism or from intolerable living conditions. Many hope to find friendship, sympathy, caring; others wish to find persons with whom to share their problems and experiences, for bureaucratic totalitarianism has little time for the individual as a person. Some join the church to assert their national culture or to rediscover their historical roots. A few join because of a concern for peace.

Nationalism is a potent force, and both church and state have had to come to terms with it. In Romania and Bulgaria the state has allowed the institutional Orthodox churches to be identified with nationalism. In the 1983 Luther quincentenary, the German state authorities jumped on the church bandwagon. Even Albania has grudgingly allowed the religious allegiance of past heroes to be mentioned in its literature. In Poland the majority are proudly Catholic and very proud that the Pope is one of their countrymen. In Slovakia the government has magnified and overreacted to the nationalist element in religious revival; whereas in Yugoslavia, nationalism, allied to different religions, is a real threat to a fragile, artificial unity, and the authorities exaggerate it when it suits them.

Some seek fertile ground for the seeds of their dissent in the churches. Religious institutions are the only legally existing bodies not inspired by the Party, run by the Party, and under the direct rule of the Party; there are no independent trade unions, no independent political parties, no independent social organizations. The church hierarchies in Poland, in the GDR, and, increasingly, in Yugoslavia, are acutely aware of the danger of being identified with political movements, though in Yugoslavia the Serbian Orthodox Church has not completely distanced itself from potentially disruptive politics. They nevertheless speak out in defense of human rights and freedom.

Church-Related Groups

Some people find what they seek in the institutional church; other gravitate toward church-related groups, which may be either official and openly backed by the church, encouraged, disapproved of, or clandestine. The institutional churches are hamstrung by state regulations, and usually restricted to worship in the church, whereas the groups attract those who are probing social, political, and existential problems and thrive on personal contact. Many young people, less inhibited by memories of past repression and eager to maintain their integrity, find their way into church-related groups.

Since they are almost the only places for people to exchange views, these groups—notably in the GDR—draw some people who, in the West, would never come near a church. Some participants do not become believers but respect and sympathize with them. In Czechoslovakia and the GDR, people with very disparate views, dissident Marxists included, may become close friends through their common participation in a religious group. In Hungary, however, Christians have, until recently, made only a marginal impact on the considerable number of dissidents.

The regimes in the GDR, Poland, and Hungary nowadays tacitly permit secular youth groups often associated with rock music, partly as a counterattraction to church groups and partly to let the young work off their frustrations. But these are essentially superficial protest manifestations, aping Western phenomena.

In many of the religious groups, people of integrity, goodness, and deep spirituality are inspired and led by older, experienced believers, including priests and nuns whose faith has withstood many trials and often imprisonment. The groups provide islands within the secular ocean in which people study, pray, discuss issues, and try to live a Christian life together. Like the churches, the groups tend to be theologically conservative, though some experiment with fresh forms of worship.

Some of the groups are official, openly backed by the church; examples of these are seen in Poland and the GDR. Others have aroused such hostile reactions from the authorities that they have to meet in secret. Czechoslovakia presents fascinating examples. In what was formerly one of the most sophisticated countries in the world, a country in which secularism had long eroded religious belief, persecution has, paradoxically, been a factor in the revival of religion, even among the intelligentsia, and has led to the formation of a parallel "catacomb" church, comparable to that in Lithuania. Czechoslovakia serves as a prime example of the counterproductive nature of religious oppression.

Some groups belong to a network; others are independent. They are potential breeding grounds of ecumenism in countries where deep historic divisions have worked against interchurch relations, and where the promotion of ecumenism by state-sponsored church leaders has inspired fear that it is only a government ploy to get the churches to neglect local concerns in favor of prestigious international contacts. Frequently, Vatican II reforms and personal contacts with Protestants have persuaded Catholics to study the Bible and to discover how much the two branches have in common.

The groups, though never likely to attract the majority of churchgoers, are an invaluable stimulant to church and society as well as a challenge to the Communist system. Western Christians could learn much from them and from the writings they produce.

Celebrations and Pilgrimages

Many East European believers are demonstrating their faith by participating in major church celebrations and in pilgrimages to holy places. The traditional pilgrimage centers are attracting more people than ever, and from a greater range of churches. No country—not even Albania—has been able to prevent the people from going.

State authorities are uneasy with this unabashed expression of religious fervor, not least because it allows the people to show their dissatisfaction with their government. Yet they cannot arrest thousands of peaceful citizens.

The churches themselves are anxious that these events not explode into provocative demonstrations, especially of nationalism, and they do their best to make them both physically and spiritually demanding. This is certainly the case in Poland and Yugoslavia; in Czechoslovakia the authorities themselves can be relied on to make them demanding.

Even in the highly secularized GDR, the numbers turning out for the annual Kirchentag (100,000 in one day) can hardly please the government, which only recently thought religion was on its way out. In Romania great numbers express and deepen their faith by visiting monasteries, while renewal is visible in the packed evangelical churches. Even the Serbs and Bulgarians, not noted for their religious fervor, visit their national shrines in droves.

New pilgrimage centers have emerged since 1980, each an embarrassment to the authorities. The most controversial is Medjugorje in Yugoslavia, the ultimate contradiction—Fatima in a Communist land. For the new one in Poland, the authorities have only themselves to blame: the thousands who flocked to Father Popiełuszko's Masses for the Fatherland now flock to his church, St. Stanisław Koska, where his mutilated remains lie buried.

Celebrations were held in 1985 in several countries to mark the eleven hundredth anniversary of the death of St. Methodius. The Bulgarian celebrations, generously sponsored by the state, emphasized the cultural rather than the religious achievements of the missions of Methodius and his brother, Cyril. The Yugoslav celebrations at Djakovo had greater religious significance. The celebrations inspired tremendous popular enthusiasm in Croatia, where the Glagolitic Western rite, a legacy of St. Methodius, has never completely died out.

But it was in Czechoslovakia, at Velehrad, where the saint died, that the celebrations took on a new dimension. Pilgrimages there had not previously been permitted. The largest public gathering in Czechoslovakia since the advent of Communism gave the government a sharp demonstration of the failure of its anti-religious policy.

The Pope and Saints Cyril and Methodius

What the Pope said in his 1985 encyclical *Slavorum Apostoli* (Apostles of the Slavs)—as distinguished from what the Communist authorities imputed to him—is important to the churches of Eastern Europe. The Pope's letter urged greater unity among Europe's Christians and their countries. His text was based on St. Cyril's last prayer: "Increase, O Lord, the numbers of your church and gather them all together in unity, and direct your chosen people in your true faith and right belief." He called on all European countries to overcome their ideological conflicts on the basis of their common Christian roots. He also prayed that Christians would be able to profess their faith without hindrance and that their dedication to the Kingdom of God would not be misinterpreted as contradicting the interests of their earthly countries.

By proclaiming the Western monk Benedict and the Eastern monks Cyril and Methodius as co-patrons of Europe, John Paul II put across the message of the essential spiritual unity of Europe. It is a message that at least some Czechoslovak Christians are taking to heart—the Catholic underground there circulates cards showing the three saints superimposed on a map of Europe (depicted also on the cover of this book). There is still, however, a long way to go, and centuries of suspicion and hostility between the churches to be overcome.

Vatican Ostpolitik

Vatican policy has had a surprising continuity. The Vatican always works within the limits of the possible. Pope John Paul II did not, as many expected, replace Cardinal Casaroli, head of the Secretariat of State and chief negotiator of Vatican *Ostpolitik*. The Pope's insistence that the church take a public stand on human rights neatly complemented Cardinal Casaroli's diplomatic, long-term approach—that Communist regimes are here to stay and the church must learn to coexist with them. *Ostpolitik* must be judged by its diplomatic success or failure and by what improvements it has brought to local churches. It should be noted that what is involved in each country is not a bilateral but a trilateral relationship, involving the church hierarchy, the regime, and the Vatican.

In the GDR there are no major problems; the church can appoint its own bishops. Because it is small, it is regarded as rather insignificant.

In Bulgaria—where the church is even smaller—the little progress that had been made was halted by the intransigent attitude of the authorities after the "Bulgarian Affair" (the alleged Bulgarian involvement in the attempt to assassinate the Pope), despite the Vatican's conciliatory behavior. With only four priests under the age of fifty, the future of the institutional church seems unpromising.

Limited progress has been made in Romania in filling the vacant dioceses. Interim bishops are working out a charter for legal status. But as long as the Eastern Rite Catholic Church is banned and the religious situation in general is so troubled, the prospects for Catholics are depressing. With the deteriorating status of Hungarians in Romania, the Vatican is apprehensive of making matters worse.

In Hungary, with bishops in all the dioceses and with some state concessions besides, relations with the government are fairly cordial. Many Catholics feel, however, that the Vatican has supported an authoritarian and compliant hierarchy to the detriment of real church unity and greater concessions. Only in 1988 did the bishops at last exhibit some independence.

The Pope has brought a breath of fresh air to the previously demoralized church in Czechoslovakia. Accommodation is no longer a priority; the papacy has given precedence to the best interests of ordinary believers. Cardinal Tomášek, backed by the Pope, is speaking out with courage, and the new Vatican line has the support of a growing number of Catholics who are convinced that collaboration achieved nothing. Key problems are filling the inordinate number of vacant dioceses, and finding someone to succeed Tomášek after his death, as the authorities would veto anyone of comparable stature.

As for Albania, the Pope has repeatedly drawn the attention of the West to the unparalleled plight not only of the Catholics but also of the Orthodox and the Muslims. The response among Western Catholics, however, has been disappointing.

At the other end of the scale, the Vatican's long-standing protocol with the Yugoslav government has freed the church from government interference, except where Croatian nationalism is suspected.

In Poland, the church under Cardinal Wyszyński worked out its own highly successful response to the regime without much reference to the Vatican. There is still no concordat between the Vatican and the state. Glemp lacks something as a leader, although his eight years as primate have been exceptionally difficult because they coincided with the suppression of Solidarity. But any weakness of his is counteracted by the extraordinary strength and unity of Polish Catholicism. The Pope is still regarded as a Polish bishop; whatever he says is wholeheartedly followed.

Outside Contacts: Catholics and Protestants

It is, of course, very difficult if not impossible for most Eastern-bloc Christians—Yugoslavia and to a lesser extent Poland and Hungary are the exceptions—to visit the West, although the Catholic bishops in all countries except Albania are allowed to make *ad limina* visits (obligatory visits to the pope once every five years) to Rome.

Official papal visits to East European countries are not welcome. The Polish government could hardly refuse to allow John Paul II to return to his native land in 1979 and 1983, and by 1987 his stabilizing influence had been recognized. No other government has felt secure enough to allow him to set foot on its soil, though by 1988 influential party members in the Catholic republics of Yugoslavia were pushing for a visit.

Despite travel restrictions, the days of acute isolation of the churches are over except for Albanians and, to a lesser extent, Bulgarians, Romanians, and Czechs. Visits by Western church leaders (the Pope excepted), particularly to conferences hosted by East European churches, have become an accepted part of life. In many cases the host country has profited from them. Romania, for instance, sought a better image—and extra cash—through the Billy Graham visit. Although Graham has been criticized for ignoring human rights, his visits have raised the morale of local Baptist churches and fostered the growth of the evangelicals.

Membership in the World Council of Churches (WCC) may have provided valuable personal contacts for some East European churchmen, but in general the WCC has limited East European churches to a very low profile in the organization, for fear, ostensibly, of antagonizing their governments.

Visits from charismatic figures such as Mother Teresa and Brother Roger of Taizé, though shunned by the media, have had a profound effect on large numbers of people. In the GDR and Czechoslovakia, for instance, such visits have brought Catholics and Protestants together at a deeper level of understanding.

Muslim Contacts Outside

Only Yugoslavia and Bulgaria have sizable worshiping Muslim communities, and their approaches could hardly be more different. Yugoslavia has promoted links with Muslim countries and allowed free travel. Oil-rich states have subsidized Muslim institutions in Yugoslavia generously. With the fall in oil prices the flow of cash may be reduced. This would not in fact displease the authorities, who have become wary of the spread of Muslim fundamentalism. Taken as a whole, Yugoslav-style Muslims and Communists coexist peacefully. That does not exclude a possible upsurge in fundamentalism among some Muslims in Yugoslavia. The unrest of the Kossovo Albanians is an ethnic, not a religious, issue.

The brutal Bulgarian campaign against the Pomaks and recently against the Turks has rightly caused an outcry, and not only in the Muslim world. No help is in the offing, however, since for the Bulgarian government it is a *fait accompli*, and since Turkey, the nearest Muslim neighbor, has many reasons for maintaining tolerable relations with Bulgaria.

Orthodox Contacts Outside

The Orthodox are the least favored in their outside contacts. The Orthodox are as badly persecuted in Turkey, where the headquarters of Orthodoxy—the Ecumenical Patriarchate of Istanbul—is located, as in any Communist country with the exception of Albania. Since most Orthodox personnel there are refused passports, they cannot properly fulfill their international responsibilities. And so Orthodoxy, already sadly divided by ethnic differences, suffers the immense handicap of having its headquarters patriarchate virtually inoperable. It has had to set up alternative facilities in Geneva as part of the WCC, where the Russian Orthodox Church dominates.

Except for the Serbian Orthodox Church, the East European churches are all subordinate to the interests of the Moscow Patriarchate, following its lead in foreign relations, while paying due respect to the ecumenical patriarch as senior. Their bishops turn up obediently at peace conferences and ecumenical gatherings and make the required noises. On the other hand, the Russian connection ensures that where they are in a minority, as in Czechoslovakia, they gain a few advantages. Contacts with other Orthodox could lessen their isolation. Some promising small ventures are being initiated, but the Orthodox cannot count on anywhere near the same level of moral and material support from abroad as other religious bodies.

The CPC and the Peace Movements

The Christian Peace Conference (CPC), with its new, modern headquarters in Prague, continues to operate, along with many state-sponsored ecumenical meetings held under the aegis of the Moscow Patriarchate, at which "peace" pronouncements are compulsory. Western participants tend to exaggerate the importance of such meetings. Most East European Christians rate them as what they are—Communist propaganda exercises.

The new grassroots peace movements that have emerged in the GDR and Hungary, uniting Christians and non-believers, are very different. Most East Europeans, having known devastating wars and with missiles stationed on their territory, genuinely want to avoid war, but they distrust Soviet-style peace. They are only too well aware that the armies on their soil are there not because their rulers fear the West but because they fear their own subjects.

The genuine peace movements have met with differing responses from the churches. The East German church has encouraged and sheltered peace and environmental initiatives—discussions, concessions for conscientious objectors—but has wisely stopped short of becoming identified with peace activities. The failure of the Hungarian Catholic Church, until 1988, to support its beleaguered conscientious objectors discredited it in the eyes of many.

Prospects for the Churches

Everywhere churches face daunting problems. Some suffer from internal rifts, often accentuated by state interference. The future of sacramental life and pastoral care has been jeopardized within some by a shortage of clergy, whether caused by the state or by lack of vocations or both. This puts a great responsibility on the laity. With regard to Hungary, for instance, Bishop Cserhati has warned, "Without the active assistance of the laity, within ten years the care of souls will not be possible." In this respect the Hungarian church is more fortunate than some others, for the authorities now permit the laity to help; in countries like Romania and Czechoslovakia, believers who undertake religious outreach on their own initiative are still often exposed to considerable risks.

Almost everywhere there is still a shortage, sometimes acute, of basic religious literature, Bibles and prayer books. Trust between believers and the state, a prerequisite for progress, is almost non-existent. Even in the GDR, where the churches as institutions are allowed considerable scope, the state has failed to honor its modest 1978 pledges to end discrimination against members. By still, on occasion, resorting to brutal extra-judicial methods—at times even murder—to remove awkward clergy and dissidents, the Polish, Czechoslovak, and, in particular, Romanian authorities have forfeited any hope of trust. Some improvements have occurred in the treatment of religious dissidents, thanks largely to protests and adverse publicity from the West against unjustified arrests. This Western pressure has helped reduce the number of "religious" prisoners in Czechoslovakia, Romania, and Yugoslavia to almost nil, though the problems of conscientious objectors are still unresolved.

Nevertheless, no East European signatory of the Helsinki Accords has fulfilled its "Basket Three" promises. Western delegates to the 1988 meeting in Vienna of the Conference on Security and Cooperation in Europe (which produced the Helsinki Accords in 1975) complained that the Soviet Union and several East European delegations, especially Romania, still refused to be tied down in detail to commitments in human and religious rights. Bulgaria, in its treatment of Muslims, and Albania, in its treatment of all dissent, religious or political, remain impervious to world opinion.

Glasnost and Perestroika

With Gorbachev's "openness" and "restructuring," a new and unexpected element arrived in the East European scene. What effect had it had as of mid-year 1988?

Most leaders were dragging their heels. They are efficient bureaucrats. Their outlook is limited, for Communism rarely produces leaders with vision or imagination—Gorbachev is very much an exception. Not surprisingly, the leaders are unwilling to take any steps that might lead to their loss of power and the considerable perquisites dependent on it. Only too conscious that they have no mandate from the people, they are unwilling to allow open discussion that might lead to radical reform. As long as there is any doubt about Gorbachev's ability to last the course—and everyone remembers what happened to Dubček and his reforms in Czechoslovakia exactly ten years ago—any definitive change of policy from Eastern-bloc leaders is unlikely.

Glasnost refers to openness, willingness to allow public discussion of awkward current problems and of history—which is falsified and distorted under Communism—without the threat of dire consequences to those who speak out. Its possible implications are infinite. *Perestroika*, restructuring, applies to the economic situation.

Faced with economic crises, Eastern-bloc leaders have been forced to try a little *perestroika*. The two exceptions are the GDR, where Honecker, very much in control and backed by a strong economy, maintains that neither *glasnost* nor *perestroika* is necessary, and Romania, where Ceauşescu has his own unique solution for his nation's problems. The only places where Romanians can read Gorbachev's speeches is on a notice board outside the Soviet embassy in Bucharest. The Czechoslovak government, with a less shaky economy than most, and knowing that liberalization would lead to a complete discrediting of the government, is doing its utmost to limit change to minor *perestroika*. Hungary, with some experience of a freer economy and public discussion, has taken steps to implement *glasnost* as well as *perestroika*. So to a lesser extent have Poland and Bulgaria, though Bulgaria is limiting its reform to reshaping its Party and economy.

Non-aligned Yugoslavia is in quite a different category. At a historic symposium organized by Freedom House in New York in June 1987, leading Yugoslav scholars, émigrés, and dissidents claimed that their country has had *glasnost* for thirty years! Their government has no problem letting people travel, they said. Frank discussion in the press has existed for some time, and for several years people from different republics have been able to publish memoirs revealing the shady past of the Party. Basically, they felt, Yugoslavia is more liberal than the other Communist states, though in religion, especially its access to the media, they thought Poland was ahead. Tolerance toward religion is becoming more widespread in Yugoslavia, and revision of official policy is keenly discussed in the press. But, they agreed, anyone looking at Yugoslavia today, foundering in its longstanding political and economic chaos, would only comment, "So *that's* where *glasnost* got you!"

Whatever else Gorbachev has promised, he has nowhere promised democracy along Western lines. *Glasnost* and *perestroika* are essentially means to an end: to enable the Soviet economy and system to function as effectively as those in the West. Gorbachev has no clearly formulated religious policy. He is an opportunist, who needs all the support he can muster when embarking on an uncertain, unprecedented course. Because religion, both in the Soviet Union and in the Eastern bloc, has proved far more tenacious and deep-rooted than ideologists expected, and because states need the cooperation of believers to overcome formidable social problems, some sort of accommodation has become essential.

Religious Changes?

By 1987 Eastern-bloc believers were looking expectantly towards Gorbachev, who appeared to be making some startling religious changes in the Soviet Union. Certainly there has been a considerable improvement in official Soviet policy toward believers, of which the release of some—by no means all—religious prisoners and dissidents is the most publicized if not necessarily the most important sign. The invaluable contribution of believers to society has been openly recognized. So has the corollary, that it is unjust to penalize them as second-class citizens.

Such a shift in outlook is long overdue in Eastern Europe. By the beginning of 1988, only the authorities in Poland and Hungary—Yugoslavia is in a different category—had rather grudgingly acknowledged that the churches and their members can act as a leaven in their communities and help lift their nations out of the mire into which they are sinking. Polish Catholics have been assertive and powerful enough, under sensible leadership, to persuade the authorities to treat them as equals. In Czechoslovakia, Catholics for the first time ever are actively lobbying for their church and for basic religious rights. The East German government doesn't admit to having any problems. It cashes in on the good will and expertise of the church as a caring agency but doesn't see fit to admit believers into other fields. In three states there have been no signs of relaxation toward religion: Romania and Czechoslovakia, where activist believers are still frequently categorized as enemies of the state, and Bulgaria, where believers have made so little impact that they are just ignored.

What improvements are made depend partly on what impact churches and believers have made on national life. But with every country except the GDR preoccupied with a deteriorating economic situation, religion currently has a low priority with the authorities.

Another problem is already obvious in the Soviet Union: a wide discrepancy between high-level pronouncements and what goes on at the grassroots level. Many local officials act in an arbitrary and autocratic way towards churches and believers whether or not their tactics reflect government policy. Even if all the East European governments relax their official policy toward religion, it could take years and a new generation of party officials to implement the new approach. Inertia and self-interest will inevitably obstruct progress. Believers, for so long victimized by petty local despots, need to be more assertive. Fear and caution are so deeply ingrained that it has taken the Czechoslovaks, for instance, forty years to rise above them. Romanians and Bulgarians are still at the mercy of informers and of the secret police.

Far-reaching legal changes are needed to improve the status of believers. Also, in Romania, Hungary, Czechoslovakia, and Bulgaria, the powers of the state office for religious affairs need to be reduced. Only in Hungary has a start been made: in March 1988, the minister of justice there proposed new laws, sanctioned by parliament, to replace outdated decrees issued arbitrarily by government ministers and state secretaries. The only precedent for such legal change so far is the situation of the Russian Orthodox Church in the Soviet Union, where vital changes in church statutes have been allowed, though by fall 1988 the laws relating to religion had not yet been modified. Bishops estimate that about 75 per cent of their demands will be met. Another needed change is an end to the practice, found in Bulgaria, Czechoslovakia, Romania, and Yugoslavia, of charging religious activists with fabricated "crimes" that bear little relationship to their real "offense."

How Westerners Should Respond

Westerners who visit an East European country owe it to those who live under Communism to be as well informed as possible. Every visitor is a potential bridge-builder who can reduce their sense of isolation, bringing information about the outside world. And every Christian visitor should take at least one religious book or Bible, even if only to leave it in a church; someone will benefit from it.

Westerners should be prepared to listen. A Christian familiar with the situation has said: "God is teaching the church to find its own way and not to become dependent on Western organizations." This is very important. Help based on mistaken assumptions can be counterproductive and can subject believers to charges of collaborating with "imperialists"; or it can deny them the opportunity of working out their own solutions. Sometimes we Westerners are required to speak out about injustice; sometimes we are asked to remain prudently silent.

Usually we can learn more than we can give or teach. Under persecution, believers have discovered their priorities; under deprivation they are discovering their basic needs. For some, it is the reassertion of their national and religious roots through pilgrimages; for others it is building the church within the family, or producing and disseminating literature, or witnessing in everyday life to the power of the Gospel, or leading the religious life in secret.

Glasnost, if and when it develops in Eastern Europe, will present Western churches with an opportunity and challenge they are, with the honorable exception of certain specialized missionary societies and the Bible societies, quite unprepared to fulfill. As Michael Bourdeaux, director of Keston College, has pointed out, Western church leaders, their thinking dominated by the needs of the Third World, hardly have the hugely disadvantaged church of the "Second World" on their agenda. It is not, as he said, as if the opportunity had never occurred before. In 1968, the year of the Prague Spring, Western churches saw the chance to supply Czechoslovak churches with religious literature they desperately needed. But when the borders quickly closed again, the Western churches' talking had hardly begun, and it was too late. The same thing could happen today. No one can predict whether *glasnost* or Gorbachev will survive. The need is not limited to books. There are many other ways in which Western Christians, with their superior technology and expertise, could help those in the East, should the situation ease appreciably. With governments forced to let prices, hitherto maintained unrealistically low, rise toward their proper levels, there has already been a considerable increase in the number of chronically poor—in Poland and Yugoslavia, for instance. Therefore financial help on a large scale might be needed; so might medical and agricultural help.

Polish Catholics in general and the Light-Life movement in particular have shown us a liberation theology very different from that propounded in the West and in the Third World. It is based on personal liberation from fear, on meeting Christ and the truth that is in him. It liberates people from enslavement—not by the use of violence, but through love and forgiveness.

The Polish liberation theology—as exemplified, for example, in the forbearance of Solidarity—is truly Christian. It has been tried and found not wanting; how otherwise could Poland have avoided a bloodbath? It has been practiced and refined by many of the finest Christian dissidents in the Soviet Union. When the Russian Orthodox dissident Anatoli Levitin was asked whether he could ever resort to violence, he said that sixty years of suffering under Soviet rule had taught him that violence achieves nothing.

Crucifixion and Resurrection

In the Soviet Union, Communism has produced a degradingly corrupt, demoralized, apathetic society lurching towards self-destruction, and demographic statistics indicate that its satellites are following in its wake. Communism has been tried and found wanting—as Gorbachev only partially indicates. In some countries the churches are virtually the only reservoir of persons with the experience and motivation to provide a constructive alternative. Individually and as institutions, East European believers have hammered some good out of evil, taught people to find inner freedom within tight political and economic constrictions, nourished hope in an apparently hopeless situation. The once monolithic Roman Catholic Church has taken the lead in teaching people to find themselves and their true freedom.

Now *glasnost* has provided a glimmer of hope for most. In Romania and Albania it has not, and the people there must not be forgotten.

Many people in both Eastern and Western Europe—more than in the United States—regard the church as a vestige of former eras when faith and superstition predominated over scientific knowledge. But to those who long to climb out of the swamp of indifference, alienation, ethical relativism, secularization, and agnosticism, the church will always be a rock that provides faith and certainty to some, shelter to those in doubt.

To Christians it is the Body of Christ, however broken or bleeding or, indeed, crucified. One has to embrace that broken and bleeding body, share to some measure in its crucifixion, as East Europeans have so fully done, to be part of the Resurrection. Having experienced crucifixion and resurrection, the churches of Eastern Europe, despite their manifold failings, have the power to gather, comfort, and heal sinful and suffering humanity.

The Plight of Religious Orders

This Charter 77 document dated December 1984 was signed by Václav Benda, Jíři Huml, and Jana Sternová, Chartist spokespersons. (Excerpts.)

Membership in a religious order automatically involves the loss of the fundamental rights that are guaranteed to all citizens, and the continual threat of penal sanctions. The rights involved are equality before the law, the right to receive education, freedom of association, the inviolability of the person and place of residence, freedom of opinion, and the right to personal property. Religious orders basically do not do anything but put into effect the principal ideals that Communism proclaims—equality and labor on society's behalf.

The liquidation of convents was a purely political act without any juridical foundation at all. The internment camps for religious were not part of the regular penal system, so its regulations did not apply. Conditions of life there were even worse than in the prisons, and in fact the political leadership was quite prepared to tolerate this since it killed them off more quickly. Their internment had no time limits—it was for life, and some served twenty years. . . . Though they worked eight to ten hours a day they were not given enough food. . . . All this represented extralegal slavery and a form of genocide, according to the U.N. definition of 1946. . . . In 1968, 8,264 religious wrote asking the minister of culture to reopen their convents; altogether they had served a total of 42,763 years in prison.

We must point out that during past and present persecution the state authorities have never brought out any law to justify the limitations imposed, nor have they tried to find one. They have relied solely on their political power, avoiding entering into discussion with the orders or anyone else over the exact juridical position. . . . The official justification they produced sounded like this: "In general it can be said that the level our society has reached doesn't provide any scope for religious orders; it is now only a matter of the gradual disappearance of the present generation, for our young people have no longer any interest in such [outdated] forms of life" (*Nová Mysl,* no. 1, 1972). . . .

The attitude of our government to the problem of orders is quite different from that of other socialist countries; even in the USSR, orders can exist legally. . . . Male orders are not allowed to function, and women's orders can function only in a very limited way. Nuns cannot live together, not even in private houses or apartments, even it they have secular employment, wear ordinary clothes, and the property belongs to them. If religious do try to live together, they lay themselves open to the risk of police proceedings, which often end up with criminal prosecution. This is what happened to the Franciscans of Liberec, Bárta and Trojan, who were condemned under Article 178 for having celebrated Mass in a private house and organized theological courses. . . . Conditions vary considerably according to the tolerance or otherwise of local party officials. . . . The sisters who, back in the 1950s, were transferred from Slovakia to Bohemia have never been allowed to return home. They can do so only by leaving their order. . . . Many very old sisters, often gravely ill, have not been permitted to go home to die among their own families.

An apparent paradox in the state's policy is that, given its severity, there shouldn't now *be* any problem of religious orders! . . . The orders have shown an extraordinary resilience and capacity to resist attempts to eliminate them by force. [After their release from prison] religious have shown themselves able to adapt creatively to new conditions. They have divided themselves into smaller groups and trained for all sorts of professions; they live in apartments like other citizens; and yet in these outwardly anonymous conditions they continue the tradition of their rules, at the same time adapting themselves to fresh forms of spirituality and new possibilities for working in very different social conditions.

The ruthless persecution by the state is illegal, and in the long run has been more damaging to society as a whole than to the orders themselves. . . . Religious orders will exist as long as there exist in society the sick and the weak, children and old people; as long as art and science endure; and as long as there is the need for people to contemplate in solitude the fundamental problems of humanity. . . .

In the long history of religious orders in our country, the last thirty-five years represent a heroic era. This period will come to an end only when the doors of the convents open again.

SOURCE: Charter 77 Document no. 21, December 12, 1984.

APPENDIX B: CZECHOSLOVAKIA

Life as a Dissident

Václav Benda

Writing before his arrest in 1979, Dr. Benda graphically portrays his life as a member of Charter 77 and of VONS (Committee for the Defense of the Unjustly Persecuted). (Excerpts.)

In about an hour I shall have to stop work and leave for my place of employment—or vice versa, depending on how you look at it. I was born a year after the end of the Second World War; I am white, a Catholic, a non-Party man, and I am irreproachable before the law. In August 1968 my wife and I, knowing full well the "unforeseeable consequences," decided not to use our valid passports but to remain in Czechoslovakia. Moreover, in 1977—after I had signed Charter 77—we several times rejected offers of an assisted passage to Austria. We live relatively happily and contentedly, considering the circumstances: after all, if a man is so eccentric as to allow himself to be thrown to the lions, it would be very silly of him to complain that their teeth were not clean enough. Let me make it very clear, though, that by saying this I am not defending either the lions or their use as a political weapon in civil life.

Since the age of eighteen I have been (often out of necessity rather than from choice) a student of philosophy, a schoolmaster, a hydrobiologist, unemployed (on unemployment benefit), a student of mathematics, a mathematician with the railways, a programmer, and a stoker. I have also had temporary jobs as a worker in a brewery and on a building site, a cowherd, an assistant arts editor, a linguist, a translator, a teacher of logic, and a computer expert. None of these enforced moves was due to any inconvenient dissident activity on my part. Rather, they occurred because I was not willing to become involved enough in the political activities prescribed in changeable directives from the top. . . . For the time being I am working in a boiler-room during the day, and trying to divide the rest of my time between sleeping, family life, civil-rights activities, mathematics, and philosophy. . . .

309

310 CONSCIENCE AND CAPTIVITY

For our four older children—five-year-old Marta, three-year-old Patrik, and the schoolboys, nine-year-old Mark and seven-year-old Martin—the occasional visits from the police are a welcome adventure. Last year their repertoire was enriched by two new games, "Belonging to the Charter" and "Being unemployed." . . . One-year-old Filip is best at being an alarm clock. . . .

The conflict with the state into which I have entered will be long, exhausting, and, by all human standards, hopeless, and in this country means that my whole family down to the third generation will also be brought into the conflict, together with all of my friends who were not quick enough to disown me publicly. . . . The state power, against which we are making our stand, has two main characteristics: it prefers to strangle its victims in deserted spots and under cover of darkness, and it never forgives or forgets. . . .

For each typewriter we possess, the state has at its disposal ten printing presses. . . . We are thrown back many centuries into an age before the invention of the motor car, the telephone, the printing press, the postal service, and so on. We have to spend several hours running around the town in order to achieve something which, in the twentieth century, would require just two short telephone calls. We spend thousands of hours repeating and copying factual details which could have been summarized in one newspaper column. We abide by the law, we act legally and publicly. The state contradicts the law, it takes action against us illegally and in a conspiratorial manner. . . .

Fortunately, the world around us is real; the children get up, get dressed and have breakfast, and go off to school, the family really exists. . . . Whereas they, these others, are mere phantoms who incongruously don a human mask and occasionally emerge from the mists, meticulously concealing their actions and especially their names. They try to ensnare us in their spiders' webs, taking advantage of the fact that everyone is afraid of them. For them, a telephone call or a short conversation is enough (now they never give you anything in writing): your rights no longer count, your claims will not be considered, your qualifications and contracts will be annulled; you will be dismissed from your job or thrown out of college without a chance of being accepted elsewhere, you will be denied medical care. . . . Out of the many hundreds of people with whom I spoke last year (discounting "conversation" with officials, of course), only three professed to be against Charter 77—and one of these latter came back to me some time later to say that he had read it and could not understand what was wrong with it.

In fact we encounter only one serious objection: we are right, but we are lunatics. . . . In the present era a system of double-truth has been almost brought to perfection in Czechoslovakia (far surpassing the 1950s and even Orwell's "doublethink"). . . .

The system is deeply immoral, for it not only causes suffering but also denies that suffering a name (and therefore a purpose). This system is dangerously stable, so stable that is eliminates historical development. . . . However, this system faces one mortal danger—it is based on the assumption that everybody must recognize the stick and carrot as an argument (and it really is a weighty argument). The cry that "the emperor is naked" can lead to quite uncontrollable and unexpected consequences and can fundamentally change the state of affairs. Of course, in an empire governed by a deceitful tailor surrounded by a host of imperial guards and courtiers—all quite naked as well—only fools or children can insist on shouting that.

Well then, I am convinced that to be a fool or a child is the only way to the Kingdom of Heaven; unless you become like these little ones, you will not enter. The wisdom of this world is foolishness and its foolishness is wisdom, but in the present circumstances it is our only temporal political hope.

SOURCE: *Religion in Communist Lands*, vol. 7, no. 4 (1979).

Condition of the Catholic Church

In a communication received in the West in 1985, a Catholic activist describes the state of his church. (Excerpts.)

There appears to be a noticeable revival of religious interest in Czechoslovakia at present, although official atheistic propaganda inevitably takes its toll—particularly amoung people with an improved standard of living in view. The main factor in this religious renaissance is the collapse of Marxism-Leninism as a credible ideology. I have yet to meet anyone in this country who would be prepared to support and defend Marxist theory on grounds that are not pragmatic or opportunistic. However, at the daily level, things are considerably less clear-cut.

Many Christians prefer to keep their beliefs to themselves, and avoid the risk of involvement in politics—which of course suits the Communist authorities very well. Yet a Christianity freely chosen can often prove itself to be astonishingly strong. Faith can hold its own against all those who have sold themselves into ideological bondage, and indeed the machinery of religious suppression has of late proved increasingly rusty. Atheistic propaganda is becoming less and less effectively transmitted, yet no attempts to improve it are being made. Even the propagandists seem unconvinced. . . .

Cardinal Tomášek is a great source of strength to us all, believers and unbelievers alike. He is a man of great integrity who will not allow himself to be pushed into a false position. He has opponents, of course, and on occasion there is even a noticeable indifference toward him from the clergy at large. This is a legacy of the years when there was no unifying figure in the church to set an example to the priesthood, and priests were left completely on their own. The cardinal therefore has a crucial unifying function, although his position is also very difficult. He is reportedly unable to rely on anyone in his immediate circle, and the government treats him as a troublesome and dangerous opponent best dispensed with. Dialogue with the authorities is a virtual impossibility.

In the final analysis, of course, the cardinal's authority is symbolic rather than actual, but even that is helpful to us. We are only too aware of the limitations of his office, but his words confirm us in our faith and are a guiding light in our lives. . . .

312

The mood and commitment of many members of the clergy leave much to be desired. . . . Many priests and believers refuse to risk any contact with supporters of the Christian resistance, to read unofficial literature, let alone duplicate it. They regard resistance as a political act, not as consistent practical Christianity. Yet surely one should recall, as Cardinal Glemp [primate of the Polish church] said at Father Popiełuszko's funeral [Fr. Jerzy Popiełuszko was murdered by Polish security police in 1984], that Christians who renounce their share of responsibility for political matters are acting in direct conflict with the social teachings of the church. . . .

While it is a simple matter for the authorities to bring a diocesan priest to heel, it is a much harder task to paralyze an entire religious order. The authorities are consequently seeking to ban orders as far as possible, and to ensure that none are revived. . . . Nevertheless the number of secret members is growing, although the strain on novices is often considerable. . . .

Churches throughout the country are visibly packed with young people despite the pressures of the atheistic propaganda in education. However, alcoholism and drug abuse are rife among the young, and there appears to be a burgeoning cult of violence sometimes based on the reawakening of a Nazi-like ideology. . . . The mood of the young tends to be one of apathy and wastage, and only Christianity seems able to provide an answer. It is by no means a coincidence that Mother Theresa of Calcutta received such an ecstatic welcome from huge crowds of young people during her visit. . . .

It seems extraordinary to us here in Czechoslovakia that Marxism continues to be attractive to people in the West—even if only as a social theory. Our own experience has shown beyond all doubt that any compromise with utopian socialism is a way to usher in the "socialism" we know, which transforms individuals into dumb collaborators or the oppressed subjects of a ruthless and faceless power, and offers no alternative other than fatalistic submission, or resistance fraught with danger and suffering.

SOURCE: Keston News Service, no. 231 (August 8, 1985).

The Secret Church

The underground monthly newspaper Informace o Církvi *(Church information) published this description of the Czechoslovak secret church in 1981. (Excerpts.)*

1. *Young people.* A growing number of young people are turning to religion and are willing, despite the threat of official sanction, to seek the company of like-minded people and to consult a priest whom they trust. . . . A church that confines itself to the performance of religious rites cannot satisfy the needs of young people interested in religion. They are looking for religious teaching and fellowship, which in Czechoslovakia today are only found in the "illegal" groups.

2. *"Worker priests."* Hundreds of priests, monks, and nuns who have been forbidden to pursue their vocation and therefore have secular jobs are having a Christianizing influence on those around them. The humane and Christian example set by these men and women often influences colleagues at work who were once believers to rethink their attitude to faith. Thus religious cells are sometimes formed in factories that in turn begin to influence other workers. These "worker" priests (and there are even some "worker" bishops) are able to achieve far more than the official parish priests, whose activities are so severely restricted.

3. *Information network.* There is a remarkable information and communications network that the authorities have been unable to destroy. Each time someone in the network is "exposed," someone else immediately steps in to take his or her place. This system means on the one hand that the "illegal" religious groups learn about one another and about events in other parts of the country, and on the other hand that people outside Czechoslovakia also learn of these events.

Especially in Slovakia, virtually every district has a Catholic layman working for this information network. Because each of them has personal contact with only a few other people, and because the network has no central headquarters, it is almost impossible for the secret police to discover more than one or two threads. Of course, the international reputation of the Czechoslovak regime is greatly damaged if the foreign media can use carefully verified facts and individual cases to show how religion is oppressed in Czechoslovakia.

4. *Rights movement.* A sort of religious civil-rights movement has emerged, whose members are no longer prepared to tolerate the arbitrary attacks made on the church without putting up some resistance. . . . Those who complain can hardly be subjected to reprisals, since they go through official channels and, far from breaking the law, are demanding that the law be upheld. True, the complaints are rarely (though sometimes) successful, but they nevertheless have an effect: other people discover that it is possible and perhaps necessary to resist injustice.

All this activity is gradually developing into a very unpleasant thorn in the flesh for the regime. Apparently, since the Czechoslovak political leadership, unlike the government of neighboring Communist states, seems to have decided against working toward better church-state relations, it sees police repression as the only way to prevent the spread of the "secret" church.

This is the only possible explanation of why such an enormous force was recently summoned to Slovakia expressly to stamp out the secret church. As a result of a decision taken by the Slovak Ministry of the Interior and the Provincial Committee, the secret police were told that all the investigative units of the secret police in Bratislava should from October 1980 onward direct their attention to the underground church and the lay apostolate. A team of thirty advisors has been attached to the city's security police. They are assisted full-time by ten advisors in each of the Slovak capital's four administrative areas. Their work is co-ordinated by a special-operations branch of the secret police.

The methods used to hunt down the secret church range from telephone-tapping and the use of informers to police action on a large scale. It is among young people in particular, as well as among the clergy—whether "legal" or "illegal"—that the secret police are looking for traces of the underground church. Many young people have recently been subjected to interrogation by the police, who have tried hard to make them name names, sometimes by threatening them (with being barred from higher education, for example) and sometimes by bribing them with promises. Often young people are asked to work for the secret police as informers; such cooperation has even been demanded of those training for the priesthood.

House searches are another method used by the police to track down the secret church. In most cases, the "aggravating material" that is unearthed during searches consists of religious writings or texts of papal documents, which are not considered subversive or anti-state anywhere else—even in other Communist countries. . . . They have to be printed underground only because the minimal amount of religious literature that the church is officially allowed to publish is utterly inadequate. Similarly, if religious orders—which are not officially banned—were not oppressed and were not forbidden to accept novices, there would be no "secret monasteries" or "illegal admissions to a religious order."

The system itself gives rise to the underground church by proscribing normal church activities that are not forbidden even in other Communist countries.

SOURCE: *Informace o Církvi*, no. 6 (1981), in *Religion in Communist Lands*, vol. 10, no. 1 (1982).

Letters From Prison

František Lízna, S.J.

Father František Lízna was sentenced in two separate trials to a total of twenty-seven months' imprisonment: in September 1981 for printing and distributing religious literature, and in January 1982 for attempting to pass on information about religious persecution to Keston College (under Article 112 of the penal code,"damaging state interests abroad"). His last letter from prison was dated June 6, 1982; he was banned from further writing because of the impact his letters made in Czechoslovakia, and was forbidden to receive letters, parcels, or personal visits. (Excerpts.)

March 14, 1982. . . . This cell and these walls are so helpless. I am sure that St. Francis would manage to talk to the cell as if it were a living thing. He would be sorry for its enduring so much foul language from its inhabitants [he had been put in a cell with several criminals] as they kick it mercilessly. . . . In all honesty, it is quite large, remarkably warm, and full of light. . . . It lets in some spring air; it is like being in a desert but surrounded by God's bounty. . . . Just think! Who would have thought that after two years of living in Prague, I would hear a bird singing under my window only in this place! . . . All this I received freely, without having to bribe the housing officials who are in charge of the distribution of accommodation for the privileged. For the last few days I have thus learned to regard this cell as my secret ally and refuse to treat it badly. . . .

April 12, 1982. Today is Easter Monday. . . . Our joy in the Resurrection is so central to our faith that it can be expressed at any time and in any situation. This joy is with us even in the face of the lion's jaws, to use a biblical image. Is it not marvelous, yet mysterious, to find that Christians radiate a joy that puts even the lions off balance? . . . As Easter follows the Crucifixion, so, too, our joy must be preceded by our suffering. . . . I can assure you that our suffering and joy are so carefully balanced that I can perceive in them the guiding hand of our good and merciful Lord.

On Good Friday I received your letters and also the one from my sister in London. Resisting the temptation to read them immediately, I waited until the early hours of the Day of the Resurrection. What a beautiful night! My cellmates went to sleep early, and in that silence I found myself among you, so that I felt I should apologize to the warden for my absence. At dawn I was coming back with Ivan; we passed St. Havel's Church along the Charles Bridge and went up toward the Royal Castle. When we parted from the others, full of joy in his Resurrection, it seemed to us that we were travelers on the road to Emmaus, so long and beautiful was that journey. . . .

April 25, 1982. It is the second Sunday after Easter, a beautiful morning. Soon the sun will penetrate our cell, so that we can again see for ourselves that the Good God never forgets us. He showers sunlight, food, and drink on everyone—the good and the bad alike. As I hear the rattle of mugs from the corridor, I realize that not only my eyes but my ears, too, were created to testify to the truth of Him who reigns above all, yesterday, today, and forever. I am even now amazed how quietly the sun comes to us, without arousing the slightest attention, in great contrast to human behavior. Observe how unobtrusively a ray of light penetrates the room, how solidly constructed and yet how delicate it seems to be. There is no shoddy work, no disorder, and the light is so meticulous that it picks up every grain of dust so that we wonder suddenly if we are alone.

I would like to extend my brotherly greetings to the newly discovered particles of dust, hated here by everyone, in gratitude for their willingness to stay with us so quietly and inconspicuously. . . . See how the dust glitters! No doubt the ability to see in this way is a precious grace, because our eyes suddenly see the rays of the invisible world. And again, I have been granted this insight in the Ruzyň prison, which, in the minds of most people, is rather an unkind place. . . . From now on, that dust which, until now, has only been a reason for irritation or anger, will have a spiritual significance for me. . . .

You can see from my letter that I almost forget that I am still in Prague. It is here that one fully realizes that it is not where we live, but rather how we live, that is important.

SOURCE: Keston News Service, nos. 154, 156, 158 (1982).

Petition by Christians, 1987

In December 1987 a thirty-one-point petition began circulating in which Augustin Navrátil enumerated the reforms Czechoslovak Christians wanted in church-state affairs. By May 1988 more than half a million people, mainly Catholics, had signed.

1. The fundamental demand is the separation of the church from the state so that the state would not interfere in the church's organization and activities.

2. The state's agencies should not hinder the nomination of new bishops; this should be an internal matter for the church.

3. The state's agencies should not interfere in the appointment of parish priests.

4. The state's agencies should not interfere in the selection of and setting of quotas for students and instructors for theological colleges.

5. The theological faculty at Olomouc should be reopened.

6. A permanent body of deacons should be allowed, in accordance with Pope Paul VI's decree of 18 June 1967.

7. All religious orders should again be allowed to function and to admit new members, as they are in the GDR and Poland.

8. Believers should be allowed to establish independent lay associations.

9. Religious instruction should be allowed to take place in churches or church premises rather than in state school buildings, as is now the case.

10. Priests should be allowed to visit prisons and hospitals when asked by patients, prisoners, or relatives. Religious ceremonies should be allowed in prisons and hospitals. Roman Catholics in prison should be allowed to take confession and spiritual counsel from priests.

11. Permission for spiritual retreats or spiritual gatherings for laymen should be granted.

12. Every parish community should be able to establish a parish council, as is the case in other countries, where laymen can assist priests in running the parish.

13. Czechoslovak Catholics should be free to get in touch with any Christian organization throughout the world.

14. Catholics should be allowed to organize and participate individually or jointly in prilgrimages abroad.

15. Catholics should have unlimited access to all religious publications; and it should be made possible to set up religious publishing houses under the guidance of church representatives.

16. The copying and dissemination of religious texts should not be considered an illicit business activity or a legally punishable act.

17. The church should be allowed to subscribe to religious literature from abroad.

18. It should be allowed to broadcast religious programs on the radio and television upon agreement with the Board of Ordinaries or with the chairman of the Bishops' Conference.

19. The jamming of the Vatican's Czech and Slovak broadcasts and of the RFE [Radio Free Europe] transmissions of Sunday Mass should be stopped.

20. Not only atheistic propaganda but also public promotion of Christian ideas by priests and laymen should be allowed. Since Marxists and other atheists criticize religion and the church, Christians and people in general should be allowed to criticize Marxist-Leninist doctrine without this being considered a criminal act.

21. All confiscated church buildings that were built with the congregation's own resources and that are needed for the church's activity should be returned to their original purpose.

22. The construction of new churches should be made possible wherever necessary.

23. The willful removal of crosses, statues, chapels, and other religious and cultural monuments should cease.

24. The power of the state Minister for Religion to interfere in the nomination, transfer, and activity of priests should be abolished.

25. Unlawfully sentenced priests, members of religious orders, and active religious laymen shoud be speedily and consistently rehabilitated.

26. Discrimination agaist Christians at work, especially in the education sector, should cease.

27. Christians should have the possibility to express their views on any subject, if it is morally justified within the right to petition.

28. All legal regulations that unjustifiably make criminal a considerable part of the activity of priests and laymen should be rescinded.

29. Articles 16, 20, 24, 28, and 32 of the constitution should be amended in accordance with the proposals made in the petition.

30. All valid laws directly or indirectly concerning religion should be

adjusted to conform with the international covenants on civil and human rights.

31. A mixed commission consisting of representatives of state bodies and the Catholic Church, including laymen nominated by Cardinal František Tomášek and by the representatives of the Catholic Church in Slovakia, should deal with these proposals and resolve outstanding problems.

SOURCE: Radio Free Europe Research, January 21, 1988.

A Christian Teacher in Atheistic Schools

Although the Hungarian state is far more tolerant toward religion today than in the 1960s, Christian educators still face many problems, both practical and theoretical. In 1985 the samizdat *journal* Beszélö *published an interview with a young teacher and a follow-up article written by another under a pseudonym. (Excerpts.)*

CONVERSATION WITH A YOUNG TEACHER

BESZÉLÖ: Doesn't the confession of faith place the teacher in direct conflict with the school?

TEACHER: We don't have to parade Christianity. However, if we are confronted with questions that demand an open answer, we must confess the faith, in the first place in front of the children. In practice many years often go by before a collision takes place. . . .

BESZÉLÖ: Are you saying that a teacher's work and Christian convictions are only temporarily reconcilable?

TEACHER: Anyone whose Christianity is not detected within a few years is not really a Christian. Of course, there are those who believe even this postponement of confrontation to be unprincipled. They say that a teacher has three options: she may fulfill her duty toward the atheistic school and cease to be a Christian; withdraw from her duty and cease to be a teacher; or else accept a compromise that deceives both the school and herself.

BESZÉLÖ: On this basis believers would exclude themselves from the teaching profession.

TEACHER: . . . I personally do not agree with an inflexibility of outlook that would bring a voluntary exodus of Christian teachers from schools. The

322

aim of teaching is the development of intellectual, spiritual, and physical strength. This must also, I think, include the shaping of one's capacity for and experience of love. A large proportion of the curriculum offers a possibility for the discussion of certain important questions. Of course, such possibilities are found mainly in the humanities, especially literature and history.

Children are curious about the "God question," the person of Jesus, the Gospel, about religion as a way of living. This is precisely because officially these things are not included in the timetable and because they have had more than enough of the atheistic answers. Moreover, they are curious to know what a believer has to say about them. We must answer these questions, but our answers are accepted only if they are endorsed by our whole personalities.

You see, the main problem with the atheistic answers is that they ring hollow. In today's schools there are probably fewer convinced materialists than believing Christians. . . . And what is meant by poverty, what is meant by violence, what is meant by omnipresent selfishness? The rousing Marxist-Leninist answers to these questions are hopelessly contrary to the children's daily experience. The Christian answer does not offer a comforting solution, but it demands something from each individual: sharing our wealth with the poor, setting non-violence alongside violence, and placing self-sacrifice against selfishness. . . .

BESZÉLŐ: How much can the children be influenced by a believing teacher?

TEACHER: It depends on how good the teacher is. Children, at least those in grammar school, are very susceptible to everything a believing teacher may tell them, because it is *different* from the precepts they are used to hearing. . . . The teacher whose Christianity is well known—that is to say, who accepts a conviction that is fraught with risks—is an example even to the child who doesn't accept his outlook on life. . . . Only some people should become teachers: those who have determination and flair for it, who can come to terms with never making a career of it, who have enough strength to bear an excess burden, and who are well aware that their employment could come to a sudden end.

BESZÉLŐ: This must be a difficult decision, especially for someone at the beginning of her career.

TEACHER: Nobody should be talked into it. But I wouldn't let myself be talked out of it.

ANOTHER TEACHER SPEAKS

The tiniest trouble—for example, an anonymous denunciation, a parental complaint, or some argument among the teaching staff—can immediately make conviction a point of indictment. . . . The honest answer given to the mild-sounding question, "Tell me sincerely, are you a religious person?," becomes a confession that can be documented: "openly admitted to be a religious person"—or, in other words, "has not yet expounded religious propaganda, but it is possible to assume that at a given opportunity he will openly proclaim his religious convictions in front of his pupils, and that is essentially religious propaganda." This crime is made worse if the person in question is a good teacher and has an attractive character.

Of course, one such report is not sufficient to merit punitive sanctions set out in written form with justifications, but it is enough to poison the air around the teacher. What head teacher enjoys a confused state of affairs among his staff, and what teacher cannot be found wanting by an alert inspector? The better the teacher's reputation, the greater the deterrent for the teaching community when their colleague's career is ruined and her life embittered by the fact that she spoke as she felt.

SOURCE: *Religion in Communist Lands*, vol. 14, no. 5 (1986).
Translated by Susanna Thatcher.

Letter to Lutheran Leaders, 1984

Zoltán Dóka

*In an open letter to executives of the Lutheran World Federation
(LWF) on the eve of the federation's 1984 meeting in Hungary,
Lutheran pastor Zoltán Dóka criticized leaders of his church and
their "diakonia theology." (Excerpts.)*

DEAR BROTHERS:
   Forgive me for burdening you with my letter. My conscience compels
me to do so. I consider it my duty to report to you without delay something
which many people in the Hungarian Lutheran Church think but dare not
say openly. . . .
   Up to the present day the leadership of the Hungarian Lutheran Church
(hereafter HLC) has misled the world Lutheran community by stating that
its pastors and congregations uniformly confess the so-called Diakonia Theology (hereafter DT). The truth is that the concept of DT has not yet reached
the consciousness of the congregations, and only a minority of pastors approve of it. Most of those who approve do so only out of personal interest
or fear, and only in a public capacity. In confidential circles they criticize
and reject the concept. . . .
   "Diakonia" is not the central theological concept of the New Testament, either in the Synoptic Gospels, or in the Johannine or Pauline literature. This bare fact makes it doubtful whether one is free to build up a theological concept that emphatically describes itself as biblical, on one individual peripheral New Testament idea. . . . This false theology makes no distinction between the acts of God and the acts of men, but mixes them and
makes them appear equal. When Bishop Káldy repeatedly stresses, "That
church which only proclaims the Gospel is not a church," it is apparent that
DT subordinates the Gospel to diakonia, or to a socioethical concept. . . .
   In the HLC there is no religious freedom. The state's church policy,
surprising though it may seem, demonstrates more concern for the interests
of the pastors and congregations than does the church leadership. . . . Theological terror reigns. . . . The church leadership maintains this terror by
telling the civil authorities that those who dare criticize DT are enemies of
the state. In this way they skillfully make theological debate impossible.
This is a real and perilous slander. . . .

Bishop Káldy's role . . . is also evident in the church press. . . . All HLC publications bear a *nihil obstat* in his name. He feels justified in censoring articles, studies, and books, striking out sentences . . . or simply inserting his own views in the text. . . . The standard of theological work in the HLC falls ever lower. Scholarly work is impossible where freedom of research is absent and where researchers must confirm already established answers. . . . Bishop Káldy upholds this situation when he says that DT is the world's best theological concept and so we have no need of foreign, especially "Western," theology. This conceited theology will do incalculable harm to the spiritual and intellectual life of the church. . . .

I ask forgiveness if with this letter I cause Bishop Káldy pain. . . . He has always rejected my criticism, or has failed to reply to me. Now I feel myself compelled to speak publicly. . . . What we are talking about here is not personalities but above all the Gospel of God. If this is taken away from us, we are all lost. The Grace of God be with us!

With brotherly greetings,

ZOLTÁN DÓKA

SOURCE: *Religion in Communist Lands*, vol. 13, no. 1 (1985).

APPENDIX I: HUNGARY

Open Letter to Catholic Dissidents, 1980

Márton Hartai

This pseudonymous letter, written in September 1980, maintains that the church has become far more subservient to the state than is realized. It depicts some typical views of participants in base groups. (Excerpts.)

I am writing this under a pen name . . . because the Communist state always tends to interpret the law according to its own interests. I must avoid becoming an entry on some "blacklist." I do not want to be followed, spied upon, exposed to harassment, limited even more in my freedom of movement—all these would prevent me from pursuing my true vocation, that is, pastoral care. . . .

Those in power . . . would like to achieve the alienation of religion. . . .This is not a very difficult task: all they have to do is to ensure that leading posts in the Church are filled by men who (willingly or not, it is all the same) are prepared to serve the interests of the secular power. Having settled this, they can even proclaim the independence of the Church—at least as far as appearances go. Once this has been achieved, they have to interfere only infrequently in ecclesiastical matters—church leaders will follow the rules of the game. . . .

The fierce "Peace Priests," the army of those tarred with a left-wing brush, are gradually fading into the background. . . . The style of state policies has become more refined: the leadership of the Church will gradually be handed over to people who are honest and sincere, who have proved their faith through imprisonment; the only snag is that they are rigid traditionalists who have not learned from their own past. These leaders would be most surprised if told that their attitudes are doing harm to the Church. . . . A distorted personality and attitude induces a kind of stupor that paralyzes the will for action, prevents the recognition of, and resistance to, disguised oppression. Is this not what we may call alienation?

The most dangerous area where this strategy operates is the manipulation of the priest's vocation. The majority of those who want to enter a seminary do not really have, strictly speaking, a priestly vocation; rather, it is that of a "prophet" or perhaps "prophet-priest": to bring good tidings to the poor, release to prisoners, sight to the blind . . . or just to proclaim the year of the Lord's grace (cf. Isa. 61:42 and Luke 4:18–19). It is true that in Hungary today there is hardly any legal possibility of responding to this vocation outside the ranks of the priesthood.

[The novice's] superiors are also talking in terms of the priestly vocation, but they mean, on their part, an identification with priestly institutions, a formal loyalty to the Church, nothing more. The novice slowly completes his five years' course and hardly notices at the end that the "priestly vocation" he had been taught is far from his original "call." Everything is in aid of this formalism: from the daily routine, through lifeless ideologies, to the virtual automation of spiritual life. . . . Unconsciously, they become alienated from their true vocation, and never realize that they are, in fact, serving the interests of the rulers. Their manipulation is so subtle that they take it for liberty.

There are some among us who do believe that the state is willing to enter into an honest dialogue with us, if only we were ready for it. The two-faced policy of the "Peace Priests" has seduced many a priest of good will. These people do not realize that every new agreement between state and church, trumpeted around the world as a great new achievement, only gives back ridiculous crumbs of the rights originally due to the Church of Christ and to all human beings.

What is the use of a flood of marvelously courageous articles, when it can happen—as it has recently—that a bishop reports a priest of another diocese because he holds catechism classes at his presbytery? When policemen surround the pupils and take their names, in order to intimidate them and their parents? When the State Church Office hold dozens of snapshots taken at religious gatherings as material exhibits against the participants? What about those ecclesiastical office-holders who are using similar underhand ways to remove "awkward" people? . . .

Another . . . aspect of the opting-out process is that of becoming an informer. Some people may be kept on a string, as a result of some moral peccadillo; they are forced to "grass" for the files of the State Church Office. Others turn informer simply because they cannot bear the constant tension. These "supergrass" priests are perhaps the most dangerous, as they are inside the Church. They are to be pitied most, too, as they are degrading both their own moral being and their vocation. . . . There is also the army of the inert, that of "loyalist" church members. They are realists too: they may reject the tragi-comic kowtowing of others, but they also avoid anything that may throw doubt upon their reliability. . . .

"He who was born lame learns to live with his lameness." . . . Our

Catholic Church, . . . burdened by a long and often dubious history, seems to accept the surrender to Caesar, the identification with the interest of the rulers of the day. It considers that its situation cannot be changed; therefore it is not worth trying to change it.

Viewing the present state of the Catholic Church, one has the impression that the Hungarian state is pioneering new methods of persecuting religion. Hungary may have succeeded in acquiring a certain respect abroad, rare among so-called socialist states; our standard of living is relatively high, there is freedom of religion, dissidents are not always thrown into prison. It is certainly true that the religious policies of our state are less crude than those of Czechoslovakia or Romania. Unfortunately, the essence remains hidden from the eyes of the innocent bystander.

Maybe the Party is attempting to shape a new, national Church—a new historical phenomenon? In addition, it strives to gain the blessing of the Vatican on its actions; the execution of its moves is usually entrusted to our religious notables. This is doubly dangerous: not only may this shake the faith of many believers—it may also undermine our trust in Rome. The Hungarian method of refined religious persecution may become the paradigm for the next decade . . . or even for the next century.

SOURCE: *Religion in Communist Lands*, vol. 11, no. 1 (1983).

Agreement: Government and Episcopate, 1950

In order to ensure the nation, People's Poland, and her citizens the best possible conditions for development and the opportunity for peaceful work in all fields, the Polish Government, which respects religious freedom, and the Polish Episcopate, which has at heart the good of the Church and contemporary Polish national interests, regulate their relations in the following way:

1. The Episcopate will urge the clergy, during the performance of their sacerdotal duties, in conformity with the teaching of the Church, to teach the faithful to respect State laws and authority.

2. The Episcopate will urge the clergy, during the performance of their sacerdotal duties, to encourage the faithful to intensified work on rebuilding the country and raising the living standards of the nation.

3. The Polish Episcopate states that economic, historic, cultural, and religious law as well as historic justice demand that the Recovered Territories [i.e. the western districts, formerly German] belong to Poland forever. Being of the opinion that the Recovered Territories are an inseparable part of the Republic, the Episcopate will request the Apostolic See to change the church administration . . . by the appointment of permanent bishops.

4. As far as it is able the Episcopate will oppose activity hostile to Poland, especially anti-Polish and revisionist activity on the part of the German clergy.

5. The principle that the Pope is the most competent and the highest church authority refers to matters of faith, morals, and church jurisdiction; in other matters, the Episcopate is guided by Polish national interests.

6. Being of the opinion that the Church's mission can be realized in various social and economic systems established by lay authorities, the Episcopate will explain to the clergy that they are not to oppose the expansion of the cooperative movement in rural areas, because the cooperative

movement in all its forms is based essentially on the ethical principles of human nature and aims at voluntary social solidarity, which has the good of the whole in view.

7. The Church, in accordance with its principles, condemning all anti-State actions, will particularly oppose the abuse of religious feelings for anti-State purposes.

8. The Catholic Church, in accordance with its principles condemning all crime, will also fight against the criminal activity of underground bands and will condemn and punish according to canon law clergy guilty of participation in any kind of underground and anti-State activity.

9. The Episcopate, in conformity with the teachings of the Church, will support all efforts to consolidate peace and will oppose as far as it is able all efforts to unleash war.

10. Religious teaching in schools:

a. The Government has no intention of restricting the present state of religious teaching in schools: programs of religious study will be drawn up by school authorities jointly with representatives of the Episcopate, schools will be supplied with the appropriate textbooks, clergy and lay teachers of religion will benefit from the same privileges as teachers of other subjects, inspectors of religious teaching will be appointed by school authorities in agreement with the Episcopate.

b. The authorities will not place difficulties in the way of pupils who wish to participate in religious practices outside school.

c. Existing Catholic schools will be maintained, but the Government will see that these schools loyally fulfill regulations and the program established by State authorities.

d. Schools run by the Catholic Church will be able to avail themselves of the privileges of State schools on general principles laid down by appropriate rules and regulations of school authorities.

e. In the event of the opening or transformation of ordinary schools into schools where religion is not included in the curriculum, Catholic parents, if they wish, will have the right and the opportunity of sending their children to schools where religion is taught.

11. The Catholic University of Lublin will be able to continue its present work.

12. Catholic associations will be able fully to avail themselves of existing privileges if they conform to demands envisaged in the decree on associations. . . .

13. The Church will have the right and the opportunity of conducting, within the framework of binding regulations, charitable activities and catechistic campaigns.

14. The Catholic press and Catholic publishing houses will benefit, just as other publishing houses, from the privileges outlined by appropriate laws and regulations of the authorities.

15. Difficulties will not be placed in the way of public rituals, traditional pilgrimages, and processions. For the sake of order, these processions will be agreed upon by church authorities and administrative authorities.

16. Army chaplains will be subject to special statutes drawn up by military authorities in agreement with representatives of the Episcopate.

17. In prisons, chaplains appointed by appropriate authorities on recommendation of the Ordinary will care for the spiritual needs of prisoners.

18. In State and self-administered hospitals, hospital chaplains will care for the spiritual needs of those patients who desire it. These chaplains will be remunerated on the basis of special agreements.

19. Convents, monasteries, and religious associations in the field of their calling and according to binding laws will have complete freedom of activity.

Bishops' Declaration on Clerical Appointments, 1953

In May 1953 the Polish government implemented a decree giving the state the right to appoint and dismiss not only priests but also bishops. The Polish episcopate responded with an unequivocal statement quite unparalleled in the Eastern bloc. (Excerpts.)

Considering it their highest duty, the Polish Episcopate draw attention to the tragic fate of the Church in Poland; to the symptoms of oppression and its causes; and to the sources from which flow the concern, anxiety, and exasperation of the broad masses of the Catholic community.

The main cause of this state of affairs is the hatred which is destroying the strength of our country. . . . We have not abandoned our desire for a peaceful solution and collaboration in the important task of a successful settlement of relations between Church and State in accordance with the agreement reached on April 14, 1950. [See appendix J.] However, in the present state of affairs, it depends solely on the sincere good will of the government whether internal peace and reciprocal harmony, which are so essential, will be genuinely achieved. It depends on the government's forsaking its radical, destructive hatred towards Catholicism, and abandoning its aim of subjugating the Church and turning it into an instrument of the State.

We wish the government to understand clearly what the decree on appointments to clerical offices really means for the structure of the Church. We therefore remind it that by this act, which is illegal according to the Constitution, the State has assumed the right of constant intrusion in the internal affairs of the Church. This intrusion sometimes interferes with priests' consciences, and involves a willful and systematic subjection of church jurisdiction to its own will.

The situation is inadmissible, from the point of view of the Church, firstly because the Church's jurisdiction pertains to strictly religious,

333

internal, and supernatural matters, such as teaching God's revelation, expounding Christian morals, administering the Holy Sacraments, organizing religious services, and providing spiritual guidance for the souls and consciences of the people. In the name of what rights could such strictly religious matters be submitted to the authority of the State, which by its nature pertains to matters exclusively secular and temporal—more especially if that authority is based on a materialistic and anti-religious ideology, and filled with destructive hatred towards the Church? Everyone, even atheists, should see that such dependence is quite impossible. That was why Lenin justly condemned the subjugation of the Church to the State as a "cursed and disgraceful" thing.

Secondly, this is an impossibility for the Church because, in accordance with its unalterable constitution, with regard to which even the Pope is helpless, there is not and cannot be in that Catholic community another juridical authority besides that which flows from above, from the Pope and the bishops.

Therefore, whenever the secular authority willfully tries to seize ecclesiastical jurisdiction, it usurps something which does not belong to it. . . .

Aware of our apostolic mission, we solemnly declare that we cannot consider this decree as legal and binding, because it is inconsistent with the Constitution of the Polish People's Republic, and violates the laws of God and of the Church. "One should obey God rather than men." We are not refusing to take into consideration the motives and the suggestions of the government. But in fulfilling church positions we must be directed by divine and by ecclesiastical law, and we must appoint only those priests whom we consider, in our conscience, as fit and worthy. We find it difficult to overlook how little worthy of their positions, especially the more important ones, are those who have yielded to external political pressure. . . . We are not allowed to place the things of God on the altar of Caesar. *Non possumus!* . . .

We are conscious of the special tasks and duties of the Catholic priest towards his country, and that is why we have often reminded our priests of them. . . . But we also demand, emphatically, that our priests should not be torn away from religious duties; they they should not be drawn into political affairs which are alien to their vocation; that political pressure aimed at using them as instruments in the struggle of the State against the Church should be stopped; and they they should not be forced to break the oath by which they pledged loyalty to the Church and their bishops. In short, in accordance with the principle of separation of Church and State, as guaranteed in our Constitution, the State must abstain from intruding in the religious, spiritual, and internal affairs of the Church. . . .

SOURCE: White Paper on the Persecution of the Church in Poland, London.

Declaration of Light-Life Principles, 1980

The renewal movement Light-Life issued this declaration of principles at its Fifth National Congress, held in March 1980. (Excerpts.)

We are all aware that the country is in an extremely serious situation. The political, economic, social, cultural, moral, and religious spheres of life are all affected: in each of these areas there is a severe and ever-worsening crisis. Clearly outlined against the background of all these crises is the problem of the individual—humiliated, denied his freedom, trapped in a web of innumerable restrictions. Against this same background looms the problem of alcoholism, accompanied by the gloomy prediction that in about ten years' time alcoholism will have caused our society to become completely degenerate (with approximately five million confirmed alcoholics and a further twenty million or so drinking to excess). . . .

Poland is unusual in that all its moral and religious crises can be largely attributed to a single cause—the present political situation, both internal and external. The question therefore arises as to whether activities aimed at liberating either individuals or the nation as a whole from all manner of evil will have to assume a political character. Certainly, from the "other side's" point of view, any activity that is effective, i.e., that leads to real changes in the existing situation, will be considered political. But how will Christians view such activity? . . .

The Pastoral Constitution of Vatican II states: "Let every citizen remember that it is his right and responsibility to take part in free elections for the benefit of all."

However, it is impossible for people who live under a totalitarian regime to engage in legal political activity without being manipulated by the prevailing political forces in a manner contrary to their Christian conscience and the Church's directives. This is why Christians in Poland tend to deride the very idea of "political involvement" and have on the whole resigned themselves to avoiding all political activity. Is there not a danger, however, that as a result of this we shall abdicate our responsibilities and withdraw into "oases" for the elite? . . . Ever since the emergence in Poland of various democratic movements formed to defend basic human rights and freedoms—movements whose members are prepared to risk persecution, imprisonment, even death—these questions have confronted us. Clearly, we can no longer evade them.

Christians have found one way which, though not "political" in the true sense of the word, does have the power to liberate individuals and even a whole nation. It is the way of Jesus Christ: "Jesus Christ meets the man of every age, including our own, with the same words: You will know the truth, and the truth will make you free (John 8,32)" (*Redemptor Hominis*). These words contain both a fundamental requirement and a warning: the requirement of an honest relationship with regard to truth as a condition for authentic freedom, and the warning to avoid every kind of illusory freedom. . . .

It is the fact that we are forced to live in a permanent state of hypocrisy that is the real source, even the essence, of our captivity. The man who lives in harmony with himself, with his conscience, with his calling, and, ultimately, with the divine concept of himself as a free spirit, is truly free. Even though he be in chains, behind prison bars, or surrounded by the barbed wire of a labor camp, the promise that "the truth will make you free" is fulfilled. . . .

On a more practical level, we should like to stress one or two instances in which a Christian is urgently required to bear witness to the truth.

First, let us take the forthcoming "election." . . . Those whose conscience does not allow them to express confidence in the government should abstain from taking part in the election, since this is the only possible way for people in their situation to witness to the truth.

In the same way, those who consider themselves Christians, but who also belong to the Communist Party or to some other association with a similar ideological basis . . . should reconsider their position. . . .

Since we are a renewal movement with "Light-Life" as our motto, we feel a special responsibility to reflect in our lives the light of truth which we perceive through faith, and to eliminate all contradiction between the faith we profess and the way we live.

SOURCE: *Religion in Communist Lands,* vol. 11, no. 1 (1983).

Letter: Cardinal Wyczyński to Minister Kąkol, 1978

In a letter to Kazimierz Kąkol, the government's minister for religious affairs, Cardinal Stefan Wyczyński defends the individual's right to truthful information.

DEAR PROFESSOR KĄKOL,

Your letter of May 29 could justifiably have been left unanswered in view of the tone and poor quality of its reproaches. However, I do not wish the correspondence between us to be maintained on this level.

Your opening "emphatic protest at the continuing misuse of sacred buildings etc." is a typical oversimplification and an unfounded generalization. It raises a few questions and calls for clarification of the following:

1. the scope of the Church's mission,
2. the definition of political activity,
3. hostility towards the socialist State.

Precise definitions of these concepts would answer the question as to whether the accusations leveled at the university chaplaincies are valid. Since you have created a problem from a few isolated cases and have drawn quite disproportionate conclusions, I am obliged, in answering these accusations directed at the Church, to treat them as a problem.

The boundaries of contemporary political life have been extended to include a vast area; they encompass all spheres of life, so that there is no room left for the individual's private concerns. The sphere of the individual's rights has shrunk almost to nothing. In addition to this limitation of his rights, the State demands that he should meet the obligations it has imposed on him. These obligations, which are mainly in the economic and professional field, are so extensive that the individual has barely any time (or place) for his private life.

As a result, the concept of "political activity" has acquired a broader meaning, and anything not connected with the obligations imposed on the individual by the State is suspect. When the various methods of political infiltration into the private life of the individual are taken to an extreme, they become intolerable. It is no wonder that resistance takes root among people whose personal and social rights are so restricted. . . . The defense of rights is not a political activity . . . ; rather, it is the duty of each individual. Still less can it be called "hostility towards the socialist State."

If therefore certain initiatives have been undertaken in this field, the question arises as to whether the State has trespassed too far into the sphere of human needs. The programming of education, particularly in schools, suggests that it has. Since programs so often give a distorted image—bordering on ignorance—of the truth about Polish history and our national culture, it is small wonder that people try to correct this view of their country's past by their own efforts. By attending lectures and using factual information drawn from academic sources, they are supplementing their incomplete knowledge of the last two centuries of Polish history, particularly the period that followed the rebirth of the State.

The damage caused by applying the method of dialectical materialism to our country's history and culture is so evident that even young students are aware of it. They can see the gaps in this interpretation and want to fill them. After all, it is not possible to interpret political events or economic, social, and moral trends that occurred centuries ago from a contemporary perspective and by this dialectical method. Conclusions drawn in such a way are obviously false.

The efforts of the "Flying University" are only modest attempts to supplement the public's incomplete education, to unearth facts about the past that had been buried in silence, to correct the glaring falsehoods that are often taught in our schools and universities. Every intelligent person has the right to do this, so there are no grounds here for accusations of hostility towards the State.

Are these lectures concerned with politics or with the humanities? Do they constitute an illegal activity? Are they "hostile towards the socialist State"? I could find no trace of hostility in the transcripts of the lectures I was given. Why then brand so many people as guilty, making more and more enemies—the State has many already, both in this country and abroad, as a result of the mistakes that it persists in making. . . .

No one in Poland today is free from the obligation to speak the truth! Anyone who keeps silent about the situation is potentially harmful to the State and the system. It is here—among these cowards who keep silent—that we must look for "the enemies of the socialist State," and not among those who want to know the truth about Poland that has been distorted by official teaching. . . .

Real harm is inflicted on the democratic system by the increasingly powerful network of police . . . and secret agents, who interfere excessively in people's lives and smell threats to the system everywhere.

I remain respectfully yours,
CARDINAL WYCZYŃSKI

SOURCE: *Kultura* (Paris), no. 1-2 (1979); reprinted in *Religion in Communist Lands*, vol. 7, no. 2 (1979).

Appeal by Six Evangelicals, 1977

This document, received in the West in March 1977, was signed by six evangelical Christians—Josif Ţon, Vasile Talpoş, Aurel Popescu, Pavel Nicolescu, Radu Dumitrescu, and Silvu Cioată. They urge a new attitude toward the regime. (Excerpts.)

We, a group of evangelical Christians, have decided that . . . we will break the guilty silence in which we have been content to withdraw and hide ourselves for many years. . . .

We speak of a systematic but masked persecution of believers, which is brutal, yet difficult to perceive from outside; extremely painful to those enduring it, yet hard to understand for an outside observer. The fact that the churches here are full to overflowing on a Sunday is no proof that there is religious freedom, but rather it is, among other things, a demonstration—mute and often unconscious—of a desire for spiritual freedom. . . .

Everywhere we are regarded as enemies. . . . We are constantly told, quite openly, that we have no place here, that we are dangerous, that we destroy the unity of the people. We are thought of as agents of capitalism and subversive to the regime. . . . An evangelical believer is not admitted to any public office of responsibility. We underline the fact that we number around one million evangelical believers in Romania. Yet among this number you will not find one headmaster or member of a local authority. . . . At all points access to these top positions is barred from us, and if anyone held such a post before he became an evangelical Christian he is immediately demoted during one of the public meetings, in an insulting and humiliating manner. . . . We are regularly classified in the lowest grades. . . . Our children are systematically insulted, mocked, and goaded at school. This starts at the most tender age of primary school. At present, measures are being taken which will close off a whole series of university faculties to our children. . . .

The laws of our country say that the exercising of the faith is free. Yet this freedom is restricted in innumerable ways. . . . In places, the place of worship is small, unsuitable, and unhealthy. Hundreds of people are forced to cram awkwardly into the church or sometimes to stand outside in rain and cold in order to catch something through the open windows. All this because the authorities have refused to give permission for them to build a proper place where they can practice their legally recognized worship.

Our pastors are . . . mocked and insulted. They are obliged to make compromises of conscience and sometimes to betray the secrets of the believers in their charge to the secret police. Thus they are broken within and become devoid of the spiritual power required to feed the church. A more tragic thing is that some of them become united with those who seek to destroy religion. . . .

Many of us have been called on numerous occasions to the secret police. . . . Who can describe to the tragedy of the hundreds . . . of brethren broken in this way, who, while preserving a knowledge of the faith and not breaking relations with the churches, like slaves fulfill in secret the sinister obligation of reporting to the secret police everything that happens in the churches and among the faithful? . . .

We are pained that, under the Stalinist terror, we were so terrified, so crushed within, that we accepted that on every public occasion, and always before the state authorities, we would thank the Party and the state for the full freedom which we enjoy! It was not just that we were persecuted and devoid of any elementary rights, but that, being fully conscious of our actions, we compelled our spirits to support and to affirm the lie that we were free, and that in Romania we had religious freedom. Not only our church leaders were guilty of committing this monstrosity, but also each one of us.

The first objective we seek in writing this document is . . . to behave . . . so that we no longer collaborate with the lie about religious liberty through our silence, nor make further public declarations which call evil good and darkness light. We want to free ourselves from the fear of speaking out the truth and only in this way oblige our country's leadership to recognize the truth themselves. If religious persecution exists in Romania, let us say so by name. And indeed it does exist here. . . .

What we ask therefore from our country's authorities is sincerity and truthfulness. . . . If you do not intend to grant evangelical Christians these rights, then say so openly. . . . In this way you will no longer force believers, even though they are terrified and devoid of courage, to live a lie. Perhaps it will mean that we shall suffer more than we do today, if it means an open persecution, but at least you will have obliged us—or at least some of us—to be men of character, and this we value more than anything else.

The call which we make to our brothers in the faith is to be daring enough to free themselves from fear. . . . Christ has called us to spiritual freedom. . . . Let us be absolutely convinced that God honors those who honor Him.

SOURCE: *Romanian Report* (Centre for the Study of Religion and Communism); published as a pamphlet by Keston College.

ALRC List of the Churches' Demands, 1978

This key document bearing twenty-seven signatures—mostly of Baptists—summarizes the basic needs of the churches in Romania. The religious-rights group ALRC was founded in 1978; through state suppression it had virtually disappeared by the mid-eighties. (Excerpts.)

1. The right of religious associations to exist undisturbed and to be recognized by law; . . . the right of the Roman Catholic Church to have a recognized juridical statute; the re-establishment of the Greek [i.e., Eastern Rite] Catholic Church, which was disbanded by the Romanian state in 1948; official recognition of the evangelical movement "The Lord's Army" within the framework of the Romanian Orthodox Church; the right of religious associations in Romania to join international religious organizations without official approval.

2. The right to practice religion in church, in private homes, and in public without official approval, as well as the right to preach, to baptize, and to officiate at open-air meetings. The right to carry out pastoral work without restriction, anywhere in our country, especially in hospitals, old people's homes, and prisons. . . .

3. The right to make church appointments; . . . the end of identity cards and permits for priests and pastors, as well as annulment of the obligation to be "recognized" or "approved" before taking up a post. . . .

4. The right to build, buy, or rent places of worship without the approval of the Department of Cults. The right to build new local churches, etc.; the right to repair or rebuild all church property affected by the recent earthquake. The end of pressure on proprietors who wish to sell or let premises to church organizations for religious purposes. The right to own church property, liturgical objects, donations. The right to receive money, donations, material help, cult objects from Christians abroad who send these either to individuals or to religious organizations.

5. . . . Free dialogue between Christians and Marxists and on the radio, television, and in the press. . . .

6. . . . The right to have a free religious press, and an end to censorship by the Department of Cults. The publication of religious magazines, regularly and in quantities necessary to meet the demand. Publicity in the magazines on all aspects of the cult, as well as on cases of religious persecution: e.g., publicity on dismissal or demotion at work, dismissal from school, fines, lawsuits, searches, interrogations, persecution of those who receive religious news from abroad, evangelistic campaigns, theological congresses, new books, ecumenical laws, inter-confessional relations, etc. The right to found a press for the printing of Bibles and religious literature in Romania. The right of any confession to have its own printing press and to own a duplicating machine. The right to disseminate and sell religious literature and the Bible in Romanian, Hungarian, German, Serbian, English, French, through colporteurs, bookshops, and kiosks attached to theological colleges, cathedrals, churches, prayer centers, monasteries, etc.

7. . . . The right of priests and pastors to hold catechism classes freely; to hold meetings for prayer and Bible study; to organize excursions. The right to give religious instruction to young Christians in school, just as classes in Marxism are held for non-believers. The right of parents to give religious instruction to their children and to have a say in the type of cultural activities their children should join. An end to the sabotage of Sundays and Christian feast-days in schools and institutions. Respect for Sunday as a day of rest. An end to forced indoctrination of children and young people with atheistic and materialistic ideas.

8. The right to carry out charitable work by collections and subscriptions; the right to found orphanages and old people's homes.

9. The right to found centers for theological instruction at university level for pastors and priests without any interference from the Ministry, and freedom for those who are chosen to be ordained. We demand—in view of the increasing interference of the Ministry in theological training—the cessation of all obstacles to recruitment for the clergy.

10. The right to hold Bible classes, religious gatherings, congresses, without the approval of the Ministry. The right to invite foreigners to take part in these . . . .

11. The right for Christians to have access to higher posts in the economy, education, university life, diplomatic service, etc. The right to be promoted. An end to ideological discrimination and religious persecution that aims to stop the emigration of those people (Christians) who see no hope for their future.

12. The right of churches and religious associations to have access to television, radio, the press, and to be able to broadcast on Sundays and other religious feast-days.

13 . . .

14. The right to reopen all closed churches, and the right of all pastors

and clergy who were dismissed arbitrarily to be reinstated. Reparations for all those who have suffered abuse and for theological students arrested.

15. The right of young Christians in the Army to have a Bible, prayer-book, etc.

16. The right of Romanian Christians to refuse to sign an oath of loyalty to the Communist Party, or an opportunity for those who do sign not to accept atheistic indoctrination.

17. The right to receive Dr. Billy Graham and other Christians in Romania.

18. The right to insist on respect for human rights in accordance with international agreements.

19. The right to give material assistance to believers who are persecuted (dismissed, arrested, demoted) for their convictions. The right to receive gifts at home and from abroad to help them.

20. The right to be visited by the clergy and to possess Bibles and religious literature. The right of prisoners to be visited by a priest.

21. The right of churches and gatherings of believers to buy, receive, and possess means of transport and to engage a chauffeur.

22. The right to advertise religious events: congresses, Bible studies. The right to organize mass gatherings.

23. The right to engage (ordain) priests without state interference; to engage priests for missionary work.

24. The necessity of reforming Church-State relations. In the last thirty years the Ministry of Cults has been a continuous source of abuses, restrictive measures, and psychological pressure on those who serve the Church; their policy of intimidation has created a deep gulf between Christians and the State. Our ideal is a free Church in a free State that would allow dialogue and cooperation between the two.

SOURCE: *Religion in Communist Lands*, vol. 7, no. 3 (1979).

A Report on Repression
of Christians, 1981

This report on repression suffered by Christians of various de-
nominations during 1981 was compiled by the Romanian Chris-
tian Committee for the Defense of Believers' Rights. (Excerpts.)

The methods of the Romanian security police differ from case to case: some
people have tasted prison life; others interrogation, beatings, and threats.
The results are intimidation, broken bones, compromises, or physical destruction. . . . We, however, find courage in the words of Jesus: "Do not
fear those who kill the body, but cannot kill the soul; rather fear him who
can destroy both soul and body in hell" (Matt. 10:28). . . .

The Pentecostal church in Rădăuți is in a critical state: its roof is
asphalted cardboard. The members bought slate for the roof, but the authorities simply stole it and put it in a state shop for sale. . . .

The faithful of the Baptist church of Bucoșnița . . . bought a house
in the name of Ioan Lazăr to serve as a meeting house, because the
congregation, who are mostly elderly, some of them invalids, could not go
on foot to the Baptist church in Petroșnița four kilometers away. Because
they met in the church in Bucoșnița, four Christians were fined up to 2,000
lei by the militia. . . .

In front of the town hall in Milișăuți a caricature mocking the faithful
of the village of Iaslovaț was pinned up. The caricature represents people in
the nude bathing in the river in the village with captions denigrating the act
of baptism. . . .

In the village of Țipeni . . . a group of fourteen Baptists were fined
1,000 lei each in 1981 because they had held a religious service. Most of
them were . . . between seventy and eighty years old. . . .

In the village of Bădăuți, on several consecutive Sundays, during religious services several people entered the church against the will of the people, read extracts from the writings of Marx, and held political discussions.
One of the faithful, Ioan Lucescu, took a stand in the face of this intru-

344

sion, and invoked the Constitution. Because of this, his children Ioan and
Maria Lucescu were put back one class at school, though they were good
scholars. . . .

Ioan Clipa of Suceava was interrogated in the autumn of 1980 because
he had distributed Bibles. He was tortured by the security police until his
psyche was destroyed and afterwards underwent nervous crises. At the beginning of 1981 the security police came again to his house and arrested him.
Ioan Clipa had suffered a trauma (he had not forgotten the torture suffered by
his friends in Botoşani and knew what he too might experience); he had a
breakdown, went into hiding, and committed suicide. . . . His wife, Eugenia
Clipa, an invalid pensioner, is left with seven young children.

Ioan Iancu, a Baptist believer from Timişoara, is well known to his
compatriots as a keen evangelist who moves around with his five children,
who form a small orchestra. On 11 June 1980 his house was searched for
seven hours by eight security police, without a warrant, on the pretext that
he was hiding arms. They confiscated . . . cassettes containing religious
material, a loudspeaker, a typewriter, a screen for projecting films, a camera,
and the like. They also confiscated religious brochures, all his Bibles, a
checkbook, and all his life savings. During the search, one of the eight, a
colonel, said to Iancu: "Now we'll see how you can go on carrying out
propaganda; you will have to do it all from memory."

Afterwards proceedings were instituted against him. At first he was accused of making religious propaganda, then of buying objects from foreigners. At length, after long-drawn-out sessions, he was sentenced in February
1981 to a year's hard labor and the confiscation of 46,000 lei for
"speculation." Not a single witness was brought to prove the accused's
speculation or that he had bought objects from foreigners. . . .

Children of Christians are . . . threatened with low marks if they go to
church on Sundays. . . . They are strangers in their own country. They are
subjected from infancy to religious discrimination, and deprived of the right
of any child in the world to delight in their childhood. Christian children in
Romania cannot have a camp where they can be protected from the violent
indoctrination of Marxism.

Many Christians have applied to emigrate, without, however, obtaining
a passport. Gheorghe Braşoveanu, an Orthodox Christian of Bucharest, an
economist, now a pensioner, is a long-standing dissident, a fighter for human rights. For that reason he has suffered much: he has been in psychiatric
hospitals several times, where he was given tranquilizers that harmed his
brain. In 1979 he was imprisoned because he founded a free trade union in
Romania. . . . Not one of his works on economics was recognized, though
Nicolai Ceauşescu himself had applied and supported some of his ideas. . . .

Dumitru Mureşan, a devoted Baptist from the village of Arcalia, has
five children. His wife is ill, and he is an invalid pensioner. From time to

time his pension is withheld. He receives no benefit for his children. They have absolutely no income. All this is because he is religious. He was interned in a psychiatric hospital, where he received "neuroleptic" injections to destroy his mind. Three years ago he asked permission to emigrate. For that "crime" his children are not allowed to attend school. The Romanian authorities also confiscated his identity card; for that reason he cannot enjoy the few small rights that are due to him. . . .

In January 1981, five believers accused of distributing Bibles in Romania and the USSR were imprisoned for periods of two to three years. . . . These were Gheorghe Hofman, Mathias Fahner, Paul Gross, Manfred Herbert, and Mihai Closs. [They were all released under the amnesty of August 1981.] Before their trial they were tortured by the security police. Paul Gross and Mihai Closs were injected with drugs to break their will and make them reveal all they knew. . . .

Simeon Lupei, a Pentecostal believer, a pensioner of Arad, was interrogated. . . . His indictment specified "religious material from abroad, received from foreigners." . . . Though an old man, Lupei was questioned day and night, threatened and mentally tortured until exhausted. Together with him . . . David Merca . . . and two Swiss citizens were interrogated for the same reason. David Merca was beaten and interrogated for two days and a night, tied to a chair and tortured until he collapsed in a pool of blood. He is summoned regularly to the security police. . . .

On 10 November 1981 in Ploieşti, several Christians were arrested and interrogated about the distribution of Bibles and religious literature. Among these were Mircea Cioată, Silviu Cioată, Toader Nelu, an engineer, and Petru Furner: all of whom were sentenced to more than five years in prison.

Klaus Wagner of Sighişoara was arrested on 1 October 1981 and later . . . sentenced to six years' imprisonment for having distributed Bibles and Christian literature. Fibia and Maria Delapeta of Carpiniş were sentenced together with Klaus Wagner to five years' imprisonment for the same reason. In connection with this, Constantin Piriu, a ship's captain, was arrested and sentenced to seven years because a cargo of two thousand Bibles was found on his barge in the Danube port of Orşova.

SOURCE: *Religion in Communist Lands,* vol. 10, no. 2 (1982).

APPENDIX Q: ROMANIA

Visit of Billy Graham, 1985

This account of evangelist Graham's visit is from a samizdat *document by a Romanian Baptist. (Excerpts.)*

As there had been absolutely no official publicity by radio, press, or television, and not even the leaders of the Christian denominations knew a week in advance what his possible itinerary would be or how he would be visiting the churches, I had to piece together the information . . . to plan my own tour. . . .

I consider that Billy Graham's journey through my country has been a blessing: for me it is the greatest public miracle I have experienced in the conditions of social and political dictatorship of Romania's Communist government. . . .

The whole tour demonstrated the organizational capacity of the Ministry of Internal Affairs, which, together with the Department of Cults, scored a great international propaganda success. On the domestic level, we Romanian citizens were shown how very well the Romanian Securitate control the foreigners' official visits. . . .

Participation in the religious meetings was "free" in a sense that only we Romanians who have lived through the years of Communist totalitarianism can really understand! Compared to the Stalinist period of history, we now have freedom! Compared to Albania or Soviet Russia, there is religious freedom in our country! Compared to Iran, it is much better here! But we were not granted the elementary right to see and hear Billy Graham, except to a limited extent. . . . The freest access we had was at the Orthodox monastery of Vorona in Moldavia, . . . where a large number saw and heard him very well. . . . At Timişoara, where he visited an Orthodox cathedral, . . . access was limited to those who succeeded in getting in three hours in advance, after waiting in front of the church since morning! The public of Oradea proved to be the most fortunate: there the hall was completely emptied of seats, allowing in a very large audience, while those in the streets could listen to the loudspeakers which had been installed. When the official delegation arrived they had to weave their way for a considerable distance through the crowds in the streets.

The Securitate remedied this situation immediately: two days later, at Arad, the official cars were protected by a large number of Securitate and three teams of traffic police so that they could reach the building, and when the delegation had gone in, a padlock and chain were put on the door so that no more people could enter! The good thing, though, was that here too external loudspeakers had been installed, and the sound quality was good. In all the other places Billy Graham visited—Sibiu, Bucharest, Timişoara—access was limited, and nobody was allowed to hear except those inside. . . .

The stupidest thing . . . was the false hospitality given to Billy Graham and his delegation. In all the towns he was to visit, the host churches received instructions to give him expensive presents—and not only for him and the foreign delegation but also for the Romanian delegation who accompanied him! The believers joyfully accepted the giving of gifts, however costly, for the sake of the foreign delegation and their message; but nobody understood why the Securitate officials employed at the Department of Cults . . . also received expensive presents.

The worst thing was the although Billy Graham had . . . subsidized his own travel and had paid for the right to have the tour televised, although he was invited by the government . . . and accommodated in hotels closed to the public, immediately after he left the towns he visited the denominational leaders were informed—and this was the last straw!—that the entire cost of the accommodation of the whole delegation had to be borne not by the government but by the believers, regardless of their denomination! The sums were extraordinarily large, and we believe that . . . there were added the expenses of hundreds of the Securitate employees who stopped believers from going into the churches to listen to him: so the believers sustained also those who were guarding them so that they would not get near to or hear Pastor Billy Graham! It is interesting to note that although the meeting took place in, for instance, a Baptist church, the Lutheran or Reformed or Pentecostal church in that town was required to pay a share even if all it had done was take part in the officially invited delegation! . . .

There was general confusion for those who did not know: I refer to the Orthodox believers who knew nothing beforehand about Billy Graham and saw him dressed in a long cloak resembling that of the Romanian priests. . . . Many of the Orthodox believers of whom I asked, "Who is the guest who is speaking?," replied that he was the Metropolitan of the Christian Orthodox in America. "How do you know?" I asked. "If his holiness the Metropolitan said 'brother,' that means he is one of us Orthodox—and he is wearing priest's clothes!" . . . Even knowledgeable people stated that Billy Graham was not a Baptist neo-Protestant but a sectarian. . . . The reason? The reduced and limited level of knowledge of religious life in our country. . . . The uninformed person receives from the . . . anti-religious newspapers just one message: all faiths are manifestations of sects and are aimed at man's undoing! . . .

All the messages I heard had an "introduction" with very many social and political points which, taking time away from the message of the Gospel, disappointed most of the audience. The non-Christians, hearing how he praised and extolled people in the leadership of a political party very well known to the entire Romanian people, were saying, "Already this man is lying, so how am I to believe his biblical message?" . . . My own thought was: Didn't Billy Graham perhaps inform himself in advance of the real nature of the "sincere, intimate relationship" between the people and their leaders? Would it not have been better to thank God publicly for the opportunity to be in Romania and preach the Gospel there? Shouldn't he have been encouraging the people? . . .

Similarly, his statement . . . according to which he believed that "the Romanian people is one of the most religious in the world" is purely gratuitous, as the Romanian people, lacking free religious education, lost its spiritual compass more than thirty-five years ago and is proceeding, rather, towards paganism! . . . And of course his advice . . . that the place of all Romanians was in Romania and that they should stop seeking to emigrate to the United States disappointed the audience. I heard it said, "Why is he making politics instead of preaching?"

SOURCE: Keston News Service, no. 245 (June 3, 1986).

Father Calciu: On His Imprisonment and 'Freedom'

Father Georghe Calciu, a member of the Lord's Army, spent first sixteen years and then five and a half years in Romanian prisons. He now lives in the West. These comments are excerpted from letters he wrote in late 1984, after his second release from prison.

ON HIS IMPRISONMENT

I am deeply moved; it is as though, in writing these lines, I were addressing the soul of the world, that same world which supported me during the period of my suffering with love and with prayers and with sharing. In my most tragic moments and when my feelings of complete loneliness overcame me, the shining thought of our spiritual solidarity brought me a healing consolation. I have come to understand that the greatest suffering is isolation—not physical or material but spiritual isolation, the soul's lost wanderings in the nothingness of solitude. But where there is love, there is also communion, in spite of walls, of bars, of terror. . . .

When . . . I was put in the same cell with two criminals who had been ordered to beat me, in the secret hope that they would kill me, there was no law to defend me. Only Divine Providence protected me, operating through the spirit of one of these prisoners, preventing him from committing a deed fatal to me and to him. They told me openly: "Father, let *them* do it. That's what they're paid for." . . .

I never ceased praying and celebrating Mass in prison, in spite of threats, terror, and beatings. If those who shut me away—laymen and clergy—thought that they could isolate my soul, they were greatly mistaken. Never for a moment did I feel cut off from the communion of the liturgy, nor from its love. I was "not afraid of them that kill the body and after that have no more that they can do" (Luke 12:4). I proclaimed to all, from the interrogator to the most lowly prisoner—on the extremely rare occasions when I met these latter—the message of Christian truth; I insisted firmly that I should be addressed as "Father," and I often succeeded; I prayed and said holy services with thieves and murderers. . . .

ON HIS 'FREEDOM'

If it were not for the love with which I was welcomed back, the tears of those who embraced me at home, on the street, in churches, of those of my parishioners and students who had suffered persecution and terror, police raids and threats, and who, in spite of all, sought me out that we might have a few moments of brotherly communion; and if it were not for the certainty of Divine Providence, though hidden, which kept me from fear, the difference between my detention and this sham freedom would be minimal. I am guarded by a far greater number of police and militia than when I was in prison, and this situation means a sort of semi-detention for all the forty families who live in the same block with us.

When we go into town—even to buy bread or milk—at least six agents follow us, shoulder to shoulder, in case we should speak to someone. Those who are not aware, and who greet us, are asked their identity, threatened, and forbidden to have any contact with us. At least thirty to forty agents and policemen . . . keep permanent surveillance on us. . . . They must be spending a monthly minimum of 100,000 to 150,000 lei absolutely uselessly, for a single policeman in the hall could do exactly the same job.

At this moment when they are forever singing the praises of fuel economy, when electricity and heating are being cut, when "working men" have to stand in the freezing cold waiting to get onto an overcrowded bus that comes as rarely as Halley's Comet is seen from the earth, what can be the reason and the aim of this enormous and senseless expenditure of money and human energy? Is it not natural that men should be indignant when they have to come from their work on foot, exhausted, frozen, and see the secret police—fat, well-fed, and well-dressed men and women needlessly burning up fuel and pocketing salaries three to four times as big as theirs, just to terrorize two people who have done no harm and who would not even be able to do any? . . .

I said in one of my sermons . . . that I knew what to expect: terror, calumny, blackmail; but reality outstripped the powers of my imagination. Nothing has changed. The power of imagination of evil is immense and varied. It will never be exhausted.

I knew that after my release my family and I would find ourselves in a larger, more subtle and perhaps more effective prison. . . . But I could never, not even in my most painful thoughts, have imagined that, only just freed from Communist prisons, . . . my soul would still have to endure an inhuman blow delivered by the hierarchy of the Romanian Orthodox Church and by my brother priests. They thought fit, by ordering my unfrocking, to take from me my priestly gifts, which not they had conferred upon me, but a great churchman who is now dead and who would have been the only one with the right to remove me from my priestly functions, for this gift is given forever. And I know that he would not have done this. . . .

I have devoted all my love and all my soul and all this immense treasury of sufferings to our country and our church. . . . Now I find myself forced to leave my country. I would not do it if I were alone. But I am not. Not only I but my family, too, is caught up in this chain of terror.

Men whom I had never met before have said to me: "Don't leave us, Father." To me, the most humble, the most oppressed, and the most fettered person in the whole country. Others have said: "Father, save yourself." The paradox is that I can follow the advice of neither: my own and my family's absolute uncertainty forces me to emigrate. The authorities keep me in total ignorance about this. The worst certainty is less bad than uncertainty.

"And now abideth faith, hope, love, these three; but the greatest of these is love." Whatever may be, I know that I shall never lack the love of my fellow men.

Questionnaires for Schoolchildren

Romanian schoolchildren have been given questionnaires about their religious habits. Although the replies are supposedly kept anonymous, some children have been identified and exposed to ridicule. Clearly the information could easily be used for other than pure sociological research. The questions below are from a compilation published in the West in 1985. Following them is a letter sent by a schoolgirl (probably a Baptist) to an older Christian.

How do you spend your free time on Sundays? Do you listen to religious broadcasts on the radio? What do you think of them? Do you go to church? What denomination is it? How often do you attend church? Why do you go to church? Who leads you there and who teaches you? Write name(s). What do you learn there? Are you told to pass on to others what you hear? Do you receive special literature at church?

What is a Christian? Are you—personally—a Christian? Do you belong to a sect? [In Romania, Protestant denominations such as Baptists and Pentecostals, as well as the "Lord's Army" movement in the Orthodox Church, are lumped together with such groups as Jehovah's Witnesses as "sects."] What is it called? Where do you meet and how long do the meetings last? What other pupils in the school do you know who go to the same sort of church? What other students do you know who belong to sects? Do all the members of your family share your Christian religious convictions?

DEAR SISTER D,

I'm writing to you because I am having problems at school because the teachers have found out that I go to church and am a born-again believer.

What do you think I should do? What should I tell them, and how?

At the "direction lesson" [weekly period in which the class is given general advice on behavior, discipline, and the like; it can also be used

353

for ideological instruction] we were given special tests about beliefs. The political-knowledge teacher told us they were compulsory and that we were not to write our names on them, but at the end they immediately took my answer and read it aloud. I cried and sat with my head on the desk, wishing the Lord would come and wishing it were the end of the world. They questioned me and told me to stand up, but I couldn't. I couldn't see anything, but I could hear the boys laughing. . . .

Mother and Father always say the Lord will take care of me and that Brother Pastor will intervene only if I am thrown out of school. But I don't want to be thrown out because I like learning and I should like to become a teacher myself, as I really like teaching others good things. I would be so pleased if you could come with the young people's guitar group on Sunday February 3. That is my birthday, and I shall be twelve.

SOURCE: Keston News Service, no. 227 (June 13, 1985).

Bibliography

Material on religion in Eastern Europe is very hard to get, and our areas of ignorance are still much greater than our areas of knowledge. Much primary source material has been destroyed or suppressed. Many works have not been translated into English; only a few of these, in German, French, and Italian, are included in this bibliography.

Periodicals and Occasional Publications

The standards and expertise of researchers at Keston College (Heathfield Road, Keston, Kent BR2 6BA, England) are unequaled. Their publications include: ◆ *Keston News Service*, fortnightly; news, analyses, shorter key documents, letters; invaluable to anyone researching affairs in Communist countries. ◆ *Religion in Communist Lands*, published two to four times a year; articles, longer documents, surveys in more depth; indispensable for scholarly use. ◆ *Frontier*, bi-monthly; short articles aimed at the general public.

◆ *Albanian Catholic Bulletin*, ed. Gjon Sinishta, published by Albanian Catholic Information Center. Occasional bulletins—five since 1980—with articles on Albanians, including those living in Yugoslavia. (P.O. Box 1217, Santa Clara, Calif. 95053.)

◆ *Amnesty International Newsletter*, published by Amnesty International Publications. A monthly bulletin with useful articles; also, occasional publications on particular issues. (1 Easton Street, London WC1X 8DJ, England.)

◆ *Catacombes: Messager Supraconfessionel de l'Église du Silence*, ed. Sergiu Grossu and Nicole Valery. A bi-monthly, in French, published since 1971. Somewhat polemical, but has useful news, articles, and, in particular, key letters and documents from Romanian Christians. (B.P. 98-92405 Courbevoie Cedex CCP 1206, 29 Paris, France.)

◆ *CSCE Reports*, published by the Commission on Security and Cooperation in Europe. Reports that have been appearing since Helsinki in 1975; some cover human- and religious-rights violations in Eastern Europe. Particularly useful: ◆ 1977 First Session, Vol. II: *Helsinki Compliance in Eastern Europe* (May 1977); ◆ *Documents of Helsinki Dissent From the Soviet Union and Eastern Europe* (May 1978); ◆ Vol. XII, *Review of East European Compliance With the Human Rights Provisions of the Helsinki Final Act* (March 1980); ◆ Vol. XIV, *Religious Rights in the Soviet Union and Eastern Europe* (May 1980), particularly the statement of Professor Bohdan Bociurkiw, pp. 3-44; ◆ *Report to U.S. Congress* (August 1980); ◆ *Seven Years After Helsinki* (November 1982); ◆ *Reports of the Implementation of Helsinki Final Act*, brief, useful, up-to-date, semi-annual summaries of the state of human—including religious—rights. (237 House Annex 2, Washington, D.C. 20515.)

◆ *Free Romanian Press*, ed. Ion Ratiu. A monthly, partly in English but mostly in Romanian, with current news of the Romanian situation; most of its religious information comes from Keston College. (54-62 Regent Street, London W1R 5PJ, England.)

◆ *Help and Action Newsletter*, published by Help and Action Co-ordination Committee, a multinational group of mostly émigré dissidents. A brief, high-quality news service, in French and English, focusing on human-rights violations in the U.S.S.R. and Eastern Europe. Items on believers are part of its coverage. Gives addresses of other sources, very useful for follow-up on specific countries or groups. (B.P. 11, 77850 Hericy, France.)

◆ *L'Altra Europa*, published by Centro Russia Cristiana. Originally restricted to the U.S.S.R. but expanded in coverage in 1985. Provides academic, philosophical, political, religious, and literary articles and *samizdat* of very high quality, looking at religion in its wider context. (Via Ponzio 44, 20133 Milano, Italy.)

◆ *Open Doors*. A popular monthly that relies mainly on Keston College and on its own couriers, who provide short, perceptive surveys of various problems in religious life. Over the years its coverage and stance, from being strictly Protestant, have become somewhat more ecumenical. Recommended for the layperson who wants regular information. A major aim of the organization, founded by Brother Andrew, is to furnish the Scriptures to people who find it difficult to obtain them through regular, legal channels. (Headquarters: P.O. Box 47, 3840 AA Harderwijk, Holland; national offices in several countries.)

◆ *Problems of Communism*, published by the U.S. Information Agency. A very high-quality academic journal, bi-monthly, with an occasional article on religion. (400 C Street S.W., Washington, D.C. 20547.)

◆ Pro Mundi Vita, a Roman Catholic study center, ecumenical in scope. Produces high-quality dossiers on specific countries. (Abdij Van't Park Abdijdreef 7A, 3030 Leuven, Belgium.)

◆ *Radio Free Europe Research: Background and Special Reports*. Furnishes keen analysis of political, economic, religious, and cultural events in Eastern Europe. (Oettingen Str. 67, Munich 22, Federal Republic of Germany.)

◆ *Religion in Communist-Dominated Areas*, published by the Research Center for Religion and Human Rights in Closed Societies. A quarterly, founded and edited by Blahoslav and Olga Hruby, providing documents and comments on the life of believers in Communist societies. (475 Riverside Drive, New York, N.Y. 10115.)

Books: General

Religion in Eastern Europe is very poorly covered. There is only one general survey that can be recommended as a handy, well-written reference book for the intelligent general reader: Trevor Beeson's Discretion and Valour *(see below), which was commissioned by the British Council of Churches. Many of the books mentioned here are not specifically about religion but provide valuable background information.*

Beeson, Trevor. *Discretion and Valour: Religious Conditions in Russia and Eastern Europe*. Glasgow: Collins, Fontana, 1982 (rev. and enl. ed.). Philadelphia: Fortress Press, 1982.

Bociurkiw, Bohdan R., and John W. Strong, eds. *Religion and Atheism in the U.S.S.R. and Eastern Europe*. Toronto: University of Toronto, 1975.

Bociurkiw, Bohdan R., et al. *Eastern Europe, Religion and Nationalism*. Washington: Wilson Center, East Europe Program, 1985.

Campana, Don Cristoforo, ed. *Luci nelle Tenebre: Considerazioni, Testimonianze, Documenti sul Cristianesimo all' Est*. Vol. I, 1971-1976; vol. II, 1977-1979. Urbania, Italy: La Chiesa del Silenzio. (Urbania, 61049 Pesaro, Italy.)

Dunn, Dennis J. *Détente and Papal-Communist Relations, 1962-1978*. Boulder, Colo.: Westview Press, 1979.

Gsovski, Vladimir. *Church and State Behind the Iron Curtain*. Westport, Conn.: Greenwood Press, 1973.

Gussoni, Lino, and Aristede Brunello. *The Silent Church*. New York: Veritas Publishers, 1954.

Hebly, J. A. *Eastbound Ecumenism*. Lanham, Md.: University Press of America, 1986.

Hösch, Edgar. *The Balkans: A Short History From Greek Times to the Present Day*. London: Faber and Faber, 1972.

Lacko, Michael, S.J. *Saints Cyril and Methodius*. Rome: Slovak Editions, 1969.

Mihajlov, Mihajlo. *Underground Notes*. New Rochelle, N.Y.: Caratzas Bros., 1980 (2nd ed.).

358 CONSCIENCE AND CAPTIVITY

Mojzes, Paul, ed. *Church and State in Postwar Europe: A Bibliographical Survey.* Westport, Conn.: Greenwood Press, 1987.

Ramet, Pedro. *Cross and Commissar: The Politics of Religion in Eastern Europe and the USSR.* Bloomington, Ind.: Indiana University Press, 1987.

_____ , ed. *Religion and Nationalism in Soviet and East European Politics.* Durham, N.C.: Duke University Press, 1988 (rev. and enl. ed.).

Richardson, Dan, and Jill Denton. *The Rough Guide to Eastern Europe— Hungary, Romania, and Bulgaria.* London: Harrap-Columbus, 1988. (Useful travel guide, one of the very few for these countries; includes historical and cultural material, with up-to-date information on locations of architecturally interesting churches and monasteries.)

Runciman, Steven. *The Great Church in Captivity.* London: Cambridge University Press, 1968.

Stehle, Hans Jakob. *Eastern Politics of the Vatican, 1917-1979.* Athens, Ohio: Ohio University Press, 1981.

Walters, Philip, and Jane Balengarth, eds. *Light Through the Curtain: Poland, Czechoslovakia, U.S.S.R., Romania—Testaments of Faith and Courage.* Belleville, Mich.: Lion Publishing Co., 1985. (10885 Textile Road, Belleville, Mich. 48111.)

Ware, Timothy. *The Orthodox Church.* Crestwood, N.Y.: St. Vladimir's Seminary Press, 1986 (rev. ed.).

Books: Countries

1. ALBANIA

Albania, Political Imprisonment and the Law. London: Amnesty International, 1984.

Durham, Edith. *High Albania.* London: Virago Press, 1985. (First published in 1909.)

Logoreci, Anton. *The Albanians: Europe's Forgotten Survivors.* Boulder, Colo.: Westview Press, 1977.

Marmullaku, Ramadan. *Albania and the Albanians.* Hamden, Conn.: Shoestring Press, 1975.

Prifti, Peter. *Socialist Albania Since 1944: Domestic and Foreign Developments.* Cambridge, Mass.: Massachusetts Institute of Technology Press, 1978.

Sinishta, Gjon. *The Fulfilled Promise: A Documentary Account of Religious Persecution in Albania.* Santa Clara, Calif.: Albanian Catholic Information Center, 1976. (P.O. Box 1217, Santa Clara, Calif. 95053.)

2. BULGARIA

Carloni, Marie Teresa. *Il Silenzio della Chiesa Bulgara*. Urbania, Italy: La Chiesa del Silenzio, n.d. (Urbania, 61049 Pesaro, Italy.)

MacDermott, Mercia. *A History of Bulgaria: 1393-1885*. London: George Allen and Unwin, 1962.

Popov, Haralan. *Tortured For His Faith*. Grand Rapids, Mich.: Zondervan, 1975.

3. CZECHOSLOVAKIA

Benda, Václav. *Lettere dal Carcere*. Bologna, Italy: Centro Studi Europa Orientale, 1981.

Havel, Václav. *The Power of the Powerless*. Armonk, N.Y.: M.E. Sharpe, 1985.

_____. *Politics and Conscience*. Stockholm: Charter 77 Foundation, 1986.

Seton-Watson, R. W. *A History of the Czechs and Slovaks*. Philadelphia: Richard West, 1980 (repr. of 1943 ed.).

4. GERMAN DEMOCRATIC REPUBLIC

Gollwitzer, Hellmut, Käthe Kuhn, and Reinhold Schneider, eds. *Dying We Live: Letters Written by Prisoners in Germany on the Eve of Execution*. Glasgow: Collins, 1956; repr. 1963.

Henkys, Reihard. *Gottes Volk in Socialismus: Wie Christen in der DDR Leben* (God's people under socialism: How Christians in the GDR live). Berlin, 1983.

_____, ed. *Die Evangelischen Kirchen in der DDR: Beitrage zu enier Bestandsaufnahme* (The evangelical churches in the GDR: Contributions toward an assessment). Munich: Christian Kaiser Verlag, 1982.

Sandford, John. *The Sword and the Ploughshare*. London: Merlin Press/ European Nuclear Disarmament, 1983.

Scheffbuch, Winrich. *Christians Under the Hammer and Sickle*. Grand Rapids, Mich.: Zondervan, 1974.

5. HUNGARY

András, Emeric, and Julius Morel, eds. *Church in Transition: Hungary's Catholic Church From 1945 to 1982*. Vienna: Hungarian Institute for Sociology of Religion, 1983.

_____ . *Hungarian Catholicism—A Handbook*. Vienna: Hungarian Institute for Sociology of Religion, 1983.

Közi-Horváth, József. *Cardinal Mindszenty—Confessor and Martyr of Our Time*. Chichester, England: Aid to the Church in Need, 1979.

Leslie, Laszlo. *Church and State in Hungary, 1919-1945*. Ann Arbor, Mich.: University Microfilms International, 1973.

Mindszenty, József Cardinal. *Memoirs*. New York: Macmillan, 1974.

6. HUNGARY AND ROMANIA (TRANSYLVANIA)

Leigh-Ferman, Patrick. *Between the Woods and the Water*. New York: Viking, 1986.

7. POLAND

Davis, Norman. *God's Playground*. Oxford: Clarendon Press, 1981.

Dissent in Poland, 1976-77: Reports and Documents in Translation. London: Association of Polish Students and Graduates in Exile, 1979.

Monticone, Ronald. *The Catholic Church in Communist Poland, 1945-1985*. Boulder, Colo.: East European Monographs, 1986.

Nowakowski, Marek. *The Canary and Other Tales of Martial Law*. London: Harvill Press, 1983.

Sikorska, Grażyna. *A Martyr For the Truth—Jerzy Popiełuszko*. Grand Rapids, Mich.: Eerdmans, 1985.

Szajkowski, Bogdan. *Next to God, Poland: Politics and Religion in Contemporary Poland*. New York: St. Martin's Press, 1983.

Tischner, Jozef. *The Spirit of Solidarity*. San Francisco: Harper and Row, 1984.

Tomsky, Alexander. *Catholic Poland*. Keston, England: Keston College, 1982.

Wyszyński, Stefan Cardinal. *A Strong Man Armed*. London: Geoffrey Chapman, 1966.

_____ . *A Freedom Within: The Prison Notes of Stefan Cardinal Wyszyński*. San Diego, Calif.: Harcourt Brace Jovanovich, 1983.

Zatko, James J., ed. *The Valley of Silence*. Notre Dame, Ind.: University of Notre Dame Press, 1967.

8. ROMANIA

Dumitriu, Petru. *To the Unknown God*. London: Collins, 1982.

Funderbunk, David. *Pinstripes and Reds*. Washington: Selous Press, 1987.

Gherman, Pierre. *Pensée Romaine, Peuple Roumain*. Paris: Spes, 1967.

Grossu, Sergiu. *Le Calvaire de la Roumanie Chrétienne*. Paris: Editions France-Empire, 1987.

Popan, Flavio. *Il Martirio della Chiesa di Romania*. Urbania, Italy: La Chiesa del Silenzio, 1976. (Urbania, 61049 Pesaro, Italy.)

Ratiu, Alexander, and William Virtue. *The Stolen Church*. Huntington, Ind.: Our Sunday Visitor, 1978.

Seton-Watson, R. W. *A History of the Romanians*. Archon Books, 1963.

Valery, Nicole. *Prisoner, Rejoice*. London: Hodder and Stoughton, 1982.

Wurmbrand, Richard. *In God's Underground*. London: W. H. Allen, 1968.

Wurmbrand, Sabina. *The Pastor's Wife*. Crowborough, England: Highland Books, 1970.

9. YUGOSLAVIA

Alexander, Stella. *Church and State in Yugoslavia Since 1945*. Cambridge: Cambridge University Press, 1979.

_____. *The Triple Myth: A Life of Archbishop Alojzije Stepinac*. New York: Columbia University Press, 1987.

Craig, Mary. *Spark From Heaven*. London: Hodder and Stoughton, 1988. Notre Dame, Ind.: Ave Maria Press, 1988. (About the apparitions at Medjugorje.)

Doder, Duško. *The Yugoslavs*. New York: Random House, 1979.

General Survey of the Catholic Church in Yugoslavia. Zagreb: Bishops' Conference of Yugoslavia, 1975.

Kindersley, Anne. *The Mountains of Serbia: Travels Through Inland Jugoslavia*. London: John Murray, 1976.

Serbian Orthodox Church, 1920-1970, The. Belgrade: Holy Episcopal Synod of the Serbian Orthodox Church, 1970.

Sussman, Leonard, and Jiři Pehe, eds. *Yugoslavia: The Failure of "Democratic Communism."* New York: Freedom House, 1987.

Index of Names